Race
and the
Social Sciences

RACE
AND THE
SOCIAL
SCIENCES

EDITORS

Irwin Katz & Patricia Gurin

BASIC BOOKS, INC., PUBLISHERS

NEW YORK   LONDON

The Authors

JAMES S. COLEMAN is Professor in the Department of Social Relations, the Johns Hopkins University. His books include *Community Conflict, The Adolescent Society, Introduction to Mathematical Sociology,* and *Adolescents and the Schools.*

PATRICIA GURIN is Assistant Professor of Psychology and a Research Associate of the Institute for Social Research at the University of Michigan. She is the author of a research monograph and several articles on the motivation and goals of Negro college students.

HERBERT H. HYMAN is Professor of Sociology and an Associate Director of the Bureau of Applied Social Research at Columbia University. He served as Program Director at the United Nations Research Institute for Social Development. His publications include *Survey Design and Analysis, Interviewing in Social Research,* and *Applications of Methods of Evaluation.*

IRWIN KATZ is Professor of Psychology and Research Psychologist of the Center for Research on Conflict Resolution at the University of Michigan. He has been a consultant to the United States Commission on Civil Rights and to the United States Office of Education. His publications include *Social Class, Race, and Psychological Development* (with Martin Deutsch and Arthur Jensen).

CHARLES C. KILLINGSWORTH is University Professor of Labor and Industrial Relations at Michigan State University. He has been President of the National Academy of Arbitrators and Chairman of the Michigan Farm Labor Panel. In addition to many articles, his publications include *State Labor Relations Acts: A Study of Public Policy.*

DONALD R. MATTHEWS, Professor of Political Science and Research Professor in the Institute for Research in Social Science, University of North Carolina, has been a consultant to the United States Commission on Civil Rights and the North Carolina Advisory Committee on Civil Rights. His books include *North Carolina Votes* and *Negroes and the New Southern Politics* (with James W. Prothro).

THOMAS F. PETTIGREW is Professor of Social Psychology, Harvard University. He has been President of the Society for the Psychological Study of Social Issues and is the author of *A Profile of the Negro American* and co-author of *Christians in Racial Crisis: A Study of the Little Rock Ministry* (with Ernest Q. Campbell).

KARL E. TAEUBER is Professor of Sociology, University of Wisconsin. He has been a consultant to the United States Commission on Civil Rights and has been on the Board of Directors of the Population Association of America. He is the author of many articles on patterns of migration and segregation. His publications include *Negroes in Cities—Residential Segregation and Neighborhood Change* (with Alma Taeuber).

Preface

There is no field of intellectual inquiry with so much potential value for dealing with racial problems as the social sciences. The gross inequalities of status, welfare, and opportunity that define Negro-white relations in America today urgently demand basic structural reforms in our society—reforms of a magnitude and complexity rarely before accomplished through orderly procedures of government in a democracy. Social science research can and must provide much of the detailed knowledge of social, economic, and political processes that will be needed in developing and carrying out rational programs of change. In the final analysis what must be changed is human behavior—with its supporting values, beliefs, and sentiments—and the institutional contexts in which the behavior unfolds.

This volume is the product of a unique interdisciplinary effort to define the seminal research issues in American race relations today. The book is less concerned with making practical recommendations for policies of social change than with formulating the research goals and strategies that are most likely to generate the basic scientific understanding needed for such recommendations. Taken as a whole, the chapters that follow present an over-all prospectus for theoretically grounded investigations of the causes and cures of racial conflict in this country.

Scholarly contributions to the improvement of race relations are still more in the realm of possibility than of actual fact. Looking beyond the recent flurry of writing and investigations, one discovers that over the past quarter-century (a period of rapid technological growth in the social sciences and also of emergent racial crisis) academicians generally have not been highly productive in attacking causes or prescribing cures for poverty and discrimination. There has, of course, been some research activity but, given the social importance of the problem and its scientific richness, the investment of effort and resources has been disproportionately low. The reasons for this neglect are not entirely clear, but surely an important factor has been a relatively low level of interest in race research on the part of many of the major funding agencies, both government and private. Happily, a more favorable trend in funding policies is now discernible. Nonetheless, there exist at present numerous glaring gaps in our comprehension of the forces that prevent the advancement of racial minorities. Indeed, social science is still largely at the stage of having to formulate the right empirical questions before it can even begin to accumulate significant new information.

The people who were involved in the preparation of this volume were moved by a desire to assess the present state of knowledge about racial inequality in the United States and to identify promising directions for future research from the standpoint of both advancing science and providing a sound basis for public policy decisions. In the interest of intensive analysis, the editors decided at the outset to limit the book's scope to six critical aspects of the Negro's plight, thereby excluding from consideration the equally important and, to some extent, unique problems of other American ethnic minorities. Six distinguished experts from sociology, psychology, political science, and economics were selected by the editors to address themselves to this task.

Herbert H. Hyman writes mainly about the aspect of Negro-white relations that has traditionally received the most attention in social psychology: white prejudice. He focuses on the effect Negro social change has on white attitudes about the Negro. Thomas F. Pettigrew defines research priorities with respect to desegregation in the public schools. Donald R. Matthews develops a broad "systems theory" model for studying race politics and demonstrates the model's ability to generate crucial empirical questions. Karl E. Taeuber asks, first, what kinds of demographic information would be most useful in breaking the "vicious cycle of Negro disabilities," and second, how the information can be obtained most efficiently. Charles C. Killingsworth suggests ways of investigating causes of and remedies for Negro unemployment and includes analyses of characteristics of the labor market. James S. Coleman formulates an overarching framework for organizing a great variety of theories and hypotheses about social change. In the last chapter the editors review all the contributions, highlighting the common themes and elaborating on important issues and policy implications not sufficiently developed elsewhere.

The book is intended to be useful to social scientists and all others who are seriously concerned with efforts to improve the condition of racial minorities. This includes government officials, civil rights advocates, administrators and other personnel in job training and antipoverty programs, urban planners, schoolmen, leaders of community organizations, and so on.

A few remarks are in order about the history of this volume. To provide the authors with an opportunity for feedback from colleagues at an early stage in their labors, a conference of about thirty-five social scientists was held at the University of Michigan in April, 1967, under the auspices of the Center for Research on Conflict Resolution. The conversations, which centered on early drafts of the papers, lasted for three days. Both the conference and the preparation of final manuscripts were made possible by a grant from the Ford Foundation. From its inception the entire project was warmly supported by John R. Coleman, formerly Program Officer in Charge of the Office of Social Development of the Ford Foundation. The authors and editors wish to thank the following social scientists, who contributed valuable suggestions in papers they prepared for the conference: Stuart W. Cook, G. Franklin Edwards, Edgar G. Epps, Leonard J. Fein, Rashi Fein, Edmund W. Gordon, Robert L. Green, Lewis W. Jones, Hylan Lewis, Stanley Lieberman, F. Ray Marshall, and Paul L. Puryear. Thanks are also due to the chairmen of the conference sessions: Eunice Grier, Vivian W. Henderson, Lewis M. Killian, Herman H. Long, and Albert J. McQueen.

I. K.
P. G.

Contents

Race
and the
Social Sciences

1 Herbert H. Hyman

Social Psychology
and Race Relations

In reviewing research on race relations in the United States conducted over a ten-year period, Blumer informs us that, by actual count, the literature "includes well over a thousand published articles and books of a professedly learned character." [1] And that was back in 1958. Certainly the rate of growth for the literature of the last decade has not declined. The Watts riots alone added another 16,000 pages of official documents to be read by any analyst who has $83 to spare. [2] To be sure, many of these writings fall outside the scope of social psychology and thus reduce the magnitude of my review. But many other writings which would not be counted in an inventory of the conventional literature on race relations fall properly within our purview and thus enlarge the task. Blumer cannot have enumerated much of the literature on the authoritarian personality, since at last count that alone totaled hundreds of items, at least some of which deserve to be read. Perhaps we should also include studies of Negro-white relations in England, South Africa, or elsewhere. If we go far enough away, we may gain a valuable perspective on the problem of race relations in the United States or find a natural equivalent to the manipulation and control of some important social condition or determinant of the phenomenon we are trying to understand here at home. And if we go back far enough in time to unearth some of the classics in our field, we may regain a brilliant insight or ingenious method worthy of current application. We may even locate a base line from long ago which permits us to examine the changes in some specific aspect of the problem in relation

3

to historical conditions.[3] Alas, one becomes weary at the mere thought of reading so much, let alone understanding it.

Confusion follows upon weariness as one begins to read the empirical studies and notes the occasional contradictory findings. Waly and Stuart Cook report "a failure to confirm" an experiment by Jones and Kohler.[4] Srole casts Adorno *et al.* into doubt, but then he is done in by Roberts and Rokeach.[5] Rokeach is called into question on another study by Triandis, and the dispute soon becomes more complicated, albeit clarified, as Byrne and Wong, and Stein, Hardyck, and Smith enter the battle.[6] Perhaps the informal, facetious advice that the late Samuel Stouffer whispered to me one night long ago—"never do a replication"—was true wisdom!

Even if we resolve our confusion, we are still afflicted with doubts about the course that current research should take if we are to understand the present and contribute to a better future. Which of the past researches should be extended? What new approaches are needed? Seeking guidance, one turns from the specific, empirical literature to the general, theoretical statements of scholars who have earned their authority in this field by rare accomplishment and long experience. Unfortunately, they do not map the royal road to knowledge of the present and future. One stands at the intersection of many roads, not knowing which direction to take, feeling panicky about the dangers along each route, which the authority is so helpful in signaling to us.

Blumer warns against the experimental, psychological road which

> has been of dubious value in the field of race relations. On one hand it cannot be said to have "paid off" in contributing noteworthy results either to a body of theoretical knowledge or, on the practical side, to the working procedures needed to change race relations. On the other hand, more significantly, the trend has led students away from a direct, naturalistic study of what is happening in race relations in the United States. Students who are following this trend are very unlikely to see the changing world of race relations with any breadth or depth or to develop any intimate acquaintance with it.[7]

Kenneth Clark cautions us about the use of opinion and attitude research which

> dabbles in reality, but avoids the real arena of action, and reflects, among other things, both a methodological sterility and a theoretical stagnation.[8]

Williams, reviewing the history of the past twenty years, remarks on the dissatisfaction that has been

> expressed concerning the tendency of many studies to concentrate upon the prejudiced majority-group individual rather than upon the object of

prejudice or even more critically, the actual relationships among ethnic-racial collectivities.[9]

And Hughes strikes at our confidence, perhaps our overconfidence, when he asks,

Why did social scientists—and sociologists in particular—not foresee the explosion of collective action of Negro Americans toward immediate full integration into American society? [10]

In the face of rapid social change in the relations between Negroes and whites, these and other writers seem to be urging us toward radically new modes of research and theorizing about the problem. Hughes urges us to liberate our "sociological imagination" and to gain "sociological foresight of and involvement in drastic and massive social changes and extreme forms of social action." [11] Williams suggests that now is the time to change our focus.

When group relations are relatively stable, the central problems that tend to monopolize research have to do with conformity, social patterning, enduring prejudices and stereotypes, and so on. When change becomes massive and rapid, one senses the lack of studies of leadership, political and legal processes, the exercise of power and authority, the sources of innovation, and the conditions generating collective protest.[12]

The many writers who examine the situational and institutional determinants of discrimination are striking against the predictive power of old-fashioned measurements of psychological or intervening variables. It is perhaps only Gordon Allport among prestigious authorities who still speaks for the value of the old psychological tradition.[13]

Thus, when I follow my own inner directive to research paths other than those suggested by the authoritative figures or the fashionable doctrines, I feel uneasy. My suggestions are intended as tentative, and my confidence is shaky. But if I draw upon the past for ideas and methods, it is because some old-timers had just the kind of social-psychological imagination we may lack and still need today. And if I do not concentrate on the immediate turbulent present, it is because such a fixation might make it harder to see the future and to formulate relevant research. As William James said: "Where is it, this present? It has melted in our grasp, fled ere we could touch it, gone in the instant of becoming." [14]

My suggestions will relate mainly to research on the white majority, with full awareness that they are only one side of the equation. Understandably, it is the side about which I know most, and the side most thoroughly explored in past research. Under six headings, I shall make some proposals that hopefully will be fruitful.

1. Studies of the current socialization of white children into patterns appropriate to integration.

2. Studies of white attitudes toward Negroes differentiated in class and other characteristics, and corollary background studies of the beliefs whites attribute to various groups of Negroes.

3. A critical review of studies of situational determinants of white behavior in intergroup relations, with the aim of improving the predictive power of attitude research and reducing the ambiguity in the case study of situations.

4. Some brief suggestions for research on reference group and relative deprivation phenomena among Negroes and whites.

5. The formulation of new areas for survey research into white attitudes and characteristics which have relevance for understanding the future of intergroup relations and which emerge out of my earlier proposals.

6. A review of a few miscellaneous methods and experiments from the past which appear to me to represent effective use of the imagination. I shall end with a brief sketch of my own research in progress, which was an attempt to liberate my imagination and learn something new about the problem of Negro-white relations.

STUDIES OF THE CURRENT SOCIALIZATION
OF WHITE CHILDREN

A quotation from a paper by Kohn and Williams provides a fine opening for my discussion and will underscore my earlier remark that the present may simply be a moment of transition toward a future on which our current research can begin to focus.

> Patterns of "appropriateness" in intergroup behavior have been changing with increasing tempo in recent years. The unthinkable of a short time ago has in many areas of life become the commonplace of today. For a brief period the transition from unthinkable to commonplace arouses extreme emotional fervor; but as the new definition of the situation becomes the socially prescribed, the fervor soon diminishes. What was for the moment an "unpatterned" situation becomes, in Karl Mannheim's terms, "built into the framework of the society." [15]

How does the unthinkable become permanently "built into the framework of the society"? It must be through the socialization of the young into a new pattern by parents who have been forced to regard the previously unthinkable as the commonplace of the future which their children will be facing.[16] Empirical studies rarely document this fact, simply because the image of the process of socialization is in terms of the transmission and preservation of the past, and the setting of most studies has been that of a stable society. Occasionally, in studies of immigrants who have been transplanted to a new world, the investigator notes that parental influences are exerted in the direction of adapting the child to his new culture.[17] In a rare study of a "revolutionary" generation of Russian adults caught between the two worlds of Tsarist and Soviet society, Inkeles documents that the values they transmitted to their children were different from the values they themselves had internalized from their parents.[18]

Do we not have a parallel in the case of those southern, or northern, prejudiced parents who may well maintain their own prejudices and yet prepare their children for a world they know is coming but do not welcome? The hypothesis takes on added plausibility in light of national survey findings by Gallup and the National Opinion Research Center that the proportion of southern and northern adults who regard integration as inevitable has risen by now to over 80 per cent from the old figure of about 50 per cent.[19] Whatever its plausibility, we should be studying the possibility, for when such socialization starts, that will be the moment when the social changes that are now under way become solidified into a new pattern of culture.

In my reading, I have not found any recent studies.[20] In a case study of the integration of the St. Louis schools in 1954–1955 Valien asked white and Negro high-school children: "Did your parents discuss integration and how you should act in an integrated school?" Consider the white child who reported of her parents that "they themselves do not believe in integration and highly object but if I had to go to an integrated school, I should make the best of it." [21] What a titillating finding! How one wishes for more systematic evidence, updated to the present, on many parents of children of younger ages. Certainly, one could begin to explore the problem on a trend basis in national surveys by appropriate questions of parents, whose own prejudices are also measured. And one could do more intensive, but systematic, research following the ingenious models of such studies as that of Horowitz and Horowitz of thirty years ago.[22]

My proposal for studies of socialization is focused primarily on the prejudiced stratum of parents. But clearly, there is an important area of inquiry into the degree to which the unprejudiced parent transmits patterns appropriate to integration. One is reminded of Park's phrase that race relations were "the relations of strangers," and Williams' more recent formulation, expressed in a book with the apt title *Stran-*

gers Next Door, that "a certain amount of intergroup prejudice does not express a specific ethnic dislike so much as a kind of generalized timidity and feeling of awkwardness in coping with unfamiliar situations and unknown people." [23] Perhaps the unprejudiced white parent, with the best will in the world, does not quite know how to socialize his child to a relationship which is utterly novel in his own experience. It is perhaps a problem in innocence rather than evil, and a problem that may be declining with time.

In Park's day and around 1950, the date of Williams' research, the observation seemed sound. How well it holds today is, of course, an empirical question, since the degree of familiarity between Negro and white is a function of changing ecological and institutional arrangements. Some empirical evidence is provided by Williams from 1951 for a sample of northern and southern cities by the simple comparison of white age cohorts on the question of whether they had had contacts with Negroes during their teenage period. Individuals in their sixties in 1951 were less than one-third as likely to report such contacts as were teenagers of that period.[24] Such simple but useful data are almost never seen in the literature. They suggest that the sophistication or the clumsiness of the parental socializer is a changing thing dependent on his fund of intimate experience or the structure of opportunity he has had for varieties of interracial contact. One could explore the problem at three levels: the interracial experience of the socializers, the patterns they try to transmit and succeed in transmitting, and the appropriateness of these patterns to the integration of white and Negro children. The protocols that Valien collected in her case study of St. Louis convey the flavor of a problem in which parents of all varieties and ethnic backgrounds tried to feel their way into an unfamiliar situation: "Be careful; watch your step"; "Be friendly without getting too thick"; "Just act like they are not there"; "Be nice about it"; "Stay with your own group of friends and if trouble seems to start leave immediately and come home"; "It's new for all of us, but it will work if we all cooperate. Be kind to everyone." [25]

Parents, of course, are not the only agency of socialization for the young. In this connection, a recent study has such intriguing and significant findings that it deserves to be replicated. Past studies of magazine fiction and of school textbooks and elementary readers have documented the stereotyped and negative image of minorities that is conveyed to the young. Gast, in a content analysis of forty-two recent children's fiction books, documents (1) a general absence of negative stereotyping, (2) occupational stereotypes of other minority groups but *not* of the Negro characters, and (3) a portrayal of Negroes as the only ethnic minority seeking higher education and attending college.[26]

My last suggestion in this particular area will illustrate the way in which comparative research may increase our understanding. Investigators in England do not all agree, but certainly there is some evidence that white English adults do discriminate and show prejudice against the small minority of West Indian and African Negroes. Yet, it was consistently reported that there were no problems of cleavage along color lines or of patterns of prejudice and discrimination being shown by the children in integrated schools or in mixed neighborhoods and playgrounds. And this is at ages where patterns of prejudice have been amply documented for American children.[27] The paradox has not, to my knowledge, been the subject of special study, but one may speculate that it has something to do with processes of socialization. At the time these studies were made, Negroes were very recent arrivals in England and very few in number. Adults therefore had no prepared, long-established patterns of conduct ready to transmit to their children, nor were the adult encounters frequent and pervasive enough for the children to learn prejudice through observation of their elders.

STUDIES OF WHITE ATTITUDES TOWARD NEGROES DIFFERENTIATED IN CLASS AND OTHER CHARACTERISTICS

All observers of the changing situation of the Negro population in the United States document the Negro's dramatic movement into higher positions in the occupational or class structure. Analysts of such social change have focused on two problems: (1) By elegant methodological treatment they have tried to describe comprehensively and to index the magnitude and rate of such occupational mobility. Then, by judicious comparisons of the status of whites and Negroes at various time points, they have documented the extent of injustice and discrimination that still operates and have made predictions as to the day when true equality will dawn.[28] (2) Stemming from these analyses, speculations flow as to the "level" of relative deprivation that Negroes are experiencing. ("Level" is dependent on the comparative reference group employed.[29] On this problem, I shall have something to say later.)

To me there has been insufficient attention to a third and important problem. The changes in occupation and class within the Negro population must have modified in some degree the Negro as an object of white attitudes; as these changes continue in the future, white attitudes may become even more radically modified. In the study of race relations now and in the future, we should try to abstract that component of prejudice, social distance, and discriminatory behavior on the part of whites which stems from the changeable class characteristics of Negroes—as they are perceived by whites—from the component due to the relatively unchanging color of Negroes.

An ironic state of affairs seems to have characterized most past research on white attitudes toward Negroes. The structure of attitude and the organization of beliefs have been conceptualized and dimensionalized to a fine point. Cognitive, affective, and conative components—images, sentiments, action tendencies of the actor—have all been highly differentiated and then measured. But the *object* to which all these refined variables have been tied has generally been left in the gross, undifferentiated state "Negro." That whites express attitudes and behave differently, depending on the characteristics—for example, the class—of the Negro presented to them symbolically, or in real life, has generally not been taken into account in the design of research. To be sure, you may quickly say that much research has documented that prejudice is more related to the psychology of the victimizer than to the characteristics of the victim; that the essence of prejudice is the lack of distinction about individuals—the very act of categorizing; and that much research from the past has demonstrated the stereotyping of an entire minority group. But to some extent we may have begged the empirical question and taken our theory to be fact. The finding may also have been an artifact of our instruments, time-bound to a period when, in fact, there was much less variability in class, education, occupation, region, and residence of Negroes and correspondingly less basis for perceptual distinctions to emerge.

Ponder the interesting difference in the findings Gilbert obtained in a study of stereotyping by Princeton students of 1950 which replicated the famous Katz and Braly study of Princeton white students of 1933. Particular traits were assigned much less frequently, and despite the constraints of the instructions, Gilbert's students spontaneously voiced "protest against the unreasonable task of making generalizations about people." [30] I am sure that as sensitive an investigator as Katz would have taken note of similar tendencies, if they had been present in the thirties. As Gilbert suggests, the times have changed, and what was once a perfectly good instrument has now become insensitive to the real phenomenon. As the authors of the encyclopedic review of prejudice in the *Handbook of Social Psychology* warn us: "It is generally impossible to tell for certain whether the subjects attributing some trait to a group are in fact ignoring individual differences or whether they are merely advancing a *statistical* generalization—and, if the latter, whether they are describing a modal group or an overwhelming majority." [31]

There are a few studies which document the general problem. In a study in Germany by Sodhi, "the subjects were requested to estimate the percentage of the members of a given nation that would, in their opinion, possess a given attribute. The results indicated that only in very rare cases was a certain attribute held to apply to all the members of a given nation. There were very large individual differences in the degree of generality estimated for certain traits." [32] In a study in England by Banton, "designed to reveal stereotypes, 59 per cent of the subjects stated that they considered the tasks meaningless, as they did not know any representatives of the nationalities concerned, and were fully aware that the picture they were being pressed to draw was probably quite unrelated to fact." [33]

Specific evidence that the white stereotype of the Negro varies with his class characteristics and of the "prepotency of class over race" in stereotyping is reported by Bayton, McAlister, and Hamer. Like Katz and Braly, they asked their white college students at a "border state university" to select from an adjective list the traits that described Negroes, but they designated the Negro as either *upper* class or *lower* class.[34] Despite the passage of twenty years, they found, just as did Katz and Braly, that the Negro was most frequently labeled superstitious and lazy, and also dirty, ignorant, and happy-go-lucky, providing he was designated lower-class. The stereotype of the upper-class Negro included none of these five adjectives; he was characterized as intelligent, ambitious, industrious, neat. By measuring the stereotypes attributed to lower-class vs. upper-class whites by the same subjects, the investigators were able to demonstrate the prepotency of class. The lower-class white was also described, although less frequently, as ignorant, lazy, happy-go-lucky, and dirty. Thus the stereotypes varied more as a function of class than of race. The larger inference they drew in 1956 was not that previous research was invalid, but that when white subjects were asked to describe *the* Negro, they assumed "that *most* Negroes tend toward lower-class status. In the present investigation no question was raised as to the relative proportions of each race that fall within the two class positions." [35]

Given these findings, it seems urgent to begin continuing examination of whites' attitudes and behavior toward Negroes differentiated in various respects, especially class characteristics, because of the rapid economic change that is occurring. Before considering the limited evidence that is now available, one prefatory remark: With respect to policy decisions, my proposal should be regarded as irrelevant. Obviously, whether whites support a human and legal *right*—for example, integrated schooling—for *all* Negroes irrespective of their class or other characteristics, rather than reserving its application to some limited class of Negroes, is an important empirical question, but has no proper place in the formulation of policy. With respect to informal social relations, it would be only reasonable to expect, in a society patterned so much along particularistic lines, that considerations of class or other factors would also govern the ties formed between Negroes and whites and to accept that as normal.

The prediction that is implicit in my proposal is that the rise of Negroes in the class structure will be accompanied by more favorable white attitudes. But others who see prejudice and discrimination as serving the economic advantage of the majority, and those who are attached to such concepts as status anxiety, might predict a worsening of race relations with the rise of Negroes.[36] The earliest social psychological study of white attitudes, in which the class of the Negro was manipulated by verbal instructions, provides a relevant datum.

In 1936, Brooks conducted a classroom experiment among students at the University of North Carolina, of whom about 80 per cent were southern. Using a social distance scale for twelve ethnic groups, Brooks attempted to discover if there would be a preferential relationship for the ethnic minority member when he was described as having "good or college education" rather than "poor or ordinary education." The attribute of education reduced the social distance from all minorities, but the net change—half a step—was least in the instance of the Negro. In that era, as Brooks put it, many of his southern subjects came "from communities where ignorant, obsequious blacks are to be preferred to 'uppity' educated Negroes." [37]

In another region, but the same era, Mintz and Horowitz reported reduction in social distance when the minority group was differentiated in "intelligence." [38] And an imaginative experiment by Razran in 1938 is suggestive of changes in prejudice as the minority group member is differentiated by class. As part of his ingenious program of reducing prejudice through a free lunch conditioning effect, Razran showed his experimental subjects photographs of girls whom they were to rate on a series of desirable attributes and toward whom they also reported their degree of general liking.[39] Two months later four types of names were attached to the photographs, Italian, Jewish, Irish, and some chosen from the "signers of the Declaration of Independence and the Social Register." General liking and desirable attributions declined when the girls were labeled as members of ethnic minorities, but the serendipitous finding that bears upon our problem was that there were reliable differences in the effects produced by different surnames: Rabinowitz vs. Kantor, or McGillicuddy vs. Flanagan. Razran suggests that the names served as stereotyped indices of social class, and the perceived lower-class status increased prejudice.

The magnitude of the effect of class rather than color, and the direction of its influence on attitude, are obviously functions of the orientation toward class as such in a given time and place and stratum and, as Brooks suggested, of the special attitude toward minorities having some class. That the cultural concern about class is relevant to these analyses and its importance in apparent color prejudice is conveyed by a sociometric study of friendship ties between white and colored children in six Liverpool schools. As noted earlier, this investigation, like others, established little or no evidence of color discrimination by English white children, but it definitely established discrimination against poorly dressed children. When class is correlated with color, the effects can be confounded.[40]

In a program of research conducted in Indianapolis in the early fifties, Westie has provided more recent and large-scale evidence on the problem, added new conceptual refinement, and explored the larger implications of his data for such varied theories of prejudice as those that draw upon notions of economic competition and status insecurity.[41] In brief, the social distance manifested toward Negroes in a variety of occupational positions by white respondents classified as to their *own* occupational position was determined. The mirror image of the research was conducted on a sample of Negroes who reported the social distance they felt in regard to whites in various occupational locations. On the basis of these data, Westie thus could test whether intimate social relations are a function not only of the class of the object of attitude but of the "status-differential" between the two parties. From his many findings, I shall cite only three for the white sample which bear upon my argument. The higher the status of the Negro, the less the social distance expressed toward him by white respondents, no matter what their own status. Differentiating the Negro's occupational position has more effect on upper-status whites than on lower-status whites. The smallest social distance is expressed by high-status white respondents toward high-status Negroes, and the greatest social distance is expressed by low-status whites toward low-status Negroes.

A study conducted by Mackenzie in 1946 provides additional supporting evidence, but has the special virtue of examining the problem in three settings, one of which was a government agency whose work force had recently been integrated.[42] Apart from the reality of the questions for these white respondents, the findings thus not only bear upon the theory we are examining but perhaps foreshadow the consequences that will flow from large-scale integration in employment. The inquiry is somewhat different from the ones previously cited. White attitudes and expressed social distance toward Negroes, as well as beliefs about the characteristics of Negro workers, were determined for the generalized, undifferentiated object "Negro," but these responses were related to the independent variable of the status of the Negroes that the white respondent had personally known. The two approaches to the problem appear to dovetail. The earlier investigations establish that white attitudes are more favorable to Negroes of higher status, and Mackenzie establishes that having known Negroes of higher status produces a generalized favorability toward Negroes.

More recently, Triandis has done a series of studies among white undergraduates at the University of Illinois in which scores on social distance and other attitudes were obtained toward Negroes and whites whose profiles of other characteristics were varied in a factorial design. In all the experiments, the Negro was identified as having either high or low occupation or some other indicator of class; and, depending on the study, certain other characteristics were varied, including religion, "philosophy of life," opinions, sex, age, and nationality.[43] Two of the five studies seem to have tenuous relevance to our discussion of attitude toward Negroes of different class, since all the Negroes in these two studies had the attribute of being foreign: They were Portuguese or French, never American. What this actually does to the construct "Negro" I do not know, but, intuitively, one senses that it has some peculiar effect. One is reminded of the many reports and anecdotes about the way in which American behavior toward a Negro changed when he was labeled as a South American or African diplomat. While there are other obscurities that reduce my confidence in reading exact conclusions out of the studies, nevertheless they add support to the findings I have already cited. Whites express significantly less social distance and more favorable attitudes toward Negroes of higher occupational status.[44]

By an ingenious technique, one other study examined the intrinsic influence of class vs. color on the social distance that young upper-middle-class white children exhibit toward other children. Thus it examines the problem in the context of developmental processes and joins the present discussion to my earlier proposal for inquiries into socialization. Epstein and Komorita prepared four types of slides— Oriental children photographed against a slum and a suburban background and white children photographed against the same two backgrounds—and then obtained social distance scores from the white children who were shown these respective stimuli. To eliminate past experience with particular minorities, all the slides were described as representing a people called "Piraneans." [45] For these upper-middle-class children attending a school "where tolerant attitudes towards minority groups are encouraged," social distance was greatest toward the lower class, whether white or Oriental, and least toward the middle class, regardless of color. An analysis of variance demonstrated that race had no significant main or interactional effect on the scores, but class had a significant effect. Much greater intimacy was shown toward the middle-class Oriental than to the lower-class white. Thus the investigators established, for this sample, that prejudice toward class, but not color, is learned early in life, and they suggested that specific aspects of the socialization process are involved. [46]

These studies, if they may be taken as substantial evidence, bode well for the future. The apprehension about closer contact and social relations will diminish as perception of the rising education and class position of American Negroes grows among whites. The relevance of such studies urges me to suggest that their obvious deficiency be remedied by further research. They are all small in scope and on highly selected populations; most of them are out of date. None of them provides any descriptive evidence on the perceptions that prevail among whites as to the class characteristics of the Negro population. Studies should be projected on a large scale through attaching appropriate questions to national surveys. Measures of feelings of status anxiety and competitive threat, and status consciousness and status loss, should also be included. Thereby this alternative body of theory will be subject to empirical test, and the possible negative as well as positive effects that may flow from the rising status of Negroes can be estimated.

In the data from the trend surveys that Sheatsley and I conducted at the National Opinion Research Center, one may find an illustration of the approach. The question we employed to measure attitudes toward residential integration referred to a Negro "with the same income and education" as the respondent's moving into the white respondent's block, in order to "eliminate the factor of social class from the discussion and leave the respondent confronted only with the issue of his potential neighbor's color." [47] In our collaborative work, we never varied by a battery of questions the class status of the potential Negro neighbor, but in 1966 NORC made one such test by using a second question which referred to a Negro without specifying any class characteristic whatsoever. This reduced approval nationally by about 9 percentage points. It seems probable that presenting in a question a Negro of sharply contrasted status would have enhanced the effect.[48]

Since race relations have been the relations of strangers, the kind of class image of Negroes that the mass media present symbolically becomes important. I think we can estimate that this has changed in a more favorable direction, but some content analytic studies would be useful.[49]

Parallel to inquiries on the changes in white attitudes and social distance when the class of the Negro is differentiated, we find a recent program of research in which the attitude or belief of the Negro is varied experimentally and the differential attitudes and behavior of whites are measured. I refer to the very exciting studies initiated by Rokeach and his associates and the experiments and controversial literature that have been stimulated by his theory.[50] The arguments leave one with perhaps a quantum of uncertainty, but the general import of the series of studies and findings is unmistakable and important. When white subjects are confronted with a range of other persons who vary in race and hold beliefs that are similar to or different from those of the subject, they show preference for Negroes of similar belief rather than for whites of opposing beliefs. This held true whether the Negro was represented in symbolic form or was a real person in contrived situations, with a high degree of verisimilitude, toward whom whites actually exhibited their preferences in choice behavior. Please note that even Triandis, the severest critic of the original work, who found that race had a *stronger effect* than similarity of belief, also documented that belief was a significant determinant of preferential behavior.[51] The implication is that the prejudice of whites toward Negroes (and Negroes toward whites) is not related to color, but to real or perceived differences in belief systems.

The two experimental programs of research, one in which Negroes are differentiated in class and the other in which they are differentiated in belief, seem to be almost identical in design and to lead to similar conclusions. But, in my judgment, they do not lead automatically to the same predictions about the future of race relations. Since the contrast I shall draw between the meaning of the two programs is based on speculation, I shall make a few suggestions for further research plus action.

In both programs of research, the class or belief of the Negro is communicated to the white respondent during the investigation, and a reduction in prejudice or discrimination is *experimentally* produced. If, in real life in American society now and in the future, whites perceive more and more Negroes of higher class, it follows from the evidence that race relations will improve. And I think this is a sound prediction, because in fact the time series on occupational mobility is moving in that direction; class is a *highly visible, directly observable* characteristic, and as the experiments show, *all* classes of whites respond more favorably to the higher-status Negro.

Consideration of the Rokeach studies along these same three lines leaves one uncertain as to what is a sound prediction of the future. Whether the belief systems of the Negro and white populations are, in fact, converging is uncertain, and part of the uncertainty stems from the obscurities in the notion of similarity. With respect to one attitude or belief, Negroes and whites may exhibit a similarity, and with respect to another component of their total belief systems, they may be dissimilar. The relative importance of different beliefs must somehow enter into the appraisal of the *net* similarity of the two groups.[52] Moreover, on any dimension of belief, similarity may be examined at the level of the two population groups or at the level of individuals. One could conceive of the Negro and white populations as having identical *distributions* of a given attitude, but given the variability within each group, it would be possible that any Negro and white pair who encountered each other might differ on that belief. In the instance of class, the evidence shows that *all* whites, regardless of their class, respond more favorably to the higher-status Negro. Here, by contrast, what is a similarity and basis of friendship to one white may be a dissimilarity and basis of enmity to another.

Move from objective similarity to the *perception* of similarity, since this is critical for the prediction. In contrast with class characteristics, the belief of any person, Negro or white, is not a highly visible, directly observable characteristic. It may be revealed in a personal transaction (as in the Rokeach experiment), but recall that race relations have been the relations of strangers and that isolation has characterized Negro and white communities. The belief of others or of a whole group may be imputed on the basis of inference or projection or learned through persuasive communication. What kinds of belief do whites actually impute to Negroes, in the absence of real encounters or experimental manipulations?

In two of the major experiments that bear upon Rokeach's theory, we find evidence. Byrne and Wong establish that prejudiced white students assume that a Negro will be *dis*similar in belief. Among teenagers in Northern California, Stein *et al.* replicate the Rokeach experimental effects, but also show that when their "white subjects are given no information at all about a Negro teenager, they apparently assume that he is different from them in values and react towards him accordingly." [53]

On the basis of these combined findings, an optimistic view of the future of race relations on the basis of the perceived congruence in beliefs of whites and Negroes seems a risky prediction, unless we hedge the risk by more evidence or by remedial action. Byrne and Wong see the phenomenon of assumed dissimilarity as partly a function of the way whites have been socialized in the past. Perhaps this will change, and I have already urged empirical studies of that. They also establish that such perceptions are a product of prior attitudes of prejudice, and here perhaps past and recent trend studies of the decline in white attitudes of prejudice are some warrant for optimism.[54] Smith and his collaborators close their inquiry with an implied suggestion for social action which will increase the likelihood that whites will learn of the common bonds of belief that they share with Negroes.

I shall suggest some inquiries which may lead us to more confident predictions flowing out of the Rokeach theory. It seems obvious to me that national surveys of both Negro and white respondents should explore periodically the perceptions each group has of the other group's beliefs and values to see whether and when and between which subgroups some bonds of belief similarity are forged. And I do not intend to limit such questions to the area of beliefs about desegregation, which is no doubt highly polarized, in contrast with many other areas in which there may be objective similarities, which are perceived. There is, of course, the possibility that Negroes and whites share many of the same beliefs, but simply have misperceived each other. If such a condition of pluralistic ignorance exists, remedial action through a program of communication may help, since it may well be that present-day media have purveyed a false image of the beliefs and attitudes of the other group to the Negro and white audiences. In this connection, content analyses of the current media would establish the contribution they have made to creation of the problem.[55]

In inquiries into the attitudes Negroes and whites impute to each other, I have one minor suggestion to make and one major recommendation to urge. The questions should distinguish between the beliefs imputed to the leadership stratum of the other group and those imputed to the rank and file of the other group, since the perceived similarity may vary. More important, whites should be asked what beliefs they impute to groups of Negroes *differentiated in class*. The findings from such an inquiry might well reveal that class provides a fundamental basis for the inference about the belief of others; they might permit more confident and optimistic predictions about the future; and they might suggest that the contrast I have drawn between the two bodies of past research is too sharp.[56] Such new research might well show that whites impute similar attitudes to Negroes of higher status and suggest that the dissimilarity imputed to "a Negro" in past investigations was based on the implicit assumption that he was lower-class. If these hypotheses are borne out, one can predict that the future rise in status will be accompanied by an increase in perceived similarity.

A BRIEF CRITICAL REVIEW OF SITUATIONAL DETERMINANTS OF WHITE BEHAVIOR IN INTERGROUP RELATIONS

If one may describe the studies of belief similarity as subject to some ambiguity, one might well describe studies of situational determinants of discriminatory or nondiscriminatory behavior by whites as surrounded by obscurity. I present my brief critical review and research proposal with a good deal of insecurity.

About the specific facts revealed by these studies there is no question. Various investigators have established that whites who harbor prejudice or exhibit discrimination against Negroes in some settings will behave in a *non*discriminatory fashion in another type of situation. For example, this has been documented in studies by LaPiere, Saenger and Gilbert, Lohman and Reitzes, Killian, Reed, Hope, Minard, and Kutner *et al.* in the United States and in England for industrial workers and ship's crews.[57] This certainly appears to be an impressive body of literature, and it introduces both a critical note that attitude measurement is not *always* predictive of behavior and a cheery note that prejudice does not *always* eventuate in discrimination. That is indubitable. However, these and other studies have led some writers to assert the general primacy in the determination of behavior of situational and structural factors over attitudinal and psychological factors and to reject the predictive power of attitude measurement. If they are correct in their conclusions, a good deal of what I have proposed thus far ought to be ignored. Just how impressive is the evidence; what does it really mean; what does it bode for the future?

The main deficiency of such studies for drawing any general conclusions seems to me to lie in the fact that the research rarely has a *sampling dimension* in its design. These are mainly case studies, and one does not know whether they have the status of "deviant cases" or typical cases.[58] Admittedly some of these studies are based on a large number of observations, but still it may be a very limited *class* of situations in terms of the many settings in which prejudice might manifest itself or nondiscrimination occur. Thus, the group of investigations listed above were all deliberately selected by me because the situation is "economic": either a consumer is caught in the act of making a purchase, an entrepreneur is trying to make profit, or a worker is trying to earn a living and nondiscriminatory behavior is the price paid for gratifying an economic need.

Imposing this principle of statistical stratification on the studies may *suggest* that the economic motive is a force that overrides prejudice and that prejudice is generally not engaged in this arena of action, and it may create optimism about the prospects for integration in work settings. Correspondingly, the class position of Negroes would gradually be elevated, and prejudice would be further reduced in accordance with the findings I have previously presented. But none of these suggestions is compelling, since the situations examined may still be some accidental sampling of persons and situations from the larger stratum.[59] For example, in contrast with Killian's study which established that uneducated, prejudiced southern "hillbilly" workers restrained themselves in Chicago, the Lohman and Reitzes case where prejudiced individuals restrained themselves in an equalitarian union setting, and the Minard study where southern coal miners restrained themselves in the mine or union setting, one can cite another case study, rarely mentioned, in which Jewish garment workers vented their prejudices against Negro and Puerto Rican workers who had been integrated into the industry and union. Note this episode, which was one of thirty-three racial grievances brought before the union. As the analyst remarks, the constellation of prejudice which the aggressor vents "is sometimes strong enough to overcome the normal fear of economic reprisal . . . and can mean the difference between paying the rent and being dispossessed from one's apartment." [60] The case certainly runs to extremes of emotion; but in the absence of some sampling, how is anyone to know whether it is more or less unusual than some of the other cases of situational determinants cited in the literature?

PLAINTIFF: I was given a new shop to control as Business Agent. I asked everyone for their union books. I had no trouble until I got to A. She looked at me and said, "Who are you?" I said, "I'm the Business Agent." She said, "You're the Business Agent? Go away; I'm an Executive Board Member of the union." Then she gave me the book and said, "How come they make garbage like you a Business Agent?" She chased me all over the shop, called me a prostitute, a street walker, a no-good scab. . . . Later she said, "A Spanish bum like you has no right to be a Business Agent in a Jewish union."

DEFENDANT: "She ran in like thunder and I fell out of the chair from fright. She tore the book from my hands and told me to go to Stalin, he would give me another book. She told the boss not to give me work. I'm walking around for two months without work;—That's my representative?"

Witness: I was at the meeting when this happened. This woman told the Business Agent, Mrs. C., "Why the hell do they have Spanish Business Agents. Go to Lenox Avenue, you'll make a lot of money."

Now, even if we do not solve the problem of how to sample natural settings so that we can generalize about the frequency with which prejudice or nonprejudice is translated into discrimination or nondiscrimination, and about the importance in the shaping of the process of various classes of situational and psychological factors, I would suggest that these types of case studies could have much to tell us. From them the sensitive analyst can detect the operation of factors which inhibit the venting of prejudice in behavior, inhibit the operation of tolerance in behavior, or quicken the flow of each attitude pattern into action. All these types of processes have been documented.

The analyst must indeed be sensitive to see through the thicket of factors, and he may well miss some relevant aspect of the situation which accounts for the phenomenon. Killian, for example, in his study of southern migrants working in Chicago plants with integrated work forces, analyzed the significance of the number and proportion of such workers in the total plant force and also the total size of the plant force. These factors might have been neglected by an analyst of another persuasion, despite their possible influence on the degree to which respective groups of workers felt strong enough to express their views.[61] He also examined the degree to which the southern workers had alternative employment opportunities in segregated settings where they could simultaneously gratify their need for jobs and their desire to behave in ways compatible with their prejudices.

In general, the studies of situational factors that prevent the translation of prejudice into discriminatory behavior show a variety of other motives interacting with the desire to manifest prejudice, the outcome then being determined by the relative strength of the forces. But this model of the process is not so very informative, since some of the motives are truly bizarre and might easily escape notice. Consider one rather offbeat finding from a study of high-school youth in Washington, D.C., responding to the desegregation of the schools. Apparently, some of the high-school leaders, governed by their crass desire for greater power, supported desegregation because they saw the Negro students as swelling the number of their supporters.[62]

Whatever long list of factors is identified by such case studies in order to establish the general importance of any particular factor, more systematic research would be needed, in which some considerations of sampling are applied. What primitive ideas on this problem might be advanced?

One can obviously pose a series of hypothetical situations to respondents in the course of a survey and ask how they *would* behave. This has the virtue of providing adequate sampling, of permitting measurements of the prior attitudes of the respondents, of varying the situational factors in a lengthy verbal description, and of measuring the other psychological characteristics which might mediate between attitude and behavior. It suffers perhaps from being too "hypothetical." [63] A variation on this approach is suggested by Tumin, who develops a series of scales that move from the one extreme of measuring inner states to the other extreme of measuring a general action tendency in interracial situations.[64] Since Tumin was interested in the readiness of southerners for desegregation, he hypothesized a series of "countervailing perspectives" which, if internalized by the respondent, would constitute effective psychological blocks against the translation of prejudice into action tendency. Then, by multivariate survey analysis, the simulated, full process comes under examination. Here, again, some may regard the approach as too "hypothetical" for their taste. Its great merit, in my judgment, is that it studies the *dependable, durable* factors that can prevent the translation of prejudice into discriminatory behavior, since without inner controls, any shift in the balance of situational factors, any untoward event, may, as Tumin notes, "allow the free flow of the prejudiced impulses previously dammed up." [65]

Beginning now and going into the future, survey research on this problem no longer need be "hypothetical." Certainly, some significant percentage of white Americans have already begun to meet Negro Americans in their neighborhoods, in places of work or recreation, in their schools, and in various public facilities. Thus, verbal reports of their past and current behavior can be obtained and correlated with their attitudes and with survey measures of the hypothesized situational variables. And as the pace of integration proceeds, the percentage of such individuals in any sample will grow, as will the corresponding yield from the method.

A specialized survey design that would seem highly appropriate is one that I have called "selective experimental empaneling." In contrast with the usual panel design in which the total sample, or a random subsample, of respondents is reinterviewed to measure the influence of events in the interim period, I have proposed what I think is a more economical and informative design for just such problems as we are discussing. From a "parent sample" that is interviewed at Time 1, the analyst selects several subgroups that exhibit contrasted profiles of characteristics. In this instance, the profile would be based on their level of prejudice and other psychological and situational variables that characterize them at Time 1. Then these subgroups would be reinterviewed at various future times to measure the differential behavioral responses to interracial events as they occur. If one is concerned about response error in such verbal reports of behavior, I do not think it would be too farfetched to obtain independent measures on the behavior of very small numbers of such contrasted types of respondents, thereby validating the procedure.

A totally different type of survey approach might be employed to obtain systematic and large-scale evidence on the situational determinants of discriminatory behavior. I have in mind surveys of knowledgeable or expert *informants* who are asked to report their observations and their inferences about a variety of situations. One can include multiple informants reporting on the same settings as a check on the reliability of report, and one can gain great coverage by broad sampling of such individuals who have had the opportunity collectively to scan many situations ranging from recreational settings and neighborhood settings to work settings and the like. There are very few instances of this type of survey in the literature, but Dean and Rosen employed it successfully with professional workers in community race relations agencies, and recently Levine, Wright, and I conducted a large survey among expert informants on problems of social change in developing countries and were greatly comforted by the results of the many methodological tests on the quality of report.[66]

Another survey design bears upon the relation between mass prejudice, or tolerance in attitude, and action taken at the level of some collective unit, such as a community. What is examined is not whether attitude issues into *individual* behavior, but into some institutional decision. A survey of the attitudes of respondents is merged with *objective* data on the events and practices in the respondents' communities. Thus, for example, Sheatsley and I measured the prejudices of respondents in a series of national surveys, classified the communities in which they lived (it could equally well have been their places of work) by the pattern of segregation, and then examined the consistency or inconsistency between prejudice and segregation, trying to tease out the intervening links.[67]

Kohn and Williams adopt a novel approach. They do not like the "hypothetical situations" approach. For them it lacks the stuff of reality. But they realize that natural situations implicating Negroes and whites are all too rare and fugitive, and the observer may not be around. Nor do they provide adequate conditions for careful data collection, or give good enough sampling, or necessarily test enough situational variables whose influence has been hypothesized. Kohn and Williams therefore initiated a series of interracial situations in a sample of settings through the use of conspirators who acted as if they were ordinary men. They had previously "cased" these settings to determine the normal behavior of the hosts, to estimate their prejudices, and to know the social context. They are most careful to qualify the generality of their conclusions, but the approach seems to me most ingenious.[68]

One final thought on the utility of surveys for understanding the likely type of behavior in a variety of situations: Whatever is learned from the study of natural situations, or posited on the basis of theory, about the determinants that normally intervene between attitude and action, one might well attempt to develop descriptive measures of them and enumerate their frequency in large samples. Then one might predict to some degree the course of future discrimination or nondiscrimination in behavior in the larger population. To take some simple examples, the relative intensity with which prejudiced and nonprejudiced individuals hold their attitudes might help predict the outcome of a situation in which such parties mingle. The propensity to violence or the courage of these two types of individuals in the face of danger might well be relevant to predicting the outcomes in various kinds of situations.[69] Rokeach suggests that there is not only an attitude toward an object or person but an attitude toward situations, with "the attitude toward situation facilitating or inhibiting the expression of attitude-toward-object." [70] This two-factor model could be the basis for more comprehensive and predictive attitude measurement. Allport suggests that the situational factors which may modify the expression of attitude are in turn dependent on personality predispositions to various types of conformity to social pressures; and this suggests that measures of such conformity tendencies should accompany the measurement of attitude.[71] In explaining the behavior of individuals in situations where there is a choice between discriminatory and nondiscriminatory behavior, various investigators have suggested that the reference group the individual holds in mind will govern his decision. But this brings me to my next proposal.

RESEARCH ON REFERENCE GROUP AND RELATIVE DEPRIVATION PHENOMENA

It has almost become a general principle in social psychology that one adopts the attitudes that he regards as the norms of his reference groups. The principle has certainly been applied to attitudes of prejudice and to acts of discrimination or nondiscrimination which are often interpreted as, respectively, identification with the felt norms of some reference group or conformity to some group with whom we interact. With respect to the future of race relations, a number of problematic aspects of normative reference behavior among whites should be explored.

The usual theory is that conformity or compliance in behavior is the price most of us are willing to pay for the approval of the group which has us under scrutiny and to avoid the punishment that might be applied against our violation of its norms. Since our attitudes are private, not subject to scrutiny, they can be oriented to the norms of some other, more distant reference group without any danger of penalty.

Certainly, the model is basically sound, but there are many qualifications, some of which are relevant here.[72] Some people may not have any abiding loyalty to a reference group. They may shed an old one, as they shed old clothes, and really identify in spirit with the new groups into which they move. In this there is a force for both good and evil in race relations, depending on whatever norms the groups espouse.

There are also some individuals who act out their cherished attitudes, prejudiced or tolerant, as the case may be, despite the group pressures facing them. Consider one such instance where this process did not work for the common good. The case is a rather compelling one, since it proceeds counter to another plausible assumption about social behavior. It is usually assumed that most of us, as we move about the world, conform to the local ways out of common courtesy for our hosts. Now recall what happened when our American troops were quartered in England during 1943–1944 and some of them encountered a rather strange etiquette in race relations. I quote from one English account of the history of the events:

> In Europe a letter was sent to all troops explaining that attitudes towards the Negro in England and France were not the same as in the United States and that the policy of the U.S. Army would not deviate from that of the local populations.
>
> By 1943 the British West Indian Negroes considered that a good deal of the prejudice and discrimination they were beginning to feel seriously could be attributed to the influence of white American troops.
>
> In November 1943 an incident occurred at a ballroom, in Liverpool, when some of our technicians came into conflict with white American soldiers. The upshot was a fight and minor injuries to one technician and a razor slash of an Englishman. The culprit has not been found and so no prosecution took place. On interview with the C.I.D. authorities, it was definitely stated that the Americans were proved to be aggressive.

At a dance hall in Warrington in December 1943 . . . a party of American soldiers demanded the ejection of one of the Jamaican technicians who was dancing with a white girl. The man in question was reported to be of good character and accepted with good feeling at factory dances, etc. The Welfare Officer at Manchester described him as a quiet and diffident fellow who attended regularly at work. The manager of the dance hall refused the request of the American soldiers that the West Indian should be ejected.

Soon after the incident the manager received a letter from the local commanding officer of the U.S. Army as follows:

"It is not our intention to dictate the policies of privately owned establishments, but in the interest of eliminating trouble in which our troops may be involved we would appreciate your co-operation in prohibiting Negroes from attending the dances."

A second important incident occurred at about the same time. . . . A series of clashes between West Indians and American white troops at a well-known dance hall in Liverpool led to the imposition of a colour bar.

[Subsequently] discussion took place with the managements of the various establishments concerned. Each pointed out that they had no personal animosity towards Colonials; in fact they had pursued an open policy until the incidents between coloured and white men (particularly Americans) became so serious that as a result their receipts were falling off considerably. The alternative of barring Americans was considered but rejected as being impracticable—largely because the latter provided a large proportion of the income of the dance establishments. Each establishment concerned said that they would be prepared to consider relaxing their bar, if other halls did likewise; but they were not prepared to act independently and be flooded with coloured men as a result. These negotiations were commenced in 1944, but it was not until the war was over and the majority of Americans had returned home that any marked change appeared to have taken place. In the present day (circa 1950) none of the dance halls or restaurants operate a rigid colour bar, although one hall prefers coloured men to bring their own partners; this minimizes the possibility of offence being taken by white girls not wishing to dance with a coloured man.[73]

As I have noted, the many varieties of reference group and conformity processes may work in any direction, dependent on the accident of which groups espouse which norms and the white individual's respective ties. We have here what seems to me to be a practical, not a theoretical, problem. How do we make the *right* reference groups more attractive and salient to more people? As William James remarked in anticipation of reference group theory: "All progress in the social self is the substitution of higher tribunals for lower; this ideal tribunal is the highest; and most men, either continually or occasionally, carry a reference to it in their breast." [74]

Perhaps a program in the engineering of reference group processes can be guided to some extent by exploratory research. I note in this connection a study by DeFleur and Westie whose main purpose was to test whether verbal reports of prejudice actually predicted behavior in an interracial situation.[75] An ingenious behavioral situation was developed in which the white subjects, whose attitudes had been previously measured by verbal instruments, indicated whether they would volunteer or not to be photographed with a Negro of the opposite sex, which picture would then be used in a range of public situations. In passing, I may note that the findings gave considerable proof that the attitude did govern the action, and similar findings have been obtained in four replications of the study by Cook.[76] What concerns me here is another aspect of the original study. On the theory that the subject's action was governed by the reference groups he held in mind, after his decision was recorded by a photograph release agreement which he signed, he was asked: "Was there any particular person or group of people . . . who came to mind when you decided to sign (or refused to sign) this document?" Nearly three-fourths of the subjects reported such reference groups, and some sixty different groups were mentioned by the forty-six experimental subjects. Some type of peer group was most frequently mentioned by these college students, who also reported clear beliefs that their actions would arouse the approval or disapproval of such peers. Certainly we have here an ingenious vehicle for inquiry into reference group processes as they mediate translation of attitude into action.[77]

But perhaps the tides are flowing in the right direction, and engineering is not necessary. Note, for example, that surveys now document that those with military experience—in contrast with the 1943 case I cited—are more tolerant than others. This has been established in Sheatsley's and my surveys and independently by Matthews and Prothro.[78] Also, consider an odd finding when northerners who move South are compared in their attitudes with southerners who go North, and both groups are compared with the stationary residents of each region. The northerners who go South remain close to the integration pole in their attitudes, but the southerners who move North also move far away in their attitudes from the segregationist pole. The latter conform to the new local group; the others hold to their old reference group.[79] Obviously the phenomenon is a welcome one, but there is a mystery of reference group processes to be analyzed.

While the explanation escapes me—and I know no research findings that illuminate the problem—I would suggest that part of the answer lies in a "national reference group" to which we are all oriented in some degree.[80] The northerner is buttressed, so to speak, by two reference groups which mutually reinforce him in his behavior against the local norm, whereas the southerner is overwhelmed by the new local group working in conjunction with the national norm. At any rate, one would like to explore the degree to which individuals adopt distant and larger reference groups rather than merely the smaller groups with which they are presently in proximity. Therein lies some of the hope for changes in southern attitudes and perhaps some of the explanation of the changes that have already occurred.

Another problematic aspect of normative reference group processes has to do with the perception of the norms of various groups. Consider the tolerant white southerner whose resolve may be weakened because he has some loyalty to a southern reference group, but perceives its norms as solidly segregationist. If only he realized that, in truth, he had some small support! But, alas, we may have a situation that Katz and Allport [81] described long ago as one of pluralistic ignorance. Matthews and Prothro demonstrate that white southerners are not aware of the attitudes and norms among southern Negroes. But perhaps some of them—especially the tolerant—do not correctly perceive the attitudes and norms of their fellow whites and underestimate the support available to them, albeit small in magnitude. Certainly, one could explore in surveys the norms imputed to various groups and compare these estimates with the distribution of actual attitudes, thus obtaining a discrepancy score. And certainly, one could then engage in some action and dissemination of the facts to remedy the underestimation of tolerant norms among groups to which individuals may feel loyal.[82]

These examples are only illustrative of what I think to be the promise for understanding and helping race relations that lies in a program of research into the normative reference groups held by whites.

Thus far, my proposals have dealt with white attitudes and behavior, but the sphere of comparative reference group theory also holds much promise for understanding the behavior of Negroes. Various analysts, as noted earlier, have interpreted the passivity or militancy of American Negroes as stemming from a sense of relative deprivation. But that sense of deprivation depends on the individuals or groups with whom Negroes compare themselves. In this area, speculation is rife and empiricism is absent. Certainly, the variety of comparative reference groups actually chosen by Negroes ought to be described and the determinants and consequences of the selection of a particular reference group analyzed. In 1953, Reid presented the problem eloquently, but it still awaits study.

> The cue and key to the problems discussed in this volume are to be found in the implied definitions of *relative status*. Almost without exception the

authors establish their comparisons between Negroes (or nonwhites) and the generalized white population. While this is an acceptable and valid method of description and analysis it certainly does not exhaust the possibilities of scientific exploration. One may raise a question as to whether or not this comparison of the *special status* group with the *generalized other* population provides the most meaningful and accurate type of analysis. The context of the analyses presented herein is an implied rather than a stated one. The relative status of the Negro population is established, in gaming parlance, the "hard way." Slight shifts in the frames of reference—the comparison of Negroes with other nonwhites, with foreign-born whites, or native-born whites, with the statuses of migrating populations, or with populations 25 years of age and over—may have indicated totally different types of status changes.[83]

I may add one final point to this discussion by formulating the odd concept of *imputed* relative deprivation. Individuals might be asked to make a judgment of the relative deprivation of a group *other than their own* and to report the comparative reference group they used as a standard in arriving at that judgment. It may well be that the reference group a Negro employs in assessing his own relative deprivation is very different from the one whites use in appraising the relative deprivation of Negroes. Perhaps some of the misunderstanding surrounding groups in conflict arises from just such differences in the comparative reference groups employed and should be explored.[84]

THE FORMULATION OF NEW AREAS
FOR SURVEY RESEARCH

By now I may have presented enough counter-evidence against the criticisms of survey research implicit in the case studies of situational determinants to warrant some confidence in the future use of surveys for the study of race relations. One could cite more evidence. For example, Cook and his associates have been engaged in a large-scale program of research on the development of nonobtrusive measures of prejudiced attitudes and discriminatory behavior. The correlations between these measures and their well-constructed but more conventional verbal scales are quite strong. The consistency with which subtle survey findings on prejudice by one agency have been replicated independently in other surveys is also comforting. For example, Matthews and Prothro find the same curvilinear pattern of attitudes of prejudice by fine age groups in the South as Sheatsley and I find independently.

So let us proceed to my proposal. I have already presented piecemeal a great many suggestions for areas of future survey research, and I shall not bother to bring these thoughts together. I shall simply note two additional areas where surveys could contribute findings that might be fruitful for race relations.

Current relations between Negroes and whites may be seen as a battle between hostile groups separated by deep hatreds and committed to the unconditional surrender of their opponents. And perhaps this picture renders the scene somewhat faithfully. But it may be an overgeneralization about the many from the behavior of the few. Perhaps a better perspective on the scene is provided by Williams' remark, "Much of the apparent ethnic prejudice in our community life is compounded by isolation, timidity, and social fear," [85] and by his observations after studying a number of cities in 1951:

> Our general picture of the majority-group population in the communities thus far studied includes a wide range of prejudice, with true bigots at one extreme and non-prejudiced persons at the other, but with a vast middle range in which reside the "gentle people of prejudice." The great majority of prejudiced persons carry prejudice at a low temperature, and much of their discriminatory behavior reflects relatively passive conformity to taken-for-granted patterns prevalent in the social groups which give them their statuses and sense of belonging.[86]

Perhaps the situation has become more polarized since that date. But, for sure, it would be highly desirable to substitute contemporary evidence for speculation.[87] The trend studies suggest to the contrary that the nonprejudiced group in the society is growing at the expense of the prejudiced. But whatever the size of the prejudiced group of whites in the population, some of the dimensions of their attitudes and the sources of their feelings ought to be surveyed on a continuing basis, since the "present . . . is gone in the instant of becoming."

Consider two sets of findings bearing on the problem. In the Cornell studies, there was a dramatic correlation between individuals reporting that they are generally uncomfortable about meeting strangers and their report that they are uneasy in the company of Negroes.[88] Understandable: Negroes and whites in the past have been strangers. Perhaps as they get to know each other better in the future, they will come to feel less distant and uncomfortable and the way toward greater integration will ease. Recently, Cook and Woodmanse, in three studies of the organization of verbally measured attitudes of whites toward Negroes, isolated repeatedly by factor analysis eleven dimensions of such attitudes.[89] One of the clearest dimensions in their data, which differentiated groups of subjects known to differ in prejudice and intergroup behavior, was that of "ease in interracial contacts," which appears to me to be very similar to the Williams dimension.

Turn away from those who are merely timid and ill at ease to those who are not "gentle people of prejudice." What will contain them or temper their hostility? Long ago, Myrdal pointed to the contradiction between American values of equalitarianism and fairness and the occurrence of prejudice and discrimination. Empirical studies suggest, unfortunately, that this contradiction is not felt by many white Americans as a source of conflict or guilt and that its psychic force toward reform is in some manner blunted.[90] Whether it is worth repeating some of these studies again as the dilemma has become more painfully apparent, I do not know. I doubt that the findings will change. But the American value of equality or justice or fairness does not provide the only moral principle and moral force toward the improvement of race relations.

Consider, for example, another value which might be phrased in a number of ways: the commitment to peaceful modes of resolving conflict, rather than violence; not fighting an underdog when the odds are too much in your favor; the use of force only in the service of a presumed just cause.[91] To be sure, our society has a streak of bellicosity also, and there is considerable evidence that the South has an exaggerated code of physical violence, but the values I have mentioned seem also to be cherished. Whatever the desire of extreme groups of whites to resist strongly Negro advancement, I should like to know the degree to which the translation of their hostility into violence is felt to be incompatible with the moral value of peaceable solutions.[92] And I believe that such an inquiry would impinge on even more important social problems: the nature of the support for or opposition to the general use of force, for example, in the solution of larger international conflicts.

STUDIES THAT EXPLORE NEGLECTED DIMENSIONS

Searching the social psychological literature on race relations, one stumbles across occasional studies which sparkle with imagination. They usually remain lost to us, buried under the massive weight of the total literature. I mention one pair of experimental studies so as to spark our own imagination, perhaps to revive the methods employed, and to suggest some of the eccentricities of prejudice. In the first study, Bray measured attitudes of subjects toward Negroes and Jews by verbal scales and then at a later date conducted an experiment on the autokinetic effect.[93] But it was a rather unusual variation on Sherif's classic experiment. In some experimental groups, a Negro confederate was introduced. In other sessions a white confederate identified as a Jew was introduced, and in still other sessions, the very same confederate was introduced and identified as a gentile. The minority membership was made salient by instructions, and the treatments were randomly assigned.

One prime hypothesis was that a prejudiced individual would be *less* influenced by the judgments reported by the minority confederates. But Bray also hypothesized that prejudice might well channel the results in other ways, since, as the stereotype went, Jews are clever and Negroes are unintelligent. And the basic findings were that the *anti-Semitic* subjects did conform more to the Jewish confederate than to the gentile, whereas those who were not anti-Negro conformed more closely to the Negro confederate than to the white gentile confederate. The experiment has a number of ambiguous findings, but it makes one ponder the paradoxical thought that accepting social influence may reflect prejudice, even though it could lead to convergence and common behavior on the part of majority and minority members.

A rather similar experiment was conducted by Malof and Lott, using as their paradigm the classic experiment by Asch.[94] The confederate was a Negro or a white individual. At the right moment, he broke away from the unanimous majority and gave rigged, contrary judgments in support of the experimental subject's own judgments of the length of line. The subjects were found to respond to the support by the confederate, whether he was Negro or white, and whether or not they were highly prejudiced. In this respect, the finding bears upon Rokeach's theory that belief similarity may override color prejudice. However, among highly prejudiced subjects, as measured by the E-scale, the white confederate's support was somewhat, although not significantly, greater in its effect.

Contemplating the difference in the effects of the Negro confederate on the white prejudiced subjects in these two similar experiments, and ignoring other differences in the two procedures, subjects, and the time interval of a dozen years, lead to one speculation. The Asch experiment creates, of course, a most stressful task for subjects in contrast to the Sherif situation. Perhaps common bonds of belief can override prejudice against Negroes best under conditions of need.

About fifteen years ago, my imagination somehow became liberated in an idle moment, and this fantasy occurred to me. If a white southerner were born totally blind, what would be his image, attitude, and behavior toward Negroes in his maturity? How about a southern Negro who had suffered the same misfortune? What would be his self-conception? His view of whites? What meaning would the traditions of southern society have for such individuals, and how would they learn to transact their lives? The same questions, of course, occurred to me in relation to the life of those who were born blind in the North. I began to think of the totally blind as a most unusual vehicle by which to explore fundamental problems of communication and socialization: knowledge, perception, and social behavior. My thoughts at that point began to move far beyond race relations, since many of our values and social patterns rest on visual cues—class distinctions, for example. Central in my focus, however, were Negro-white relations which depend, after all else is said, on the simple fact of color which, under this handicap, society must labor mightily to teach and the blind labor mightily to learn. Perhaps the blind might never learn at all!

In the design that began to emerge, there was also a place for those blinded later in life, after they had been socialized as members of a sighted world. Bereft of the cues they once used, how would they maintain their accustomed patterns of behavior? Perhaps they might learn the hard way the absurdity of social distinctions which can be erased for them simply by the adventitious fact of blindness.

For a dozen years I shackled my imagination while I pursued more conventional lines of research. But I combed the literature and could find no such studies. So, finally, I began an inquiry, and as of now have completed lengthy interviews with about four hundred totally blind adults, distributed among Negroes and whites, southerners and northerners, and those blinded early and late in life. And I have corresponding interviews with a sighted family member who functions both as an informant on the process of socialization or resocialization and also as a control subject matched in many social respects with his blind counterpart so as to isolate the intrinsic effects of blindness. I have also conducted interviews with a small sample of totally blind children and with one adult member of their family and with a sighted sibling where available. After several years, the data have been collected and processed, and the analysis is now in progress. I present this bare sketch, without findings, simply to convey the thought that new worlds of opportunity still await the social psychologist of race relations, if he will only liberate his imagination and harness his energies to the task.

•NOTES

1 H. Blumer, "United States of America: Research on Racial Relations," *International Social Science Bulletin*, X (1958), 403.

2 California Governor's Commission on the Los Angeles Riots, *Transcripts,*

Depositions, Consultants' Reports, and Selected Documents. 18 vols. Library of Congress printed card no. 66–63719, $83.00 (35 mm microfilm).

3 A good example is provided by a national survey in 1945 which employed an intensity scale in conjunction with more conventional measures of white attitudes toward Negroes. The more tolerant groups held their attitudes less intensely than the prejudiced groups. The inference was drawn that the greater intensity among the prejudiced represented their need to defend a position which was already then under attack. Certainly, this same hypothesis could be tested more effectively and unambiguously under present-day conditions. From a pragmatic point of view, it would be exceedingly valuable to know whether the adversaries on the issue are unequally matched because of the differing levels of intensity with which they hold their views. Yet this simple technique and valuable base line has been neglected by recent researchers. See H. Cantril, "The Intensity of an Attitude," *Journal of Abnormal and Social Psychology,* XLI (1946), 129–135.

4 P. Waly and S. W. Cook, "Attitude as a Determinant of Learning and Memory: A Failure to Confirm," *Journal of Personality and Social Psychology,* IV (1966), 280–288; E. E. Jones and R. Kohler, "The Effects of Plausibility on the Learning of Controversial Statements," *Journal of Abnormal and Social Psychology,* LVII (1958), 315–320.

5 L. Srole, "Social Integration and Certain Corollaries: An Exploratory Study," *American Sociological Review,* XXI (1956), 709–716; A. Roberts and M. Rokeach, "Anomie, Authoritarianism, and Prejudice: A Replication," *American Journal of Sociology,* LXI (1956), 355–358.

6 H. Triandis, "A Note on Rokeach's Theory of Prejudice," *Journal of Abnormal and Social Psychology,* LXII (1961), 184–186; M. Rokeach, ed., *The Open and Closed Mind* (New York: Basic Books, 1960), pp. 132–168; M. Rokeach, "Belief versus Race as Determinants of Social Distance: Comment on Triandis' Paper," *Journal of Abnormal and Social Psychology,* LXII (1961), 187–188; D. Byrne and T. Wong, "Racial Prejudice, Interpersonal Attraction, and Assumed Dissimilarity of Attitudes," *Journal of Abnormal and Social Psychology,* LXV (1962), 246–253; D. Stein, J. Hardyck, and M. B. Smith, "Race and Belief: An Open and Shut Case," *Journal of Personality and Social Psychology,* I (1965), 281–289.

7 Blumer, *op. cit.,* p. 430.

8 K. B. Clark, "Problems of Power and Social Change: Toward a Relevant Social Psychology," *Journal of Social Issues,* XXI, No. 3 (1965), 5.

9 R. Williams, Jr., "Social Change and Social Conflict: Race Relations in the United States, 1944–1964," *Sociological Inquiry,* XXXV (1965), 12.

10 E. C. Hughes, "Race Relations and the Sociological Imagination," *American Sociological Review,* XXVIII (1963), 879–890.

11 *Ibid.*, p. 879.

12 Williams, *op. cit.*, pp. 13–14.

13 G. W. Allport, "Prejudice: Is It Societal or Personal?", *Journal of Social Issues*, XVIII, No. 2 (1962), 120–134.

14 W. James, *Principles of Psychology* (New York: Holt, 1890), I, 608.

15 M. Kohn and R. Williams, Jr., "Situational Patterning in Intergroup Relations," *American Sociological Review*, XXI (1956), 146.

16 Aberle and Naegele remark: "All in all, child rearing is future-oriented to an important extent. The picture of the desired end product is importantly influenced by the parents' experiences in the adult world, as well as by their childhood experiences. When adult experience changes under the impact of major social change, there is reason to believe that there will ultimately, though not necessarily immediately, be shifts in the socialization pattern as well." D. F. Aberle and K. D. Naegele, "Middle-Class Fathers' Occupational Role and Attitudes toward Children," *American Journal of Orthopsychiatry*, XXII (1952), 367. That individuals attempt to socialize *themselves* to a future status and situation different from their present position has been given much recognition under the rubric of *anticipatory socialization*. That parents would anticipate a changed situation for their children and socialize them accordingly seems equally worthy of recognition and study, but ironically has been neglected.

17 See, for example, an incidental observation in a study of Italian-American immigrants: I. Child, *Italian or American?* (New Haven: Yale University Press, 1943), pp. 44–45.

18 A. Inkeles, "Social Change and Social Character: The Role of Parental Mediation," *Journal of Social Issues*, XI, No. 2 (1955), 12–23.

19 H. Hyman and P. Sheatsley, "Attitudes toward Desegregation," *Scientific American*, CCXI, No. 1 (1964), 7.

20 By contrast, there are a number of studies of the way Negro families orient their children to entering into a desegregated school. See, for example, E. A. Weinstein and P. N. Geisel, "Family Decision-Making over Desegregation," *Sociometry*, XXV (1962), 21–29.

21 Bonita Valien, *The St. Louis Story: A Study of Desegregation* (New York: Anti-Defamation League, 1956), p. 31.

22 E. L. Horowitz and R. Horowitz, "Development of Social Attitudes in Children," *Sociometry*, I (1938), 301–338, especially pp. 332–336. See also O. Quinn, "The Transmission of Racial Attitudes among White Southerners," *Social Forces*, XXXIII (1954), 41–47, for data on socialization practices before 1944. Also see C. Bird, E. Monachesi, and H. Burdick, "Studies of Group Tensions: III, The Effect of Parental Discouragement of Play Activities Upon the Attitudes of White Children toward Negroes," *Child Development*, XXIII (1952), 295–306; Marian Radke-Yarrow, Helen G. Trager, and J. Miller, "The Role of Parents in the

Development of Children's Ethnic Attitudes," *Child Development,* XXIII (1952), 13–53; R. C. Schaffer and A. Schaffer, "Socialization and the Development of Attitudes toward Negroes in Alabama," *Phylon,* XIX (1958), 274–285.

23 R. Williams, Jr., *Strangers Next Door* (Englewood Cliffs, N.J.: Prentice-Hall, 1964), p. 100.

24 *Ibid.,* p. 160. Williams also establishes that variation in interracial contact in the course of development predicts interracial contact in later life. See p. 184.

Interracial contact during childhood was found in another study to increase activity in support of integration of their churches among a group of clergymen matched in attitude and in the level of segregation of their parishes. See K. C. Garrison, Jr., "The Behavior of Clergy on Racial Integration as Related to a Childhood Socialization Factor," *Sociology and Social Research,* LI (1967), 209–219.

25 Valien, *op. cit.,* pp. 31–32.

26 D. Gast, "Minority Americans in Children's Literature," *Elementary English,* XLIV (1967), 12–23. This finding bears on our later discussion of the rising occupational status of Negroes and the perception by whites of the Negro's changing class.

27 See, for example, K. Little, *Negroes in Britain* (London: Kegan Paul, 1948), pp. 8, 69; L. Silberman and B. Spice, *Colour and Class in Six Liverpool Schools* (Liverpool: The University Press, 1950); D. Wood, "A General Survey," in *Coloured Immigrants in Britain,* issued under the auspices of the Institute of Race Relations (London: Oxford University Press, 1960).

28 See, for example, papers by P. M. Hauser, D. Moynihan, and R. Fein, in *Daedalus,* XCIV (Fall, 1965). See also P. M. Siegel, "On the Cost of Being a Negro," *Sociological Inquiry,* XXXV (1965), 41–57.

29 Fein, *ibid.;* T. F. Pettigrew, *A Profile of the Negro American* (Princeton: Van Nostrand, 1964).

30 G. Gilbert, "Stereotype Persistence and Change among College Students, *Journal of Abnormal and Social Psychology,* XLVI (1951), 251. For other recent evidence that measures of prejudice and stereotyping based on check lists and forced-response formats obscure the uncertainty respondents feel, inflate consensus on specified traits, and miss such aspects of the white's cognitive structure of the Negro as his poverty and oppressed status, see H. J. Ehrlich and J. W. Rinehart, "A Brief Report on the Methodology of Stereotype Research," *Social Forces,* XLIII (1965), 564–575; H. J. Ehrlich, "Instrument Error and the Study of Prejudice," *Social Forces,* XLIII (1964), 197–206.

31 J. Harding *et al.,* "Prejudice and Ethnic Relations," in G. Lindzey, ed., *Handbook of Social Psychology* (Cambridge: Addison-Wesley, 1954), II, 1025. Apropos the warning, note especially the remarks of one of Gilbert's

subjects: "In most of these I must, unfortunately, base my decisions on my acquaintance with only one or two representatives, or, even worse, on movie or magazine stock characters. Thus, I write everything with extensive reservations. Secondly, I wish to point out that I most definitely do not consider any characteristics which I hesitantly assign to one ethnic group as necessarily applying to an individual within the group. I merely think that one group would tend more toward containing such an individual than another."

32 K. S. Sodhi, "Federal Republic of Germany: Research on Racial Relations," *International Social Science Bulletin*, X (1958), 392.

33 M. P. Banton, *White and Coloured* (London: Jonathan Cape, 1959), p. 37.

34 J. A. Bayton, L. B. McAlister, and J. Hamer, "Race-Class Stereotypes," *Journal of Negro Education*, XXV (1956), 75–78. I omit the very interesting findings also reported in which Negro experimental subjects were asked to stereotype the same four stimulus groups, white and Negro upper and lower classes.

35 *Ibid.*, p. 77.

36 The apparent plausibility of the prediction stems from the exclusive attention to the one limited factor, status *anxiety*, which might be heightened by the rise of Negroes in the class structure. But other neglected aspects of status-related behavior might be affected by the rise of Negroes in just such a way as to reduce prejudice. For a more elaborate conceptualization of status concerns and a comprehensive theory of the relation between status needs and prejudice, see H. M. Blalock, Jr., *Toward a Theory of Minority-Group Relations* (New York: Wiley, 1967), pp. 51–70. Blalock theorizes that whites with a high degree of status *consciousness* now avoid Negroes out of fear of the status *loss* they will suffer from contact with what is at present a lower-status group.

37 L. M. Brooks, "Racial Distance as Affected by Education," *Sociology and Social Research*, XXI (1936), 131. Woodward reminds us that if we go further back in history, we find that southern white behavior and attitudes toward Negroes were *more* favorable in relation to upper-class Negroes. For example, he quotes from a Charleston, South Carolina, paper in 1885: "It is a great deal pleasanter to travel with respectable and well-behaved colored people than with unmannerly and ruffianly white men." Twelve years later the same paper said: "The common sense and proper arrangement, in our opinion, is to provide first-class cars for first-class passengers, white and colored. . . . To speak plainly, we need, as everybody knows, separate cars or apartments for rowdy or drunken white passengers, far more than Jim Crow cars for colored passengers." C. V. Woodward, *The Strange Career of Jim Crow* (New York: Oxford University Press, 1955), pp. 30–31.

38 E. L. Horowitz, "Race Attitudes," in O. Klineberg, ed., *Characteristics of the American Negro* (New York: Harper, 1944), p. 148.

39 G. Razran, "Ethnic Dislikes and Stereotypes: A Laboratory Study," *Journal of Abnormal and Social Psychology,* XLV (1950), 7–27.

40 Silberman and Spice, *op. cit.* It is relevant to report here old studies which showed the early awareness of white American children of the impoverished class position of Negroes. See for example, Horowitz and Horowitz, *op. cit.,* or Radke and Trager who showed by doll-play techniques that white children dressed Negro dolls in poor clothes and assigned the doll to a poor house. Marian J. Radke and Helen Trager, "Children's Perceptions of the Social Roles of Negroes and Whites," *Journal of Psychology,* XXIX (1950), 3–33. Another investigator of Negro-white relations in England reports the following protocol which conveys the way in which class can override color in a setting where class values have great potency. She reports the remark of a college servant to a Negro student: "You know, sir—I always call you sir, don't I now?—yesterday Bill heard me calling you 'Sir' and he said to me 'Oh' he said 'why do you call *him* sir? I wouldn't call him 'sir'—not a nigger I wouldn't.' I says to him, 'Bill, we're servants of the university, aren't we, and it's our job to serve him as well as the others. It isn't *their* fault that these fellows are coloured. They can't help it.'" Judith Henderson, "A Sociological Report," in *Coloured Immigrants in Britain,* issued under the auspices of the Institute of Race Relations (London: Oxford University Press, 1960).

41 F. R. Westie, "Negro-White Status Differentials and Social Distance," *American Sociological Review,* XVII (1952), 550–558; F. R. Westie and M. L. Westie, "The Social-Distance Pyramid: Relations between Caste and Class," *American Journal of Sociology,* LXIII (1957), 190–196; F. R. Westie and D. H. Howard, "Social Status Differentials and the Race Attitudes of Negroes," *American Sociological Review,* XIX (1954), 584–591.

42 Barbara K. Mackenzie, "The Importance of Contact in Determining Attitudes toward Negroes," *Journal of Abnormal and Social Psychology,* XLIII (1948), 417–441.

43 Triandis, *op. cit.,* pp. 311–312. As a result of such a design, Triandis can play off the effect of race vs. class. For example, will there be less social distance toward a Negro of high status than toward a white of low status? One is reminded of the parallel in the early study by Horowitz and Horowitz in which young white southern children were asked whether they would rather play with a "rich colored" or a "poor white," the investigators taking the precaution initially to determine empirically whether poverty or riches was in fact the preferred attribute. While similarity in race overrode the effect of undesirable status for 29 children, it should be noted that 17 children chose on the basis of class.

44 H. Triandis and L. Triandis, "A Cross-Culture Study of Social Distance," *Psychological Monographs,* LXXVI (1962), whole of No. 540; H. Triandis and L. Triandis, "Race, Social Class, Religion and Nationality as Deter-

minants of Social Distance," *Journal of Abnormal and Social Psychology*, LXI (1960), 110–118; H. Triandis, *op. cit.*; H. Triandis and L. Triandis, "Exploratory Factor Analyses of the Behavioral Component of Social Attitudes," *Journal of Abnormal and Social Psychology*, LXVIII (1964), 420–430; H. Triandis and W. D. Loh, "Race, Status, Quality of Spoken English, and Opinions about Civil Rights as Determinants of Interpersonal Attitudes," *Journal of Personality and Social Psychology*, III (1966), 468–472. In this last experiment, the stimulus persons were presented not by verbal descriptions but in the form of color slides accompanied by a tape-recorded voice purporting to be the person depicted and presenting his views. In this fashion the stimulus person approximated more to a real person, and class position could be conveyed both by style of dress and style of speech. It should be noted that Triandis demonstrates that particular characteristics of the stimulus person—for example, class, belief, race—vary in the specific dimensions of prejudice that they determine.

45 R. Epstein and S. S. Komorita, "Parental Discipline, Stimulus Characteristics of Outgroups, and Social Distance in Children," *Journal of Personality and Social Psychology*, II (1965), 416–420. The technique Hartley invented in his classic studies of the generality of prejudice of using a fictitious or "Nonesuch" group is thus reincorporated into the modern research repertory. For that early use, see E. L. Hartley, *Problems in Prejudice* (New York: Kings Crown Press, 1946). A similar design, employed by two other investigators, implicitly provides additional evidence on the contribution that class makes to prejudice against Negroes, although the study was inspired by a different theory and is interpreted accordingly. Each of four Negro faces was superimposed on two backgrounds, and the series of eight pictures was then shown to a group of white undergraduates who answered questions about the pictures and described the characteristics of the Negro. Some of the backgrounds were contrasted in class; for example, a yacht club or luxurious home vs. a rural slum. The descriptions of the very same Negro were more derogatory in the stereotyped and lower-class setting. See A. B. Riddleberger and A. B. Motz, "Prejudice and Perception," *American Journal of Sociology*, LXII (1957), 498–503.

46 Their experimental design provided a test of one specific factor in socialization—perceived severity of parental punitiveness—which was found not to have any significant interactional effect on the direction of prejudice toward class or color, although it had a significant effect on generalized social distance toward others. In a program of research now in progress under the direction of S. Cook, a similar experiment is being conducted. Photographs of a Negro, a white, and a Japanese person, to which are attached verbal descriptions of his low or high occupation as well as other desirable or undesirable attributes, are shown to experimental subjects who then record their reactions on a social distance scale and a semantic differential. The findings have not been reported in detail, but "the results clearly show that the ratings of the person de-

scribed are strongly influenced by the number of factors that are high in the personality sketch." See S. W. Cook, *Studies of Attitude and Attitude Measurement, Progress Report* (Boulder: University of Colorado, October 1, 1966, mimeographed), pp. 4–10.

47 Hyman and Sheatsley, *op. cit.*, p. 4.

48 Personal communication from Sheatsley.

49 TV monitoring studies conducted in 1962 and again in 1964 document an increase in the number of Negro appearances, albeit still low, and a drop in stereotyped characterizations. A more recent study conducted in the fall of 1966, in which sports programs were monitored and accompanying commercials classified, documented that Negroes appeared in only 5 per cent of the commercials. The finding is compelling in light of the fact that the audiences for such programs are predominantly male sports fans favorably attuned to watch Negro star athletes. See L. Plotkin, *Report on the Frequency of Appearance of Negroes on Televised Commercials* (New York: City College, 1967, mimeographed).

50 M. Rokeach, *The Open and Closed Mind* and "Belief Versus Race." See also M. Rokeach and L. Mezei, "Race and Shared Belief as Factors in Social Choice," *Science,* CLI (1966), 167–172; M. Rokeach, "Attitude Change and Behavioral Change," *Public Opinion Quarterly,* XXX (1966), 529–550.

51 In his most recent study, H. Triandis presents a resolution of the contradiction between his and Rokeach's findings. For some dimensions of interracial behavior, difference in race is the important determinant; for other dimensions, difference in belief is the important determinant; for still other dimensions, both race and belief are important. He also isolates two types of white subjects who vary in whether or not they are consistently more sensitive to the race or the belief of the other person. See H. C. Triandis and E. E. Davis, "Race and Belief as Determinants of Behavioral Intentions," *Journal of Personality and Social Psychology,* II (1965), 715–725. All the Triandis studies were conducted among northern subjects, for whom race would be expected to be a less prepotent characteristic than for southern subjects. Rokeach had included among his subjects one group from Texas for whom he had found that belief also outweighed race in determining preferential responses. Some six years after his southern study, a new investigation conducted in three regions in 1966 found that belief congruence was more important than race for whites living in the North or border region, but that race was the more important factor for the Louisiana sample. See C. R. Smith, L. Williams, and R. H. Willis, "Race, Sex, and Belief as Determinants of Friendship Acceptance," *Journal of Personality and Social Psychology,* V (1967), 127–137.

52 The study by C. R. Smith *et al.* provides some evidence in support of the argument. The stimulus persons presented some eight different beliefs. Similarity with respect to some beliefs (such as Communism) was far

more important in eliciting friendship from the white subjects than similarity in other beliefs. The investigators also suggest that the behavior of the southern subjects may be explained by the fact that they assumed that the Negro stimulus person who had been presented as holding *one* similar belief differed from them in his other beliefs. *Ibid.*

53 Stein *et al., op. cit.*

54 A sad finding by Matthews and Prothro in their large-scale surveys of the white and Negro populations of eleven southern states is, in this special context, perhaps some cause for comfort. They find little awareness among whites, especially those in the deep South, of the true attitudes of southern Negroes on desegregation (as objectively revealed by their own survey). As they remark, the dominant white group "may respond to those demands if they know what they are. . . . Even whites who are appalled at Negro demands may be forced at least to recognize that the demands exist." To be sure, this is so, and the only note of optimism to be derived—*given this vantage point*—is the greater awareness of the demands among whites living in the border states. But, from the vantage point of the Rokeach theory, perhaps lack of awareness is better than correct recognition of the differences in belief and the deep-seated resentment Negroes feel about segregation. One is reminded of Tumin's phrase, "the social functions of ignorance." What *net* balance of optimism and pessimism should be derived from their finding, I would not attempt to estimate. D. Matthews and J. Prothro, "Southern Racial Attitudes: Conflict, Awareness, and Political Change," *Annals*, CCCXLIV (November, 1962), 117, 119.

55 Judging from Carter's study of southern newspapers in 1957, the obvious and pessimistic expectations one might harbor might be shattered. These papers, at that time, did not purvey an extreme segregationist view. R. Carter, Jr., "Segregation and the News: A Regional Content Study," *Journalism Quarterly* (1957), pp. 3–18.

56 I am indebted to Pettigrew for his suggestion that class may be the indicator individuals use in inferring the attitude of another, and thereby merging the two bodies of research which I had seen in such sharp contrast.

57 R. T. LaPiere, "Attitudes vs. Actions," *Social Forces*, XIII (1934), 230–237; G. Saenger and E. Gilbert, "Customer Reactions to Integration of Negro Sales Personnel," *International Journal of Opinion and Attitude Research*, IV (1950), 57–76; J. D. Lohman and D. C. Reitzes, "Deliberately Organized Groups and Racial Behavior," *American Sociological Review*, XIX (1954), 342–344; L. M. Killian, "The Effects of Southern White Workers on Race Relations in Northern Plants," *American Sociological Review*, XVII (1952), 327–331; B. A. Reed, "Accommodation between Negro and White Employers in a West Coast Aircraft Industry, 1942–1944," *Social Forces*, XXVI (1947), 76–87; J. Hope, "Industrial Integration of Negroes: The Upgrading Process," *Human Organization*,

XI (1952), 5–14; R. D. Minard, "Race Relations in the Pocahontas Coal Field," *Journal of Social Issues,* VIII, No. 1 (1952), 29–44; B. Kutner, C. A. Wilkins, and P. R. Yarrow, "Verbal Attitudes and Overt Behavior Involving Racial Prejudice," *Journal of Abnormal and Social Psychology,* XLVII (1952), 649–652; J. Henderson, *op. cit.;* Banton, *op. cit.,* p. 226. Most of these studies were conducted prior to the passage of antidiscrimination laws. Obviously, there is no great mystery to be solved when people restrain their prejudices in the face of law or the threat of punishment.

58 For example, the study by Kutner *et al., op. cit.,* which is frequently cited as evidence, is based on the behavior of eleven restaurant owners in a "northeastern community."

59 One of Killian's southern workers, transplanted to Chicago, illustrates the strength of the economic motive, but also reveals that the situation may not always be stacked so neatly that the prejudiced person has to pay the price of not discriminating in his actions. He remarks: "I guess I've just been lucky, but I aint never worked in a place where they hired Niggers. I would if the job was a good one, but I just never have." *Op. cit.,* p. 330. One may also recall many instances from the past where discrimination against workers from a minority group has served to protect the economic advantage of a white labor force.

60 I. Stuart, "Minorities vs. Minorities; Cognitive, Affective and Conative Components of Puerto Rican and Negro Acceptance and Rejection," *Journal of Social Psychology,* LIX (1963), 96–97.

61 Hope, *op. cit.* In his study of nondiscriminatory behavior in a southern plant, Hope is thoughtful enough to tell us that the plant was new; white and Negro workers were recruited at the same time; and therefore the whites did not feel displaced by the Negro workers.

62 R. T. Bower, "The Role of Opinion Research in Desegregation," in *The Role of the Social Sciences in Desegregation* (New York: Anti-Defamation League, 1958), p. 23.

63 One should not jump to such conclusions too quickly. Schuman and Harding developed a verbal instrument which presents discriminatory incidents in which the respondent can either yield, so as not to offend the feelings of other whites implicated in the description, or support the minority and offend the other whites. They present evidence of its correlation with other measures. See H. Schuman and J. Harding, "Sympathetic Identification with the Underdog," *Public Opinion Quarterly,* XXVII (1963), 238.

64 M. Tumin, *Desegregation: Resistance and Readiness* (Princeton: Princeton University Press, 1958).

65 M. Tumin, "Some Problems for Sociological Research in Desegregation," in *The Role of the Social Sciences,* p. 35.

66 J. P. Dean and A. Rosen, with the assistance of R. B. Johnson, *A Manual*

of *Intergroup Relations* (Chicago: University of Chicago Press, 1955); H. Hyman, G. Levine, and C. Wright, "Studying Expert Informants by Survey Methods: A Cross-National Inquiry," *Public Opinion Quarterly,* XXXI (1967), 9–26.

67 Hyman and Sheatsley, *op. cit.* See also Bower, *op. cit.*

68 Kohn and Williams, *op. cit.* In two of the other studies cited above (LaPiere, and Kutner *et al.*), test teams were also introduced into a range of establishments, but the main concern was to document the frequency of discrimination, rather than to analyze a variety of situational factors.

69 R. Coles, "It's the Same, But It's Different," *Daedalus,* XCIV (Fall, 1965), 107–132; M. Deutsch, "Courage as a Concept in Social Psychology," *Journal of Social Psychology,* LV (1961), 49–58.

70 Rokeach, "Attitude Change and Behavioral Change."

71 Allport, *op. cit.* He states it eloquently: "All theories of social causation have as their unacknowledged silent partner the psychological fact of *conformity.*"

72 For example, by interviewing the hillbilly southern workers, Killian established that "the South continued to be their principal reference group and they followed its practice of racial segregation and exclusion when it was conveniently possible. When confronted with situations in which these ways could not be adhered to without personal sacrifice, however, they tended to make the necessary behavioral adjustments even though changes in attitudes did not necessarily occur." *Op. cit.,* p. 331.

73 A. H. Richmond, *Colour Prejudice in Britain* (London: Routledge and Kegan Paul, 1954), *passim.* Reprinted by permission of the author. Whether the case study reveals that the young and vigorous, who are trained in violence, are most likely to express their inner sentiments despite external pressures; whether it reflects an extra quotient of felt power that goes with large numbers, group cohesiveness, and the military uniform, permitting the soldiers to act out their desires; or whether the actions stemmed from the stamp of legitimacy conferred by higher military authorities, I do not know. But the case certainly would be fruitful to re-examine in detail. It is also worthy of note that in some of the race riots in major American cities of that era military personnel were at times major participants. See, for example, Rose's account of the 1943 Los Angeles riot. A. M. Rose, "Race and Ethnic Relations," in R. K. Merton and R. A. Nisbet, eds., *Contemporary Social Problems* (New York: Harcourt, Brace, and World, 1966), p. 463.

74 James, *op. cit.,* p. 316.

75 M. L. DeFleur and F. R. Westie, "Verbal Attitudes and Overt Acts: An Experiment on the Salience of Attitudes," *American Sociological Review,* XXIII (1958), 667–673. In another phase of these studies, Westie and DeFleur recorded various autonomic responses of the subjects while they were being shown colored slides of Negroes and whites, later de-

scribed as like the pictures for which they would volunteer to pose. The physiological responses of subjects varied systematically with the prejudice scores obtained by the verbal instruments and with the race and sex combination depicted in the photograph. What is suggested is that both the behavioral test and the verbal instrument do tap a deeper level of feeling. See F. R. Westie and M. DeFleur, "Autonomic Responses and Their Relationship to Race Attitudes," *Journal of Abnormal and Social Psychology,* LVIII (1959), 340–347.

76 Cook modified the DeFleur and Westie procedure and varied certain conditions over his four studies so as to determine the influence of particular variables and to develop the best and most efficient instrument for indirect attitude assessment. However, from the point of view of the general hypothesis that verbal attitudes predict interracial behavior in public situations, all five studies may be regarded as replicative, and all provide positive evidence. In his final study, an experimental manipulation provides a technique to test our earlier hypothesis of the interaction of class and race in the determination of prejudice. A Negro accomplice is introduced into the situation as the agent of the publishing company requesting the photograph of the white subject in the interracial situation. Under one experimental condition the accomplice exhibits high socioeconomic status and under a second condition low socioeconomic status. See S. Cook, "Studies of Attitude and Attitude Measurement," Progress Report, National Science Foundation, October 1, 1966 (mimeographed). Another investigator recently modified the DeFleur and Westie procedure in a similar respect, introducing two Negro accomplices, one light-skinned and one dark-skinned, who acted as the representatives of a psychological testing company and a civil rights organization soliciting the photographs for scientific and political uses, respectively. He finds substantial discrepancies between verbally measured attitude and behavior. In addition to this main variable, the procedure was changed in so many other respects from the original design that it is difficult to account for the opposed findings. The difference in the characteristics of the subjects should be stressed, being limited in this instance to very young girls enrolled at the University of Wisconsin. Such subjects might well have less stable attitudes, their verbal responses might be sensitive to the prevailing tolerant norms of that campus, and they might well exhibit unusual reluctance to pose with a Negro of the opposite sex. See L. S. Linn, "Verbal Attitudes and Overt Behavior: A Study of Racial Discrimination," *Social Forces,* XLIII (1965), 353–364.

77 One may also conceive of the DeFleur and Westie experiment as a design for testing the relative contribution of reference groups and situational pressures to the translation of attitude into action. The situational pressures are manipulated by the range of public settings in which the subject will allow his photograph with a Negro to be shown. The potential audience presumably will react in various ways and may include more or less significant others. To be sure, the student was in fact

alone with the experimenter, even though he was making a decision about an act which would at some future time reveal him to a particular public. The pressure from that public thus is in the realm of the future and is a matter of conjecture. In the sense that these publics have to be carried in the mind (represented symbolically), they have similarity to reference groups. But these social groups with their imputed reactions were very different from the reference groups which the subjects spontaneously brought to mind as guiding their decisions to face or not face the brunt of the specified publics who would see the photograph. By contrast, one of the experimental modifications of the design introduced by Cook actually introduces situational pressure right into the laboratory, by having the volunteering done in a setting of a group or organization.

78 Matthews and Prothro, *op. cit.*

79 Hyman and Sheatsley, *op. cit.*

80 In this connection, note the application of such a concept to the behavior of local elites and professionals involved in intergroup relations by Dean and Rosen. They remark: "Many national organizations provide special intergroup training for the professionals who will staff their local chapters. Where such training is well planned and extensive, the local leader appears to evaluate his professional progress on the basis of national standards. To the extent that these become important reference points for the local staff member, we can expect him to give leadership to his board and other local community people in intergroup relations. If, on the other hand, the national organization does not establish itself and what it expects firmly in the mind of its local professionals but leaves them largely autonomous, then the local professionals will tend to set their patterns of intergroup relations in conformity with other local practices rather than ahead of them. This appears to be a major reason why two organizations with apparently parallel programs can differ considerably in their effectiveness in getting movement in intergroup relations." Dean and Rosen, *op. cit.*, pp. 135–136. See also Tumin, *Desegregation,* p. 86. Other interpretations may be entertained to explain the differential behavior of the geographically mobile northerners and should be subjected to empirical test. For example, differential types of selective migration must be considered.

81 D. Katz and R. L. Schanck, *Social Psychology* (New York: Wiley, 1938), p. 174.

82 The model for such an inquiry is provided by Breed and Ktsanes, who found in New Orleans in 1957 that the integrationist whites underestimated the extent of such sentiment, whereas the segregationists indulged in what Allport has labeled the "illusion of universality," believing that everyone was segregationist, when "in fact 27 percent of their fellow townsmen" were integrationist. See W. Breed and T. Ktsanes, "Pluralistic Ignorance in the Process of Opinion Formation," *Public Opinion Quarterly,* XXV (1961), 385.

83 I. D. A. Reid, "The Relative Status of the Negro in the United States— A Critical Summary," *Journal of Negro Education,* XXII (1953), 442.

84 See a discussion of "differing frames of reference: a source of conflict" by L. Levine, "The Racial Crisis: Two Suggestions for a National Program," *American Journal of Orthopsychiatry,* XXXVII (1967), 238. That we should not make a quick prejudgment about these matters is suggested by the finding of the Cornell studies that when asked to make subjective judgments of their class position around 1950 the Negroes in the sample much more frequently designated themselves as "upper class" than did the white respondents. This suggests that they were employing other Negroes as a point of comparison, rather than whites. *Op. cit.*

85 R. Williams, Jr., *Strangers Next Door,* p. 200.

86 *Ibid.*

87 That our images may be shattered by the evidence is suggested by one of Williams' findings: "Our data indicate that only 28 per cent of the 665 adult Negroes interviewed [in Bakersfield, California, Savannah, Georgia, and Elmira, New York] agree with the statement '*Sometimes I hate white people.*' This may appear to be one of the more remarkable findings of this study, the more so because the item says 'sometimes,' and the responses were given, without exception, to Negro interviewers." *Ibid.,* pp. 280–281.

88 *Ibid.,* p. 100. In this connection, recall that Bogardus, on the basis of the administration of his social distance scale in 1926, 1946, and 1956, documents a decline in white feelings of social distance toward Negroes over the thirty-year period. E. S. Bogardus, "Racial Distance Changes in the United States During the Past Thirty Years," *Sociology and Social Research,* XLIII (1959), 286–290.

89 S. Cook and J. J. Woodmanse, "Dimensions of Verbal Racial Attitudes: Their Identification and Measurement," *Journal of Personality and Social Psychology,* VII (1967), 240–250.

90 Large-scale negative evidence, albeit only suggestive, was collected in the course of national trend studies conducted between 1944 and 1956. A large majority of white Americans stated that "most Negroes were being treated fairly"; an even larger majority of southern whites took this position; and over that considerable span of time, the finding was highly stable despite the changing position of the Negro and the variations in the prominence of the problem. See H. Hyman and P. B. Sheatsley, "Attitudes on Desegregation," *Scientific American,* CXCV, No. 6 (1956), 39. An intensive empirical study in Indianapolis in 1957 provided considerable positive evidence that the contradiction between the general democratic values endorsed by the individual and his expressed negative attitudes toward Negroes was experienced as a conflict which he resolved by revising his initial prejudiced statements. But there was also evidence

that some individuals maintained their prejudice and resolved the conflict by other psychic mechanisms. Ironically, another type of dilemma seemed to be experienced by some who sensed a conflict between their own democratic treatment of Negroes and the patterns of prejudice which they took to be normative in their communities. This moral dilemma might well be resolved in the direction of prejudice. See F. R. Westie, "The American Dilemma: An Empirical Test," *American Sociological Review*, XXX (1965), 527–538. For another local study in a suburb of New York City, see R. W. Friedrichs, "Christians and Residential Exclusion: An Empirical Study of a Northern Dilemma," *Journal of Social Issues*, XV, No. 4 (1959), 14–23. In one empirical study in the South, limited to social science students enrolled in a university in the deep South in 1957, some evidence is presented that the students realize that their negative attitudes toward Negroes are not the proper, moral attitudes to exhibit and thus, inferentially, might be classified as harboring some "guilt." Yet, the investigator also establishes that students who were *born* in the deep South are less likely, by this index, to be classified as guilty, and he qualifies his general conclusions in light of the fact that the sample is drawn from a universe likely to be more sensitive to the dilemma than the ordinary population and that many other moral norms might be invoked to justify one's prejudices. See E. Q. Campbell, "Moral Discomfort and Racial Segregation—An Examination of the Myrdal Hypothesis," *Social Forces*, XXXIX (1961), 228–234.

91 In this context it may be relevant to note that earlier findings on the relation between religiosity and prejudice have been found to be an artifact of the crudeness of the measure of religiosity. When respondents are classified by levels of religiosity instead of being dichotomized into the religious and nonreligious, moderate religiosity, an indicator of conventional conformity, correlates with prejudice; but greater religiosity, an indicator of personal values, correlates with nonprejudice. See Allport, *op. cit.;* G. Lindzey, "Differences between the High and Low in Prejudice and Their Implications for a Theory of Prejudice," *Journal of Personality*, XIX (1950), 28–29; Tumin, *Resistance and Readiness*, pp. 64–66. One recent study provides contradictory evidence. See P. B. Sheatsley, "White Attitudes toward the Negro," *Daedalus*, XCV (Winter, 1966), 226–229.

92 Such inquiries could also explore the degree to which whites regard the exercise of violence by Negroes as undermining their moral claims to an improvement in their situation. Ideally the same inquiry should explore the views of the white population on the exercise of violence both by themselves and by Negroes. Thus one could establish the prevalence and social location of various types of individuals: whites who feel that violence is improper whether exercised by a white or a Negro, those who regard white violence as legitimate but violence by Negroes as improper, whites who regard violence by Negroes as justified and that by whites as improper, whites who now regard violence by both parties as justified.

93 D. W. Bray, "The Prediction of Behavior from Two Attitude Scales," *Journal of Abnormal and Social Psychology*, XLV (1950), 64–84.

94 M. Malof and A. Lott, "Ethnocentrism and the Acceptance of Negro Support in a Group Pressure Situation," *Journal of Abnormal and Social Psychology*, LXV (1962), 254–258.

2 *Thomas F. Pettigrew*

The Negro and Education:
Problems and Proposals

The full inclusion of Negroes into American society must certainly rank first on any agenda of domestic priorities. And no institution is more central to this process of inclusion than Horace Mann's "balance wheel of the social machinery": public education. Yet problems mount faster than progress in this realm. The plain truth is that American education is failing in this critical task and at present shows few signs of becoming more effective in the future.

This chapter, then, will focus on the problems and potential of public education's contribution to the full inclusion of Negroes into American society. In particular, it will seek to highlight the role which social science theory and research can play in aiding educational policy and change. Such a broad topic must be narrowed to be treated at all, so higher education will be omitted from the discussion. Four basic questions concerning the Negro and education are posed: Where are we now? What special difficulties beset research in this area? What do we know to date? And what do we need to know? Fully satisfying answers to such sweeping questions cannot be provided at this point, of course, but these queries at least focus and organize the discussion.

WHERE ARE WE NOW? [1]

"Racial isolation in the schools," concludes the United States Commission on Civil Rights, ". . . is intense whether the cities are large or small, whether the proportion of Negro enrollment is large or small,

49

whether they are located North or South." [2] Thus, in the fall of 1965, 65 per cent of all Negro pupils in the first grade of public schools and 48 per cent of all Negro pupils in the twelfth grade of public schools were enrolled in schools with 90 to 100 per cent Negro student bodies. Moreover, 87 per cent of all Negro pupils in the first grade of public schools and 66 per cent of all Negroes in the twelfth grade of public schools were enrolled in predominantly Negro schools.

Though different in magnitude, the regional discrepancies do not change the picture significantly; in 1965, while 97 per cent of Negro first-graders in the public schools of the urban South attended predominantly Negro schools, the figure for the urban North was 72 per cent. White children are even more segregated. In the fall of 1965, in all regions, 80 per cent of white public-school children in both the first and twelfth grades were located in 90 to 100 per cent white schools.[3]

Moreover, the separation is increasing. In Cincinnati, for example, seven out of every ten Negro elementary children in 1950 attended predominantly Negro schools, but by 1965 nine out of ten did so. And while Negro elementary enrollment had doubled over these fifteen years, the number in predominantly Negro schools had tripled.[4] This pattern of growing separation is typical of American central cities —the very cities where Negro Americans are concentrated in greatest numbers.

There are at least four major causes for this growing pattern of *de facto* school segregation: (1) trends in racial demography, (2) the antimetropolitan nature of school district organization, (3) the effects of private schools, and (4) intentional segregation similar to the older problem of *de jure* segregation.

The first two of these factors become apparent as soon as we compare public-school organization and current racial demographic trends. There are approximately 27,000 school districts in the United States, with almost all of the recent consolidation of districts limited to the rural areas. Thus, there are over 75 school districts in the Boston metropolitan area and 96 in the Detroit metropolitan area.[5] There is pitifully little co-operation between central city and suburban school systems; and there are vast fiscal and social disparities between districts— especially central city and suburban. Add to this the fact that over 80 per cent of all Negro Americans who live in metropolitan areas reside in central cities, while over half of all white Americans who live in metropolitan areas reside in suburbs, and the racial separation by district becomes intense. Racial housing trends are not encouraging and offer no hope for relief of educational separation in the next generation.[6] Consequently, America would face an enormous problem of *de facto* school segregation even if there were no patterns of intradistrict separation by race.

But, of course, the nation also faces the task of overcoming sharp racial segregation within school districts. For example, 90 per cent or more of the central city enrollment of Negro elementary-school children are found in 90 to 100 per cent Negro schools in Richmond, Virginia; Atlanta; Little Rock; Memphis; Gary; Omaha; Washington, D.C.; Tulsa; Oklahoma City; Baltimore; and Chicago. In cities with large Roman Catholic populations this intradistrict segregation is unwittingly increased by the absorption of many white children into the parochial system. Since only about 6 per cent of Negro Americans are Roman Catholics,[7] a large church school system necessarily limits the available pool of school-aged white children for a central city public-school system. In St. Louis and Boston, about two of every five white children go to private schools; and in Philadelphia, roughly three out of every five white children go to private schools.

In addition, blatant racists make the problem of intradistrict segregation worse by open advocacy of separation, careful misplacement and zone-drawing of new facilities, and steadfast refusal to take the measures which would at least begin to ease the problem. The Civil Rights Commission provides in its report two pointed examples from Chicago and Cincinnati of *"de facto"* segregation by design.[8] And bad-faith school resistance to racial change is, of course, frankly demonstrated in much of the rural South, where almost one-fifth of all Negro Americans still reside.

But the public resistance of anti-Negro political figures gains the headlines, while the more important structural barriers (demographic trends, antimetropolitan school district organization, and private-school effects) are often the critical factors.

WHAT SPECIAL DIFFICULTIES BESET RESEARCH IN THIS AREA?

One might think that a problem so ominous and widespread would have been rigorously and thoroughly researched. Such is not the case. While there is a growing research literature of importance, enhanced in large part by the recent Coleman and Civil Rights Commission publications, there is a paucity of independent work in relation to the gravity of the situation. The reasons for this paucity are not difficult to discern: some are political, others technical. We must consider these special difficulties before reviewing what is known to date in this realm.

Political Difficulties

The researcher in race relations in general, and school desegregation in particular, is by definition a threatening disturber of political equilibriums. To paraphrase President Truman, it's hot in the kitchen and one can be easily burned.

Ideological constraints are not subtle; and no set of findings can possibly please the chief ideologists involved. Thus, "the unqualified integrationists" will question any study which does not find racial desegregation of all types of significant and lasting value to all the children involved. Members of the "educational establishment" in good standing will not easily accept findings which suggest that compensatory education programs in ghetto schools are not the answer to the typically low academic achievement of impoverished Negro children. Garden-variety "white segregationists," North and South, will reject any research data which indicate that white children are not academically harmed by interracial classrooms. And "black power advocates" will brand as "racist" any results which reveal below-grade-level performance of children in all-Negro schools. Yet all four of these ideology-violating findings are commonly uncovered by competent investigations. Little wonder, then, that few areas in social science have such an attentive, hostile, and varied audience.

The most common political barrier to conducting meaningful research on race and education is the refusal to co-operate. This impediment leads to a serious bias in the systems and schools in which studies are made, for there is, naturally, a strong tendency for the better systems to welcome independent research and the poorer systems to reject it. Compare the following lists of urban public-school systems. New Haven, White Plains, Berkeley, and Riverside are prominent among areas where significant investigations on desegregation have been performed. By contrast, Boston, Cleveland, Columbus, Cincinnati, Chicago, Los Angeles, Houston, and Wichita, among others, all refused to allow the Equal Educational Opportunity survey ("the Coleman Report") to test their children even though it was ordered by Congress in the 1964 Civil Rights Act. These are *not* random lists of American school systems.

The same phenomenon is evident in the recent controversy over national testing. A cynic might observe that perhaps half of the country's systems would be found by standardized national testing to be below the median grade levels in achievement; while virtually all systems now claim to average above median grade level—a rather amazing psychometric phenomenon when you think about it!

The bias created by refusal to co-operate is not just a simple function of "something to hide." The Coleman procedure purposely sampled schools within metropolitan areas rather than school districts and thereby rendered it impossible, together with solemn guarantees of confidentiality, for any one system to be singled out. Yet a number of cities, such as Cincinnati, maintained they could not participate in the Coleman study because they were at that time in the courts defending against charges of racial discrimination and segregation. Such claims remind anyone who has ever served as an expert research witness in such cases of the favorite retort to his testimony: studies showing the damage of segregation are all from other places and do not, it is argued, hold for the city in question. No definitive answer to this assertion is possible, of course, since such systems typically never allow outside research in the first place.[9]

Sample biases almost always operate in social experiments in the field. Unable to control events to fit his research purposes, the social scientist often attempts to ensure that the bias works *against* his hypothesis so that positive support is, if anything, made all the more impressive. Such is generally the case in this instance. The central hypothesis under test in most desegregation investigations is that segregation is academically and attitudinally harmful to children. Such an idea should have its most rigorous test in such highly regarded school systems as those of Riverside, Berkeley, and White Plains, rather than in such systems as those of Boston and Cincinnati. The bias in co-operation, then, often operates against the central hypothesis of research in this area and may therefore not be as serious as it first appears.

Another widely employed political device to thwart meaningful studies involves "managed research." Similar to "managed news," this technique may simply exclude any independent work and allow only in-house investigations. In a sense, the in-house studies are frequently not research at all; rather they consist of contrived demonstrations to support a conclusion or program to which the system was firmly committed before the work even began. Such studies are often hastily commissioned for use in court; and cases concerning *de jure* and *de facto* school segregation contain classic examples of this phenomenon in their defense briefs.

Another form of "managed research" consists of inviting outside evaluation, especially when required by federal grants, but attempting to dictate the conclusions by manipulating and restricting the research itself. One instance of this phenomenon occurred in a Negro-led movement to bus children out of the ghetto to underutilized schools in other parts of the system. The leader of the movement stoutly maintained its aim was only to obtain better education, and not to achieve desegregation. When research on the effort was begun, the leader insisted that only a Negro social scientist could conduct the study. Furthermore, it was insisted that mothers in the movement should do all the interviewing of each other—not a rigorous technique, to be sure. Despite all these precautions, one of the chief findings of the study countered the leader's ideological position: most of the mothers in the bussing movement liked the idea in part because racial desegregation was a result of the effort. At that point, the beleaguered researcher was accused of having asked the wrong questions!

A final political barrier to meaningful work is offered by the use of "double bookkeeping" of contrasting standards to evaluate findings. The technique is quite straightforward: if the findings fit the political necessities, fragile studies are accepted as rigorous; if the findings do not fit the political necessities, rigorous studies are disparaged as inconclusive. The United States Department of Health, Education, and Welfare provided an unfortunate prototype of this technique during 1967. To support the politically expedient programs of "compensatory education," the department issued an essentially anecdotal report and claimed it proved the success of Title I programs under the Elementary and Secondary Education Act of 1965.[10] In truth, the department has yet to undertake a rigorous evaluation of this $1.5-billion annual national investment. By contrast, however, the department regarded the United States Commission on Civil Rights report, *Racial Isolation in the Public Schools*, as "not definitive" in its research indicating the benefits of the politically inexpedient process of racial integration of the schools. *No* scientific study is ever "definitive" of course; nor, as we shall see shortly, are the commission's conclusions subject to only one interpretation. Nevertheless, the "double bookkeeping" in standards in evaluating the two different reports was, to say the least, striking and instructive.

Design Difficulties

Apart from political problems, research on race and education is subject to an array of design difficulties. While none of these difficulties is unique to this area, together they constitute a formidable challenge.

Nonrandom Assignment of Students
to Various Types of Schools

The ideal experiment involves random assignment of subjects to the tested conditions. The field situation rarely allows this ideal arrangement. And in school research the nonrandom distribution will typically reflect the extreme clustering effects of homogeneous residential areas. One example of this phenomenon in the race and education realm concerns which Negro children are most likely to be found in predominantly white classrooms. Whether the assignment is done on an "open choice" or "neighborhood" basis, middle-class Negro children are most often found in disproportionate numbers in interracial school settings. This occurs because middle-class Negro parents tend to be more ambitious for their children, better able to afford the expenses involved in realizing their plans, and more likely to live on the fringes, rather than in the core, of the ghetto. No control on class, then, would find the desegregated Negro children doing markedly better than their peers in all-Negro classrooms; but the class bias in assignment would prevent an assessment of the desegregation effect directly. Desegregation research now under way in Riverside, California, under the direction of social psychologist Harold Gerard thus acquires special interest, for it is one of the first studies where the experimenter has a voice in the assignment of students.

Nonrandom Selection of Communities
by Various Types of Parents

A second bias enters with the selection of the community and school system by parents. The knowledge of an effective school system, desegregated schools, or special residential status attracts certain types of families and repels others. And when a large parochial educational system exists, church members who send their children to it differ from members who still send their children to the public schools. These nonrandom selection factors add to the importance of both replicating findings in a wide variety of communities and analyzing data aggregated from a range of communities throughout the country.

Nonrandom Treatment of Students Within Schools

A third type of nonrandom selection is introduced by such devices as "ability tracking" and "interest grouping" within schools. These biasing factors in classroom composition are rare in the primary grades, become more prevalent in the middle grades, and are widespread in the advanced grades. Careful attention must therefore be paid to these classroom assignment devices as well as to the differences between classroom and school effects.

The High Loss of Sample Members over Time

Yet another bias results from the high turnover of students in many school systems. The most glaring example is the high-school dropout, a phenomenon that makes research at the eleventh and twelfth grades especially difficult. But the problem exists at all grade levels from the high horizontal mobility of Americans. While an estimated one out of five American families moves annually, the ratio is even higher among young families with school-aged children. And since longitudinal investigations are particularly appropriate for work on race and education, this extensive student turnover and mobility raises genuine problems.

The Need to Control for Initial School Performance

Any study of changes over time ideally should have measures of the change variable sampled before, during, and after the intervention hypothesized as the cause of the shift. Educational investigations are typically change studies; yet surprisingly few of them have "before measures"—that is, measures of the students as they entered schools for the first time. Such data are not readily obtainable. In addition to the mobility across systems described above, many schools lack a thorough testing program for entering students. Complicating the matter further, the racial composition of the testing situation often affects performance of even young Negro children. Thus, Negro children entering a biracial school may score higher on achievement tests, for instance, than comparable Negro children entering an all-Negro school before the effects of their diverse schools can even operate solely because of differential testing climates. These are not mere methodological refinements. The necessity to control for initial school performance will become evident from research on desegregation discussed in the next section.

Special Difficulties in Controlling and Measuring Such Variables as Social Class across Race

The critical importance of controlling social class in this research has already been illustrated. But just how one controls social class and similar variables across race is not a simple matter. Income equilibration is especially questionable, for the Negro floor of deprivation extends below that of the white floor in areas outside of Appalachia. Consequently, social-class controls across race generally employ educational and occupational indices, though problems of true comparability remain. The harsh truth is that this methodological complication accurately reflects a condition of American society: racial oppression against Negro Americans has been so extensive for so long that race and class are intimately intertwined.

Hawthorne Effects

Evaluation studies, whether in education or not, are plagued by "Hawthorne effects." Put simply, the Hawthorne effect occurs when experimental groups that receive special attention improve not so much as a function of the experimental variable as of the special attention. Uncovered initially in industrial research at the Hawthorne wiring plant of Western Electric,[11] the phenomenon is common in educational research. Most educational innovations, for instance, generally appear at first to be beneficial, because their evaluations do not consider the operation of the Hawthorne effect. Almost *any* intelligent intervention appears to increase academic achievement in schools for a year or so as a function of higher teacher morale, more attention to the children, and other indirect consequences of the new intervention. But typically these increases are not sustained, once the Hawthorne effect begins to wear off. Evaluation cannot, therefore, reach positive conclusions after just a year or so of a new educational program; the real test must be concerned with *sustained* improvement.

Rosenthal Effects

"If the Hawthorne doesn't ruin an evaluation," goes one pessimistic slogan of the trade, "the Rosenthal will!" The Rosenthal effect is directly related to the Hawthorne phenomenon.[12] It involves unintended experimenter biases that favor the hypothesis under investigation. Often the bias results from nonverbal communication between the experimenter and the subject. In an experiment in a San Francisco school, Rosenthal demonstrated dramatically that these biases are common phenomena of the classroom:

All of the children in an elementary school were administered a nonverbal group test of intelligence which was disguised as a test that would predict academic "blooming." There were 18 classes, 3 at each of all 6 grade levels. Within each of the grade levels one of the classes was of above average ability children; a second class was of average ability children, and a third class was of below average ability children. A table of random numbers was employed to assign about 20 percent of the children in each of the 18 classes to the experimental condition. Each teacher was given the names of those children "who would show unusual academic development" during the coming school year. That was the experimental manipulation. At the end of the school year the children were retested with the same group intelligence test. For the 18 classes combined, those children whose teachers expected them to gain in performance showed a significantly greater gain in IQ than did the control children, though the mean relative gain in IQ was small. Teachers' expectancies, it turned out, made little difference in the upper grades. But at the lower levels the effects were dramatic. First graders purported to be bloomers gained 15.4 IQ points more than did the control children, and the mean relative gain in one classroom was 24.8 points. In the second grade, the relative gain was 9.5 IQ points, with one of the classes showing a mean gain of 18.2 points.[13]

Rosenthal's work has important implications for both educational practice and evaluation. It calls into strong question ability grouping, since so-called "low-ability" pupils are likely to receive training congruent with the low expectations their teachers necessarily have for them. This work also underscores the need for "double-blind" evaluation studies in which neither the teachers nor the on-the-scene experimenters are aware which children are in the experimental condition.

One might think after considering this array of political and methodological problems that meaningful research in the race and education realm is impossible. Competent work *is* rare, but the two recent federal studies related to the problem have provided us with a data-based perspective with which to place in context many of the policy-critical issues. Nonetheless, we shall be returning to these design difficulties when we discuss the interpretation of these federal data.

WHAT DO WE KNOW? WHAT DO WE NEED TO KNOW?

A start toward answers to such sweeping questions can be made if we direct our attention to a number of key issues: (1) What are the chief correlates of Negro academic achievement? (2) Is there a racial composition effect on Negro performance apart from social-class effects? (3) What useful definitional distinctions can be drawn between the terms "segregation," "desegregation," and "integration"? (4) What are the racially optimal environments for performance? (5) Is there a critical age for initiating desegregation? (6) Are there lasting consequences into adulthood of interracial schooling? (7) Is "compensatory education" in predominantly Negro schools an effective substitute for school desegregation? (8) What are the politics of school desegregation? (9) What is the racial relevance of educational alternatives to the public schools? (10) What ideas exist for "ultimate solutions"?

What Are the Chief Correlates of Negro Academic Achievement?

No short summary of Coleman's *Equality of Educational Opportunity* survey can do justice to this massive and complex work. But combined with the extended analysis of the Coleman data performed by the United States Commission on Civil Rights, a few rough generalizations can be ventured about Negro academic achievement in public schools.

Two basic correlates of achievement emerge from the Coleman data: "home background of the child" and "student body quality of the school." Though each of these factors is measured in the report by a number of indicators, both basically involve social-class differences and are effectively represented by parents' education. Home background can be tapped by the average education of the parents of each student; and student-body quality can be rated by the education of the parents of all the students comprising a particular school. Measured in this manner, it is perhaps more accurate to speak of these two major correlates as *individual social class* and *school social class*.

The individual social-class factor is often said to be *the* principal correlate of achievement in the Coleman study, but this flat statement requires qualification. Individual social class proved a more important predictor of test scores for white than for Negro children.[14] And it proved of declining importance from the sixth to the twelfth grades.[15] As shown in considerable research on adolescents in American society, the influence of the family recedes as the influence of peers strengthens. Consequently, the *school* social-class variable becomes particularly powerful in secondary education; and it is a far more important correlate of Negro than white achievement.

These trends can be detailed with data from the metropolitan Northeast. By the twelfth grade, lower-status Negro children attending higher-status schools perform as a group slightly better than higher-status Negro children in lower-status schools.[16] Combining the two variables for the scores of these children, their verbal achievement averages range from slightly below an eighth-grade level for low-status students in lower-status schools to almost an eleventh-grade level for high-status students in higher-status schools—a decisive difference of three full grades.[17]

School social class, then, is easily the most important *school* correlate of achievement scores, white as well as Negro, although Coleman also looked closely at teacher-ability and school-facility variables. Teacher variables, ranging from years of teaching experience to years of formal education and vocabulary test score of the teacher, prove important, however. In ways similar to the school social-class factor, the teacher factor is a stronger correlate of Negro than white student verbal achievement scores and is much more powerful in the secondary than elementary years.[18]

By contrast, school facilities do not relate highly to pupil performance. Once individual social class is controlled, for example, per pupil instructional expenditure in grades six, nine, and twelve is not significantly associated with achievement save in one notable case: Negro children in the South.[19] Nor do such variables as pupil-teacher ratio, library volumes, laboratories, number of extracurricular activities, comprehensiveness of the curriculum, strictness of promotion, ability grouping, and school size reveal any important and consistent relationships with achievement.[20] These essentially negative findings concerning the influence of school facilities have received great attention and have apparently threatened many educators who ponder what chances for success their next school-facilities bond referendum will have. Much of this concern, however, is caused by a misreading of these results. The chief finding is that school social class is such a critical achievement correlate that with a gross survey approach it will simply overwhelm any smaller school effects.

Moreover, the Coleman data do *not* mean that school facilities are unimportant. What they do signify is that the range of facilities now found in the nation's public schools is not great enough to explain wide differences in student performance. Consider the pupil-teacher ratio variable. Most American classrooms range between twenty and forty students per teacher; and teachers are typically not provided with teaching techniques aimed at exploiting smaller classes. Within this relatively narrow range, Coleman could not show any consistent relationships with achievement scores. Yet one can still reasonably argue that it makes a major difference whether one is teaching five or five hundred students, especially with teachers able to adapt their teaching styles to small groups of children. But Coleman could not test this proposition, since actual pupil-teacher ratios of five and five hundred are virtually nonexistent. In short, Coleman could only test the effects of variables as they range in present-day schools. Just where below twenty and above forty pupils per teacher the instructional ratio variable becomes crucial for student performance must await better-trained teachers and more detailed experimental studies.

One final set of variables, however, did correlate highly with verbal achievement. "Student attitudes" included measures of interest in school and reading, academic self-concept, and a sense of control of the environment.[21] Interestingly, student-attitude variables are important correlates of performance for all groups of children at all three of the grade levels tested (sixth, ninth, and twelfth grades). Yet different attitude measures predicted white and Negro achievement. The academic self-concept variable (measured by such items as "How bright do you think you are in comparison with the other students in your grade?") proves far more significant for white achievement. But the sense of environmental control (indicated, for example, by disagreeing that "good luck is more important than hard work for success") is much more significant for Negro achievement.

Clearly, these attitude-achievement findings result from tapping into a complex process involving a two-way causal pattern. Not only do Negro children with a sense of environmental control subsequently do better in their school achievement, but those who do well in school achievement undoubtedly begin to gain a sense of environmental control. Nevertheless, it is tempting to speculate with Coleman that each child faces a two-stage problem: first, he must learn that he can, within reasonably broad limits, act effectively upon his surroundings; and, second, he must then judge his own relative capabilities for mastering the environment. The critical stage for white children seems to be the second stage concerning the self-concept, while the critical stage for Negro children seems, realistically enough, to involve the question of manipulating an often harsh and overpowering environment. In any event, more detailed work seems justified to follow up Coleman's fascinating speculation:

> Having experienced an unresponsive environment, the virtues of hard work, or diligent and extended effort toward achievement appear to such a [minority] child unlikely to be rewarding. As a consequence, he is likely to merely "adjust" to his environment, finding satisfaction in passive pursuits. It may well be, then, that one of the keys toward success for minorities which have experienced disadvantage and a particularly unresponsive environment—either in the home or the larger society—is a change in this conception.[22]

The Coleman report's conclusions should, of course, be interpreted only within the context of the type of data on which they are based. The report is already the target of considerable criticism, and it will surely be the target of still more criticism in the future. In truth, the analysis and writing were necessarily performed in great haste; there exist major methodological problems ranging from a relatively large school system nonresponse rate to special issues involved with a massive regression analysis; and a number of the report's interpretations are open to strong challenge. Furthermore, careful reanalysis uncovers such difficulties as high percentages of children who did not know the educational levels of their parents, a key variable. And further reanalysis will undoubtedly reveal other such problems.

Yet all of this careful scrutiny and criticism is in its own way a high tribute to the significance of this ambitious study. The Coleman group achieved a landmark accomplishment in an amazingly short span of time; and the report and its data will influence the direction of American education for years to come. And this is as it should be, for the report's major conclusions will almost surely survive the reanalysis and criticisms.

The soundness of Coleman's chief conclusions is attested to by two lines of supporting evidence. First, the United States Commission on Civil Rights' report on *Racial Isolation in the Public Schools* presents an extensive reanalysis of the Coleman data. Using more detailed contingency analyses on the metropolitan northeast subsample, the commission replicated the central findings of Coleman's extensive regression analysis on the entire national sample: namely, the crucial importance of both individual social class and school social class as correlates of Negro and white achievement. Second, these central findings are substantiated by an array of more detailed, though less extensive, educational studies that employed methods and samples different from those of Coleman's survey.

Three such earlier studies lend confidence to the Coleman emphasis on school social class. In a study published in 1959, Wilson demonstrated the special significance of school social class in determining college aspirations in eight high schools in the San Francisco–Oakland Bay area of California.[23] He found higher percentages of college aspirants in higher-status schools even after controlling for other determinants of college aspirations—father's occupation and education, mother's education, median academic grade, and intelligence test score. For example, among boys whose fathers and mothers were high-school graduates and whose fathers held manual occupations, 60 per cent in upper-status schools wanted to go to college, compared to 54 per cent in the medium-status schools and only 32 per cent in the lower-status schools. Likewise, among boys with a modest C academic grade record, 72 per cent from upper-status schools aspired to college, in contrast to only 55 per cent from medium-status schools and 41 per cent in lower-status schools. Finally, for those in the 100 to 119 IQ test range, for instance, 93 per cent in the upper-status schools, 72 per cent in the medium-status schools, and 51 per cent in the lower-status schools aimed for college.

Differential college aspirations were not the only outcomes of school social class uncovered in this Wilson study. Controlling for father's occupation, both occupational aspirations and political party preferences are also influenced. Hence, among boys whose fathers occupied manual positions, 44 per cent in the upper-status schools wanted to be professionals and 50 per cent preferred the Republican party, compared with 31 per cent and 32 per cent in the medium-status schools and 27 per cent and 24 per cent in the working-status schools, respectively.

A second early attack on the problem was mounted at Harvard University, though it substituted the social-class level of nine Boston suburbs for a direct measure of the schools' social-class levels.[24] Controlling for father's occupation, boys from the higher-status communities were found to be more likely to go to college. In addition, community status, which determined the status level of the schools, had its crucial impact only at the high-school level—the level at which Wilson was working. Consequently, community status predicted neither primary-school grades nor the entrance into the college preparatory courses in high school from junior high school, a finding that resembles the Coleman result that school social class gained in predictive value in the secondary-school grades.

The most definitive early study was conducted by Michael.[25] He analyzed the aptitude test scores as well as the career and college plans of 35,436 seniors in a nationally representative sample of 518 American public high schools. Together with the students' scores on a scholastic aptitude test not unlike those that were used by Coleman, Michael classified the students on an index of family social class, using such information as the father's occupation and education and whether older siblings had attended college. Further, he classified the high schools into five status ranks according to the percentage of seniors in each school who fell into his two top family status classifications—a method similar to the school social-class measures of Coleman.

The first finding showed that, with family status controlled, the higher the status of the school, the higher the average score on the scholastic aptitude test. Further analysis revealed that the variation in the percentages of students scoring above the national average on the test was about equally attributable to the individual and school social-class indices. But the variation in the percentages scoring in the top quarter was considerably more related to individual social class than school social class: a result directly in line with Coleman's finding that school social class is most important for the more deprived students and in line with the commission's reanalysis finding that, among whites in the metropolitan northeast school, social class was least important for the highest-status students.[26]

Turning to plans to attend college, Michael, as did the Wilson and the Harvard investigators, demonstrated that school social class makes a difference. But Michael's larger sample allowed deeper analysis and —as in the Coleman analysis—revealed that these effects are strongest for students from lower-class backgrounds. Consider first seniors who score in the top quarter of the aptitude test distribution. Among these talented youngsters from the lowest individual social-class group, only 44 per cent who attended the lowest-status high schools planned to go to college, compared with 57 per cent who attended the highest-status high schools. By contrast, among the talented seniors from the highest individual social-class group, 80 per cent who attended the lowest-status high schools planned to go to college, compared with 86 per cent who attended the highest-status high schools. In other words, the high-status school exerts a far greater influence on college plans among talented lower-status than talented higher-status children.

Much the same phenomenon is true for Michael's entire sample. The percentage differences in college plans between individual social-class groups is essentially the same at each type of school; but the percentage differences in college plans between scholastic aptitude test levels is far higher in the high-status than the low-status high schools. Put simply, attendance at a low-status school does not deter seniors from upper-status families in planning for college, but attendance at a high-status school is an important aid to able seniors from lower-status families.

All three of these earlier studies, then, demonstrate the significant consequences of attending high schools of varying social-class compositions. Yet as Coleman himself pointed out in an earlier paper,[27] these initial studies did not differentiate between the effects of school social class per se and those of some variable, or combination of variables, strongly related to school social class, such as school facilities, which (as Michael has demonstrated) did covary with school social class. It remained, then, for Coleman himself to answer his own query; for the Coleman report was able to provide the relevant controls and demonstrate that these effects were indeed associated with school social class per se even after the other relevant types of factors were controlled.

In addition, these three earlier investigations suffered from the inter-related methodological weaknesses that also limit the Coleman survey: the results are neither longitudinal nor corrected for initial achievement and aspirations upon entering school in the primary grades. These weaknesses open the studies to the possibility that their findings are merely the result of special selection biases. That is, lower-class children in predominantly middle-class schools may achieve more and aspire higher, not because of the school climate, but because they are as a group brighter and more ambitious at the outset than lower-class children in general.

A number of critics of the Coleman report have challenged the social-class climate finding on precisely these grounds of possible selection biases. They apparently choose to ignore a fourth replication of the Coleman result reported at length in the Civil Rights Commission's report.[28] Wilson, in a follow up to his earlier research, studied the school social-class variable with a probability sample of junior and senior high-school children in Richmond, California. He had the advantage of both longitudinal data and initial scores upon entering school, thus overcoming the critics' objections. And Wilson found a strong effect of the social-class climate of the elementary school on subsequent academic success at higher grade levels, even after "allowing for individual differences in personal background, neighborhood context, and mental maturity at the time of school entry." Thus, three earlier investigations and a later, well-controlled study by Wilson closely agree with the major conclusion of the Coleman report concerning the pre-eminent importance of a school's social-class climate.

To sum up, the Coleman study is a broad-gauged survey of what exists now in American public schools. It could neither detail precise learning processes nor test what American public schools could potentially become in the future. Similar to the naked eye compared with an electronic microscope, the Coleman report outlined the gross facts of American education today, while the precision of the specific experiment is now needed to detail the processes that go unseen by the survey.

Hopefully, the direction of future educational research will be strongly influenced by this landmark study. The Coleman report sets the broader context within which more limited data must be interpreted, and it provides a rich variety of exciting leads with obvious policy implications. In order to minimize the operation of individual social-class factors, for example, would boarding schools be an effective intervention for especially deprived youngsters in the early grades? Are there *any* truly effective public schools which are overwhelmingly attended by lower-status children? And if so, by what means do such schools overcome the typically powerful effects of school social class? What precisely is the process underlying the high association between the Negro child's sense of environmental control and his achievement scores? And how might this sense of control of the environment be learned in school? These and scores of other questions spring to mind from a careful consideration of the Coleman report. Systematic funding, both public and private, is needed to encourage and make possible a systematic research attack on these vital questions.

Is There a Racial Composition Effect Apart from Social-Class Effects?

The Coleman report provides only spotty and somewhat conflicting evidence on a focal issue of race and education: the academic consequences of desegregation apart from social-class considerations. At one point in the report, the text reads:

> The higher achievement of all racial and ethnic groups in schools with greater proportions of white students is not accounted for by better facilities and curriculum in these schools (to the extent these were measured by our questionnaires). . . . The higher achievement of all racial and ethnic groups in schools with greater proportions of white students is *largely, perhaps wholly, related* to effects associated with the student body's educational background and aspirations. This means that the apparent beneficial effect of a student body with a high proportion of white students comes not from racial composition per se, but from the better educational background and higher educational aspirations that are on the average found among white students. The effects of the student body environment upon a student's achievement appear to lie in the educational proficiency possessed by that student body, whatever its racial or ethnic composition.[29] [Italics added.]

However, in a later, brief section entitled "Integration and Achievement," the language is softened to read that the positive effects on Negro achievement "appeared to be less than, and *largely accounted for* by, other characteristics of the student body than the racial composition of the school per se."[30] (Italics added.) Moreover, this section provides contingency analyses using regional samples from the metropolitan Midwest and Northeast that show the beneficial effects of desegregated schooling for both Negro and white pupils.[31] A footnote assures the reader that the beneficial effects are not a function of individual social class,[32] though nothing further is said about controls for other school social-class variables. The section consists of less than four pages of the 737-page report—one-half of 1 per cent of the total space; this seems remarkably scant attention to pay to the racial composition factor in a report on "equal educational opportunity." At any rate, the five tables published on this critical subject are most suggestive.

The first table reveals that in eleven out of twelve comparisons Negroes in the sixth, ninth, and twelfth grades from classrooms with

"more than half" white classmates scored highest on reading comprehension and math achievement. The second table extends the analysis
for the ninth and twelfth grades by controlling for the grade in which
each Negro student began attending interracial classrooms. In eleven
out of fourteen comparisons, Negro students from more-than-half
white classrooms once again scored highest in reading comprehension.
Interestingly, too, the Negro students who began their desegregation in
the first three elementary grades scored highest in twelve out of sixteen
comparisons. A third table provides the standard deviations for the
reading and math test scores of Negro children in the sixth, ninth, and
twelfth grades. Here the significant finding is that in ten out of twelve
comparisons the scores of Negro children from more-than-half white
classrooms have larger standard deviations than those from classrooms
with fewer white pupils. In addition, the scores of the few Negroes
whose classmates were all white tend to record the highest standard
deviations of all groups, though, of course, this is at least partly a function of the smaller cell sizes.

The final two tables concern the percentages of white students in the
ninth and twelfth grades who choose all white "close friends" and prefer all-white classrooms. The positive effects on white attitudes of early
desegregation are quite consistent. In all eight comparisons, white children who began their interracial school experiences in the first three
grades tend *less* than other white students to prefer all white friends
and classes.

The Civil Rights Commission directed much of its reanalysis of the
Coleman data at the relatively neglected question of the effects of desegregation. Employing parents' education as the chief social-class indicator, the commission's work attempted to control for both individual
and school social class while testing the relationship between racial
composition of the classroom and Negro verbal achievement. This reanalysis uncovered relatively large and consistent differences in favor
of the twelfth-grade Negro students in the metropolitan Northeast who
came from more-than-half white classrooms.[33] For instance, among
lower-status Negro children in lower-status high schools, those from
more-than-half white classrooms scored at the eight-and-a-half-grade
level, compared to only a seventh-grade level for those from all-Negro
classrooms. At the other end of the scale, among higher-status Negro
pupils in higher-status schools, those from more-than-half white classrooms scored at the ten-and-a-half-grade level, in contrast to the ninth-
grade level of those from all-Negro classrooms.

The commission also found evidence to suggest the special efficacy
of early desegregation. With control again for both individual and

school social class, ninth-grade Negro children in the metropolitan Northeast who had been in interracial classrooms in the first three grades consistently scored from a half to a full grade above comparable Negro students.[34]

A number of explanations can be offered for these commission findings which maintain that racial composition of the classroom itself is not the crucial variable, but rather other factors which covary with racial composition are crucial. Each of these explanations deserves examination. Thus, it could be maintained that even in the metropolitan Northeast predominantly Negro and predominantly white schools vary sharply in school quality, especially teacher quality, and that it is these quality distinctions that are responsible for the improved scores in predominantly white institutions. This argument could be challenged by the failure of the Coleman study to uncover sharp quality differences between "Negro" and "white" schools in the metropolitan Northeast; but Coleman's finding itself can be seriously questioned.[35] In any event, school-quality controls narrow slightly the performance differentials attributable to desegregation, but do not by any means exhaust them.[36]

A second type of explanation involved selection biases discussed earlier as a typical difficulty besetting research in this area. One special form of the selection argument involves ability grouping. It can be argued that all the commission found was that schools in the metropolitan Northeast do a reliable and accurate job of placing Negro students in ability groups or "tracks." Given the social handicaps many Negro children bring to the school situation, goes the argument, only the very brightest do well; and these gifted Negro children eventually are assigned to high-ability groups where most of their classmates are white. But less exceptional Negro students find themselves assigned to low- or medium-ability groups where many or most of their classmates are other Negroes. Consequently, Negroes with mostly white classmates score highest on academic achievement tests simply because they were brighter to begin with.

Another form of the selection explanation concerns parental choice of community and school. It maintains that *within a given social-class group* more ambitious Negro parents will somehow manage to live in communities with interracial schools. Thus, what appears to be an advantage wrought by interracial schools is actually a result of the self-recruitment of especially motivated children of educationally minded Negro parents within each Negro social class. A third possible selection argument, involving the relatively larger number of dropouts of poorly achieving Negro students from predominantly white schools, is not viable here, because the commission results can be replicated at the ninth-grade level, while the vast majority of future dropouts are still in school.

These and other selection explanations receive some limited empirical support from the Wilson research in Richmond, California, conducted for the commission and mentioned earlier.[37] He found that "Negro students who attended integrated schools had higher mental maturity test scores in their primary grades, and came from homes better provided with educative materials." [38] Thus, when Wilson held constant the early elementary achievement of these students, he found that the school-class effect remained, but that "the racial composition of schools, while tending to favor Negro students in integrated schools, does not have a substantial effect." [39]

Wilson's conclusion is limited, however, in five ways. First, test scores in the early grades, as described previously, can be highly influenced by the setting in which the tests are administered. The ideal control for initial scores, not available to Wilson, would consist of results from tests administered to all the children under the same conditions. Second, the conclusion applies to *schools*, not *classrooms*—the principal unit of the commission's analysis. This is not an unimportant distinction, of course, since formally desegregated schools often have largely segregated classes within them.

Third, unlike the Coleman data, the number of Negro students in desegregated schools in Wilson's study of Richmond, California, is quite small. The eighth-grade verbal reasoning test data, for example, are available for only 128 Negro children in predominantly white schools, compared with 777 Negro children in predominantly Negro schools.[40] Fourth, among these 128 desegregated eighth-graders, only 8 of them (6 per cent) were in lower-status schools; but among the 777 segregated eighth-graders, 378 of them (49 per cent) were in lower-status schools. In other words, there is not enough variance in school social class among desegregated eighth-graders for Wilson's statistical procedures to separate the school social-class and racial composition factors convincingly. Fifth, another type of Negro child critical to Wilson's analysis is in especially short supply. While he has Negro students with both high and low test scores when they entered segregated primary schools and others with high test scores when they entered desegregated schools, he lacks many examples of Negro children with *low* test scores when they entered *desegregated* primary schools. This missing group is the most crucial of all for analytical and practical purposes.

Since the Wilson study leaves open the question about the effects of desegregation on the more disadvantaged Negro students, the commission employed Coleman's data to check on the effects of interracial classrooms on the verbal scores of less gifted Negro ninth-graders in the metropolitan Northeast.[41] These students had poorly educated parents and reported themselves to be in low- or medium-ability tracks. Both in high- and low-status high schools, these Negroes, who were from predominantly white classrooms, performed on the average from one-half to two-thirds of a grade better than comparable Negroes from predominantly Negro classrooms.

The ability-grouping argument is directed at the finding that predominantly white *classrooms* are associated with higher Negro scores. But it does not address itself to the additional finding that multiple-tracked, predominantly white *schools* are also associated with higher Negro performance. More importantly, the ability-grouping contentions lose force from the time sequence involved. Recall that the largest effects of interracial classrooms occur when the experience begins in the earliest elementary grades. Yet ability grouping does not typically begin in American public schools until the middle-school grades and does not become nearly universal until the high-school grades. Therefore, desegregation would appear to afford a better explanation for who gets into the high-ability tracks than ability tracks do for desegregation effects. A Negro child of medium ability who begins his education in a desegregated school, for instance, has a far higher probability of being selected later for a high-ability track than a Negro child of comparable ability going to a school of similar social status who began his education in an all-Negro school. Ability grouping, then, can serve as a magnifier of the differences already begun by classroom differences in racial composition, a catalyst adding to the cumulative deficits of the segregated Negro.

The parental choice of community and school explanation is in some ways the reverse of the ability-grouping contention. It aims to account for the fact that predominantly white *communities and schools* are associated with higher Negro achievement; but it cannot fully account for the fact that the commission shows that interracial *classrooms* are also associated with higher Negro achievement, unless one is willing to assume that there is widespread selection by Negro parents of classrooms as well as communities and schools. There are other assumptions, too, that this particular line of reasoning must make that are at best dubious. Since lower-status, low-ability Negro pupils also benefit from desegregation, these contentions require that poor Negro families possess a sophisticated knowledge of where to go to find the better interracial schools and also have the funds and freedom of mobility to move accordingly. All that is known about the extreme residential discrimination practiced against Negroes, especially poor Negroes, in American metropolitan areas today makes such assumptions most improbable.[42]

Two additional explanations argue that at least some of the apparent racial composition effect revealed by the commission's reanalysis still reflects the operation of the powerful school social-class effect. One chain of reasoning is based on the difficulty of controlling for social class across racial groups. Since the floor of Negro deprivation is below that of whites, for example, it can be maintained that lower-class Negroes who attend a predominantly white school comprised largely of lower-class whites are still benefiting from a higher social-class student climate than lower-class Negroes who attend a predominantly Negro school comprised of lower-class Negroes. While there is some merit in this reasoning, it should be remembered that the differences for twelfth-graders which were associated with racial composition of classrooms in the commission's report (averaging about one and a third grades when the two class variables were held constant) were approximately 80 per cent as large as those attributable to school social class directly (averaging about one and two-thirds grades, holding the individual social-class and racial composition variables constant).[43] Since the racial effect is almost as large as the *entire* class effect, it follows that the small school class residual under discussion could account for only a small portion of the racial composition effect. Besides, the two factors prove most important at different grade levels. The racial composition of classrooms is most powerful for the achievement scores of children in the beginning grades, while school social class is most powerful in the high-school grades.

The other class explanation is limited but, perhaps, more subtle. It applies only to certain lower-status Negro students who attend predominantly white, lower-status schools. Even if the lower-status Negro child is of fully equivalent status to that of the whites, he might well benefit from membership in a minority comprised largely of middle-class Negroes. This possibility is not as remote as it may sound, for a larger percentage of middle-class than lower-class Negroes attend predominantly white schools, and the argument only assumes that the Negro minority will serve as a more positive and salient reference group than the white majority. Though of limited scope, this ingenious possibility elegantly illustrates the subtleties and difficulties inherent in this type of research.

None of these counter explanations, taken singly or together, appear to eliminate the relatively large relationship found by the commission between the racial composition of the classroom and Negro test performance. If it is not an artifact of other covarying factors, what could be the reasons for this association? The process is undoubtedly complex, but a number of empirical clues are suggestive at this point, and detailed, experimental research will have to follow them up. For example, Coleman found that Negroes in interracial schools are somewhat more likely to feel they can control the environment—the attitude that proved such an important predictor of Negro scores. The commission noted that predominantly Negro schools often become stigmatized in the community as "bad schools" by Negroes and whites alike even when at least the physical facilities are the equal of supposedly "good schools" for whites. Moreover, there are effective and ineffective interracial schools, and the difference between them points to the importance of interracial acceptance for high achievement and aspirations. A number of these considerations will be discussed in detail later in this chapter.

A practical educator might well wonder what the policy implications are of this extended discussion about a racial composition effect separate from those of social class. Is it not true that the relatively small size of the Negro middle class makes desegregation an educational imperative even if *all* the benefits of interracial schooling for Negroes are a direct result of the school social-class factor alone? For most practical purposes, the answer to this query is *yes*. There are, however, cases of predominantly Negro, high-status schools with empty seats. Can one expect the same benefit for a lower-status Negro child from attendance at such a school as he would receive from a predominantly white school of comparable status? The commission report suggests that the child would receive much, *though not all*, of the benefits of racial desegregation.

But this lengthy discussion had two purposes. One was to illustrate in depth the operation of many of the special problems that plague race and education research mentioned briefly in a previous section. A second reason for this discussion is that the issue is in fact of vital theoretical and practical significance. While it is not critical for determining the *need* for desegregated schools, it is crucial for determining the *actual processes* through which desegregation affects both Negro and white children. If it is merely a school social-class effect, that fact limits our search to nonracial processes that should not be unique to interracial schools. If, however, there is also a racial composition effect, then our net must be cast wider to include specifically racial considerations. The writer believes that the present evidence, tentative as it is, points to the operation of *both* social-class and racial composition factors. This belief is further bolstered by the additional evidence presented in the sections below.

What Useful Definitional Distinctions Can Be Made between "Segregation," "Desegregation," and "Integration"?

The Coleman and Civil Rights Commission results suggest some empirically based definitional distinctions that could prove clarifying in this semantically confused realm. To begin with, the legal distinctions between *de jure* and *de facto* segregation are of no practical importance for the consequences of racial isolation in the schools. The commission's data speak to this issue directly; they suggest effects of *de facto* school segregation just as negative as those reported earlier for *de jure* school segregation. The legal distinction has little relevance for the Negro child in the all-Negro school.

Indeed, a realistic look at so-called *de facto* school segregation in cities today calls into question even the legal separation of the two forms of segregation. While *de jure* segregation has its roots in blatant state legislation, so-called "*de facto*" segregation generally has its roots in state action, too. Such state action may include anything from school board decisions to urban renewal plans and zoning ordinances. At some future time in American history, as Paul Freund has suggested, the judiciary will have to come to terms with the implications of the state action similarity between the *de jure* and *de facto* forms of school segregation.

The Coleman and commission data also have implications for the question of numbers and percentages. Two major alternatives had been previously proposed. One manner of defining "segregation" and "desegregation" is to peg the definition to the nonwhite percentage of the area's over-all school population. Thus, if 12 per cent of a system's students are nonwhite, ideally each school in the system would approach a nonwhite student composition of 12 per cent. There are at least two criticisms of this approach: it is often impractical in all but reasonably small areas; and it treats the individual school as a simple reflection of the community, rather than as an integumented institution with its own dynamics and requirements.

A second definition of a racially desegregated school attempts to meet these criticisms with a relatively fixed, rather than variable, gauge. On the basis of several social-psychological considerations, the ideally desegregated school is one whose student body includes from roughly 20 to 40 per cent nonwhites. The disadvantage here is that uniracial schools could still result in systems with fewer than 20 or more than 40 per cent nonwhite children.

The federal studies suggest a simpler set of definitions: a segregated school is one whose student body is predominantly nonwhite; while a desegregated school is one whose student body is interracial but predominantly white. Such definitions stem from the basic finding that the beneficial effects of interracial schools for the academic performance of Negro children are not linear; that is, Negro test scores do not rise evenly with increasing percentages of white children in the classroom. Rather, both the Coleman and commission analyses point to a discontinuity past the mid-point, with the highest Negro verbal test scores reported from *more-than-half* white classrooms.[44] Indeed, enrollment in classes with less-than-half whites is associated with scores not significantly different from those of all-Negro classrooms.

These simpler definitions receive further support from white test performance. As long as the class is predominantly white, the achievement levels of white pupils in interracial classrooms do not differ significantly from those of white pupils in all-white classrooms.[45] But attendance in predominantly Negro classes is associated with lower white test scores. In other words, the same classes relate to higher scores for both Negro and white children; and these classrooms are predominantly white and may usefully be defined as "desegregated." Similarly, the same classes relate to lower scores for both Negro and white children; and these classrooms are predominantly Negro and may usefully be defined as "segregated."

The ideological difficulties of such definitions are readily apparent. As mentioned before, Negroes can rightfully argue that such definitions indicate that "white is right," that predominantly Negro schools cannot be "good schools." Commissioner Frankie Freeman of the Civil Rights Commission addressed herself specifically to this issue:

> The question is not whether in theory or in the abstract Negro schools can be as good as white schools. In a society free from prejudice in which Negroes were full and equal participants, the answer would clearly be "Yes." But we are forced, rather, to ask the harder question, whether in our present society, where Negroes are a minority which has been discriminated against, Negro children can prepare themselves to participate effectively in society if they grow up and go to school in isolation from the majority group. We must also ask whether we can cure the disease of prejudice and prepare all children for life in a multiracial world if white children grow up and go to school in isolation from Negroes.[46]

The two federal reports also suggest that another useful distinction can and should be made between "desegregated" and "integrated" schools. Note that the definition of desegregation involves only a specification of the racial mix of students, namely, more than half whites. It does not include any description of the *quality* of the interracial contact. Merely desegregated schools can be either effective or ineffective, can boast genuine interracial acceptance or intense interracial hostility. In short, a desegregated school is not necessarily a "good school."

Recall that the Coleman report revealed consistently larger standard deviations for the test scores of Negro children in desegregated (that is, more-than-half white) classrooms.[47] Many of these children are doing extremely well, but others are not doing nearly so well. What accounts for these wide differences? The commission's reanalysis of these Coleman data suggests that the intervening variable is *interracial acceptance.* In desegregated schools where most teachers report no tension, Negro students evince higher verbal achievement, more definite college plans, and more positive attitudes than do students in tense desegregated schools.[48] White students also evince benefits from the interracially harmonious school.

The term "integrated school," then, might usefully be reserved for the desegregated school where interracial acceptance is the norm. With these usages, "desegregation" becomes the prerequisite, but "integration" is the ultimate goal.

What Are the Racially Optimal Environments for Performance?

The special efficacy of the desegregated school with interracial acceptance and low levels of tension is completely consistent with the growing body of experimental evidence on racially optimal performance environments. The basic work in this realm has been conducted by Irwin Katz.[49]

Katz first studied biracial task groups consisting of two Negro and two white students. In a variety of conditions, the Negro subjects "displayed marked social inhibition and subordination to white partners." The Negroes made fewer remarks than did whites, tended to accept the whites' contributions uncritically, ranked whites higher on intellectual performance even after equal racial ability had been displayed, and later expressed less satisfaction with the group experience than did the whites. These compliant tendencies were modified only after a situation was presented which required the Negro subjects to announce openly correct problem solutions to their white partners. That this procedure did work suggests the general technique for the interracial classroom of making sure that the Negro members have the opportunity to display personal competence publicly.

Katz also demonstrated performance effects of the biracial context on his white subjects. Accustomed to all-white situations, the white subjects often failed to utilize the abilities of their Negro partners, even when they could expect a monetary bonus from the experimenter for good teamwork.

A second series of experiments by Katz reveals further effects of racial isolation by introducing threat into different racial environments. Thus, students at a predominantly Negro college in the South performed better on a digit-symbol substitution task under conditions of low stress when tested by a white stranger, but under conditions of high stress when tested by a Negro stranger. Likewise, Negro students in another experiment scored higher on a digit-symbol code with a white tester as long as they believed the code to be a research instrument for studying hand-eye co-ordination—a nonintellectual capacity; but they did better with a Negro tester when they thought the code was an intelligence measure.

Katz has also isolated some of the effects on Negro Americans of anticipated comparison with white Americans. Students at a Negro college in the South were given easy and difficult versions of a digit-symbol task by a Negro experimenter who used three different instructions: one set of instructions described the task as not being a test at all, another set described it as a scholastic aptitude test with norms from the Negro college itself, and a third set described it as a scholastic aptitude test with national (that is, predominantly white) college norms. The Negro subjects performed best when they anticipated comparison with other Negroes, less well when they anticipated comparison with whites, and least well when no comparison at all was anticipated.

Another study again varied the race of the anticipated comparison group, other Negroes; but at the same time it varied the race of the experimenter and the probability of success. The results of this experiment are consistent with those just cited. The Negro subjects performed best when tested by a white with a reasonable expectation (60 per cent) of success and anticipation of comparison with Negro norms; they performed worst when tested by a white with a low expectation (10 per cent) of success and anticipation of comparison with white norms.

Katz believes these findings are consistent with a four-factor model of Negro American performance in biracial situations. On the negative side of the ledger, he lists (1) *lowered probability of success*. Where there is marked discrepancy in the educational standards of Negro and white schools, or where Negro children have already acquired strong feelings of inferiority, they are likely to have a *low expectancy of academic success* when introduced into interracial classes. This expectancy is often realistic, considering the situation, but it has the effect of lowering achievement motivation. The practical implication of this factor is to avoid its operation by beginning interracial instruction in the earliest grades, an implication consistent with the Civil Rights Commission's finding that desegregation in the earliest grades generally has the most positive effect on the achievement of Negro children.

(2) *Social threat* is involved in any biracial situation for Negro Americans; because of the prestige and dominance of whites in American society, rejection of Negro students by white classmates and teachers often elicits emotional responses that are detrimental to intellectual functioning. This Katz finding, too, is consistent with the commission finding that Negro academic achievement is highest in integrated schools featuring cross-racial acceptance.

(3) *Failure threat* arises when academic failure means disapproval by significant others: parents, teachers, or peers at school. Low expectancy of success under failure threat may also elicit emotional responses detrimental to performance. But this need not always be the case. Sometimes experiences in the interracial classroom act to dispel feelings of failure threat and group inferiority. When one of the nine Negro children who, under the glare of world publicity, desegregated Central High School of Little Rock, Arkansas, in 1957 was asked what she had learned from her arduous experience, she exclaimed: "Now I know that there are some stupid white kids, too!" This insight into the white superiority myth could never have been acquired in an all-Negro high school.

On the positive side of the ledger, Katz notes that acceptance of Negroes by white classmates and teachers often has (4) *a social facilitation effect* on their ability to learn, apparently because it reassures Negro children that they are expected to be fully as talented in the classroom as anyone else. This anticipation, that skillful performance will win white approval rather than rejection for not "knowing your place," endows scholastic success with *high incentive value*. Katz believes this factor explains why his Negro subjects tend to perform better with white investigators on tasks which are free of severe threat.

A more recent Katz experiment adds another dimension.[50] Heretofore, Katz had employed primarily Negro college students for his subjects. But when he now uses as subjects truly isolated, grade-school Negro boys from a New York City slum, the social facilitation factor previously evident with white testers disappears. In a verbal learning task, performance was superior with the Negro experimenter under all conditions of the study including the use of approval. This result suggests that the original Katz model must be placed in a larger context of the past racial experience of the Negro subjects. It also underlines once more the need for early interracial experience.

A further complication is introduced by what Thibaut and Kelley call "the comparison level for alternatives." [51] Clark and Plotkin, for example, have shown that Negro pupils on scholarship in high-quality, predominantly white colleges generally achieve *lower* dropout rates than better-prepared white students.[52] Clark and Plotkin argue that this finding is a result in part of the fact that the alternatives of the Negro students, should they drop out, are far more limited.[53] A similar explanation can be provided for the far greater re-enlistment rates of Negro servicemen.

Similarly, in the desegregated elementary or secondary school, Negroes may respond differently as a function of the status and experience they would have had were they in a segregated school. The Commission on Civil Rights, in its reanalysis of the Coleman data, turned up some intriguing sex trends that may well be explained by this process of "comparison level for alternatives." Both in achievement scores and college aspirations, Negro girls as a group do not seem to benefit from desegregation as much as Negro boys. That is, the differences between Negro girls in desegregated and segregated classrooms tend to be less striking and consistent than those for boys. One might speculate about the contrasts in sex roles between the two settings. Hence, it may be that girls lose status in the shift from segregated to desegregated schools, while the boys gain. In the less accepting, predominantly white schools, many Negro girls may rank relatively low in those matters of special concern to school-aged girls: beauty as judged by Caucasian standards and membership in social cliques. By contrast, Negro boys may improve their status in the shift to desegregation, for they are less likely to be closed out of such male concerns as athletics. In any event, these leads deserve research attention with more finely grained tools than surveys, for such leads offer the promise of elucidating the larger interaction process sketched out by Katz.

Two promising bodies of middle-range, social psychological theory have yet to be applied to this area: contact theory and attraction theory. Gordon Allport, in his book on *The Nature of Prejudice*,[54] stated flatly the contentions of contact theory for intergroup relations. Contact reduces intergroup conflict and prejudice when there are (1) equal status for members of the two groups in the situation, (2) common goals, (3) no intergroup competition, and (4) the support of authorities, law, or custom. These conditions are consistent with the findings of a large number of research studies on Negro-white contact in the United States—contact ranging from public housing to the armed services.[55] But contact theory has not been systematically applied to school desegregation research. How is cross-racial acceptance encouraged? How can the "social facilitation" effect from interracial situations of low stress be maximized? These questions raised by the Coleman, Civil Rights Commission, and Katz results need research answers, and contact theory offers important leads for this work.

Further leads are provided by the extensive social-psychological work, both theoretical and empirical, on interpersonal attraction. Newcomb states the fundamental tenet as follows: "Insofar as persons have similar attitudes toward things of importance to both or all of them, and discover that this is so, they have shared attitudes; under most conditions the experience of sharing such attitudes is rewarding, and thus provides a basis for mutual attraction." [56]

Rokeach has applied these notions to American race relations with some surprising results. Rokeach maintains that white American rejection of Negro Americans is motivated not so much by racism as by assumed value differences. In other words, whites generally perceive Negroes as holding conflicting values, and it is this perception, and not race *per se*, that leads to rejection. Indeed, save for one sample of whites in the deep South, a variety of subjects have supported Rokeach's ideas by typically preferring a Negro with similar values to themselves over a white with contrasting values.[57]

The Allport, Newcomb, and Rokeach principles are clearly consistent, highly relevant to the interracial classroom, and deserving of further application and testing. Taken together, they suggest a broad social evaluation hypothesis: *Many of the consequences of interracial classrooms for both Negro and white children are a direct function of the opportunities such classrooms provide for cross-racial self-evaluation.*[58] It follows from such a hypothesis that the more opportunities for cross-racial self-evaluation a school provides, the greater the consequences. And it also follows that children for whom peers of the other race become referent should evince the largest changes.

These predictions are consistent with the analyses of the Coleman and commission reports and with the conceptual framework and experimental results on biracial performance of Katz. Hence, the repeated indications of the special potency of desegregation in the early elementary grades fit well with the self-evaluation view. Young children have less rooted self-conceptions and have not yet adopted uniracial school cliques as their chief peer referents. So, too, do the Coleman conclusions that the most significant school correlate of test scores is the social-class climate of the school's student body and that this factor is especially important for Negro children. Schools with a middle-class milieu furnish higher comparison levels for achievement and aspirations; and these higher levels will be especially influential for disadvantaged Negro youngsters whose referents otherwise might well have lower levels. And the special efficacy of more-than-half white classrooms and schools, particularly those characterized by cross-racial acceptance, is also consistent with these predictions. The integrated class and school are unique in the range of opportunities they provide Negro children for maximal self-evaluation against higher comparison levels.

Just how higher white comparison levels can benefit Negro children of varying achievement levels is indicated in a new Katz paper.[59] His earlier factor of social facilitation appears of greater importance to relatively high achievers; while his newly derived factor of "rigidly high internalized standards" is more appropriate to low achievers. He finds in recent experiments that poorly achieving students in a virtually all-Negro school in Detroit have adopted rigid standards so rigorous that they lead inevitably to perceived failure. Consequently, the high, but more realistic, comparison levels typically established by predominantly white schools may well serve paradoxically to *lower* and make more realistic the internalized standards of many poorly achieving Negro pupils; when white children are discovered to have more modest definitions of success, the Negro child's self-imposed standards become less rigid and anxiety-producing.

The inclusion in Coleman's student schedules of a question about cross-racial friendships makes possible direct tests of the social evaluation hypothesis. All students tested in the sixth, ninth, and twelfth grades were asked: "Think now of your close friends. How many of them are white? None, less than half, about half, more than half, all." Assuming "close friends" to be the referent, the social evaluation hypothesis predicts that the major consequences of interracial schools for both Negroes and whites will be found among those who report "close friends" of the other race.

The published analyses employing the "close friend" variable confirm this hypothesis. Thus, with the family and school social-class variables controlled, Negro children with close white friends far less often prefer all Negro friends and an all-Negro school than other Negro children, regardless of the racial composition of their classrooms.[60] Classrooms with half or more white students relate strongly to these interracial preferences solely because Negroes in them more often have close white friends.[61] In addition, Negroes who participate in extracurricular activities more frequently report close white friends.[62]

Negro achievement scores and college aspirations present a somewhat different picture from the attitude data. Having close white friends is related neither to higher scores nor aspirations in all-Negro classrooms. But in more-than-half white classrooms Negro students with close white friends tend to have both higher achievement scores and higher college aspirations.[63] That the critical mediating factor for desegregation benefits for Negro children is cross-racial friendship is further supported by the fact that Negro students in half or more white classrooms report more close white friends than other Negro students.[64]

Friendship operates in a similar fashion for white students. Hence, with father's education controlled, having close Negro friends is strongly and positively related to white preference for an interracial school.[65] And recall that white pupils who begin their interracial schooling in the early grades are more likely to have close Negro friends when they reach the ninth and twelfth grades.[66]

Is There a Critical Age for Initiating Desegregation?

During the 1950's, the White Citizens' Councils of the deep South provided a noteworthy example of being wrong for the right reasons. They sternly opposed the racial desegregation of the public schools and particularly objected to beginning the process in the primary grades. "It's not fair," they argued; "the very young children simply wouldn't know any better than to become friends!"

The relevant data on the subject support the Citizens' Councils' observation, if not their conclusion. Recall that the Coleman and commission reports both showed the largest achievement gains for Negro children who began their interracial schooling in the first three grades. Recall also that the Coleman report indicates that the most positive attitudes toward having interracial classes and Negroes as close friends were evinced by white children who had begun their interracial schooling in the early grades.

Racial isolation is a cumulative process. Its effects over time on children of both races make effective desegregation increasingly more difficult. Separation leads to different interests and values and consequently makes less likely the conditions specified by Allport, Newcomb, and Rokeach as those most likely to lead to intergroup acceptance. Separate schooling also enhances the likelihood of the operation of the three factors Katz found to depress Negro performance in biracial situations: lowered probability of success, social threat, and failure threat. In addition, the research on the development of racial recognition and preference initiated by the Clarks and since replicated throughout the country by many investigators provides yet another reason for the importance of early desegregation.[67] The dawn of racial awareness occurs in the third and fourth years of life, and the beginnings of racial prejudice appear by the fifth and sixth years. In short, from many perspectives, early interracial intervention seems most desirable.

The cumulative nature of racial segregation is dramatically illustrated by data from Louisville, Kentucky, supplied in an earlier report of the United States Commission on Civil Rights. In 1962, Louisville had six public high schools, all with some Negroes, and an open choice of enrollment. One of the high schools, Central, had been designated for Negroes before the end of the city's *de jure* pattern of school segregation and remained in 1962 virtually all-Negro. The commission checked on whether the percentages of Negroes in the junior highs were systematically related to the selection by Negroes of the homogeneously all-Negro Central High. The relationship turned out to be very close: a Spearman rank order correlation of $+.82$. The commission sums up the findings tersely: "The inference is strong that Negro high school students prefer biracial education only if they have experienced it before. If a Negro student has not received his formative education in biracial schools, the chances are he will not choose to enter one in his more mature years." [68]

Evidence from a variety of directions, then, consistently points to the conclusion that the youngest years are the most effective during which to initiate desegregation. Separation produces further separation. This is not to imply that there are no positive benefits of high-school desegregation when the students involved have not had the opportunity of prior desegregation; the commission results suggest some positive effects from desegregation at all levels. But it is to imply that the elementary grades are critical for the most beneficial desegregation.

Are There Lasting Consequences into Adulthood of Interracial Schooling?

If the research on desegregation's consequences for current students is difficult to execute, research which attempts to trace these consequences into adulthood is even more difficult. Yet suggestive survey data from the Commission on Civil Rights report indicate that this is an important and fruitful area for intensive research.

The commission had three survey studies performed on this and related questions, all three of which employed similar questionnaires.

The National Opinion Research Center, University of Chicago, drew a national white adult sample and a Negro adult sample from the urban North and West. In order to maximize the number of respondents who had as children attended interracial schools in the Negro sample, the South and persons over 45 years of age were omitted and smaller cities and middle-class Negro neighborhoods were oversampled. In addition, the Dumbarton Research Council, of Menlo Park, California, conducted an intensive study of 1965 high-school graduates, Negro and white, who had spent their entire school careers in the Oakland, California, school system.

Complete controls are not possible in the analyses of such data, but region of birth, region of schooling, amount of education, and social and economic characteristics of the family of origin were held constant as far as possible whenever appropriate. Within these limits, Negro adults from desegregated schools were more likely as adults to have white-collar jobs and to be earning more money than comparable Negroes from segregated schools.[69] Interestingly, these trends did not hold for those who had attended college, which suggests that higher education can often compensate for elementary- and secondary-school segregation.

The most striking results, however, involved the racial attitudes and behavior of both Negro and white adults. Negro adults who as children had attended interracial schools, when contrasted with comparable Negroes from all-Negro schools, were more likely to trust "a white as much . . . as another Negro," more willing to live in an interracial neighborhood even if they would have to "pioneer" to do so, more eager for their children to attend desegregated schools, and less likely to think that Negro children have a difficult time in desegregated schools. For their part, white adults from desegregated schools expressed more willingness to reside in an interracial neighborhood and were also more favorable than other whites toward the elimination of discrimination against Negroes in employment.[70]

The study of recent high-school graduates in Oakland corroborated in large part the findings of the larger samples. For example, while the desire to send their children to desegregated schools was widely shared among the Negro sample members, it was those from desegregated Oakland schools who were willing to sacrifice to achieve it. Thus, 75 per cent of the Negroes with backgrounds of interracial education, compared to only 52 per cent of the Negroes from segregated schools, agreed that they would be willing to send their "child out of the neighborhood to go to an integrated school." Similarly, 70 per cent of the desegregated Negroes were willing to go out of their way to live in an interracial neighborhood, but only half of the isolated Negroes expressed such willingness.[71]

Behavioral differences, as well as those of attitude, appear in the commission's results. Negro adults who were educated with whites were more likely to be living in mostly white neighborhoods, to be sending their children to mostly white schools, and to have close white friends.[72] Likewise, white adults who were educated with Negroes were more likely to be living in interracial neighborhoods and to have close Negro friends.[73] Thus, the cumulative nature of segregation is not just limited to the school career of the child but tends to span generations.

The consistency of these results and their practical importance commend further and more detailed work in this area. Longitudinal research and more sensitive methods than crude surveys seem indicated. Again, the central focus of such research should not be so much a specification of the long-term consequences of interracial schooling as a clearer conception of the *process* by which these effects are generated. One hint as to a mediating factor appears in the commission's data: namely, many of the attitude and behavioral consequences appeared to be mediated by cross-racial friendship as predicted by social evaluation theory. Consistent with the ideas expressed earlier on the importance of such friendship for a truly *integrated* school, many of the adult results were greatly enhanced if the respondent had had interracial schooling *and* a close friend of the other race. Those who had received a desegregated education, but who had not had a close friend, often showed few if any positive effects.

Is Compensatory Education in Segregated Schools an Effective Substitute for Integrated Education?

Since the initiation of the widely publicized Higher Horizons project in New York City and similar early programs elsewhere, so-called "compensatory education" has been put forward as an effective alternative to racially integrated education.[74] Now the roughly $1.5 billion annually invested by the federal government in this type of strategy through Title I of the 1965 Elementary and Secondary Education Act makes this alternative even more attractive and widespread. Moreover, it is politically expedient, for it solves—temporarily, at any rate—a real dilemma many school superintendents and boards of education in urban districts face: on the one hand, one must act to upgrade the incredibly ineffective education of impoverished Negroes that has been occurring for years; but, on the other hand, racial desegregation of public schools is often a controversial and stoutly resisted action. Compensatory programs allow one to act and to avoid controversy, especially if federal funds pay the bill.

There is only one difficulty with this "solution": there is no rigorous evidence that it works. Indeed, there is mounting evidence from throughout the nation that it resoundingly fails. This is not to say that these enthusiastically initiated programs do not improve for a time the tenor of many ghetto schools—not an unimportant achievement. Nor does it deny that Hawthorne and Rosenthal effects often lead to improved academic performance for a while. But it is to say that it remains to be demonstrated that these programs can lead to *lasting* and significant academic gains. So far, the record of these programs is not encouraging.

To account for repeated failures in this realm, one need only recall the chief finding of the Coleman report: the principal resource a school can offer a disadvantaged child is close association with advantaged children. As we have seen, a major reason why integration leads to lasting significant academic gains for Negro children seems to be the association with middle-class children that it often provides for working-class Negro children. Compensatory programs for disadvantaged youngsters without such contact are, to put it mildly, struggling uphill to achieve meaningful effects under the same isolated conditions as before. One may speculate that this is one of the reasons for the Coleman report's unpopularity in some quarters. Striking as it does at the heart of a politically expedient strategy which is supported by $1.5 billion, the report (understandably, perhaps) has been suppressed and irresponsibly criticized. Released late on a rainy Saturday afternoon of a July Fourth week-end, the Coleman report is now out of print, and one is told by both the Government Printing Office and the United States Office of Education that it will not be reissued.[75]

The Commission on Civil Rights report explored this crucial area further.[76] Though widely misinterpreted as attacking "compensatory education" in general, the commission expressed skepticism over the efficacy of such programs *in ghetto schools*. It came to this conclusion after studying in detail such programs in St. Louis, New York City, Syracuse, Philadelphia, Berkeley, and Seattle. It noted with interest that comparable Negro children in the last four cities who were bussed out to predominantly white schools did show *sustained* academic gains, whereas those who had remained behind in the ghetto schools for special programs did not.

The commission's conclusion is obvious: Why not have both integration and remedial education as needed? Of course, the two intervention strategies are often pitted against each other as "either-or" alternatives, since realistically they compete for the same funds, have rival educational ideologies undergirding them, and have different political constituencies. The reasons for not combining them are political, for in educational terms there is every reason to co-ordinate both measures into a single strategy.

Finally, it should be said in fairness that the general failure of ghetto compensatory programs to date does not necessarily mean failure of future and radically different programs. One cannot evaluate a program yet to be tried. It is the responsibility, however, of those who honestly believe that compensatory education can in fact be a viable alternative to racial integration to reject the null hypothesis with rigorous data; that is, the advocates of compensatory education have the burden of proving that it can work.

What Are the Politics of School Desegregation?

If one accepts "a shifting pendulum" notion of social change, the arc of the civil rights pendulum in America must be seen as a particularly wide and violent one. Early in the 1960's, building to the climax of the march on Washington of 200,000 Americans in 1963, and culminating in the Selma march in 1965, the push for racial desegregation in all public realms appeared certain of both its direction and ultimate triumph. Public opinion agreed that this should be the national course; two-thirds of adult Americans, for example, supported the passage of the sweeping 1964 Civil Rights Act. The resisters to racial change, especially such southern segregationists as Bull Connor, of Birmingham, and Sheriff Jim Clark, of Selma, became isolated and negative symbols of a vanishing age.

But the civil rights pendulum began to swing violently in the other direction soon after the Selma march. History will note that 1966 was the year when the full domestic effects of the Viet Nam War came to be felt by the civil rights struggle. Not only was domestic spending cut back, but the liberal coalition became confused and split over both the war and the newly articulated ideology of "black power." Moreover, the anti-Negro elements of the population gained new mobilization and legitimization as Negro frustration and desperation spilled over into destructive riots and calls for separatism.

The events of 1966, 1967, and 1968, from war to riots, frightened white America. And most significant of all, the United States Congress reflected the retreat to the point of leading it. The same Congress that enacted the 1965 Civil Rights Act reverted to the racist policies of earlier times: weakened civil rights acts were rejected; requests for needed jobs to enforce previous civil rights legislation were refused; a clause calling for affirmative moves against housing and school segregation was stricken summarily from the Model Cities Act; and the Senate even approved an appropriations rider that allows hospital segregation in some cases. In addition, congressional committees roundly castigated the United States Office of Education and its distinguished commissioner, Harold Howe, II, for their timidly modest southern school desegregation guidelines (which were, after all, merely a too restrained attempt to enforce Title VI of the 1964 Civil Rights Act fashioned by Congress itself). The lowest point arrived when the distinguished House of Representatives publicly laughed down a needed rat-control bill.

The popular mass media description of this sad scene is "white backlash." But this vague term is too variously defined and too simple to be helpful or accurate.[77] The implication is that there is a massive shift toward negative white attitudes about Negroes. Relevant research data, however, point to a different, though equally dangerous, process with at least three dimensions: (1) a political mobilization of a united right combined with a political demobilization of a divided left; (2) a rising salience of racial concerns among both white and Negro Americans; and (3) a growing resistance to the pace of change, though not generally toward the goals of the change, among white Americans— especially among the mildly prejudiced.

Roughly speaking, about 30 per cent of white Americans are reasonably solid segregationists, and about 30 per cent are reasonably solid integrationists. The shifts in survey data over time particularly reflect the variable mood of the middle 40 per cent, whose typically mild prejudice against Negroes is usually not nearly as salient as their desire for "law and order." When it appeared in 1964 that racial peace could be achieved by a civil rights act directed at the South, the mildly prejudiced joined the then-mobilized integrationists in supporting that statute. Now that riots and black power slogans threaten the peace, the mid-group joins the now-mobilized segregationists in demands to slow racial change.

This mid-group's generally negative attitude toward interracial housing is especially significant. This negative attitude is not new: the mid-40 per cent combined earlier with segregationists to form consistent two-to-one majorities against antidiscrimination housing referendums in Akron, Detroit, and Seattle as well as in California on Proposition 14 in 1964. In 1966, Negro protests in Chicago and the housing title of the defeated civil rights act centered special attention on housing. These developments made more salient and triggered already-existing housing fears. Indeed, the cry for "neighborhood schools" seems less related to the noun "schools" than to the adjective "neighborhood." [78]

Against this national backdrop, the local politics of school desegregation have become more complex. Coalition groups which press for desegregation and consist largely of middle-class Negroes and liberal whites still exist in more communities than the national scene would suggest. Resistance groups of status-threatened, lower middle-class whites, such as the Parents and Taxpayers in New York City, can still be found, too.[79] And the educational bureaucracies of many big cities continue to destroy the effectiveness of even token efforts toward racial balance.[80]

But there are new elements: black power Negro militants who ridicule interracial schools as a further device to destroy "Negro culture"; less federal pressure for school desegregation; and more talk among disenchanted "liberals" about the "impossibility" of achieving urban school desegregation.[81] None of these elements, of course, is entirely new: there has traditionally existed an understandable Negro ambivalence over integrated education, especially among the lower class; actual federal pressure on local school boards never approached the force of Washington rhetoric; and some white "liberals" have sought for some time an excuse to turn their attention to other issues.

Nor are all the new elements damaging to the future of school desegregation. Many educators, especially in smaller cities and suburbs, are evincing a surprising new interest in desegregation. Influenced by the Coleman and commission reports and the growing awareness that compensatory efforts in ghetto schools are failing, the whole tone of professional discussion has shifted in recent years from "Why desegregate?" to "How can we desegregate?"

A uniquely valuable study of the school desegregation process in eight major cities points up the importance of this recent shift among many professional educators.[82] The eight cities—including Baltimore, Boston, Buffalo, Newark, Pittsburgh, St. Louis, and San Francisco—represent cities outside of the South between one-quarter of a million to a million in population with at least 10 per cent Negro citizens; and each had its desegregation politics studied intensively by a research team from the University of Chicago. Thus, the sampling excluded the largest cities where the problem is most intense—New York City, Houston, Cleveland, New Orleans, Los Angeles, Atlanta, Chicago, and Philadelphia—but included others more typical of the central range of American metropolitan areas.

A principal finding of the study was the consistency of the pattern with which the issue arose and was handled in the various cities. Typically, the first stage of the school system's reaction to desegregation demands involved the school superintendent. In the majority of instances, the superintendent flatly rejected the demands. He was likely to argue for "color blindness" and a narrow definition of the school's function as "educational" and not "social." Often, too, the superintendent displayed "an extreme defensiveness and an intolerance for 'lay' criticism."

This standard reaction must be seen in historical perspective to be understood. As part of his needed ideological protection from political pressures, the urban superintendent must jealously guard his role as a professional and stress the significance of his credentials as the boundary between his expert knowledge and the layman's ignorance. Moreover, the pressure for special treatment of a particular group attacks a basic and hard-won principle of big-city school systems developed out of the progressive era: all groups must be "treated alike," with no special favors for one ethnic or political segment. That truly equal treatment is *not* a fact for the Negro child only makes the official reaction to civil rights demands all the more defensive. The Chicago study also uncovered the fact that big-city superintendents frequently have backgrounds that are not likely to equip them to play a leadership role in urban change. Of those in *Who's Who,* they averaged 57 years of age and generally came from small towns or farms, attended little-known colleges, began their teaching careers in small towns, and gained their administrative experience outside the large cities.

The second stage of the controversy witnesses the school board taking over decision-making from the superintendent. After the superintendent's rejection of their demands, desegregation groups step up their demonstrations, and the school board begins to consider this issue as serious. Its first reaction, the Chicago study notes, is crucial, for it sets the tone for the remainder of the conflict. If the board rejects the demands for racial change, as in Boston, the controversy flares up to headline proportions. Demonstrations and threats have little effect on the board at this point for it is politically "locked in." Only intervention from higher authority—the state or the federal government—can break the deadlock.

Yet in many cases the school board accepts, at least in part, the racial demands. This may not represent major concessions. Indeed, most of the "positive" board responses studied were more symbolic than real. A ringing statement of integrationist intent often clears the air; but the ability of even a sincere board to act on the statement is severely limited by factors beyond its immediate control. The authoritarian structure of most school systems is a chief barrier, and few boards are willing or able to attempt the radical reorganization necessary to achieve basic structural alterations. Moreover, central city school boards generally face demographic, tax base, and state aid restrictions quite beyond their control.

The Chicago research also found that the types of key responses to civil rights pressures—flat rejection or symbolic acceptance—could be predicted from the composition of the boards themselves. Negative responses emanated from four boards, all of which were comprised of low-status, political members. In the Boston instance, the school committee is usually employed by unknowns as a political steppingstone to higher office. Positive board responses, on the other hand, came from boards comprised largely of high-status, nonpolitical members, such as corporation executives or lawyers and professionals. In the three most positive instances (Pittsburgh, Baltimore, and St. Louis) the cities have elites which are highly involved in a variety of local policy issues.

This pattern of the mid-sixties must now accommodate a new and unlikely coalition in resistance to school desegregation. The white segregationist politicians of the South and North find new allies among the most ardent black power separatists and the disenchanted white "liberals." Each segment of this emerging coalition, in an interesting way, needs and exploits the other two segments; yet one wonders how long after the close of the Viet Nam War such an unstable coalition can be maintained.

The points at issue, of course, are *choice* and the *future* of American race relations. Spokesmen, white or Negro, who glibly announce what "Negroes" would do if a truly honest choice were provided them between racial segregation and integration reflect only their own feelings. A true choice has never been provided to the great majority of Negro Americans.

In education, the continuation of ghetto schools for some time is certain; but will Negro parents also be provided integrated schools for their children should they prefer them? If they are offered such a choice, there will undoubtedly be some who opt for segregation, others for integration. What the proportion is of each will be a function of the local conditions and which segments of Negro America are involved. But the results might well be surprising. Who would have guessed, for example, that 96 per cent of the parents of randomly chosen Negro children, most of them poor and all of them in ghetto schools, would accept the invitation to have their offspring bussed long distances to previously all-white schools in the suburbs of Hartford? Yet precisely this happened in the Project Concern integration move in the fall of 1966. This may indicate that under prestige conditions that do not require parental initiative (as in so-called "freedom of choice" or "open enrollment" plans), integrated schools may well be preferred if they are viewed as the best schools. Lomax could possibly still be correct in his speculation that "school integration isn't something large numbers of Negroes get excited about." [83] But we shall not know until real choice is offered.

More is at stake, of course, than providing choice. Integrated schools are not devices "for Negroes" or, for that matter, "for whites." Recall that, apart from academic benefits for Negro children, interracial training is associated with markedly more positive racial attitudes among white and Negro children and adults. The future of American race relations depends on our schools' ensuring that the nation will not have yet another generation of bigots.

What Is the Racial Relevance of Educational Alternatives to the Public Schools?

If our present schools are failing Negroes, why not think of educational alternatives to the public schools? Increasing numbers of specialists, from Kenneth Clark to James Coleman, have asked themselves this question and come up with a variety of suggested possibilities. This thinking has been stimulated by the implications of military test data and the relative success with the disadvantaged of such institutions as the armed forces and the Job Corps.

The enormity of the public-school failure, in lieu of adequate national testing, is best spelled out by the results on the Armed Forces Qualification Test (AFQT) administered to all draftees and enlistees.[84] Consider the 383,000 18-year-olds examined in late 1964 and 1965. One-fourth of these men failed to meet the minimum intellectual standards of the armed services (mental groups IV and V). The racial differences are striking. Whereas 19 per cent of white testees failed, 67 per cent of Negro testees did so.

Part of this racial difference is attributable to regional concentration. The majority of Negro draftees and enlistees are from the South, where state rates of white failures range up to eight times more than in northern states (for instance, 5.5 per cent in Washington State contrasted with 43.7 per cent in Tennessee). Thus, the Negro failure percentage in Washington state was only two-thirds as much as the white percentage in North Carolina. Part of this racial difference is socioeconomic, for which the armed services' data supply no satisfactory controls. And part of this racial difference reflects the greater number of years of formal training enjoyed by the white 18-year-olds. Nevertheless, a significant amount of this racial difference on the AFQT is a function of the public schools' lack of success with Negro youth. Two out of three of the Negro failures had attended at least some high school, compared with less than half of the white failures; and they averaged one more year of schooling than white failures.

The intriguing armed forces contribution to this bleak picture, however, is the increasing willingness to accept these "test failures" and train them in basic military skills.[85] The services, like industry, have always been willing to relax test standards in times of war and manpower shortages. In World War II, for example, the army set up Special Training Units and successfully provided a basic fourth-grade education in eight weeks for 254,000 previously illiterate soldiers—roughly half of them Negroes and the great majority southerners.[86] And in 1966, with the Viet Nam War heating up, then-Secretary of Defense Robert S. McNamara launched Project One Hundred Thousand. The project was so named because it aims to admit 100,000 into the services annually who would not normally be accepted because of extremely low AFQT scores. McNamara stated his position bluntly:

> There is now ample evidence that many aptitude evaluations have less to do with how well the student can learn than with the cultural value system of the educator. Too many instructors look at a reticent or apathetic or even hostile student and conclude: He is a low-aptitude learner. In most cases it would be more realistic for the instructor to take a hard, honest look in the mirror and conclude: I am a low-aptitude teacher. . . . Clearly, the way to measure the low-test scorer's "aptitude" is to place him in a situation that offers the encouragement he has never had before. That means a good teacher and a good course of instruction, well supported by self-paced audio-visual aids. It also means less formal, classroom, theoretical instruction, and more practical on-the-job training. Under these conditions, the so-called low-aptitude student can succeed.[87]

It appears that the services succeed with these castoffs of the public schools. The army's Basic Combat Training centers graduate more than 95 per cent of all their trainees and move them up to more advanced training; and the low test scorers have the *same* ratio of graduates as other groups.[88] No easy analogies can be made, of course, between the army's training centers and central city schools: army personnel are older; the army provides "a total institution" environment separated from home influences; the army trains for a more limited set of skills; and so on. Yet its distinct success with the schools' mistakes commands our attention. Any institution that can make productive citizens out of the very Americans our public schools gave up on must have some elements that are transferable to the school setting.

Note some of the army's training techniques: male instructors for young male students; direct reward in rank and prestige for learning; more "hands on" than book training; greater use of group spirit and competition as sources of motivation; more "masculinity" identification with learning; constant checking and supervision of instructors; and the assumption that "if the student is failing to learn, the instructor is failing to teach." [89] Note, too, that the army provides a racially integrated training situation and is "categorically against any kind of ability groupings." [90] Do these contrasts with the typical public school account in part for the army's greater success with the disadvantaged? Do they explain in part, too, why Negro youth drop out of high schools in far greater percentages than white youth, yet re-enlist in the army with twice the frequency? Should the armed forces continue to accept these men, even in peacetime, as an important effort for American society? Applied research is obviously called for along these lines.

Encouraged by such efforts of institutions other than public schools, many observers are casting around for additional alternatives. The popular phrase "open schools" has been coined for this purpose, though it has diverse meanings for those employing it. For Clark, "open schools" mean centers not administered by present school systems.[91] In addition to armed services schools, he believes state and federal regional schools, college- and university-sponsored schools, and corporation- and union-sponsored schools could all become stimulating competitors for public education. Racial and socioeconomic balance of the student bodies would be a requirement for public funds.

The Clark proposal assumes that the competition of alternatives will act to upgrade the public schools. This assumption is by no means inevitable in the economic market place; nor have the present alternatives, private and parochial schools, conspicuously acted in this fashion. Indeed, present alternatives have typically drained off both select students and financial resources from public education. Clark's ideal alternatives, however, would contrast sharply with today's private and parochial institutions of learning by demonstrating the efficacy of new approaches in racially and socioeconomically mixed schools. He is currently proposing to major corporations that they take up this challenge now as one visible means of aiding the central city.

James Coleman's idea of "open schools" involves, in effect, subcontracting specific educational tasks to private interests.[92] A parent would be given the choice of having his child take fourth-grade mathematics at his regular school or from any number of private subcontractors—I.B.M., General Learning, or others—who also provide the course in racially and socioeconomically balanced settings. Contract remuneration from public funds would be based on the test score increases of the children enrolled in a corporation's course. Like Clark, Coleman assumes that competition would stimulate, rather than flatten, public instruction.

One does not have to have a 1984 nightmare to visualize problems in Coleman's scheme. First, business competition for parental choice could easily assume irrational proportions. Since parents would typically not have access to the basic information necessary for a truly rational choice, their selection could become not unlike choosing toothpaste. Advertising would aid the irrationality: "Be the first on your block with R.C.A. computer instruction!" Second, contract remuneration pegged to test scores assumes testing procedures more advanced than anything now available. Present-day measures are easily manipulable; students can be taught "for the tests" (as in the New York Regents exams) and for "testwiseness" so that scores are influenced apart from true achievement. With remuneration based on the scores, the temptation to resort to such devious devices would be enormous.

In any event, the moral of these ideas is clear: in casting about for means by which to halt the growing educational genocide of Negro children in deteriorating central city schools, we are not limited for solutions to public education as currently organized. Adopting the successful and transferable procedures of the armed services and Job Corps, developing alternative schools, and subcontracting particular tasks are among the many possibilities.

What Ideas Exist for "Ultimate Solutions"?

Whether or not "open schools" of any variety are in the future, the critical first order of business is meaningful structural change of public education as it now exists. Is it possible to achieve effective racially and socioculturally balanced student bodies? Are there any "ultimate solutions" for our big-city school systems? Is not integration really a nice but impossible notion? What about Washington, D.C.; Harlem; South Side, Chicago?

Initially, we must make a clear distinction between *small-ghetto* and *big-ghetto situations*, for what is possible and useful in the former may well be counterproductive in the latter. The small-ghetto situation generally involves a city with less than a seventh or so of its public-school population Negro. Its high schools and often even its junior high schools are naturally desegregated, and with good faith it can correct its elementary-school segregation *within* its borders. There are many such communities throughout the United States, and together they account for a surprisingly large minority of Negro children. They should not be confused with the Washingtons and Harlems, as such apostles of segregationist doom as Joseph Alsop are given to do.

The elementary schools in these small-ghetto cities can usually be desegregated with a plan custom-styled to the system utilizing a unique combination of the following within-district methods: (1) the district-wide redrawing of school lines to maximize racial balance (positive gerrymandering); (2) the pairing of predominantly white and Negro schools along the borders of the Negro ghetto (the Princeton plan); and (3) a priority for and careful placement of new and typically larger schools outside the ghetto (the rebuilding plan). If there is a need to desegregate at the junior or senior high levels, two other devices are often sufficient: (4) the alteration of "feeder" arrangements from elementary grades to junior highs and from junior highs to senior highs in order to maximize racial balance (the balanced feeder plan); and (5) the conversion of more schools into district-wide specialized institutions (the specialized school plan). Controversy is typically minimal because the small-ghetto situation can usually be accommodated without widespread subsidized transportation of students (bussing).

The real problems of implementation occur for the big-ghetto situation. The small-ghetto devices are generally mere band-aid remedies for the city system with a substantial and growing percentage of Negro students. Thus, pairing schools along the ghetto's borders would have to be repeated every few years as the ghetto expanded. Or a new school built outside the ghetto last year may only result in a nearly all-Negro school within the ghetto next year. Even in Boston, with only 26 per cent nonwhites in its public-school system, a sophisticated redistricting plan for elementary schools would have only minor effects. In a computer-assisted system analysis, the ultimate limit of redistricting was tested with the rules that children in grades one through three would not be assigned more than a half-mile from their homes, and children in grades four through six not more than three-quarters of a mile. Yet the proportion of Boston's nonwhite elementary students attending predominantly nonwhite schools would only be reduced from 78 to 66 per cent, and for nonwhite junior high students from 65 to 50 per cent.[93] Clearly, for Boston—not to mention the really enormous ghetto cities of New York, Philadelphia, Washington, Chicago, and Los Angeles—more sweeping measures are required.

If the criteria for these sweeping measures are specified, the form and direction of future efforts begin to take shape. And these criteria were suggested earlier in the discussion of the causes of *de facto* school segregation. In planning for big-ghetto desegregation, larger educational complexes drawing from wide attendance areas will be essential. These attendance areas will generally have to include both central city and suburban territory in order to ensure the optimal stable racial mix. The sites for these facilities must be not only convenient to the mass transit network but also on racially neutral turf. Such locations would avoid immediate public labeling of the school as "white" or "Negro."

Racial specifications are by no means the only criteria for future remedies. Public schools in our largest cities have lost their former pre-eminence as the innovative educational leaders. Berkeley, California, Newton and Brookline, Massachusetts, and a host of other smaller communities are now the pacesetters. Thus, the plans for the future should accent and facilitate innovation. Indeed, future public schools should possess facilities which could rarely be duplicated by expensive private schools if they are to compete effectively for the children of advantaged parents. Such arrangements, of course, will cost considerable money; thus, a final criterion must be significant federal support of capital costs.

Several designs would meet these criteria; but one can serve as illustrative. Ringing our major cities with educational parks, each of which serves both inner city and suburban students, offers one basic plan— *the metropolitan park plan.* Each park would be located on neutral turf in an inner-ring suburb or just inside the central city boundary; [94] and it would be so placed that the same spoke of the mass transit system could bring both outer-ring suburban children into the park and inner-city children out to it. The attendance area of each part would ideally cut out a metropolitan pie slice containing a minimum of 12,000 to 15,000 public-school students, with the thin end of the slice in the more dense central city and the thick end in the more sparse suburbs.

But what incentive could generate the metropolitan co-operation necessary for such a plan? A number of systems have considered educational parks, but they usually find the capital costs prohibitive. Moreover, many systems are currently hard-pressed for expansion funds, especially as referendums for school construction bonds continue to be defeated throughout the nation. Federal funding, then, on a massive scale will obviously be needed, though it must be dispersed in a far more careful and strategic manner than the everybody-gets-his-cut, "river and harbors bill" principle of the 1965 Elementary and Secondary Education Act.

The educational park idea is not a panacea; there can be elegantly effective or incredibly ineffective parks. Yet ample federal funding combined with the nation's planning and architectural genius should be able to set a new standard and direction for public schools. This combination has successfully been applied to public facilities ranging from interstate highways to magnificent airports. Now the combination should be applied for the benefit of children.

From high-rise structures to multiple-unit campuses, educational parks themselves can be planned in a variety of ways. The most widely discussed design would involve a reasonably large tract of land (80 to 100 acres as a minimum) and no fewer than fourteen or fifteen schools serving grades from kindergarten through high school. One educator has visualized a campus design for 18,000 students consisting of two senior high, four junior high, and eight elementary schools.[95] If the park were to serve an especially densely populated section, it would be best if it did not include the entire grade spectrum so that it could still cover a reasonably expansive and heterogeneous attendance area. In general, however, an educational park resembles a public university. Both include a variety of educational programs for a large group of students of varying abilities.

Apart from offering racial remedies, the metropolitan park concept has a number of distinct advantages. First, there are considerable savings that accrue from consolidation; centralized facilities, such as a single kitchen, need not be duplicated in each of the park's units. Savings on capital costs, too, would result from simultaneous building of many units at one location. These savings, however, do not necessarily mean that the total construction and operating costs would be less than those for the same student capacity spread out in traditional units. The advantage is that for essentially the same cost metropolitan parks could boast significantly better facilities than traditional schools. Consequently, each child would be receiving far more per educational dollar in the metropolitan park.

Many innovations made possible by the metropolitan park extend beyond the equipment realm. For instance, the teaching profession today suffers from being one of the most undifferentiated by rank of all professions, a characteristic which discourages a lifelong orientation to the field. While the medical profession has a graded rank order of roles from intern and resident to chief of a service, teachers must either enter administration and become principals or shift to more prestigious schools in order to move up the ladder. By concentrating a large number of teachers in a relatively small area, far more role differentiation becomes possble. Thus, a teacher might progress from an apprentice in a team-teaching situation, to a master teacher in a team, to a supervisor of master teachers, and so on. Faculty concentration also allows more intensive across-school, in-service training. Concentration of students also allows wider course offerings. Specialized classes, from playing the lute to seventeenth-century English literature, become economically possible when the students electing them are gathered from units throughout the park.

In addition to the natural resistance to change, four major objections have been raised to the park concept: (1) excessive capital costs; (2) the phasing out of existing schools; (3) the problem of impersonalization in the large complexes; and (4) the loss of neighborhood interest and involvement in the school. Each is a serious objection and deserves comment.

The park *is* expensive, and major federal funding is necessary. Furthermore, mistakes in design and location could be disastrous. A park is an enormous commitment of resources, and, if poorly conceived, it could stand for years as a major mistake in planning. This is precisely what would happen if parks were operated totally within central city systems. Demographic projections prove the folly of building parks for a single central city system as a desegregation device.[96] It is for this reason that the parks of the future must be *metropolitan* in character.

Present schools were expensive, too, and raised the problem of phasing out existing facilities. For many urban districts this is not a problem; they have already overutilized schools with double shifts and rising enrollments or old schools long past their usefulness. But some urban districts have many new schools and would be hesitant to join a park consortium. The program, however, is a long-term one. Hopefully, by the early 1970's, most of the nation's leading metropolitan areas would boast of one or more parks; these in turn could serve as models for completing the park rings in the decade. Moreover, elementary and secondary student enrollments will rise rapidly: from 48.4 million in 1964 to a projected 54.9 million in 1974 and 66 million in the fateful year of 1984.[97] Metropolitan parks, then, could be phased in as older facilities are phased out and enrollments swiftly rise.

The third objection to parks centers on the impersonalization of organizational bigness, "the Kafka problem." Indeed, much of the park's description (15,000 students, a staff approaching 1,000, the latest electronic equipment) has a frightening Kafka ring; and one can easily imagine how an ill-designed park could justify these fears. But such a prospect is not inherent in the park plan; nor is bigness a park problem alone. Many of today's huge urban high schools accommodate many thousands of students in a single unit and arouse the same uneasiness. In fact, imaginatively designed parks could act to counter the urban trend toward ever larger public-school units. *Smaller* schools at each level can be economically built as units within the park; and careful planning can afford a reasonable degree of privacy for each unit while still providing access to the shared facilities of the park.

Some critics are particularly concerned about the park's loss of neighborhood interest and involvement. The criticism assumes that most urban public schools today are neighborhood-based and that they generate considerable neighborhood involvement. Serious doubts can be raised about both assumptions: we may well be worrying about the loss of something already lost. In any event, there is no evidence to indicate that only a neighborhood-based school can generate parental concern, that a metropolitan park could not duplicate this feat, or that there is a close and negative association between the size of the attendance area and involvement.

In summary, then, those who say there is nothing we can do about the educational segregation of our major cities are, fortunately, wrong. This is not to say that desegregation progress will be easy or even that we will do what is necessary to achieve such progress. But it is to say that potentially it *can* be done for a significant number of urban Americans, white and Negro.

PROPOSALS

Among the proposals which flow from this lengthy discussion of the Negro and education are those involving an action-oriented Commission for Metropolitan Education, a major demographic simulation of the problem's future dimensions, an effort toward methodological upgrading of evaluation studies, and many varieties of process research in interracial education. Each of these proposals deserves brief discussion.

A Commission for Metropolitan Education

Either established by a single large foundation or a consortium of foundations interested in education, an action-oriented Commission for Metropolitan Education is imperative to set the model for future federal efforts in education. If well budgeted and staffed, this commission could pursue a range of significant thrusts markedly different from such ill-fated and unfortunate private programs as the Ford Foundation's Great Cities compensatory education endeavor or its present "community control" program in three New York City schools.

First, and most important, the commission could experiment in the making of strategic grants to metropolitan consortia for a variety of cross-district co-operative schemes. Remarkably little co-operation exists today between districts within metropolitan areas, even in such obvious spheres of mutual benefit as common procurement of supplies. The Great High School plans in Pittsburgh, for instance, have been drawn up with virtually no communication with surrounding suburban districts. Not even the richest nation on earth in peacetime can expect to fund adequately over 25,000 separate school districts that largely compete against one another.

Multidistrict grants should make quality education for *all* of a metropolitan area's children its primary goal, keeping a careful check that this includes expanding opportunities for racial and class integration. At present this focus would mean, among other possibilities, support for the spread of Boston's METCO (Metropolitan Council for Occupational and Educational Opportunities) and Hartford's Project Concern to other metropolitan areas. Though transporting relatively small numbers of Negro children to empty seats in suburban schools offers no long-term solution in itself, it represents the beginnings of metropolitan co-operation, helps to mobilize metropolitan thinking and political pressures, and, as in Massachusetts, may lead to planning for state-operated demonstration schools in urban areas.

As indicated throughout this paper, public-parochial school coordination should be a focus of the commission. Especially in such cities as Philadelphia and St. Louis, where large proportions of the school-aged white children attend church schools, the commission could encourage new and more meaningful methods of joint operation. High in priority among these methods would be those involving physical proximity of public and private facilities and individual, rather than group, participation of parochial students in public programs.

A Commission for Metropolitan Education would have many points of entry and leverage. One is provided for by the New Model Cities program. Though Congress stripped the program of metropolitan and desegregation requirements, it nevertheless presents opportunities to lay the groundwork toward these goals. Relatively small but carefully designed grants to critical local agencies working with Model Cities planning in particular cities could exploit this possibility. In this regard, the metropolitan planning councils that exist in most urban areas make promising starting points.

Another point of entry and leverage is the university. Urban study programs at Chicago, Columbia, Harvard, and other universities in major centers have already received significant foundation funding and provide bases for both research and direct involvement of higher education. The commission could ensure that metropolitan educational concerns not be left out of the work and action of these urban programs; this means at the minimum that the schools of education at these institutions be directly linked in organization and be given responsibility for drawing up operational proposals for local metropolitan co-ordination.

Still another point of entry is through the architectural, design, and planning professions. Large educational complexes, whether in the park form described here or not, are definitely in the future. They could be enormous monuments to poor planning; or they could introduce an entirely new and upgraded level of facility for public education. So critical, then, is the effective use of America's best architectural and planning genius that the commission might well assign a high priority to this area. Special grants to innovative members of these professions for work with educators in creating a range of skillful designs to meet varied situations and specifications could prepare the ground for effective utilization of future federal school construction funds.

Plans, no matter how imaginative, are never as convincing as the concrete example. This suggests that the commission should invest in the development of at least one well-conceived metropolitan educational complex. There is actually no metropolitan complex in existence today meeting the criteria discussed in this chapter, so that any such model development would undoubtedly receive considerable attention. To increase its impact, the complex should be located in a region where racial and class issues exist in a not too atypical form. Thus, Washington, D.C., and New York City on one end and Salt Lake City and Spokane on the other would not be ideal hosts for this model venture. More typical would be, say, Providence, where interest in the idea has already developed throughout the metropolitan area, state educational officials are favorable, and the Negro percentage is similar to that of all but the heaviest centers of concentration.

Finally, the commission might well consider establishing a land bank of ideal metropolitan sites for future educational complexes. Such an effort could consist of interest-free loans to school district consortia to purchase strategic sites for building metropolitan complexes in the future. Ask urban superintendents with long-range views about such sites, and they will immediately provide you with one or more ideal locations which could be purchased if only the capital funds were available. Ask urban planners about such sites, and they are likely to tell you that such locations are in short supply and rapidly disappearing, especially in the older eastern cities. These opinions suggest that a land bank of even modest proportions might prove of critical significance.

A Major Demographic Simulation of the Problem's Future Dimensions

Much of today's debate over the public education of Negro American children resembles the proverbial blind men describing the elephant. Each commentator generalizes broadly from his own limited slice of the problem. Yet the critical context for any intelligent approach to the issue is basically demographic. Integrationist ideologists make it sound as if total school desegregation could be accomplished next fall if it were not for segregationist politicians. Most observers of the urban scene can eye the growing densities of Negro population in central cities and cast aside such contentions as naïve. But the same observers are susceptible to an equally naïve reading of racial demography that characterizes virtually all educational integration efforts as futile.

Earlier it was noted that Negro Americans are represented in the nation's metropolitan areas in a similar proportion to that of white Americans: that is, about two out of every three Negroes and two out of every three whites live in a metropolitan area. And it was noted that Washington, D.C., and Harlem are *not* typical of Negro communities throughout urban America. In addition to disregarding these facts, the apostles of demographic doom must also (1) assume that Negro ghettos will not extend into suburbs (as Pittsburgh's eastern ghetto already has and Chicago's western ghetto is about to); (2) project that the single-site model of so-called "neighborhood" schools will dominate future school plans despite its increasingly uneconomic future; (3) contend that the overwhelmingly white parochial systems in key central cities will not co-operate more and more with public systems; (4) hold that virtually all school district and municipal boundaries will remain as they are; and (5) maintain that metropolitan co-operation in public education will not grow despite its economic attractions and the possibility of future federal incentives. None of these sweeping assumptions appears fully justified.

As usual, the truth seems to lie somewhere between the two extreme interpretations. On the one hand, with all the good faith, metropolitan co-operation, and federal construction funds imaginable, school integration as a realistic alternative for virtually all urban Negroes is a long-term goal. On the other hand, vastly expanded integrated education in metropolitan America not only is possible but could be achieved by means of devices known now. Yet these two statements do not delimit the problem sufficiently. How many urban Negroes and whites could be integrated with various alterations in present school organization?

What would be the Negro demand for such integration? What would be the Negro demand for separate schools? And what is the range of possible answers to these queries for 1980, 1990, or 2000? While no precise estimates are possible, current thinking is now unaided by even the order of magnitude and range of possibilities. With the growing technology of computer-assisted simulation of social processes, however, work on these issues would be valuable for planning not just in education but in all realms of American race relations.

We know enough now to realize that the resulting models would be complex. For example, Negro demand for integration is not just a simple function of central city concentration but also highly dependent on the realistic opportunities available for integration. Not unlike the increase in total automobile travel attracted by new turnpikes, any model would have to contain feed-back components of ever increasing integrationist demand with expanding actual integration. Likewise, estimates would be necessary of rising demand for racial separatism with increased segregation. Recall the Civil Rights Commission data on Negro and white adults which strongly suggest that adult interracial behavior, as well as interracial attitudes, are importantly a function of integrated or segregated school experience. Recall, too, the surprisingly favorable response of lower-status Negro parents to having their children participate in Hartford's Project Concern and integrated schools once it became a viable possibility. But these data are rare. Hence, such a full-scale simulation project would not only provide a valuable context for political decisions but also lead to significant research aimed at providing the model with values for its vital parameters.

Methodological Upgrading of Evaluation Studies

Attention has been drawn throughout this chapter to the typically weak, often misleading, nature of evaluation research in education. In part, these weak investigations stem from a failure to apply the control procedures and newer analysis techniques that have been devised. But much of the problem is also related to the need for still more sophisticated procedures and techniques. And such methodological upgrading of social evaluation work would have significant benefits for many areas outside of education and race relations; indeed, the spread of the requirement for rigorous evaluation to increasing numbers of federal and state programs makes this upgrading essential.

An earlier section detailed the principal design problems faced by research in this area: nonrandom student assignment to various schools, nonrandom parental selection of communities, nonrandom treatment of students within schools, high loss of sample members over time, the need to control initial school performance, the difficulty of equating across race such key variables as social class, and both the Hawthorne and Rosenthal effects. All these difficulties are subject to some degree of correction or control now. But further work to estimate and correct for sample biases, to devise methods of analysis with missing observations, to measure key variables, and to restrain the Hawthorne and Rosenthal effects is badly needed.

To start, an over-all strategy is required for approaching the evaluation of ongoing programs which seldom if ever allow directly for the elegant designs of the laboratory. Rossi has advanced one such approach similar to that implicitly followed in this chapter.[98] He contrasts "soft" correlational designs, such as that of the Coleman report, with "hard" controlled experimentation, such as Katz's laboratory studies. Rossi argues that "soft" designs are adequate first steps, especially in testing programs whose effects are expected to be massive. In an extreme instance, if the goal of a new birth-control technique is to eliminate totally the chance of conception in the experimental group, control groups are unnecessary; for the practical question is not whether the experimental subjects have fewer conceptions than the control subjects, but whether the experimentals have any conceptions at all.

Think of the opposite case. Suppose a "soft" evaluation shows little or no effects; it is very unlikely that "hard" methods will uncover significant effects. This is the case today with the results of "soft" investigations on compensatory education programs in ghetto schools. But the desegregation studies present an example of where more precise evaluation is called for. "Soft" research, including the two federal reports and numerous evaluations of local interracial schools, strongly suggests that desegregation has sustained and marked effects on the achievement of Negro children and the racial attitudes of both Negro and white children. Now we need more Katz-like experimentation employing "hard" designs on the subject.

More Process Research in Interracial Education

A useful way to conceptualize what is needed by way of "hard" evaluation of school desegregation is to accept the "soft" results as initial evidence of achievement and attitude benefits requiring investigation into the precise *processes* by which these outcomes evolve. Throughout this chapter theoretical and empirical leads for this process research have been highlighted. In capsule form, these leads include:

A. Developing social psychological theory, especially that centered on social evaluation, intergroup contact, interpersonal attraction, and value congruity, promises to furnish the broader theoretical context for work on the desegregation process.

B. Katz's four-factor model, broadened to include the subject's previous history of racial contact and his newest factor of rigidly high aspirations, promises to provide the direct operational framework for understanding the process.

C. The intriguing survey findings of the Coleman and Civil Rights Commission studies suggest experimental entry points into the study of the desegregation process. Among such findings given particular emphasis in this chapter are:

1. School social class appears to be the most important school correlate of academic achievement for children of all regions, races, and social classes. This suggests detailed, longitudinal work on the learning experiences of children precisely matched in family social class but in radically diverse social-class schools. It also points special attention to the deviant cases: the predominantly lower-status schools whose students achieve well and the predominantly upper-status schools whose students achieve poorly.

2. A strong sense of personal "fate control" is associated with high Negro achievement and is found most often in interracial schools. This suggests research on the acquisition and maintenance of this sense of control along the lines begun by Rotter and his students.[99]

3. "Integrated" schools characterized by cross-racial acceptance and low racial tension are associated with higher academic performance and more positive interracial attitudes than merely "desegregated" schools. This finding argues for careful work on the learning and social evaluation consequences of cross-racial acceptance, especially as it articulates with the previous empirical work of Katz.

4. For Negro and white pupils and for academic achievement and interracial attitudes, the benefits of desegregation are maximized when it begins in the primary grades. This result points to future comparative investigations of desegregation processes at various grade levels as well as longitudinal designs with children who enter interracial classrooms at different stages of their school careers.

5. The academic consequences of interracial education tend not to be linear. Negro students in interracial but mostly Negro schools typically do no better than comparable students in all-Negro schools, while Negro children in mostly white schools score significantly higher than comparable Negroes. In turn, white students in interracial, mostly white schools do as well as comparable whites in all-white schools,

though white students in mostly Negro schools score lower than comparable whites in mostly white schools. These results beg for future research directed at isolating what qualitative differences exist between mostly Negro and mostly white schools. Is there a racial "stigma" involved, as hypothesized in this chapter? And, if so, how does it operate to depress performance in the mostly Negro institution? Social-class backgrounds of both individual students and school student bodies will have to be rigorously controlled in such work if truly racial factors are to be uncovered. And deviant case analyses of both students and schools which do not fit these generalizations offer a promising start.

6. Negro boys appear to benefit more from desegregation than Negro girls in terms of both academic achievement and college aspirations. Hypotheses immediately spring to mind to explain this result after the fact; but none of them have received adequate empirical test as yet. Thus, this finding may well be directly related to the "fate control" and cross-racial acceptance trends listed above. At any rate, comparative and deviant case analyses of sex role differences in mostly Negro in contrast to mostly white schools might well shed light on subtle, sex-role processes involved in desegregation. In addition, this work could check out the applicability to the desegregation process of "the comparison level for alternatives" notion of Thibaut and Kelley described earlier.

7. Compensatory education programs in ghetto schools generally fail to produce sustained and significant gains in academic performance. Yet there are reports of similar programs that are successful with comparable students when these efforts take place in interracial settings. If these reports are accurate, a four-way research design might well prove enlightening: (a) segregated schools without compensatory programs; (b) segregated schools with compensatory programs; (c) integrated schools without compensatory programs; and (d) integrated schools with the same compensatory programs as in (b). Current evidence strongly suggests that Negro academic performance in the long term is not significantly different between (a) and (b) but rises in (c) and still further in (d). Yet process comparisons between (a) and (c) and between (b) and (d) are important, especially the latter when the compensatory programs are, at least formally, identical. As noted before, integration provides an established means of sustained academic improvement for Negro pupils; yet it alone does not close the typical racial gap in performance. Hence, research aimed directly at determining the optimal compensatory programs *in integrated schools* appears of unusual practical importance.

8. Many of the armed forces training techniques and principles

seem to be unusually effective with "low performers," Negro and white, for whom the public schools did little. Could at least some of these techniques and principles be usefully adapted for public-school utilization? Some basic as well as applied research is required to answer this query. Rigorous evaluation of typical military instruction needs to be made by independent researchers. Such work could isolate the truly effective techniques; then applied work could attempt to transplant and evaluate these devices in the public-school setting.

These are but a few of the proposals necessary for beginning the task of providing genuine educational opportunities to Negro youth. But when will we begin the task? America failed to offer fourteen generations of Negro Americans a first-class education, and the nation is paying a heavy price for that failure now. Will we fail the fifteenth generation, too, and pay an even greater price?

•NOTES

1 This section constitutes in large part a terse restatement of Chapters 1 and 2 of U.S. Commission on Civil Rights, *Racial Isolation in the Public Schools* (Washington: Government Printing Office, 1967), Vol. I.

2 *Ibid.*, I, 7.

3 J. S. Coleman *et al.*, *Equality of Educational Opportunity* (Washington: Government Printing Office, 1966), pp. 3–7.

4 U.S. Commission on Civil Rights, *op. cit.*, I, 8.

5 *Ibid.*, p. 17.

6 K. E. Taeuber and A. F. Taeuber, *Negroes in Cities* (Chicago: Aldine, 1965).

7 N. Glenn, "Negro Religion and Negro Status in the United States," in L. Schneider, ed., *Religion, Culture and Society* (New York: Wiley, 1964), pp. 623–639.

8 U.S. Commission on Civil Rights, *op. cit.*, I, 48–49.

9 The author, when faced with this situation in an NAACP case in Springfield, Massachusetts, was moved to respond: "These matters have been repeatedly found to be true elsewhere, but not, it is true, in Springfield itself. Yet we've never, thank goodness, had an atomic bomb dropped on Springfield either, but we are reasonably certain that it would operate about the way it has done over Japan and under the Nevada desert!"

10 U.S. Department of Health, Education, and Welfare, *First Annual Report. Title I. Elementary and Secondary Act of 1965* (Washington: Government Printing Office, 1967). This report consists largely of testimonials from state departments of education in unabashed praise of Title I: "an

educational revolution," "a new vision," and so on. But to ask the states to evaluate their Title I windfalls is like asking a recent winner of the Irish sweepstakes what he candidly thinks of horseracing.

11 F. J. Roethlisberger and W. J. Dickson, *Management and the Worker* (Cambridge: Harvard University Press, 1939).

12 R. Rosenthal, *Experimenter Effects in Behavioral Research* (New York: Appleton-Century-Crofts, 1966).

13 *Ibid.*, pp. 410–411.

14 Coleman, *op. cit.*, p. 300. Replicated by Wilson in his work in Richmond, California: see U.S. Commission on Civil Rights, *op. cit.*, II, 172–174.

15 Coleman, *op. cit.*, p. 300.

16 U.S. Commission on Civil Rights, *op. cit.*, I, 85.

17 *Ibid.*

18 Coleman, *op. cit.*, pp. 316–317.

19 *Ibid.*, pp. 312–313.

20 *Ibid.*, pp. 312–316.

21 *Ibid.*, pp. 319–325.

22 *Ibid.*, p. 321.

23 A. B. Wilson, "Residential Segregation of Social Classes and Aspirations of High School Boys," *American Sociological Review*, XXIV (1959), 836–845.

24 S. Cleveland, "A Tardy Look at Stouffer's Findings in the Harvard Mobility Project," *Public Opinion Quarterly*, XXVI (1962), 453–454.

25 J. A. Michael, "High School Climates and Plans for Entering College," *Public Opinion Quarterly*, XXV (1961), 585–595.

26 U.S. Commission on Civil Rights, *op. cit.*, I, 85.

27 J. S. Coleman, "Comment on Three 'Climate of Opinion' Studies," *Public Opinion Quarterly*, XXV (1961), 607–610.

28 A. B. Wilson, "Educational Consequences of Segregation in a California Community," in U.S. Commission on Civil Rights, *op. cit.*, II, 165–206.

29 Coleman *et al.*, *op. cit.*, pp. 307, 310.

30 *Ibid.*, p. 330.

31 *Ibid.*, pp. 331–333.

32 *Ibid.*, p. 331.

33 U.S. Commission on Civil Rights, *op. cit.*, I, 90.

34 *Ibid.*, p. 107.

35 *Ibid.*, p. 94.

36 *Ibid.*, pp. 98–100.

37 *Ibid.*, pp. 100–101.

38 *Ibid.*, p. 100.

39 *Ibid.*, p. 101.

40 *Ibid.,* II, 185 (Table 23).

41 *Ibid.,* I, 101.

42 Taeuber and Taeuber, *op. cit.*

43 U.S. Commission on Civil Rights, *op. cit.,* I, 90.

44 *Ibid.,* p. 90; Coleman *et al., op. cit.,* p. 332.

45 U.S. Commission on Civil Rights, *op. cit.,* I, 160.

46 *Ibid.,* p. 214.

47 Coleman *et al., op. cit.,* p. 333.

48 U.S. Commission on Civil Rights, *op. cit.,* I, 157–158.

49 I. Katz, "Review of Evidence Relating to Effects of Desegregation on the Intellectual Performance of Negroes," *American Psychologist,* XIX (1964), 381–399.

50 I. Katz, T. Henchy, and H. Allen, "Effects of Race of Tester, Approval-Disapproval, and Need on Negro Children's Learning," *Journal of Personality and Social Psychology,* VIII (1968), 38–42.

51 J. W. Thibaut and H. H. Kelley, *The Social Psychology of Groups* (New York: Wiley, 1959), pp. 21–24.

52 K. B. Clark and L. Plotkin, *The Negro Student at Integrated Colleges* (New York: National Scholarship Service and Fund for Negro Students, 1963).

53 Negro dropout rates are higher at the high-school level than white rates even though the same limited set of alternatives awaits the Negro. The difference between the two levels is probably a dual result of the highly motivated selection of scholarship Negro students at the college level and a goal-gradient phenomenon of a college degree being far closer than a high-school one to attaining ambitious aspirations.

54 G. W. Allport, *The Nature of Prejudice* (Cambridge: Addison-Wesley, 1954), Chapter 16.

55 T. F. Pettigrew, "Complexity and Change in American Racial Patterns: A Social Psychological View," in T. Parsons and K. B. Clark, eds., *The Negro American* (Boston: Houghton Mifflin, 1966), pp. 325–359.

56 T. M. Newcomb, R. H. Turner, and P. E. Converse, *Social Psychology: The Study of Human Interaction* (New York: Holt, Rinehart, and Winston, 1965), p. 40.

57 M. Rokeach and L. Mezei, "Race and Shared Belief as Factors in Social Choice," *Science,* CLI (1966), 167–172; M. Rokeach, P. W. Smith, and R. I. Evans, "Two Kinds of Prejudice or One?", in M. Rokeach, ed., *The Open and Closed Mind* (New York: Basic Books, 1960), pp. 132–168; C. R. Smith, L. Williams, and R. H. Willis, "Race, Sex, and Belief as Determinants of Friendship Acceptance," *Journal of Personality and Social Psychology,* V (1967), 127–137; D. D. Stein, "The Influence of Belief Systems on Interpersonal Preference," *Psychological Monographs,* LXXX (1966), whole of No. 616; and D. D. Stein, J. A. Hardyck, and

M. B. Smith, "Race and Belief: An Open and Shut Case," *Journal of Personality and Social Psychology*, I (1965), 281–289. One of these investigations (Smith *et al., op. cit.*) suggests, too, that Rokeach's contentions prove most accurate in racially desegregated settings, least accurate in racially segregated samples.

58 T. F. Pettigrew, "Social Evaluation Theory: Convergencies and Applications," in D. Levine, ed., *The 1967 Nebraska Motivation Symposium* (Lincoln: University of Nebraska Press, 1968).

59 I. Katz, "The Socialization of Competence Motivation in Minority Group Children," in Levine, *op. cit.*

60 U.S. Commission on Civil Rights, *op. cit.*, II, 97–99.

61 *Ibid.*, p. 103.

62 *Ibid.*, p. 102.

63 *Ibid.*, pp. 100–101.

64 *Ibid.*, p. 103.

65 *Ibid.*, p. 141.

66 Coleman *et al., op. cit.*, p. 333.

67 K. B. Clark, *Prejudice and Your Child*, 2d ed. (Boston: Beacon, 1963); M. E. Goodman, *Race Awareness in Young Children* (Cambridge: Addison-Wesley, 1952); J. K. Morland, "Racial Recognition by Nursery School Children in Lynchburg, Virginia," *Social Forces*, XXXVII (1958), 132–137; H. W. Stevenson and E. C. Stewart, "A Developmental Study of Racial Awareness in Young Children," *Child Development*, XXIX (1958), 399–409; and H. G. Trager and M. R. Yarrow, *They Live What They Learn* (New York: Harper, 1952).

68 U.S. Commission on Civil Rights, *Civil Rights USA: Public Schools, Southern States, 1962* (Washington: Government Printing Office, 1963).

69 U.S. Commission on Civil Rights, *Racial Isolation in the Public Schools,* I, 108–109.

70 *Ibid.*, p. 112; II, pp. 221–241.

71 *Ibid.*, I, pp. 111–112.

72 *Ibid.*, p. 113.

73 *Ibid.*, II, pp. 221–241.

74 For a recent example of vast claims made for a compensatory education program and the realistic evidence, see the following exchange concerning the More Effective Schools program of New York City: J. Alsop, "No More Nonsense about Ghetto Education!", *New Republic*, CLVII (July 22, 1967), 18–23; and R. Schwartz, T. Pettigrew, and M. Smith, "Fake Panaceas for Ghetto Education," *New Republic*, CLVII (September 23, 1967), 16–19.

75 Repeated inquiries finally elicited the information that the entire report has been placed on "microfische" and is available from Bell and Howell Corporation. The point remains: the U.S. Department of Health, Educa-

tion, and Welfare has not exerted itself to disseminate the report widely.

76 U.S. Commission on Civil Rights, *Racial Isolation in the Public Schools,* Vol. I, Chapter 4.

77 T. F. Pettigrew, "What White Backlash?", *Nieman Reports,* XVIII (December, 1964), 7–9.

78 J. M. Ross, T. Crawford, and T. Pettigrew, "Negro Neighbors—Banned in Boston," *Trans-Action,* III (September, 1966), 13–18.

79 For enlightening analyses of this status-threat phenomenon, see D. Rogers and B. Swanson, "White Citizens Response to the Same Integration Plan: Comparisons of Local School Districts in a Northern City," *Sociological Inquiry,* XXXV (1965), 107–122; and K. Lang and G. Lang, "Resistance to School Desegregation Among Jews," *Sociological Inquiry,* XXXV (1965), 94–106.

80 The classic example of such a bureaucracy is found in New York City. See D. Rogers, "Obstacles to School Desegregation in New York City: A Benchmark Case," in M. Gittell, ed., *Educating an Urban Population* (Beverly Hills: Sage, 1967), pp. 155–184.

81 Examples of this phenomenon include W. H. Ferry, "Farewell to Integration," Century 21 Lecture of Stanford University, November 8, 1967; and J. Alsop, "Ghetto Schools," *New Republic,* CLVII (November 18, 1967), 18–23. For a reply to the latter article, see R. Schwartz, T. Pettigrew, and M. Smith, "Is Desegregation Impractical?", *New Republic,* CLVII (January 6, 1968), 27–29.

82 R. L. Crain, *et al., School Desegregation in the North: Eight Comparative Case Studies of Community Structure and Policy Making* (Chicago: National Opinion Research Center, Report No. 110A); and R. L. Crain and D. Street, "School Desegregation and School Decision-making," in Gittell, *op. cit.,* pp. 136–154.

83 L. E. Lomax, *The Negro Revolt* (New York: Harper and Row, 1962).

84 R. de Neufville and C. Connor, "How Good Are Our Schools?", *American Education* (October, 1966), 1–11 (Superintendent of Documents Catalog No. FS 5.220:20096).

85 C. Braddock, "The Armed Forces Have Their Ways for Low-Achievers," *Southern Education Report,* II, No. 7 (March, 1967), 2–9.

86 G. Bradley, "A Review of Educational Problems Based on Military Selection and Classification Data in World War II," *Journal of Educational Research,* XLIII (1949), 161–174.

87 R. S. McNamara [Secretary of Defense], Address at the Convention of the Veterans of Foreign Wars, New York City, August 23, 1966.

88 Braddock, *op. cit.,* p. 7.

89 *Ibid.;* and T. F. Pettigrew, *A Profile of the Negro American* (Princeton: Van Nostrand, 1964).

90 Braddock, *op. cit.,* p. 5.

91 K. B. Clark, Address at the U.S. Commission on Civil Rights Conference, Washington, November 17, 1967.

92 J. S. Coleman, "Toward Open Schools," *Public Interest*, IX (Fall, 1967), 20–27.

93 Joint Center for Urban Studies of M.I.T. and Harvard, "Changes in School Attendance Districts as a Means of Alleviating Racial Imbalance in the Boston Public Schools," unpublished report, August, 1966.

94 Other convenient and racially neutral sites would be appropriate to specialized metropolitan educational parks. Rather than be near the central city and suburban boundary, sites near the art museum, the science center, the music center, and colleges and universities could possess enough appeal and status to attract suburban children into the central city despite the longer commuting.

95 G. Brain, "The Educational Park: Some Advantages and Disadvantages," in N. Jacobson, ed., *An Exploration of the Educational Park Concept* (New York: New York Board of Education, 1964), p. 16.

96 The Philadelphia Urban League, in proposing nonmetropolitan parks for a central city system whose student body is already majority nonwhite, has advanced just such a plan.

97 F. Keppel, *The Necessary Revolution in American Education* (New York: Harper and Row, 1966), p. 19.

98 P. H. Rossi, "Boobytraps and Pitfalls in the Evaluation of Social Action Programs," Address at the Annual Meeting of the American Statistical Association, Los Angeles, August 16, 1966.

99 J. B. Rotter, "Generalized Expectancies for Internal Vs. External Control of Reinforcements," *Psychological Monographs*, LXXX, No. 609 (1966); E. Battle and J. B. Rotter, "Children's Feelings of Personal Control as Related to Social Class and Ethnic Group," *Journal of Personality*, XXXI (1963), 482–490; and P. M. Gore and J. B. Rotter, "Personality Correlates of Social Action," *Journal of Personality*, XXXI (1963), 58–64.

3 Donald R. Matthews

Political Science Research
on Race Relations

Until recently, political science enjoyed—some might say suffered from—the reputation of being the most reformist, prescriptive, and applied of the social sciences. "Even when research workers are most alert to the exactions of objective investigation," David Easton wrote fifteen years ago in his influential critique of the discipline, "[political scientists] gather their material with the immediate objective of putting it to use in suggesting some projected reform." [1]

Paradoxically, this concern for immediate and practical benefits did *not* lead American political scientists to conduct research on race politics or race relations. Despite the fact that the Negro problem was the most important unresolved domestic problem confronting the nation, exactly six articles containing the word "Negro" in their titles were published in the *American Political Science Review* between 1906 and 1963. Four other articles included the word "race" in their titles (including one on "Nationalism and the Uralo-Altaic Race"), and another three were on "civil rights." During the same period 2,601 other articles were published by the profession's leading journal. [2]

But political science has changed in recent years. The discipline now is far more positivistic, theoretical, and quantitative than before World War II. Today the dominant mood is "behavioral" and "scientific." [3] But, if I may engage in paradox one last time, this commitment to the canons of science seems to be leading to *more*, rather than less, research on the Negro problem by American political scientists. A cursory examination of recent doctoral dissertations, for example, shows

113

that at least some of the upcoming generation of political scientists are interested in such problems as "The Political Implications of Race," "The Politics of Poverty," "Consensus, 'Rules of the Game' and Democratic Politics: The Case of Race Politics in the South," "The Negro Vote as a Political Resource," "Southern Negro College Student Participation in the Protest Movement," and "The Right to Vote: The Effects of Negro Enfranchisement in Selected Mississippi Counties." [4] There is still a long way to go before political scientists begin to give this subject the attention it deserves, but the trend seems to be in that direction. And, as I shall argue below, there are reasons for believing that this shift in attention may well accelerate in the future.

Under these circumstances relatively little of this chapter will be devoted to summarizing and criticizing research already done by political

A POLITICAL SYSTEM

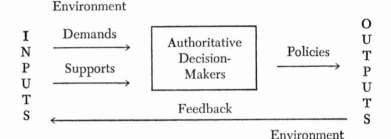

Figure 3–1

scientists on the racial problem in America. Instead I intend primarily to point out lines of inquiry which seem especially promising both for potential pay-off to policy-makers and for potential contributions to a verified general theory of politics. A second aim will be to suggest the possible relevance of a number of widely accepted political science concepts, theories, and findings to future research on racial politics in the United States.

I shall try to order these remarks by casting them within the framework of what is known in political science as "systems theory." [5] While this approach is far from a "theory" in any very meaningful sense, it is the closest thing political science now has to a generally accepted paradigm.[6] Briefly and superficially put, an increasing number of political scientists view political life as a system of interrelated activities which influence the way in which authoritative decisions are formulated and executed for the society as a whole. In its simplest form, this "system" is viewed as having the following major components: *inputs* from the *environment*, which take the form of either *demands* or *supports;* a set of *authoritative decision-makers* who convert these inputs into *outputs*, or *policies*. A portion of these outputs *feed back* through the environment, becoming future inputs (Figure 3–1).[7]

I do not wish, here, to argue the merits and demerits of this conceptual scheme.[8] Given its growing popularity among political scientists, however, I believe that the study of Negro politics is most likely to enter into the mainstream of American political science if it can be shown that the subject can be analyzed in systems terms.

POLITICAL DEMANDS

The Content of Negro Political Demands

What do American Negroes want? What kinds of demands are they making on the American political system?

At first blush, the answers to these questions seem obvious: American Negroes want both a psychological sense of and the reality of equality. But the history of ideas contains more than a few divergent conceptions of social, economic, and political equality. Even in the absence of argument over what "equality" is, the best ways to achieve such an abstract and generalized goal are highly problematical. It is a mistake, therefore, to assume the existence of a clear, unchanging, unidimensional goal for Negro political activity.

The rhetoric of today's race politics, for example, leads one to wonder if racial separatism or black supremacy has supplanted desegregation and racial integration as the dominant goal of Negro politics. Most of the evidence which points in this direction consists of statements by the Malcolm X's, Floyd McKissicks, and Stokely Carmichaels of contemporary America: electoral research has taught us how very risky it is to infer anything about mass attitudes from elite behavior. And what little systematic research we have on the subject—outdated and limited in scope as most of it is—shows little support for racial separatism and black nationalism among American Negroes.[9] But perhaps nationwide studies conducted today would show a sharply different picture.[10] Ordinarily mass attitudes do not change very rapidly, but the Negro is scarcely an ordinary American, and these are scarcely ordinary times.

While it is important that we know more about the attitudes and desires of the Negro masses, the attitudes of Negro political elites undoubtedly will have greater impact on policy outputs in the short run.[11] Most political scientists today feel that this is probably "functional" for American democracy: that political leaders in the United

States tend to be more ideological and policy-oriented, better informed, and more committed to the preservation of the democratic "rules of the game" than the relatively uninterested, ill-informed, and potentially antidemocratic man in the street.[12] It is at least possible that the opposite is true in the Negro subcommunity: that the ordinary American Negro is more willing to accept the delays, compromises, and limited victories of democratic politics than are his leaders.

Even if the vast bulk of American Negroes still seek racial integration, the many dimensions of this objective create serious political difficulties. Some of these have been brilliantly described and analyzed by James Q. Wilson in his *Negro Politics: The Search for Leadership*.[13] Writing in 1960 on the basis of his study of the role of Negroes in big-city politics (especially Chicago), Wilson distinguishes between *welfare* and *status* political goals. As the labels imply, the first set of objectives stress the provision of more and better governmental outputs for the Negro community, even if these bread-and-butter gains are achieved, as they usually are, within the confines of a segregated society. Status goals, on the other hand, are symbolic breaches in the wall of segregation with primarily psychic pay-offs for all save the few middle-class Negroes who benefit personally from token desegregation. The main point of Wilson's useful distinction is that these two sets of goals are rarely achieved together; the attainment of welfare goals requires a type of Negro leadership and white political structure quite different from and incompatible with ideological and conflict-prone status politics. The results of these contradictions can be weak Negro leaders whose legitimacy and integrity are always in doubt, sharp internal conflict within Negro communities, and sudden and seemingly inexplicable shifts in Negro political tactics. Most of the Negroes Wilson talked with denied that such a thing as "Negro leadership" existed: one reason for this widespread view is these internal contradictions in integrationist goals.

Negro goals and political objectives should not be studied in isolation, but in terms of their relationships to white opinions and political demands. The most widely cited work on this question still seems to be Myrdal's optimistic speculations on the "rank order of discriminations." According to Myrdal, the areas of life in which Negroes most want desegregation are the areas in which white men are most likely to give in to their demands, and vice versa.[14] Obviously the effect of this is greatly to reduce the conflict and tension surrounding the Negroes' struggle for acceptance and equality. In today's world, this happy congruence can no longer be assumed to exist; indeed, the Matthews-Prothro study of Negro and white attitudes in the eleven states of the former Confederacy shows that today's race politics, at least in the South,[15] is more nearly a zero sum game. It would be well to know whether this is true in the North and West as well.[16]

A final aspect of Negro political demands is the *rate* at which Negroes expect their goals to be achieved. The Matthews-Prothro interviews conducted in 1961 demonstrate that a large number of southern Negroes expected extraordinarily rapid, indeed revolutionary, progress toward racial equality.[17] In contrast, while few southern whites disagreed about the *direction* of change in race relations in the region, most expected these changes to occur at glacial speed. If these expectations remain unchanged, someone is going to be bitterly disappointed.

It is quite possible that this expectation gap has broadened rather than narrowed since 1961. The substantial gains made by Negroes in recent years have almost certainly led to a rapid escalation of Negro hopes and impatience; there are fewer signs that these same events have led to counterbalancing shifts in white expectations.

Be that as it may, I hope enough has been said here to demonstrate that the content of Negro political demands cries out for systematic study *on a continuous basis*. Neither policy-makers nor social scientists can any longer afford to guess about Negro goals from the contents of yesterday's newspapers.

Traditional Modes of Articulating Demands

Wants must be expressed in meaningful ways before they become political demands. Historically, this conversion has been partial and ineffective for American Negroes because of the group's limited resources and because Negroes have been barred by a hostile white majority from taking full advantage of the resources they did possess.

A number of resources can be translated into political power: votes, money, prestige, information, skill, organization, and so on.[18] Individuals and groups possess varying amounts of these resources. The amount of *potential* political power they have is *not* directly determined by the amount of *any one resource* they have. Rather, it depends on how much of *all* these resources they control. (Often there may be a good deal of dispersion, with those having a great deal of one resource not having much of the others.) People's actual power depends, further, not just on the level of their total resources but also on whether they choose to expend these resources to further their political goals. The local millionaire, for example, may have a tremendous power *potential* because he is wealthy, but little actual power because he is more interested in chasing nubile blondes and buying yachts than in seeking political influence. It is therefore possible for individuals and groups with limited political resources who invest them heavily in politics to be more influential than those with vast power potential but no inclination to use their resources for political purposes. In the usual case, the proportion of all resources actually used for political purposes tends to be small. The result is a great deal of "slack," or unexpended resources, in the political system.

The resource American Negroes have had in abundance is numbers; this gives the group substantial *potential* power at the polls. But until quite recently most Negroes lived in the South and, after about 1900, were effectively barred from the ballot box. Under these circumstances, the principal mode of political expression available to Negroes was litigation—a way of making political demands for which their resource base was ill suited. Only after many long legal battles were won—and millions of southern Negroes "voted with their feet" by migrating to the North and West—were Negroes to begin expressing their demands effectively through the more normal processes of electoral politics.

Litigation

Lawsuits are not an easy way for a large and impoverished group to make sweeping demands on a political system.[19] According to American legal doctrine, courts decide disputes between individual litigants, and not "political" conflicts between groups or classes. They do not make general policy determinations, but decide specific "cases and controversies" *after* an individual can demonstrate that he actually has suffered harm. At least as compared to legislators and executives, then, the judges' policy-making role is passive and circumscribed. American judges place heavy stress on the importance of precedent and the need for consistency in their decisions over time; the Negro community sought nothing less than to overturn all the leading precedents and interpretations of the Constitution since the end of Reconstruction. The dual (federal and state) organization of American courts, their highly complex and technical procedural rules, the monopoly of direct access to the courts enjoyed by a conservative and almost entirely white legal profession, added to the staggering dimensions of this task.

That American Negroes now have won this courtroom battle is a testament to the extraordinary skill and persistence of a tiny minority of the Negro middle class, the National Association for the Advancement of Colored People lawyers. Despite their small numbers, limited resources, constant harassment by barratry suits and statutes, to say nothing of the frustrations and delays inherent in the judicial process, they succeeded in revolutionizing the court's interpretation of the federal constitutional document in the course of sixty years. Neither this elite group nor the politics of this process has been fully described and explained.[20] Nor—as we shall develop at some length below—has much attention been paid to the actual consequences of these decisions on human behavior.

Voting and Electoral Politics

Negroes are no longer dependent on litigation as their primary mode of expressing political demands. A number of questions about Negro voting are deserving of attention; of these, three have been singled out for comment here:

1. *How much* voter participation can reasonably be expected from an impoverished and undereducated group, such as American Negroes?

2. *How united* can and will this vote be?

3. Can these votes be *converted into favorable policies*?

While studies of mass participation in politics are both numerous and of impressively high quality,[21] most of what we know is based on the analysis of all-white samples or of national samples in which the Negro component is too small to permit detailed analysis. Thus these questions remain largely unanswered for the nation as a whole.

Matthews and Prothro do seek to answer these questions for the eleven states of the former Confederacy. They find—addressing themselves to the first of these three questions—that southern Negroes participate in political life at surprisingly high levels when compared to southern whites of approximately equal socioeconomic status, *except when it comes to voting*. The racial gap in this one form of participation seems to be largely the result of the special barriers and inhibitions to Negro voting which have characterized southern politics since 1900 and should largely disappear as these barriers are gradually eliminated through federal action. Nonetheless some of the barriers to Negro voter participation are quite subtle and difficult to change: the absence of political candidates favorable to Negro goals, the lack of structure and cognitive confusion which characterize southern politics, the desperate shortage of Negro leadership and organization, and so on. And the fact remains that so long as southern Negroes remain lumped at the bottom of the region's social and economic structure, and so long as most southern whites remain hostile to Negro self-advancement, it is unlikely that the group's full voting potential can be mobilized.

On the second question, Matthews and Prothro find the southern Negro vote to be highly cohesive and, in a rudimentary sense, highly "rational." This is not to deny that in a few areas the Negro vote is corrupted and manipulated by white politicians for their own ends.[22] But on a regionwide basis "[Negro] majorities as great as 60 per cent may be expected without any organized bloc voting at all. Where organizations reinforce these common tendencies, cohesion in voting approaches the 90 per cent level." [23] Whether this astounding degree of voting cohesion can be maintained as Negro communities achieve more power and are characterized by greater internal diversity of status and life style is another matter.

On the third question—the extent to which Negro votes can be converted into favorable public policies—the Matthews-Prothro study is relatively pessimistic, at least so far as the South is concerned.

> Political pundits have assumed that the vote will automatically give southern Negroes influence over public policy commensurate with their numbers. Once Negroes are voting in substantial numbers, the argument goes, southern state and local officials will either respond to Negro demands or suffer at the polls. Negroes will then be able to use their political leverage to force governments to eliminate segregation in other realms of life. Hence the special significance of the vote to southern Negroes.
>
> Attractive as this argument is, it is much too simple. The linkages between mass attitudes, as expressed in elections, and public policy are exceedingly complex and little understood. The best research we have suggests that the translation of votes into power, and power into policy, is by no means automatic, and that public officials and political leaders have far more freedom of maneuver in dealing with their constituents than had been initially realized.[24] The governmental response to Negro votes, then, may not be at all automatic in the South or anywhere else. The experience of northern Negroes—who have been voting in large numbers for many decades and yet are still distinctly "second-class citizens"—is not very comforting to those who would place primary reliance on the vote as the "solution" to the Negro problem in the South.
>
> Southern Negroes have but one political resource in abundance—votes. Southern whites, most of whom still oppose the Negro's political objectives, tend to have the lion's share of *all* political resources, including votes. The competition between the two groups for control over public policy will tend to be very uneven unless southern whites fail to use their overwhelmingly superior resources for political ends. No doubt there has been a great deal of "slack" in the utilization of political resources by southern whites in the past. But the more threatened they feel by evidence of rising Negro political power in the future, the more their disproportionate resources will be invested in politics and the less "slack" there will be. Racial inequalities in political resources other than the vote, then,

NOTE: From *Negroes and the New Southern Politics* by Donald R. Matthews and James W. Prothro, © 1966 by Harcourt, Brace & World, Inc., and reprinted with their permission.

probably will result in southern Negroes' receiving less influence over policy than their proportionate share of the electorate would seem to dictate.

Even the vote itself has limitations as a political resource for southern Negroes. They are in a minority almost everywhere in the South. (In the relatively few communities where Negroes are potentially a clear majority of the electorate, white resistance to Negro voting tends to be most vehement, and the barriers to the effective use of the ballot, once achieved, are likely to be greatest.) In order to win, southern Negroes generally have to enter into coalitions with at least some white politicians and voters. In situations characterized by an overwhelming white consensus in favor of segregation, biracial coalition-building is almost impossible. A good many Negroes in the South may finally win the right to vote only to find themselves in a more or less permanent political minority.

Where a significant minority of moderate and integrationist whites is in being Negro-white political coalitions are easier to arrange. But opponents of biracial coalitions need merely take steps to increase the salience of the racial issue to the electorate at large, and the Negro-white coalition usually dissolves. In view of the corrosive effects of the racial issue and the lack of other stable political structures in one-party systems, Negroes in the South may have to rely primarily on joining *ad hoc* coalitions on an issue-by-issue basis. . . .

Such a complex and fluid political situation, characterized by high tension levels and limited "slack," places heavy demands on political leaders. For one thing, bargaining and negotiations between white and Negro leaders must be almost continuous and call for highly developed political skills. In the second place, followers may become confused by rapidly shifting strategies and alliances. They must be given clear cues and constant guidance lest they inadvertently throw their votes away. All these things southern Negro leaders must be able to do, and do well, before the Negro vote can have a major impact on public policy, even in areas where biracial coalitions are formed. The desperate shortage of capable Negro leaders and the possibility that this shortage will become even more severe in the future not only affect how often Negroes go to the polls, but how effectively they use their votes once they get there.

Southern Negroes seem to have a better chance of achieving some types of racial objectives than others by way of the ballot box. Other modes of attack—litigation, demonstrations, and federal intervention—are likely to be more fruitful than the vote in grappling with many kinds of civil rights problems.

First, Negro votes are an effective resource in altering segregationist practices when *the costs of abandoning segregation are relatively low for the white community*. For example, police brutality tends to decline and, to a lesser extent, the entire administration of justice tends to improve after southern Negroes become active members of the electorate.[25] The psychic and monetary costs of such reforms for whites are modest. Where, on the other hand, the white community perceives the costs of abandoning segregation as high—such as in the areas of housing or school desegregation—the Negro vote seems to have little impact. The coefficient of correlation between the proportion of the Negro adult population registered to vote and the existence of desegregated schools, by county, in 1958 was +.03! Change in this area tends to be brought about through litigation and federal action. Negro political muscle demonstrated at the local polls seems entirely irrelevant.

A second factor that affects the ability of the Negro vote to bring about desegregation is the *visibility of the issue to the white community*. If the benefits of the reform are confined to the Negro ghetto, and if the change can be brought about without a great deal of publicity, then the Negro vote seems to carry more punch. Negro policemen, for example, have been hired in many southern communities and assigned to responsibilities in Negro residential areas with scarcely any publicity or controversy. Hiring Negro firemen, however, tends to be much more difficult. Either Negro and white firemen must share the same living quarters or else the community must build a new firehouse. And a new firehouse takes money, often a bond issue. So hiring Negro firemen is both more costly and more visible, and hence harder to achieve.

Third, the power of the Negro vote increases to *the extent that whites perceive the issue as involving matters of fairness and impartiality*. One of the greatest resources of Negroes in their struggle for equality is the obvious congruence of many of their demands with the "democratic" and "good government" ethos. Reforms that can be justified by simple and clear appeals to the whites' sense of fair play and impartiality have a relatively good chance of being adopted. Thus nondiscrimination in public hiring practices is far easier to achieve than a policy of compensatory opportunities that seems, on its face, to discriminate in favor of Negroes. Police brutality and discrimination in electoral administration are obviously unfair, and very few white southerners are prepared to defend either practice as inherently desirable.

Finally, the vote can help southern Negroes to achieve racial equality only in the *public sector of community life*. Even a responsive government is of little help in altering injustice in areas where the government has no legal authority or informal influence. As the more blatant, legal, "southern" forms of segregation are replaced by more subtle, *de facto*, "northern" forms, the vote as a weapon in the civil rights struggle will become less and less potent.[26]

The Matthews-Prothro study was written as of 1961. Portions or all of it could and should be replicated soon. Longitudinal and quasi-experimental tests of the model of Negro political participation it proposes are badly needed. Above all, comparable studies of Negro participation and its consequences need to be conducted outside the South.

Negro Leadership and Organization

Studies of Negro leadership and organization are relatively numerous. This no doubt reflects the intrinsic importance of the topic as well as the fact that such studies can be carried out by one or a few scholars with modest financial resources.

Most of these studies have been conducted on the local level and are surprisingly similar in their concepts and findings. Johnson,[27] writing in the late 1930's, distinguished between two types of Negro leadership, gradualist and revolutionary, on the basis of their attitudes toward segregation; Myrdal[28] writing in the next decade and Wilson[29] almost twenty years later make essentially the same distinction under different labels (Accommodationist-Protest and Moderate-Militant). Thompson,[30] writing on New Orleans; Burgess,[31] on Durham, North Carolina; Ladd,[32] on Winston-Salem, North Carolina, and Greenville, South Carolina; Killian and Grigg,[33] on Tallahassee and other Florida cities; and Matthews and Prothro,[34] for the South as a whole, use somewhat more complex typologies which still preserve the same underlying attitudinal dimension as the criterion of classification.

Moreover, if their idiosyncratic embellishments are overlooked, most of these studies agree on the other attributes associated with these differing leadership styles, despite the fact that they were independently conducted over a period of thirty years in widely different communities. Table 3–1 is an attempt to summarize this rough consensus. Today this typology may be much less useful than it once was: there are very few "traditional" or "moderate" Negro leaders left, and the "militant" type of leader includes an extremely disparate group of men ranging from, say, Roy Wilkins to Eldridge Cleaver. It is time for us to begin thinking about Negro leadership in terms of new categories.

Another leading hypothesis in this area is that the structure and style of Negro leadership are largely determined by the characteristics of the community within which the Negro minority is embedded. Thus Wilson, for example, convincingly accounts for the manifest differences in leadership styles of Adam Clayton Powell, Jr., and William L. Dawson largely in terms of the structural differences in the politics of New York City and Chicago. He writes:

> We will argue, first, that the most important single factor in creating or modifying the political style of each leader is the character of the organization which supports the leader and the nature of the incentives which he must distribute to sustain it. Each political leader acts so as to maintain the strength of his organization. The strength of the organization is

TABLE 3-1   *Characteristics of Varying Types of Negro Leaders*

	TRADITIONAL *"Accommodationist"* *"Conservative"* *"Uncle Tom"*	MODERATE *"Gradualist"* *"Moderate"* *"Liberal"* *"Race Diplomat"*	MILITANT *"Protest"* *"Revolutionary"* *"Radical"* *"Race Man"*
1 Recruitment (Relative social-economic positions from which type of leader is drawn)	High or low	High	High or low
2 Goals	Ameliorative action within segregated system; few beneficiaries	Improvement of welfare of all Negroes; gradual desegregation	Status goals; symbolic victories for all Negroes; immediate and total racial equality or black supremacy
3 Strategies and Tactics	*Ad hoc*, covert, individual approaches to white leaders; ingratiation and supplication	Continuous, overt, organized efforts; legal attacks on segregation; bargaining	Protests and demonstrations; tend to be intermittent and sometimes violent
4 Bases of Influence with Whites	Usefulness as means of communication with and control of Negro community	Control over Negro votes and legal challenges	Fear of adverse publicity, boycotts, violence, federal intervention
5 Bases of Influence with Negroes	Access to whites and/or prestige	Ability and performance in conventional politics	Ability and performance in unconventional, protest politics

measured in terms of the number and size of the contributions to it, the extent to which a single undisputed leadership can control it, and the extent to which it can attain its collective goal (in this case, the retention of political office). To maintain the flow of contributions (the time, money, and energies of organization workers and the votes of the electorate), incentives must be distributed by the leader. In the case of Powell, these are largely intangible (nonmaterial or "ideal") incentives; in the case of Dawson, these are largely tangible or material.

The second argument will be that the character of the organization which the leader must maintain is largely determined by the nature of the local political system. The aspects of that system most relevant here include the size and composition of the political districts and the relative strength and unity of the city-wide political organization. The maintenance of a Negro political organization is intimately bound up with the maintenance of the political system of the community as a whole.[35]

There is danger that this point of view may be pushed so far as to deny the possibility of change in Negro leadership patterns and performance within a given community. Little attention has been focused on this critical question.

I also believe it is possible to do a much more adequate job of describing and explaining the tactical and strategic problems faced by Negro political leaders than has been done to date.

Outside the central cities of a few metropolitan areas in the North, Negroes are a more or less permanent political minority. The political demands of a cohesive minority with intensely felt goals can have a substantial impact on policy outputs in the United States when confronted with relatively passive and indifferent majorities. But the white majority is far from indifferent in many areas and about many problems of central concern to American Negroes. And, for a good number of purposes, policy pay-offs are unlikely unless Negroes are able to become a part of a biracial majority coalition which is able to win elections.

In city politics of the South, for example, Negro leaders are usually confronted with the option of forming coalitions with the white working class and organized labor, as in Houston, Texas, or attempting to piece together a winning coalition with downtown business interests and that portion of middle-class suburbia still contained within the city limits, as in Atlanta, Georgia. In statewide politics the tactical choices are often far more numerous, ambiguous, and changeful, while the Goldwater campaign and the overwhelming preferences of Negro southerners for the Democratic party seem to leave little room for discretion and bargaining in Presidential politics.

Wilson describes an equally complex picture in the northern cities:

The Negro is in need not of a single grand alliance, but of many different and often conflicting alliances which take into account the different bases of support available for different kinds of issues. Nationally, organized labor may support civil rights and income-transfer measures but locally it is often likely to support (at least tacitly) segregated housing and economy in government. Religious groups are very effective when the issue is voting rights; they are much less effective in dealing with economic questions where simple morality is not at issue. Upper-class businessmen may support Negro voting claims in Southern cities and Negro oriented public works programs in Northern cities, but nationally they will oppose large-scale income redistribution. A grand Negro-liberal coalition, if achieved, may so rationalize these inconsistent positions as to deliver the leadership of would-be allies into the hands of those elements who are least in favor of (or least effective on behalf of) Negro causes. Nowhere are these problems better seen than in the relationship between Negro and white workers in our major industrial cities.

While it may be true that Negroes and whites have a common interest in ending unemployment, improving housing and education, and resisting technological displacement, a stable and enduring alliance to attain these objectives will not be easily achieved. The only major political mechanism by which poor whites and Negroes have in the past been brought into alliance—the big-city machine—is collapsing; except for a few large industrial unions, no substitute has yet appeared.[36]

So far, at any rate, research has not gotten much beyond the state of describing the strategic and tactical alternatives which confront Negro leaders. The applicability of the theoretical work on coalition formation, bargaining, and rational strategy under varying conflict situations, as represented by theorists with as widely varying orientations as Riker, Downs, Lindblom, and Schelling,[37] has yet to be explored. It is time to see whether the models developed by these men can help us better understand Negro leadership problems. I think they can.

Efforts to estimate the effectiveness of Negro political leadership and organizations are almost nonexistent.[38] Admittedly this is an exceedingly difficult research problem which has yet to be solved outside artificial laboratory environments, but, in this area, satisfactory studies of leadership and organizational effectiveness would have great practical as well as theoretical and methodological utility.

The brilliant, if polemic, insights of Frazier's *Black Bourgeoisie* [39] also cry out for rigorous testing. Frazier's devastating picture of the alienation of the Negro middle class from the black masses in an anxious effort to become carbon copies of the middle-class white bears a striking resemblance to Michels' analysis of the embourgeoisement of socialist party leadership in western Europe.[40] A gulf between the elite and the masses may, in fact, be a quite widespread phenomenon which becomes particularly acute among underprivileged groups of all colors. If this holds true for American Negroes under present-day conditions, much of the literature on Negro leadership recruitment, which assumes that only middle-class Negroes are in social positions from which effective leadership may be exercised, needs drastic rethinking and revision.

Finally, studies of Negro leadership and organization in action on the national level of politics are almost nonexistent.[41] The intense struggle for national leadership of the Negro masses deserves more than the journalistic treatment it has received so far. Students of leadership can find few more intriguing figures than Martin Luther King, Jr., more ironic events than the loss of Negro confidence in the NAACP following *Brown* v. *Board of Education,* more breathtaking events than the rise and fall of the Negro protest movement between 1960 and 1966, or the emergence of the black power leaders of today. The top-level leadership of American Negroes is in such a state of flux that the analyst can observe changes in power, organization, personnel, style, and objectives which take generations to occur in other groups. This rapidity of change creates severe political tensions and problems, but can be a boon to researchers.

Nontraditional Modes of Articulating Political Demands

Because, as we have seen, the traditional modes have been of limited effectiveness in meeting the political demands of American Negroes, the latter are no longer content to press their claims for favorable policy outputs in traditionally legitimate ways. Beginning in 1955 with the Montgomery bus boycott and especially after the 1960 Greensboro sit-ins, the Negro protest movement invented, revived, and popularized an array of unconventional and provocative political techniques— boycotts, strikes, sit-ins, lie-ins, freedom rides, mass demonstrations and marches, passive resistance—to further its own ends. The use of these coercive and violence-inspiring tactics is now commonplace, and not just by Negroes. Few political scientists have paid much attention to these revolutionary changes in the ordinarily bland style of American politics.

Political protests are efforts by small, intensely dissatisfied groups with limited resources to force favorable government action by bringing third parties with greater power potential into the controversy on their side.[42] The protesters, in a sense, create or "borrow" new resources by arousing the sympathies or fears, sense of fair play, or common interest of potential allies who have more power over policy outputs than the protesters themselves. The protest is a highly dramatic and symbolic form of political action which seems to presuppose an advanced system of mass communication, consensus on basic values, a politically responsive government, and a highly interdependent society which may be easily disrupted by the actions of an intensely motivated small minority. It also seems to be a political tactic that can become self-defeating if used too often or for trivial ends, for after a while the protests no longer are "news," and originally responsive third parties become uninterested or alienated.

Active protesters are generally assumed to be frustrated, angry, and alienated. Matthews and Prothro found quite the opposite to be the case among the southern Negro college-student generation which began the protest movement: the students actively involved in the protests were more optimistic about race relations and tolerant of whites, less bitter and alienated, than the students who took no part in the protests.[43] They also tended to come from higher-status urban families and to attend the academically better Negro institutions. A number of independent studies of white students have found the same patterns of social advantage, emotional stability, and absence of frustration and hostility among active protesters.[44] The hard-core professionals of protest politics, however, may be rather different types of people than the volunteers who make up the membership of protest movements. Only more and better research will tell.

The few case studies of Negro protests [45] tell us little about their success at goal attainment or their psychological impact on participants and onlookers. Certainly the initial sit-ins and freedom rides were spectacularly successful in affecting federal civil rights legislation and in heightening efforts to enforce federal antidiscrimination statutes and administrative rulings already on the books. But the costs in heightened racial tensions, white fears, and white "backlash" was high. Adequate funding and staffing for implementing and enforcing these new rules may thereby have been precluded during the prolonged hangover. Whether concrete, long-range progress can be won through protest politics is still an open question.

An analytic distinction can and should be drawn between racial protests, rioting, and rebellions: the first are more or less self-conscious and organized attempts to bring pressure to bear on governments as described above; the second are goalless and leaderless outbursts of mob violence; the third are a relatively mild form of "interval" or guerilla warfare analogous to the civil disorders in the Philippines or Algeria after World War II. It is not always easy to distinguish between these ideal-types in specific cases, but ever since the Birmingham, Alabama, riots on Mother's Day, 1963, outbursts of Negro violence and looting have taken place in the ghettos of New York, Chicago, Los Angeles, Detroit, Rochester, Boston, Nashville, Cincinnati, San Francisco, and most of the other larger cities in America.

There are no indications that these riots are about to become less frequent or severe in the future. Still—and to me this is quite shocking —these outbursts and their causes have not yet received serious and searching analysis by political scientists.[46] The reports of the *ad hoc* study commissions regularly appointed by frightened officials in the wake of the rioting are written too quickly and in too "political" an atmosphere to be anything but superficial or to draw heavily upon the special skills and insights of social scientists.[47] So far, at any rate, efforts to ameliorate the conditions thought to bring about rioting in the ghettos are based on guesswork as to their precise causes and have been spectacularly unsuccessful.

It would be a mistake to overestimate how well equipped political scientists are to study these phenomena. As a profession we have been preoccupied until very recently with the internal politics of modern stable democracies—a very rare type of political system. Save in the international realm, the control and use of violence have not been a major professional concern, despite the intimate connection between violence, law, and government which (following Max Weber) we regularly point out to our freshman students and then proceed to forget. Nor are we, as a profession, particularly experienced at analyzing rapid or revolutionary change. But in recent years, political science has discovered the non-Western, nonindustrial, nondemocratic nations. Some of the most exciting work in the discipline is now being done on political modernization and change in the underdeveloped world.[48] It is time that American political scientists directed comparable ingenuity and energy to our own domestic crises of governmental effectiveness and legitimacy in the violent politics of the American ghetto.

POLITICAL SUPPORTS

A colleague of mine likes to observe that the billboards in areas of die-hard opposition to civil rights read IMPEACH EARL WARREN, and not ABOLISH THE SUPREME COURT. Even under conditions of extreme frustration with policy outputs, he argues, the southern whites still support the system, if not the temporary incumbents of its offices.

Far more amazing is the degree to which American Negroes apparently have supported the American political system *despite* its failure for centuries to produce favorable policy outputs.

Negroes "apparently" support the system since we have almost no hard evidence on the attitudes of Negroes toward the political system or their place in it.[49] Matthews and Prothro do find a surprisingly high sense of political efficacy and political competence among their sample of Negro adults in the South,[50] and Marvick suggests, on the basis of a secondary analysis of the Almond-Verba data,[51] that northern and younger Negroes have just about as much confidence in the fairness of their government as their white socioeconomic counterparts.[52] But these are mere scraps of evidence which need to be supplemented and/ or supplanted by major studies. Signs of Negro alienation from the political system are all about us; Negro support for the system may be drastically on the decline.

In the absence of policy outputs which satisfy demands, the processes of political socialization become critical to the stability of the system. Ineffective political systems may be able to survive if their members have been thoroughly socialized to accept them as legitimate and to support the system. All of this speculation suggests the need to study Negro political learning as a rather special case of political socialization in America. What, how, and by whom are American Negroes taught about political life? So far as I know, no one is studying these theoretically intriguing and exceedingly practical questions about political life in America. We now know enough about the political socialization of the white majority to have some useful bench marks.[53]

AUTHORITATIVE DECISION-MAKERS

The systems paradigm tends to focus one's attention on the environment and how the political system copes with the changing demands and supports emanating from other systems of action which make up this environment. It does not, at least so far, seem to throw much light on what goes on in "the black box" or how demands and supports are converted into policies. And yet older research traditions in political science stress that the behavior of decision-makers and structural and institutional arrangements in the black box are by no means neutral in processing the conflicting claims of groups for favorable public policies.

Thus, for example, the President of the United States is more likely to be responsive to Negro demands today than other authoritative decision-makers largely for structural-institutional reasons. The Electoral College makes his selection depend on winning a plurality of votes in a handful of "swing" states with large electoral votes; the bulk of the nonsouthern Negro population resides in the big cities of these states. The election of Presidents by direct popular vote, or the elimination of the "winner-take-all" manner of apportioning the electoral votes of the states, would tend to reduce the power of American Negroes in national politics.[54] (It is no accident that former Presidential campaign managers—Herbert Brownell and Robert Kennedy—have been among the most aggressive champions of Negro causes in Washington.[55])

The Congress has been a far less sympathetic target for Negro pressures for equally mundane reasons: the underrepresentation of urban areas in the allocation of seats in both chambers;[56] the relative lack of articulation between Presidential and congressional elections;[57] the seniority system for distributing committee seats and chairmanships;[58] the opportunities for delay and parliamentary obstruction provided by the Senate's cloture rule and the House's Committee on Rules;[59] the tendency of legislative bodies to develop norms of behavior which discourage their members from attempting to alter their internal *status quo* and legitimize the disproportionate influence of senior members socialized into traditional legislative ways.[60]

The inflexibility of the bureaucracy, when confronted with changes in policy mandates emanating from the President,[61] and the tendency of executive agencies to make their peace with the more powerful segments of their clientele [62] are well documented. Both tend to work to the disadvantage of low-resource groups demanding rapid and basic changes in the fabric of public policy. Finally, the relative autonomy enjoyed by state and local governments under the American system of federalism encourages the response of these governmental units to the prevailing biases of their localities and permits almost endless opportunities for delay when national opinion-majorities confront strongly held local prejudices.[63]

The creation and implementation of important public policies require the co-operation, or at least acquiescence, of *all* these governmental agencies, with their differing political outlooks and maintenance needs. This tends to result in incremental changes in policies backed by broad coalitions of supporters. Advocates of change must "win" in a large number of decision-making arenas of quite different complexions; the opponents of change usually need win only once. Under these conditions massive coalitions far in excess of simple majorities are ordinarily required to change important public policies, and then not very much at any one time. The battle for adequate appropriations, effective administration, and facilitating court interpretations of new statutes and rules can go on for many years after the basic policy "mandate" has been formally determined by the President and Congress. There is, therefore, a certain indeterminacy about policy change in the United States which reformers neglect at their own peril. Eventually, of course, controversies over policy are settled (or at least lose their primacy for the actors involved), the administration of the policy becomes routinized, and the bureaucracy carries out the policy, backed by great institutional momentum and resistance to change. The chances are that the substance of the policy has been somewhat altered in the process!

Most students probably would agree on this listing of the gross structural biases and decision-making properties of the American political system. But they are overly general and admit of too many exceptions and qualifications to be of much use in specific cases. The processes of decision-making in specific policy areas can change drastically almost overnight (the election of a new President, the death of a congressional committee chairman, a change of mind of a single member of the Supreme Court), and highly stable decision processes can be very different for one area of public policy—say, agricultural price supports—than for another—say, urban affairs.[64] We therefore need a series of detailed descriptive case studies of the processing of Negro political demands by federal, state, and local government officials and agencies before we can speak with confidence about the response (and nonresponse) of the black box in the systems paradigm to Negro inputs in the United States.

Along with this essentially descriptive task should go a fresh look at problems of institutional reform. If political demands from Negroes fail to evoke adequate responses from American governmental units—with the possible consequence of massive alienation of Negroes and a drastic reduction in their support of the system—what sorts of institutional-structural reforms might alter this situation? What would be the costs, in terms of other values sacrificed and possibly undesirable side effects, of making these institutional changes? And what are the probabilities that these institutional changes can be brought about in time to be of help? The vast literature on the reform of American political institutions is often characterized by a lack of concern for political feasibility, naïveté about the actual operation and maintenance needs of the institutions to be reformed, a failure to consider the unintended consequences of reforms, and confused or unarticulated value premises.[65] We can and must do better in the future.

All of this discussion of what goes on in the black box is an overly general appeal for very specific studies of the interaction between American Negroes and officialdom and for hard-nosed estimates of the political consequences of institutional arrangements for the conversion of Negro demands into public policies.

POLICIES AND FEEDBACK

Perhaps the most important consequence for political science of the adoption of a systems perspective is the attention it directs toward outputs. To the systems analyst, public policies become the dependent variable; everything else becomes significant only insofar as it explains what comes out of the black box.

This implies a radical reorientation in our thinking and a redirection of much of our effort. For, up to now, political scientists have focused almost all their attention on independent variables and almost none on what these independent variables purport to explain. This odd imbalance in political science research now seems in the process of change.

The most obvious sign of this reorientation is the recent flurry of quantitative studies which seek to relate socioeconomic independent variables ("the environment" in the systems paradigm) and political-institutional intervening variables (the black box) to the policy outputs of state and local governments in the United States.[66] These studies have their unresolved problems: good statistical indices of political-institutional arrangements are hard to come by; the allocation of dollar expenditures to specific purposes and the determination of the source of funds spent are exceedingly difficult in the complex fiscal environment of American federalism; the problems of casual inference in the research design are more confounding than they at first appeared to be. Yet these studies are a first step in the analysis of "who gets what and why?" It is to be hoped that this mode of analysis will soon be applied to race relations policies.

At the same time, the *direction* of policy—"who gets what?"—is not the only dimension of the problem we should investigate. The *rationality* of public policy (Is policy A the most efficient route to goal *x*?), *coherence* (Do policy A and policy B have reinforcing impacts or tend to cancel each other out?), *consistency* (Is policy A pursued over a long period of time or frequently changed?), *costs* (Is goal *y* sacrificed in an effort to achieve goal *x*?), and the *impact* of public policies (Will policy A actually bring about the changes in individual behavior and attitude which were intended?) are also important. To answer these questions with any degree of scientific rigor is not now possible. But if policy outputs are to be our dependent variables, we must be able to grapple successfully with questions of this sort. Race relations, as our most pressing domestic problem, seems to be an especially promising policy area in which to make this attempt.

Undoubtedly the most central of these questions about public policy is that of *impact,* for answers to most of the other questions depend on an ability to predict the actual consequences of individual behavior and attitudes of new laws, court decisions, and administrative rulings. At least some of the variables which seem to affect the probabilities that new race relations policies will have impact are presented in Table 3–2. A few comments on their possible interrelationships and relative weight might also be hazarded.

T A B L E 3 - 2   *Variables Affecting Impact of Civil Rights Policies*

A. Governmental Resources
1 *Legitimacy:* of perceived source of policy
2 *Availability of Uncommitted Resources:* to be used as incentives or to support coercive enforcement; information and expertise necessary to use other resources skillfully and to enhance legitimacy of policy
3 *Intensity:* willingness to use resources
4 *Allies:* attitudes and resources of other governmental agencies and of private "third parties"
B. Target Group
1 *Status:* federal officials, state-local officials, private citizens
2 *Race:* Negro or white
3 *Attitudes:* direction and intensity
4 *Resources:* size, organization, geographical location, prestige, etc.
C. Change Required by Policy
1 *Type:* behavioral or attitudinal
2 *Magnitude:* large or incremental
3 *Costs:* of change to government and to the target group

The most important factor influencing the probability of success of a civil rights policy is probably the type and amount of change the policy requires: overt behavior is a great deal easier to change than attitudes (C–1); small and gradual change is easier to bring about than large or abrupt alterations in established ways (C–2); reform is more easily achieved when the costs to the government and to the target group are relatively small (C–3). All of this seems self-evident. But it still helps to explain why the federal government has been relatively successful in abolishing discrimination in public accommodations and at the polling booth and much less so in the areas of public schooling and housing.[67]

Efforts by government to diminish white racial prejudice—an attitudinal rather than a behavioral change—generally take the form of enforcing behavioral compliance with antidiscrimination rules in the hope that this will lead in time to attitude change. The evidence in support of this hypothesis is not overwhelming,[68] but we do know that a great deal of *voluntary* compliance with civil rights laws can be obtained even in the face of great hostility toward the substance of the rules.[69] Whether this dissonant posture can be maintained for long is an open question.

The impact of enforced behavioral conformity on attitudes becomes centrally important in another way. Increasingly the goals of race relations policy are defined in psychocultural terms (erase the scars of slavery,[70] abolish the "culture of poverty," [71] change Negroes from "parochials" and "subjects" into "participants" [72]) and are aimed at changing Negro attitudes. Ever since John Stuart Mill, men of good will have assumed that participation in the political community has an educational effect on the participant, that a democratic-participant society tends to produce informed, responsible, self-respecting individuals. The "maximum feasible participation" policy of federal poverty programs and the federal government's efforts to ensure southern Negroes free access to the ballot box may, or may not, have this important effect on Negroes. These programs and events provide political scientists with a wide variety of natural experimental situations in which to study a subject of great theoretical and practical significance: the complex relationships between individual behavior and attitudes and the ability of governments to alter both.

Another class of variables which affects the probable impact of governmental race relations policy is the nature of the group whose behavior or attitudes the policy seeks to change. Up to now, a great deal of civil rights policy has sought to change the behavior of public officials —judges, policemen, voter registrars, and the like—rather than of private persons (B-1). Ordinarily we would assume that officialdom would prove to be a relatively easy target for such measures. But favorable responses, even from federal officials, cannot be assumed [73] and are most likely to be achieved in relatively authoritarian and hierarchical structures, such as the armed forces. When the targets of race relations policies are state and local officials, a positive impact may not be achieved without a full-scale political battle, even the use of the ultimate sanction at the command of the federal government—military forces.[74] State and local officials are necessarily and properly responsive to local prejudices; often they can justify defiance of federal directives in terms of conflicting state-local constitutions, statutes, and ordinances; they control the resources of state and local governmental units (B-4). In areas of strong hostility toward civil rights policies (B-3), they are likely to be more resistant than local private citizens.

Finally, governmental resources affect the probable impact of civil rights policies on citizen behavior and attitudes. Between 1900 and 1957, most new race relations policies were promulgated by the federal courts. The main resource at their command was the tremendous prestige and legitimacy of the United States Constitution and Supreme Court (A–1), but both suffered as a consequence of these controversial decisions. So long as the other branches of the federal government were unable or unwilling to commit their resources heavily to the struggle to achieve conformance to the decisions (A–4), and while the opposition to the new decisions was intense and in control of southern state and local governments (B–1, 2, 3, 4), the courts themselves did not have the available resources (A–2) to enforce their new rulings even with "deliberate speed"(C–2).

Voluntary compliance with the civil rights legislation enacted by Congress since 1957 seemingly has been more widespread, despite the fact that the changes in policy contained in the legislation were relatively drastic (C–2). No doubt the threat of coercive sanctions and remedial action contained in the statutes (A–2) contributed to acceptance. So too, apparently, did the high legitimacy of legislative outputs (A–1), especially among the opponents of the civil rights movement, and the demonstration—which a successful legislative campaign provides—that a large and powerful coalition was willing to invest heavily of their resources in order to see the new policy carried through (A–3, 4).

Executive orders and administrative rulings do not enjoy as much legitimacy as do legislation or court orders (A–1), except in highly technical fields in which the administrators' superior information and expertise may generate respect and acquiescence (A–2). The original Fair Employment Practices Commission (FEPC) which was established by executive order, for example, was throttled by a hostile Congress for want of legitimacy and sufficiently intense and powerful allies (A–3, 4). When the opposition to a new civil rights rule is large and intense and controls substantial resources (B–3, 4), legislation is unlikely, and administrative or judicial attacks on the problem become the only practical course. Neither is likely *by itself* to bring about large-scale change in racial attitudes and behavior, for exclusively administrative efforts usually lack legitimacy and supportive allies, while courts take drastic action only at the risk of eroding their main resource, legitimacy. On the other hand, this does not mean that Negro demands inevitably will be frustrated now that the judicial and legislative phases of the struggle seem to be drawing to a close. Backed by widespread popular acceptance and high legitimacy, powerful allies, plentiful resources, and the awesome momentum of governmental agencies once their policies become locked into bureaucratic routines, administrators are in a powerful position to bring about behavioral change. But this presupposes, of course, the existence of popular support for administrative policies and that enforced behavioral compliance with them eventually will bring about attitudinal change.

Thus we return full circle to the extraordinary importance of the attitudes which undergird American racial patterns and the still mysterious processes by which governments may be able to contribute to their change.

CONCLUDING REMARKS

In choosing topics for research, social scientists often are confronted with a choice between rigor and relevance, between making a contribution to a body of systematic theory and providing information and knowledge of use to practical men of affairs. These dilemmas are largely absent for researchers in the field of race relations: it is quite possible to be scientific and socially and politically relevant, too. I hope that in these pages I have pointed out some ways in which political scientists can contribute to the alleviation of racial injustice in America while, at the same time, developing a verified general theory of politics. Both tasks are staggeringly difficult. But few modern political scientists are willing to concede that either is beyond our grasp.

•NOTES

NOTE: Professors Leonard Fein, Lewis Jones, Albert McQueen, and Paul Puryear made numerous and especially helpful comments on the working draft of this chapter presented at the Conference on Social Science Research in Race Relations. Three of my friends and colleagues at North Carolina—Frederic Cleaveland, William Keech, and Lewis Lipsitz—were kind enough to read and comment on a subsequent version. Many of my ideas on this subject have grown out of my long and close collaboration with James Prothro. None of these men should be charged with the shortcomings of this chapter; all contributed to whatever merit it may have.

1 D. Easton, *The Political System* (New York: Knopf, 1953), pp. 78–79.

2 K. Janda, *Cumulative Index to the American Political Science Review: Vols. 1–57: 1906–1963* (Evanston: Northwestern University Press, 1964). Of course, a number of articles without these words in their titles must be, at least in part, concerned with the racial problem in America.

3 See R. A. Dahl, "The Behavioral Approach in Political Science: Epitaph

for a Monument to a Successful Protest," *American Political Science Review*, LV (December, 1961), 763–772. Dahl may exaggerate the extent to which the "behavioral-scientific" mood has captured the profession, but his analysis of the causes of the methodological rebellion is excellent.

4 W. C. Seyler, comp., "Doctoral Dissertations in Political Science," *American Political Science Review*, LX (September, 1966), 778–803. I am indebted to Professor L. Fein for pointing out to me the number of recent dissertations on topics related to race.

5 See especially the latest work by the pioneer of this approach, D. Easton, *A Systems Analysis of Political Life* (New York: Wiley, 1965). Also, G. Almond and J. Coleman, eds., *The Politics of Developing Areas* (Princeton: Princeton University Press, 1960), Introduction. Presents a somewhat different formulation.

6 See T. Kuhn, *The Structure of Scientific Revolutions* (Chicago: University of Chicago Press, 1965), and G. Almond, "Political Theory and Political Science," *American Political Science Review*, LX (December, 1966), 869–879.

7 This figure is drawn, slightly revised, from Easton, *A Systems Analysis,* p. 32.

8 Systems theory is sometimes criticized for being too broad and all-inclusive. In fact, if "authoritative decision-makers" are thought of as the legal government, as I shall do in this chapter, the paradigm excludes from the realm of "the political" all power relationships between private persons which do not at least indirectly effect demands on, or support for, the government. This represents a substantial narrowing of the concept of "politics" from that used in everyday speech and by many political scientists. While this is probably desirable—political science as a discipline has been overly ambitious in the past—the narrower scope of the phenomena worthy of study according to this approach may, if we are not careful, lead us to overlook the political significance of new, quite unconventional behaviors which characterize race relations today. See text, p. 8 ff. An even more telling criticism of the systems paradigm is that it is so abstract and general that it is of little use to empirical researchers. This very weakness, however, contributes to its utility for this study and other efforts to organize numerous and disparate ideas and facts and in a coherent way.

9 See D. R. Matthews and J. W. Prothro, *Negroes and the New Southern Politics* (New York: Harcourt, 1966), Chapter 12, and W. Brink and L. Harris, *The Negro Revolution in America* (New York: Simon and Schuster, 1964), *passim*. G. T. Marx, University of California, Berkeley, found, on the basis of random sample surveys of Negro adults in Chicago, New York, Atlanta, and Birmingham conducted in 1964, that less than one-third of those Negroes interviewed were strongly anti-white. He also reports little change in attitudes in subsequent years. (*The New York Times*, May 26, 1967.) See the full report: G. Marx, *Protest and Prejudice: A Study of Belief in the Black Community* (New York: Harper and

Row, 1967). See also C. E. Lincoln, *The Black Muslims in America* (Boston: Beacon, 1961).

10 One of the easiest and most economical ways to increase our understanding of the attitudes and opinions of the mass of American Negroes would be for one or more foundations to make funds available to survey research organizations to permit the routine oversampling of Negroes in all or most of their studies. Most surveys now conducted contain too few Negro respondents to permit separate analysis of the Negro component of the sample. A relatively modest additional expenditure would result in a very large increase in data available to students of race relations.

11 Cf. V. O. Key, Jr., *Public Opinion and American Democracy* (New York: Knopf, 1961), Chapter 21.

12 J. W. Prothro and C. M. Grigg, "Fundamental Principles of Democracy: Bases of Agreement and Disagreement," *Journal of Politics*, XXII (1960), 276–294; S. A. Stouffer, *Communism, Conformity and Civil Liberties* (Garden City, N.Y.: Doubleday, 1955); H. McCloskey, "Consensus and Ideology in American Politics," *American Political Science Review*, LVIII (1964), 361–382; R. A. Dahl, *Who Governs?* (New Haven: Yale University Press, 1961), Chapter 28. This line of interpretation has not gone unchallenged. See, for example, J. Walker, "A Critique of the Elitist Theory of Democracy," *American Political Science Review*, LX (June, 1966), 285–295.

13 J. Q. Wilson, *Negro Politics: The Search for Leadership* (Glencoe, Ill.: The Free Press, 1960).

14 G. Myrdal, *An American Dilemma* (New York: Harper and Row, 1944), Chapter 3, Part 4.

15 Matthews and Prothro, *op. cit.*, pp. 332 ff.

16 Cf. Brink and Harris, *op. cit.*, for some clues as of 1964.

17 Matthews and Prothro, *op. cit.*, pp. 375 ff.

18 This discussion of political resources and their relationship to power follows Dahl, *Who Governs?* Chapters 19–28.

19 The study of the judicial politics and policy-making, as distinct from legal doctrines, is a recent development in political science. Writing in 1955, Peltason made the following telling contrasts: "Traditional approaches to the judiciary often fail to draw attention to important data. Consider the results if the legislative process were described in the same manner as judicial activity is now detailed. Biographies of leading congressmen would be the main staple of research. Discussion of statute-making would concentrate on activity within the legislative chamber. Legislators would be seen as an isolated group. A congressman's vote, say, for the Taft-Hartley Act would be explained as reflecting his conviction that such a law was a reasonable regulation of commerce designed to promote the national interest. Studies of the legislative process would deal primarily with legislators' speeches and contain critical comments

on their arguments. Attention would be focused upon formal rules of procedure. Students in courses on legislation would be assigned readings from the *United States Code*. Little attention would be paid to the consequences of legislative decisions.

"The study of legislators as participants in the group struggle has been fruitful. Perhaps it will be useful to study judges in the political process also. We can find out only by trying."—J. W. Peltason, *Federal Courts in the Political Process* (Garden City, N.Y.: Doubleday, 1955), pp. 1–2, *passim*, and G. A. Schubert, *Constitutional Politics* (New York: Holt, 1960).

20 The standard sources on the NAACP's strategy and tactics are C. E. Vose, "Litigation as a Form of Pressure Group Activity," *Annals*, CCCXIX (September, 1958), 20–31, and *idem, Caucasians Only: The Supreme Court, the NAACP, and the Restrictive Covenant Cases* (Berkeley and Los Angeles: University of California Press, 1959). L. Miller, *The Petitioners: The Story of the Supreme Court of the United States and the Negro* (New York: Pantheon, 1966), is a good, readable history stressing legal doctrine, by an NAACP attorney. A. Lewis, *Portrait of a Decade: The Second American Revolution* (New York: Random House, 1964), is a valuable account of the decade following *Brown vs. Board of Education* by *The New York Times'* able Supreme Court reporter.

21 For useful summaries of this literature see R. E. Lane, *Political Life* (Glencoe, Ill.: Free Press, 1959); L. Milbrath, *Political Participation*, (Skokie, Ill.: Rand-McNally, 1965); S. M. Lipset *et al.,* "The Psychology of Voting," in G. Lindzey, ed., *Handbook of Social Psychology* (Cambridge: Addison-Wesley, 1954), II, 1126–1134.

22 A. Clubok, J. DeGrove, and C. Farris, "The Manipulated Negro Vote: Preconditions and Consequences," *Journal of Politics,* XXVI (1964), 112–129; H. Holloway, "The Negro and the Vote: The Case of Texas," *Journal of Politics,* XXIII (1961), 542 ff.

23 Matthews and Prothro, *op. cit.,* p. 231.

24 The following dozen paragraphs are drawn virtually verbatim from, *ibid.,* pp. 477–481.

25 See, for example, L. A. Dexter, "The Representative and His District," *Human Organization,* XVI (1947), 2–13; Key, *op. cit.,* Chapter 21; W. E. Miller and D. Stokes, "Constituency Influence in Congress," *American Political Science Review,* LVII (1963), 45–56.

26 This section relies heavily on W. R. Keech, "The Negro Vote as a Political Resource: The Case of Durham," unpublished dissertation, University of Wisconsin, 1966. See also "Voting," in U.S. Commission on Civil Rights, *1961 Report* (Washington: Government Printing Office, 1961), I, part III, 143–199; H. S. Whitaker, "A New Day: The Effects of Negro Enfranchisement in Selected Mississippi Counties," unpublished dissertation, Florida State University, 1965; A. Sindler, "Protest Against the Political Status of the Negro," *Annals,* CCCLVII (1965), 48–54.

27 G. B. Johnson, "Negro Racial Movements and Leadership in the United States," *American Journal of Sociology*, XLII (July, 1937), 56–72.

28 Myrdal, *op. cit.*, Part IX, Chapters 34–35.

29 Wilson, *op. cit.*, Chapter 9.

30 D. G. Thompson, *The Negro Leadership Class* (Englewood Cliffs, N.J.: Prentice-Hall, 1963), 58–79.

31 M. E. Burgess, *Negro Leadership in a Southern City* (Chapel Hill: University of North Carolina Press, 1962), 176–186.

32 E. C. Ladd, Jr., *Negro Political Leadership in the South* (Ithaca, N.Y.: Cornell University Press, 1966), Chapters 4–5.

33 L. Killian and C. Grigg, *Racial Crisis in America: Leadership in Conflict* (Englewood Cliffs, N.J.: Prentice-Hall, 1964), Chapter 4.

34 Matthews and Prothro, *op. cit.*, Chapters 7–8.

35 J. Q. Wilson, "The Negro Politicians: An Interpretation," *Midwest Journal of Political Science*, IV (1960), 346–369; and reprinted in H. A. Bailey, Jr., ed., *Negro Politics in America* (Columbus: Merrill, 1967). The appearance of this "readings book" indicates an awakening interest among political scientists in Negro politics.

36 J. Q. Wilson, "The Negro in Politics," *Daedalus* (Fall, 1967), 949–973. Quote from pp. 960–961.

37 W. Riker, *The Theory of Political Coalitions* (New Haven: Yale University Press, 1962); A. Downs, *An Economic Theory of Democracy* (New York: Harper and Row, 1957); C. E. Lindblom, *The Intelligence of Democracy* (New York: The Free Press, 1965); T. C. Schelling, *The Strategy of Conflict* (Cambridge: Harvard University Press, 1960).

38 Matthews and Prothro, *op. cit.;* Chapters 7–8; Keech, *op. cit.;* and Whitaker, *op. cit.*, are the principal exceptions.

39 E. F. Frazier, *Black Bourgeoisie* (Glencoe, Ill.: The Free Press, 1957).

40 R. Michels, *Political Parties* (Glencoe, Ill.: The Free Press, 1949). First published in 1911.

41 The major exceptions are L. C. Kesselman, *The Social Politics of FEPC: A Study in Reform Pressure Movements* (Chapel Hill: University of North Carolina Press, 1948), and H. Garfinkel, *When Negroes March* (Glencoe, Ill.: The Free Press, 1959). Professor R. Wolfinger is at work on a study of the politics of recent federal civil rights legislation which should prove illuminating.

42 Cf. J. Q. Wilson, "The Strategy of Protest: Problems of Negro Civic Action," *Journal of Conflict Resolution*, V (September, 1961), 291–303. This passage has also been influenced by my reading of an unpublished paper by Professor M. Lipsky of Wisconsin University.

43 Matthews and Prothro, *op. cit.*, Chapter 14. See also J. M. Orbell, "Protest Participation among Southern Negro College Students," *American Political Science Review*, LXI (June, 1967), 446–456; R. Searles and

J. A. Williams, "Negro College Students' Participation in Sit-ins," *Social Forces*, XL (March, 1962), 215–220; J. A. Gerchwinder, "Social Structure and the Negro Revolt: An Examination of Some Hypotheses," *Social Forces*, XLIII (December, 1964), 248–256.

44 J. Katz of Stanford University has analyzed eight studies of student protestors at different American universities conducted by separate investigators and concludes: "The amazing fact is that the results of all these studies converge, that they do not contradict each other in the major findings. . . . Studies agree that most campus activists are comparatively intelligent, stable and unprejudiced" (*The New York Times*, June 19, 1967).

45 See J. L. Walker, "Protest and Negotiation: A Case Study of Negro Leadership in Atlanta, Georgia," *Midwest Journal of Political Science*, VII (May, 1963), 99–124; J. L. Walker, *Sit-Ins in Atlanta: A Study in Negro Protest* (New York: Eagleton Institute Case Studies, No. 34, 1964); A. P. Sindler, *Negro Protest and Local Politics* (New York: Eagleton Institute Case Studies, No. 37, 1965); J. Ehle, *The Free Men* (New York: Harper and Row, 1965); Thompson, *op. cit;* Burgess, *op. cit.;* Killian and Grigg, *op. cit.*

46 Professor H. M. Scoble of the Department of Political Science at UCLA is conducting research on the Watts riots. No doubt other political scientists (and a larger number of sociologists and psychologists) are similarly engaged in cities which have suffered through comparable experience. The importance of the subject, however, argues for massive large-scale research programs and, to my knowledge, there are none which include political scientists.

47 See R. Blauner, "White-Wash over Watts," *Trans-Action* (March, 1966), pp. 1–9, 54; and H. M. Scoble, "The McCone Commission and Social Science," 1966 (mimeographed).

48 See Almond and Coleman, *op. cit.,* and the other studies sponsored by the Committee on Comparative Politics of the Social Science Research Council for examples of the better work on political development. C. Johnson, *Revolutionary Change* (Boston: Little, Brown, 1966), and H. Eckstein, ed., *Internal War, Problems and Approaches* (New York: The Free Press, 1964), provide a useful introduction to recent research on purposive political violence.

49 See G. Almond and S. Verba, *The Civic Culture* (Princeton: Princeton University Press, 1963), for the leading work on this subject. The authors find an extraordinarily high level of support for the American political system as compared to that in Britain, Germany, Italy, or Mexico.

50 Matthews and Prothro, *op. cit.,* Chapter 10.

51 Almond and Verba, *op. cit.*

52 D. Marvick, "The Political Socialization of the American Negro," *Annals*, CCCLXI (1965), 112–127, reprinted in Bailey, *op. cit.*

53 Cf. H. Hyman, *Political Socialization* (Glencoe, Ill.: The Free Press, 1959); F. I. Greenstein, *Children and Politics* (New Haven: Yale University Press, 1965); D. Easton and J. Dennis, "The Child's Acquisition of Regime Norms: Political Efficacy," *American Political Science Review*, LXI (March, 1967), 25–38, and "The Child's Image of Government," *Annals*, CCCLXI (1965), 40–57.

54 For an exhaustive and illuminating discussion of this question see the debate on the Lodge-Gossett and Mundt-Condert-Daniel proposed Constitutional amendments in the U.S. Senate, *Congressional Record*, March 20–27, 1956. See also L. Wilmerding, Jr., *The Electoral College* (New Brunswick, N.J.: Rutgers University Press, 1958).

55 See J. Anderson, *Eisenhower, Brownell and the Civil Rights Bill of 1956* (University: University of Alabama Press, 1964), a fascinating case study.

56 A. Hacker, *Congressional Districting* (Washington: Brookings Institution, 1963); G. E. Baker, *The Reapportionment Revolution* (New York: Random House, 1966). Recent research on state politics suggests that the policy consequences of malapportionment may have been greatly overestimated. See T. R. Dye, *Politics, Economics, and the Public* (Skokie, Ill.: Rand-McNally, 1966), pp. 270–281, and the sources cited therein.

57 M. C. Cummings, Jr., *Congressmen and the Electorate* (New York: The Free Press, 1966).

58 G. Goodwin, Jr., "The Seniority System in Congress," *American Political Science Review*, LIII (1959), 412–436.

59 H. E. Shuman, "Senate Rules and the Civil Rights Bill," *American Political Science Review*, LI (1957), 955–975; F. Burdette, *Filibustering in the Senate* (Princeton: Princeton University Press, 1940); J. A. Robinson, *The House Rules Committee* (Indianapolis: Bobbs-Merrill, 1963).

60 D. R. Matthews, *U.S. Senators and Their World* (Chapel Hill: University of North Carolina Press, 1960), esp. Chapter 5.

61 The consequences of this for the U.S. Presidency are fully explored in R. Neustadt, *Presidential Power* (New York: Wiley, 1960).

62 See P. Selznick, *TVA and the Grass Roots* (Berkeley: University of California Press, 1949), and J. L. Freeman, *The Political Process* (Garden City, N.Y.: Doubleday, 1955).

63 W. H. Riker, *Federalism: Origin, Operation, Significance* (Boston: Little, Brown, 1964). Particularly concerned with the consequences of American federalism for Negroes and other low-resource groups.

64 See F. N. Cleaveland, "Congress and Urban Problems: Legislating for Urban Areas," *Journal of Politics* (1966), 289–307. Professor Cleaveland has directed a series of legislative case studies on this topic to be published by the Brookings Institution. Urban and Negro problems are linked, and the political and institutional barriers to effective policymaking are similar in many ways.

65 For one of the few works on institutional reform which avoids these difficulties, see R. H. Davidson, D. M. Kovenock, and M. K. O'Leary, *Congress in Crisis: Politics and Congressional Reform* (Belmont, Calif.: Wadsworth, 1966).

66 The first of these articles was R. E. Dawson and J. A. Robinson, "Inter-Party Competition, Economic Variables, and Welfare Policies in the American States," *Journal of Politics*, XXV (1963), 265–289. Dye, *op. cit.*, is the latest and most definitive work in this genre.

67 Several quantitative analyses of the implementation of *Brown vs. Board of Education* exist: T. F. Pettigrew, "Demographic Correlates of Border-State Desegregation," *American Sociological Review*, XXII (1957), 683–689; T. F. Pettigrew and M. R. Cramer, "The Demography of Desegregation," *Journal of Social Issues*, XV (1959), 61–71; D. R. Matthews and J. W. Prothro, "Stateways versus Folkways: Critical Factors in Southern Reactions to *Brown vs. Board of Education*," in G. Dietze, ed., *Essays on the American Constitution* (Englewood Cliffs, N.J.: Prentice-Hall, 1964), pp. 139–156. The response to court decisions and legislation seeking to provide southern Negroes access to the polls is described in Matthews and Prothro, *Negroes and the New Southern Politics*, Chapter 1.

68 See M. Berger, *Equality by Statute: Legal Controls over Group Discrimination* (New York: Columbia University Press, 1952), esp. Chapter 5 and the works cited therein.

69 M. E. Tumin, *Desegregation: Resistance and Readiness* (Princeton: Princeton University Press, 1958).

70 S. M. Elkins, *Slavery: A Problem in American Institutional and Intellectual Life* (Chicago: University of Chicago Press, 1959).

71 O. Lewis, *La Vida* (New York: Random House, 1966).

72 Almond and Verba, *op. cit.*

73 J. W. Peltason, *58 Lonely Men* (New York: Harcourt, 1961). A sensitive analysis of the difficulties federal judges in the South faced in implementing the *Brown* decision.

74 An excellent case study of one of these: C. Silverman, *The Little Rock Story* (revised), Inter-University Case Program No. 41 (University: University of Alabama Press, 1959).

4 *Karl E. Taeuber*

Negro Population and Housing: Demographic Aspects of a Social Accounting Scheme

The social sciences have documented the prevalence and persistence of a wide variety of white-Negro differences—in income, occupation, education, housing patterns, mortality, fertility, migration, and many other items. The grand culmination of this effort occurred a quarter of a century ago with Myrdal's *An American Dilemma*. Subsequent work has continued to emphasize the historical and social context of racial differences, but a new focus has developed on the northern and urban scenes. As attention has shifted from the rural South, race relations literature has tended to become less historical, less concerned with a traditional social structure, more concerned with functional relationships in a changing society and with an ongoing vicious cycle of disabilities.

Political controversy over civil rights and increasing newsworthiness of race relations have renewed concern with white-Negro differences. This concern might lead to such an emphasis on racial differences that similarities are glossed over, thus perhaps fostering the very racism that produces differences. Nevertheless, I suspect that an emphasis on problems may still be valuable. For example, although Harrington's *The*

145

Other America helped popularize the concept of the "culture of poverty" and the notion that the "lower classes" really exist and really are different, it is acclaimed for the political stimulus it gave to the "war on poverty." Moynihan has argued that top policy-makers become complacent about continuing problems and routine statistical indicators. He viewed his report on *The Negro Family*, a forceful dramatization of white-Negro differences in family welfare, as an essential spur to action.

A rather different reaction to renewed emphasis on white-Negro differences has been the call for a summary "index of race relations." It is assumed that trends in a few key indicators could tell as much about the state of race relations as trends in a few, key economic indicators are presumed to tell about the state of the economy. Such a view overlooks the complex array of economic indicators currently in use and the intricate and still controversial theory specifying interrelations among indicators. Perhaps sociologists should take it as a public compliment that their knowledge of American society is thought to be as well developed as economists' knowledge of the economy. But my reaction is one of concern that pleas for simple indicators represent a search for simple answers to extremely difficult social problems.

Sociological research no longer need be engaged simply in spelling out the sad state of "the Negro." Statistical documentation of the anguish of race relations is ample. What is now necessary is increasingly sophisticated analysis of the various ways in which race is a factor in social change in the United States. I endorse Coleman's argument in another chapter that the most urgent need is for a comprehensive social accounting system. Such a system involves much more than simply a set of indicators. The basic need is for "methods, models, and materials suited to disentangle the causal relationships among indicators." [1]

With respect to housing, for example, researchers have provided measures of segregation, crowding, and quality with which to measure white-Negro differences. These are useful, but we must also attempt to determine how the entire process of provision of shelter is affected by race and racism. What role is played by racial residential segregation and change in racial occupancy? Are there strategic points at which planned intervention might be particularly feasible or effective? These are illustrative of the kinds of questions to which a useful social accounting system must be addressed.

It is tempting to say that we know the problems; what we lack is the solutions. But this is too simple. For example, Negroes receive less income than whites; one solution to such economic differentials is to give more money to Negroes. This, indeed, is the most direct of all answers to the poverty problem, but it is not the only answer nor necessarily the one that should guide policy. Raising the income of Negro families could be done directly, as by federal transfer payments; the direct and indirect consequences of such payments must be anticipated through social and economic research. Getting more money to Negroes may also be accomplished, one would suppose, by getting Negroes into better jobs. Better jobs might be obtained in part by providing Negroes with better education. Better education might be obtained in part by accelerating the pace of school desegregation. And so on. Each aspect of the social situation of Negroes is involved to some degree with every other aspect. These relationships must be uncovered if policy is to be rational. This is the justification for emphasizing a social accounting *system.*

Some degree of control over the complexity of an endlessly ramifying system may be gained by first examining the individual life cycle. Roughly speaking, various aspects of family background precede formal education, which in turn precedes occupational choice and the receipt of earned income. At various times in the life cycle crucial alternatives are selected. The nature of these choices—occupational choice, for example—is determined by the previous preparation of the individual and by the nature of the job market at that time. If there were no discrimination in the job market, Negroes would still fare more poorly than whites if they were less well prepared educationally or in other ways.

The life cycle may be viewed as a series of games, each played according to society's rules. The rules of most of the crucial games are unfair to Negroes. But even if a particular game is played fairly, the outcome for Negroes is likely to be unfavorable because of the handicaps with which they enter the game. To improve the outcome of a game, it is necessary to discern which rules need changing and the extent to which the players need extra coaching. The need for extra coaching before any given game may be reduced in two ways. One is to alter the rules (as by reducing discrimination) so that player characteristics have less effect on the outcome. A second is to alter the outcome of preceding games by rule changes, extra coaching, or introduction of new compensatory games. To illustrate briefly, a firm may hire few Negroes because of discrimination in evaluating applicants and because few Negro applicants pass a test. The discriminatory practices of the personnel office may be identified and corrected, thus changing the rules of the game, but Negroes may still need special coaching to pass the test. To avoid this, attention may be directed to the formal educational process; the test may be revised to be less "culture-bound";

or the test may be dropped and an on-the-job training program instituted to compensate for any lack of preparation.

Direct policy on civil rights ordinarily is designed to ensure that one
or another game is played fairly, or, in Coleman's terms, to enlarge the
freedom of social action of Negroes. But many other policies are necessary if the position of Negroes in American society is to be improved
rapidly. Identifying discrimination—its locus, causes, and consequences—is only part of the social science research problem. The concern must be with analysis of the entire life cycle, the context in which
it takes place, and the forces that impinge on it. Here, then, is the need
for Negro population studies. Birth and death, marriage and family
formation, are not often perceived as civil rights problems, but any social accounting system must be concerned with such vital events.

SOURCES OF DATA

A separate section on sources of data tends to become an obstacle
intervening between the introduction to and the real substance of a
discussion, but the quality of data on Negroes has itself been viewed as
a substantive issue.

> The term alienation may by now have been used in too many ways to
> retain a clear meaning, but it will serve to sum up the equally numerous
> ways in which large numbers of Negro youth appear to be withdrawing
> from American society. One startling way in which this occurs is that the
> men are just not there when the Census enumerator comes around.[2]

The more one attempts to work with data on Negro population and
housing, the more concerned he becomes over the quality of currently
available data. Moynihan developed concern to such a degree that in
mid-1967 he organized a national conference to focus attention on the
problem. Papers at the conference presented new information on
sources of difficulty and possible solutions. The proceedings have been
published, so it will suffice here to quote the opening paragraphs of the
"Resolutions" of the conference:

> The Conference on Social Statistics and the City, convened by the Joint
> Center for Urban Studies of the Massachusetts Institute of Technology
> and Harvard University, meeting in Washington, D.C., June 22–23,
> 1967, by general concurrence resolved the following:
> While American population statistics are among the very finest in the
> world, papers presented to the Conference have established beyond rea-
> sonable doubt that the Decennial Census, the Current Population Survey,
> and to a lesser degree, the Vital Statistics of the United States, seriously

and significantly under-enumerate or under-estimate the size of the Negro, Puerto-Rican, and Mexican-American populations. As much as 10 percent of the Negro population may not have been counted in the 1960 Census, and there is considerable probability that the Puerto Rican and Mexican-American were similarly under-counted.

In 1960 as many as one Negro male in six within the age group of 20 to 39 years may have been omitted altogether.

In a modern society statistical information is not only a primary guide to public and private actions; in itself it profoundly influences patterns of thought and basic assumptions as to the way things are and the way they are likely to be.[3]

The usual approach of researchers to data of poor quality is a brief discussion followed by a dismissal of the problem as "probably not affecting the results" of the study. In most studies utilizing large-scale data on Negroes, however, such a conclusion is likely to represent a pious hope or desperate assertion rather than a reasoned assessment. Rates of underenumeration are very high in selected areas. Rates of nonreporting, and probably of misreporting, are also likely to be high in the same areas. The missing persons cannot be presumed to resemble the enumerated population, nor should we assume their characteristics to be distributed in the same fashion as those recorded. We may be missing a very large proportion of a particular segment of the Negro population.

It is easy for social scientists to formulate hypotheses about the enumeration process and Negro attitudes, but facts are harder to come by. We are not at all sure just who is missed or whether "alienation" or "man-in-the-house" rules or other "obvious" explanations are relevant. Efforts by the Census Bureau to improve enumeration of Negroes have achieved some success with simple procedural modifications. More careful enumeration of all residential structures and greater efforts to secure information on units with no one at home uncover additional Negro population. Hence, it is entirely possible that much of the underenumeration stems from field procedures which are inadequately designed and administered for the kinds of neighborhoods and housing arrangements in which many Negroes live.

The need for caution in jumping to conclusions about sources of census errors is best illustrated by the example of census underenumeration of infants. Prior to the 1950 Post-Enumeration Survey, it was thought that respondents tended to overlook new babies in the family, perhaps because of a social-psychological perception problem. The survey showed that most missed babies were in households which were missed altogether. The principal solution to the underenumeration lay in improved census coverage of dwellings rather than in improved questionnaire design or better interview rapport.

The resolutions of the aforementioned conference urged upon the Bureau of the Census a number of procedural devices for improving enumeration of minority populations. But neither the resolutions nor the conference discussions emphasized sufficiently the central need to determine who is being missed. The Census Bureau can tinker with procedural modifications, and to the extent that coverage is improved it furthers its understanding of the problem. But rational modification of census procedures to effect major improvements in coverage requires prior knowledge of who is missed and why.

I would give priority to a series of test enumerations in various types of areas, each enumeration to be preceded and/or followed by a frontal assault on the task of determining who should have been enumerated. This assault might use field workers who live in the area for some time, local residents and other informed persons, or matching of the enumeration list against welfare, selective service, and other lists. Efforts of this type have not yet met with a great deal of success, but I urge their continuance as our best hope for uncovering the nature of the problems for which it is necessary already to be designing solutions.

Although I have written so far of *census* data, the same problems exist in every survey operation. The decennial census is but the largest of all data-producing surveys. Problems of coverage, reliability, and validity are found in local studies and in national sample surveys. It matters not whether the sample is a few dozen or a few thousand, whether the sampling procedure is designed by the Survey Research Center, National Opinion Research Center, Louis Harris, or the Bureau of the Census. Not only surveys but vital statistics registration and most other record sources of information are also seriously deficient, although the character and source of errors must be determined separately for each type of information.

The Conference on Social Statistics and the City formulated an argument that underenumeration of a group might be a violation of constitutional rights, of the one-man one-vote principle, or of equal protection of the laws. Regardless of the legal merits of the argument, it is obvious that poor data can lead to misguided or unfair policy. In the simplest instance, a program may falter if it is planned and budgeted on the assumption that there will be 200,000 eligible recipients in a given city, and 300,000 eligible recipients claim benefits.

For social science research, as opposed to policy, absolute numbers are often of little interest. The focus is on relative numbers—percentages and rates—or on multivariate statistical formulations. If errors in the numerator and denominator of a percentage or rate are compensating, the percentage or rate will nevertheless be correct. But any assumption about compensating errors must be regarded with great skepticism until proven. We know that patterns of underenumeration and errors in data for Negroes differ from those for other groups and that within the Negro population errors are concentrated among persons with certain characteristics.

For multivariate statistical formulations, the problems are equally great and often unrecognized. Random errors in any single variable affect results. Large nonrandom errors in each variable, particularly when the errors in one variable are correlated in some unknown pattern with errors in another variable, can wreak havoc. "The degree of association between any two cross-classified variables is governed in very large part by the pattern of association between their errors of classification and . . . without knowledge of this pattern we are almost at a total loss to know what interpretation to place upon the classification." [4] Statisticians and econometricians have paid more attention to these problems than have demographers and sociologists. It is essential that additional work be carried out to develop the appropriate statistical theory and to facilitate its application to the routine kinds of analyses of census, survey, and other data conducted by social scientists. Until this is done, we must remain uncertain of the range of error in our analyses. "No one would accept a sample estimate that did not include an estimate of the sampling error involved. We believe that the same criterion should be applied to errors of classification, where these can be measured." [5]

Improvements in completeness of enumeration and in quality of data are necessary but not sufficient. The utility of census and other survey data on Negroes could often be improved in the tabulation process. The following suggestions are not novel, but they are in need of wider implementation.

Foremost with respect to all census, vital statistics, and other mass data programs is the need for tabulations for Negroes. The concept of "color" and the split between white and nonwhite has become embedded in our statistical systems. Data on nonwhites are rarely of interest unless they can be regarded as approximately equivalent to data on Negroes. An assumed equivalence of Negro and nonwhite is satisfactory in many instances, but such an assumption is ridiculous in studies of residential segregation in Los Angeles, of the movement of Negroes to suburbs, or the assimilation of Negroes in upper occupational levels. Acknowledging that any simple categorization is a crude abstraction, I believe a distinction between Negroes and non-

Negroes is the most useful division of the United States population. In our society, "Negro" is a meaningful social identification; "nonwhite" is not. Even the term "white," as familiar as it is, today seems less meaningful than non-Negro. Social scientists rarely provide a rationale for the "majority" category they choose as a basis for comparison with Negroes. The case for non-Negroes is certainly as good as the case for whites, for it permits a comparison of Negroes with the aggregate of all other groups in our society.

The equivalence between white and non-Negro is much greater than that between nonwhite and Negro. Classifying a few hundred thousand persons of "other races" together with the white population causes much less theoretical or empirical distortion than does classifying them with the Negro population. I think the most serious barrier to immediate substitution of "non-Negro–Negro" for "white–nonwhite" throughout official data systems is the awkwardness of the name "non-Negro" and an unwillingness to lump together "whites" with "Chinese," "Japanese," and "American Indians." Another barrier is the desire to maintain continuity and facilitate comparisons through time. One solution would be to tabulate data for total, white, and Negro. Data for Negroes would be available, and figures for nonwhites or non-Negroes could be obtained by subtraction. But problems of comparability can be overemphasized. Where nonwhites are predominantly Negro, there is no problem. Where nonwhites are a mixture of diverse groups, comparability may not be worth preserving.

It has been common for census and other agencies with very large data files to prepare many of their special-purpose and research tabulations on a sample basis. Frequently this results in too few Negroes to permit repeating the detailed tabulations by race. To avoid this, corresponding tabulations for Negroes could be made from a larger sample. Thus, where a special tabulation is prepared from a 1 per cent sample, corresponding tabulations for Negroes could be prepared from a 10 per cent sample. This oversampling in the tabulation process is analogous to the increasingly common practice of collecting data originally for stratified samples in which Negroes are overrepresented. Recognition of a national need for data on the Negro population carries with it an obligation to provide detailed tabulations.

The Bureau of the Census and many other agencies, public and private, have valuable data files which have not been exploited for the information they might provide on Negro population and race relations. In some instances it may be necessary to add a question or two to periodic questionnaires or to modify current coding procedures before usable data are available. In many instances, the problem is simply a lack of appropriate tabulations. Information by race is so important that collectors and tabulators of data, even if their own immediate purposes do not require a division by race, should seek to make their data useful and available for exploitation by others.

For small surveys, or in other instances where the cost of special tabulations is slight, it may suffice to include race in the basic data file. For census data and other large files, tabulation by race should be as common as tabulation by region or by urban-rural residence. Capability for tabulations by race should be built into virtually all survey operations and registration systems, government and private.

THE NATURE OF DEMOGRAPHY

The population occupying a specified territory may increase by birth or in-migration and may decrease by death or out-migration. This basic demographic equation has given rise to a workbox full of techniques for assessing and describing the growth and territorial redistribution of populations. Included are not only the mathematical techniques of the demographer but the survey methods of the census taker and the recording techniques of the vital statistics registrar. Despite the complexity involved in elaboration of the basic demographic equation, that equation is too narrowly defined to encompass most of the interests of the social science demographer. Members of a population have a wide variety of characteristics which define their position in society. Hence, the demographer must be prepared to examine selective fertility, selective mortality, selective migration, and—most important and difficult of all—social mobility.

Demographic analysis, broadly conceived, may be applied to many different topics in the social sciences. A particularly apt example may be taken from the chapter by Killingsworth in this volume: changing numbers of Negroes and whites in the labor force may be understood only by an accounting scheme embracing numbers in the armed forces, numbers in various other government programs, selective migration to cities, and occupational and industrial mobility, all delimited by age, sex, and race.

As a mode of analysis, therefore, demographic analysis may be utilized by an economist or other specialist. The demographer may be particularly skillful with the mathematics of the demographic equation, but as soon as he begins to work with real data he is impelled to adopt the stance of one or another substantive discipline, be it economics, sociology, public health, or whatever. My approach is that of a sociologist preferring a demographic mode of analysis and concerned with selected aspects of social change. These aspects include those pertaining to the basic demographic equation—fertility, mortality, and migration—together with related topics that must be taken up in a sociological discussion.

FERTILITY

In the demographic equation, fertility is the fundamental source of population increase. Hence, the study of Negro fertility plays a key role in assessing and anticipating Negro population trends. Other reasons for studying Negro fertility are more closely and concretely connected to major social problems and the formulation of policy. Children are consumers, and the family which has many children must allocate a greater proportion of its economic resources to food, clothing, housing space, and medical care. Opportunities for saving are diminished, and the likelihood of financial crisis is increased. The demands children impose on their parents' time and energy reduce further the likelihood that either parent will acquire additional education or on-the-job training or make other investments in their own human capital. The association between poverty and large families is well known. There is every likelihood that the causation is reciprocal.

From a policy perspective, social problems associated with high fertility have a particularly useful trait. A small target population in the parent generation accounts for a large share of the target population in the child generation. Consider a group of forty families with adequate incomes and two children each and ten poor families with eight children each. Fifty per cent of the children are reared by poor families, but these may be reached by economic or social assistance programs directed to only 20 per cent of the families.

Throughout the period for which reasonable estimates have been made, fertility rates in the Negro population have exceeded those among whites. At a detailed level there have been numerous divergencies in trends. Unfortunately, there has been little work at a detailed level. The major fertility studies of recent decades have deliberately confined their attention to the white population. The principal methodological innovation, the development of concepts and techniques for cohort analysis of fertility, was initially applied to data for whites.[6] A review of existing studies, mainly based on unrefined techniques or highly aggregated data, reveals a number of puzzles. Many of these are amenable to further research, and their solution would contribute to an understanding of contemporary trends.

Historical evidence suggests that fertility must have been at very high levels among the slave population.[7] Despite high mortality and low rates of in-migration during the nineteenth century, Negro population increased rapidly. Beginning with the Civil War and continuing until the 1930's, Negro birth rates fell sharply. A very abrupt postwar rise—the "baby boom"—was followed eventually by a downward trend which became very distinct in the early 1960's.[8]

Negro fertility declined after the Civil War in the South as well as the North, in rural as well as urban areas. In fact, much of the decline occurred while the overwhelming majority of Negroes remained concentrated in the rural South. Among whites, fertility declined throughout the nineteenth century. Urbanization and economic development clearly cannot be adduced as direct causal factors in these fertility declines, but other factors are difficult to specify, especially for the Negro population. Currently available data are so limited as to preclude any thorough analysis. Farley considered and rejected an argument that the decline in Negro fertility was associated with changing age at marriage or marital patterns, but he was unable to develop a positive case for other factors:

> This discussion has not isolated the precise reasons for declining Negro fertility. The abrupt change in the social system which followed emancipation and the continued exclusion of Negroes from the dominant white society obviously influenced the reproductive practices of Negroes. These disruptive changes along with the prevalence of fertility inhibiting diseases apparently were the chief factors accounting for the declining fertility rates.[9]

The role of disease requires further study to specify a range of magnitude for its impact on fertility. Farley's estimates indicate some deterioration in mortality rates among the Negro population in the post-Civil War years, presumably because of deterioration in economic circumstances, diet, and general health. Debilitating disease, especially pellagra, may have contributed to lower rates of childbearing. During the twentieth century, Negro life expectancy rose. Although general improvements in health might have tended to enhance fertility, it is only after 1940 that marked increases occurred in the proportion of births in hospitals and, presumably, in the extent of formal maternal health care. By contrast, military health records from both World Wars reveal a high prevalence of venereal disease among Negro examinees. These data are consistent with a variety of other indications that venereal disease may have produced high rates of complete and partial sterility and that these medical factors may account for a substantial share of the childlessness observed among Negro families. The medical control of venereal disease might help explain the marked reductions in childlessness in recent years and sustained high Negro fertility during the 1950's.[10] Although it seems quite likely that trends in medical infertility are related to trends in Negro fertility, more work should be done to estimate plausible ranges for the magnitude of the association.

During the 1950's, Negro fertility remained sharply higher than white fertility and apparently did not begin to decline until several years after a fall in rates for whites. Unfortunately, absence of regular and prompt preparation of cohort fertility series for Negroes precludes precise specification of trends. But it is important to know the degree to which trends for Negroes correspond with those for whites, the degree to which they are similar except for a time lag, and the degree to which they diverge. It would then be possible to test alternative interpretations. For white fertility, estimates have been developed of the impact of changing rates of marriage, changes in age at marriage, changes in the timing of births within marriage, and changes in the total number of children ever born.[11] Some of these changes have been linked to changes in the economic outlook confronting young couples.[12] Similar estimates could be prepared for Negro fertility, and they might present a quite different picture from that garnered from the crude measures currently available.

In recent years, some of the special fertility studies which collect a broad range of attitudinal and behavioral data have included Negroes. The 1960 "Growth of American Families" study collected interviews for nonwhites in its sample.[13] One chapter of the published report was devoted to fertility of "nonwhites": 256 Negroes, 10 Japanese, 1 American Indian, 1 Chinese, 1 Eskimo, and 1 native of Guam. The general conclusion was that fertility attitudes and behavior of nonwhites in many respects resemble those of whites.

> If we combine couples in the college group with noncollege couples who have had no Southern farm background, we find that whites and nonwhites have approximately the same past and expected number of births. Inasmuch as this group contains 63 percent of the nonwhite couples, we may say that a majority of nonwhite couples have and expect about the same number of births as similar white couples.[14]

This conclusion corroborates analyses of census data showing the locus of Negro high fertility to be among poorly educated rural southern Negroes, particularly farm residents. During the 1940's and 1950's, there was a rapid displacement of Negroes from agricultural employment, first as tenants and then as laborers. Extensive urbanization of Negro population occurred in the South as well as the North, and educational levels improved markedly. Throughout these years, the proportion of Negro couples in the high fertility category should have been diminishing and the proportion in the group with fertility similar to whites should have been increasing. Hence, declining fertility among Negroes, or at least convergence between white and nonwhite rates, might have been anticipated but has not occurred.

Reviewing the trends in the late 1950's, Lee and Lee saw the persistence and widening of differences as a temporary aberration, a result of factors which would soon diminish in importance: "These include the continued improvement in general health and the lowering of the incidence of venereal disease, the decrease in maternal and fetal deaths, the possibly increasing stability of the Negro family, and the probably continuing economic development." [15] I must note again the need to specify estimated magnitudes for hypothesized effects. It is within the technical capacity of demography to estimate the effects on fertility of changes in the incidence of venereal disease or the stability of the Negro family. Improved data are necessary also to enhance the possibilities for fruitful analysis.

Census questions on number of children ever born have been asked only of ever-married women. Many fertility surveys restrict their universe even more narrowly, to women married once, husband present. Census analyses and other survey approaches, therefore, overlook a portion of fertility that is particularly significant among the Negro population. Farley has estimated that 2 per cent of the increase in the nonwhite general fertility rate 1940–1960 "is attributable to high proportion of women married, 54 percent to more childbearing by married people and 44 percent to rises in the illegitimate birth rate." [16] There is an air of unreality about (or at least a severe restriction on the utility of) studies which ignore illegitimate births. Analyses using vital statistics are not hampered by this limitation. Birth certificates are issued for all babies, and the marital status of the mother is confined to the confidential portion of the certificate.

Illegitimacy has been discussed more as a separate social problem than as an aspect of reproductive behavior. An unusually broad analytic approach was outlined in provocative fashion in an attack on the Moynihan report:

> The authors of *The Negro Family* take at face value Census Bureau statistics that record illegitimacy for whites at about 3 percent, for Negroes at about 22 percent. More careful consideration, in the context of other well-known facts, would reveal not so much a careless acceptance by Negroes of promiscuity and illegitimacy, as a systematic inequality of access to a variety of services and information.[17]

This view directs attention away from the end result of illegitimate births to the prior occurrence of what might be termed illegitimate intercourse.

> From the known data, we can conclude only that Negro and white girls probably engage in premarital intercourse in about the same proportions, but that the white girl more often takes Enovid or uses a diaphragm; if she gets pregnant, she more often obtains an abortion; if she has the baby, first she is more often able to conceal it, and second, she has an infinitely greater opportunity to give it up for adoption.[18]

The analysis consisted simply of a quick (and unreliable) guessing game to partition out the total illegitimacy differential to differentials in reporting, shotgun marriage, abortion, contraception, and so forth.[19]

More generally, illegitimate births result from a specific temporal sequence of events and nonevents: nonmarriage, coitus, nonregulation, conception, nonabortion, fetal survival, nonmarriage, birth, infant survival, nonmarriage.[20] A full analysis would have to examine racial differentials at each step. Attention should be directed not simply to explaining away racial differentials but to pulling together and elucidating available information about each of these behaviors. We should learn not only how they differ by race but how they vary by education, by residence, and by class and how the entire sequence fits in the total context of patterns of reproductive behavior in American society.

Much of the existing work on Negro fertility is devoted to specification and interpretation of white-nonwhite differentials. What should be the goal in such studies? The analyst typically tries to specify or control for the effects of white-nonwhite differences in age composition, marital status, socioeconomic characteristics, and so forth. Whatever fertility differential remains is identified as the "race effect." As a residual variable, the magnitude of the race effect may be greatly influenced by the number and variety of variables included in the analysis. Hence, there is always some question of interpretation of the race effect. In any analysis, this should be explicitly clarified by elucidating the theoretical perspective underlying the methodology.

Explicit justification of one's methodological approach is particularly important for Negro-white comparisons because of the difficulty of effectively standardizing or controlling for some of the key socioeconomic variables. Consider the 1960 fertility study, in which an attempt was made to match 270 nonwhites in the sample with whites having similar characteristics.[21] The sample contained few whites of low socioeconomic status. It was impossible to effect a complete match simply on occupational level, let alone on several variables simultaneously. Thus, the nonwhites and matched whites both had about 12 per cent living on southern farms, but the average income for these nonwhite husbands was $1,900 compared to $4,000 for the whites. Even if matching is formally possible, or if other control techniques are utilized, can the methodological objectives be fulfilled if the mere fact of being Negro affects the meaning of each status and has other pervasive social implications?

Analysis of white-Negro differences entails many sticky issues if the goal is to parcel out aggregate differences to various separate effects, one of which is a residual race effect. An alternative approach begins with an assumption that white and Negro populations may respond differently to socioeconomic and other relevant variables. Separate analyses may be carried out for each racial group, regressing a fertility measure on a common set of explanatory variables. Only in the null case that the regression coefficients for the two equations are not significantly different is it appropriate to parcel out a simple race effect. Ordinarily the regressions will differ, indicating that effects of socioeconomic or other variables differ by race. Specification of such interactions is an appropriate task, and such regression equations contribute directly to a social accounting framework.

The goal of a social accounting framework is neither to explain away race differentials nor simply to identify race effects. Rather it is to indicate the manner in which Negro fertility is responsive to other variables and the effects it in turn has on other variables. The kinds of regression analyses discussed above meet this need to an extent, but they have one serious defect: they are typically derived from cross-sectional studies. They permit us to specify how Negro fertility varies, for example, with income, but only in a static sense. To be of maximum use to policy formulation, the accounting framework must be dynamic. The more useful question to be answered is not how fertility of Negro families with incomes below the poverty line compares with that of families above the poverty line, but how does the fertility of families with low incomes change if an income maintenance program moves their incomes up. Longitudinal inferences from cross-sectional data are unreliable guides to actual dynamic relationships.

Sophisticated cohort analyses can put some dynamic character into fertility studies. The temporal character of such data typically pertains only to fertility itself, and not to the full range of socioeconomic and other associated variables. Retrospective questionnaires, in which the respondent provides a temporal history for each item of information, can overcome this problem, but errors and biases in recall together with other technical difficulties limit the scope and effectiveness of retrospective studies. We now need to invest substantial resources in longitudinal studies designed to provide direct information on the dynamics of family formation and fertility. I shall comment further on this in the next section.

New data collection is essential for pursuit of many research questions, but others can be studied profitably with existing census data, vital statistics, and governmental and private survey files. Imaginative analyses and tedious retabulation can yield a rich pay-off. A noteworthy example is Farley's utilization of historical census data to estimate trends in Negro fertility and mortality during the nineteenth century.[22] For recent decades he was able, without extensive resources or expensive special tabulations, to construct from published data the first cohort fertility series for Negroes.

Established scholars sometimes undertake this further mining of existing underexploited data, but it is necessary to rely especially on young scholars, including those writing master's theses and doctoral dissertations. They are more likely to have the time and patience to undertake the sort of work required. What is often lacking is financial support to permit the necessary retabulation and data manipulation. Considering the millions of dollars already invested in censuses, vital statistics, and other fertility data, additional exploitation comes at a bargain price. In addition to project-by-project review of appropriate proposals, a funding agency should encourage production of general samples of data files which can be put in the hands of researchers. An example is the 1/1000 sample tape from the 1960 census; a similar vital statistics sample might be feasible. For the purposes at hand, special tapes for the Negro population are essential. Thus, the census 1/1000 tape includes too few Negroes for complex analysis of most topics, but a 1/100 Negro tape could be prepared. It would be large enough to be useful and small enough to be economically processed. This approach has the potential of opening new realms of analysis to young scholars with small research budgets as well as to established scholars who want to experiment.

Contraceptive use is an important determinant of fertility levels. (It is necessary to recall, however, that large declines in European birth rates occurred long before the development and widespread use of modern contraceptive devices and that contraceptives may be used for careful spacing of a large family.) What are the patterns of contraceptive use among the Negro population? How are these patterns changing? What is the process of diffusion of the pill and other new contraceptives among the Negro population? Is this similar to the process among the white population, but with a time lag? Or is there some difference in process as well as in timing? Is the process different among Negroes than among other low-income groups? The 1965 National Fertility Study is the first large fertility study to oversample Negroes.[23] It will provide partial answers to many of these questions. It cannot bear the full burden of providing such information, but should serve as one of a continuing series of studies of the dynamics of reproductive control in the United States.

Encouragement of rational family planning has long been an active program of planned parenthood groups and other private agencies. Recently many public health, welfare, and other governmental agencies have become interested in family planning programs. Birth control is a live public issue; many decisions are being made and programs activated without waiting for sociologists to acquire additional knowledge of the basic social processes. To the activists, such knowledge is likely to be regarded as irrelevant. They think it obvious that it is easier to disseminate contraception than to seek indirect changes in fertility through dissemination of education, jobs, money, or new values.

A number of sophisticated researchers concur in the view that we already possess the knowledge needed to launch effective family planning programs on a mass basis among high fertility populations. A leading exponent of this approach, Donald J. Bogue, emphasizes the readiness, indeed eagerness, of people for knowledge of birth control. He sees great utility to mass communication and mass motivation programs which cater to this readiness. Major results can be achieved with a small expenditure of funds, man power, and time. For a first large demonstration project, Bogue chose a ten-square-mile strip of Chicago's West Side predominantly Negro slum. By extensive mailings, advertising, mobile clinics, and other inexpensive efforts, the program aimed to make birth control a topic of casual conversation to stir up the community.[24]

Because the boundaries of the target population cannot be defined with precision, the principal evaluation of the Chicago program rests on analysis of trends in Negro fertility in the core study area compared with trends elsewhere in the city and nation.

A rather careful analysis of the evidence available supports the conclusion that the birth rate among the low-income groups of Chicago, and especially the Negro population, has undergone a genuine decline in the last five years. The size of this decline is extraordinary and exceeds the changes that were occurring at the national level. It is greatest among the population group that was the principal recipient of the program of accelerated family planning service, begun by Planned Parenthood in 1960–61 and supplemented by a mass communication program conducted jointly by Planned Parenthood and Community and Family Study Center, 1962–1965. The timing of the greatest decline among this population corresponds to phases of intensive communication activity, lagged by about one year to allow for contraception to manifest itself in lowered fertility. It is difficult to avoid the inference, therefore, that these programs have had a significant effect upon fertility. This effect appears to have been not only direct, in stimulating people to come to Planned Parenthood Centers for service, but also much more pervasive and indirect. During the two and a half years of mass communication treatment, the low-income population has adopted contraception as a permanent part of its culture, via a process of private discussion and evaluation, provoked and stimulated by newspapers and other mass publicity.[25]

From a policy perspective, such a conclusion is highly welcome and encouraging. It suggests that a program with low costs per potential mother reached can nevertheless have a quick and major impact that continues permanently. Unfortunately, it is not yet certain that the program had the impact claimed for it. Estimates of fertility trends require assumptions about population trends as well as information on births. Alternative methodological procedures can produce more or less rapid rates of decline in the estimated rates of Negro fertility in Chicago.

The fact that such disparities in analyses are possible suggests perhaps that the only honest conclusion is that without better knowledge about net migration patterns after 1960 no one can reliably ascertain whether Negro fertility in Chicago has declined more, less, or by about the same percentage as white fertility in Chicago or nonwhite fertility in the nation.[26]

It is usually assumed that the test of a fertility control program is the trend in the birth rate, but examination of trends in birth rates is hardly sufficient evaluation of a program. For which women does the program accelerate the rate of adoption of effective contraception—those who already have four or five children or those with none, those with a stable marriage and a measure of economic security or those with no firm family ties and a bleak economic future? How has the family planning program altered or accelerated the ongoing processes of change in reproductive attitudes and behavior? Several studies arising out of the West Side Mass Communication Experiment have been issued, but the full set of evaluative studies has not yet been subjected to independent scrutiny. For the moment it is necessary to be cautious about drawing sweeping conclusions from limited data. Other contraception-dissemination programs have not been studied as intensively.

It is only because of the importance of discovering effective programs for fertility control that it is necessary to emphasize the obvious caveat that no single study can provide a sound basis for rational policy formulation. At best a single study can demonstrate some degree of effectiveness for a particular approach and can provide some experimental evidence for the comparative utility of minor variations within that approach. In a mass communications program, for example, a well-designed study can provide comparative evaluations of different types of mailings and procedures for following contacts. But a single study cannot pit against each other all the approaches suggested by current knowledge of reproductive behavior. Hauser has spelled out a number of considerations for a broad series of experiments in fertility control, and he has recently reasserted the need for research as well as action programs.

> The family planning movement is in a hurry and well it might be. No reasonable person can take issue with the objective of bringing about fertility control as rapidly as possible. But the wish does not necessarily produce the objective. And the possible quarrel with the present family planning movement is not with what it is attempting to do or with what it is doing. It is rather with what it is failing to do—and, that is, it is failing to explore or to administer longer range as well as the short range programs against the possibility that its fundamental assumption and basic premise . . . may prove to be erroneous. The family planning movement is failing to insure itself against the failure of its present rationale and methods. This is dangerous because at the present time it is not known whether the direct approach being used will in fact turn out to be a short cut in inducing social change. It is not yet known whether a birth control communications program and a birth control clinic will, in fact, bring about a more rapid decline in the birth rate than improved and universal general education, or new roads facilitating communication, or improved agricultural methods, or a new industry that would increase productivity, or other types of innovations that may break the "cake of custom" and produce social foment.[27]

That Hauser is concerned with world-wide, high fertility populations does not negate the relevance of his perspective to the Negro population in the United States. What seems to work on Chicago's West Side may not work on the near South Side or far South Side, nor may it be the most efficient or effective procedure in Atlanta or the Mississippi Delta. Experimentation in broad approach as well as in detailed refinement should be a part of any sizable investment in action programs. Only in that way can sufficient knowledge be developed to permit not only long-run economies but long-run successes.

FAMILY PATTERNS

A fascinating account of the controversy stirred up by the Moynihan report on *The Negro Family* has been published by Rainwater and Yancey.[28] Not the least virtue of their volume is its reprinting of many documents central to the public debate. For all the statistical trappings of the original report, a hard appraisal of this literature reveals a strikingly small body of facts on which to base such a large amount of political discussion. There is no doubt that a higher percentage of Negro than of white households has a female head, that the incidence of family breakup among Negroes is higher, and that many Negro children do not spend their entire childhood in a single intact family. But in the study of family patterns (as in the study of fertility) there has been little penetration beyond gross indicators to analysis of underlying processes. "The great classic studies of marriage and family among Negroes in the United States—those by Frazier, Davis, Dollard, Johnson, Warner, Reid, Sutherland, and Drake and Cayton—are now at least a generation old. No one can afford to reject or even to ignore them, but they do not reflect current situations." [29]

We cannot be content with invocation of the heritage of slavery and resurrection of the insightful case studies of the rural South. Rather we must accept Jessie Bernard's charge, made by way of prefatory explanation for her audacity in writing at book length on *Marriage and Family among Negroes*: "The major contribution of the present book may be its greatest defect: the data for most of the chapters are extremely thin. There are serious gaps in our knowledge of marriage and family among Negroes, and it is hoped that—by focusing attention on these gaps—this book will encourage researchers to fill them." [30]

As with fertility research, I shall emphasize approaches to family research that exploit existing data, and then sketch some requirements for new data. I shall conclude this section with a brief review of other types of needed family studies, particularly those relevant to current policy considerations.

Census and similar survey data are well suited to many investigations of family composition (relationships among persons living with relatives) and household composition (relationships among persons living in the same housing unit). These data underlie current knowledge of the prevalence of female heads of Negro families and of the greater frequency of lodgers and other nonrelatives in Negro households. Existing census data are amenable to analysis at a much more specific level of detail than has yet been undertaken. For example, variation in the prevalence of female heads of family among Negroes (and among poor whites) in states and local communities could be related to variation in state and local welfare regulations.

A number of other topics are amenable to demographic analysis.[31] Consider the percentage of the population of each age that lives outside of households, in rooming houses, dormitories, military barracks, prisons, and other institutional arrangements. For whites, this percentage peaks at about 15 per cent at ages 20–24, plummets to near zero through middle age, and rises slowly in old age. For nonwhites, the percentage peaks in much the same fashion, but drops only gradually through adulthood and fails to rise during old age. For whites, then, nonhousehold living is concentrated at the ages of transition from parental to independent family status and of widowhood. But who are the Negroes living outside of households? Where are they? What are their living arrangements? What are their social characteristics? Not all questions of their social integration can be answered from census data, but a good start could be made without any further data collection.

The unusual family composition among Negroes is not confined to the prevalence of female heads. Nonnuclear family combinations are much more common among Negroes than whites. Inclusion in the family of relatives of the head, other than spouse and children, may represent a type of extended family system, perhaps derivative from the matriarchal family pattern. Do unattached adults simply move in with Mom? Or is this type of living arrangement primarily a response to Negro migration patterns which lead persons to new environments in which only the tie of kinship legitimates a claim for aid and friendship?

Census data reveal among the Negro population many grandchildren of the head living in families that do not include any member of the intervening generation. There are also many children not related to the head. How common a practice is it to leave the children down South while the parents (or mother) go North to establish themselves? Is this behavior concentrated among recent migrants? Does it represent a temporary adaptation to migration or other family crisis, or is it a more permanent feature of the kinship and family system?

Although many of these questions can be pursued quite usefully with current census and survey data, the limits of existing information are quickly reached. How permanent are the distinctive family and household organizations? Are the same persons repeatedly drifting into and out of these nonhousehold or extrarelative situations? Or are such arrangements utilized by any one family only occasionally and temporarily during crises? Are children who are left behind typically reunited with their parents after a few months, or is such an arrangement typically of longer duration?

For selected aspects of family structure and household composition census data provide an opportunity for significant research. For other aspects of family structure census data are inadequate or irrelevant. Much of the information currently obtained from censuses or surveys is of the snapshot variety, descriptive of a current or recent status but not of the process or timing of change. Limited flow data are obtained from questions on duration of marriage and place of residence five years before. To acquire more extensive longitudinal information it has been common to rely on the comprehensive life histories obtainable by a case study approach. Such an approach is likely to be inappropriate for specification of prevalence or incidence in the population or estimation of parameters in multivariate analysis. I believe that a variety of sensitive and difficult longitudinal information could be collected in national surveys. Such data would be of tremendous value for assessing the kinds of issues being raised about Negro family dynamics.

What is needed is the systematic collection through survey procedures of individual and family life histories. Starting with current circumstances and working backward in the life cycle, I should want to obtain a retrospective diary of certain categories of events. Each change of residence might be recorded, together with the chronicle of changing family and household composition. Education and employment histories must be correlated with the residence and family histories. Collection of such retrospective histories is feasible, if troublesome. It is necessary to formulate procedures that permit overlooking some of the endless detail in the biographies of selected individuals—the full itinerary of the traveling salesman, for example.[32]

Among many other topics that could be included in such life history surveys is one behavioral domain central to discussions of Negro family patterns, but hitherto excluded from large-scale surveys. It is essential to obtain representative empirical knowledge of periods of consensual marriage as well as legal marriage and, to the fullest extent possible, of less stable periods of cohabitation. The goal should not be to reproduce the detailed sexual histories of the Kinsey or Pruitt-Igoe studies.[33] Rather it is to delimit generalized patterns of sexual behavior in the life history so that periods of marriage, separation, and other forms of relationship may be placed in sequence with respect to one another and to other events in the life cycle. There are no studies which analyze these behaviors in any representative sample of the population or allow any magnitudes to be placed on the prevalence of behavior sequences such as true desertion or pseudo-desertion in response to man-in-the-house rules. Similar information is equally needed and equally lacking for the white population. I think a feasible approach to data collection can be modeled on fertility studies which have obtained reproductive and contraceptive histories.[34] Extension to additional topics of family formation and relationships should be possible. Most people like to talk about themselves. In appropriate circumstances they casually discuss all sorts of intimate and sensitive topics. Taboos are imposed more often by the timidity of the researcher or his financial sponsor than by his respondents.

Retrospective data have several limitations. They are subject to biases of recall. It may be difficult or impossible to rearrange the longitudinal information so as to identify the population exposed to risk of some events. The information obtained pertains mainly to the more distant rather than the more recent past. Prospective studies, in which the same population is followed up through time, overcome these difficulties to some extent and provide a more reliable basis for longitudinal analysis. Ideally a series of prospective studies should be tacked onto the retrospective surveys, and a base thus established for continuing, current, dynamic investigation of social processes.

Consider one of the most interesting findings from the Moynihan report. Male Negro unemployment rates for one year were highly correlated with indices of Negro family instability (new AFDC cases and per cent of married women reported as separated) for the following year. The original memorandum presenting these correlations noted that "the number of separated women is many times the number of unemployed men they could be separated from." [35] Such a comment may not take adequate account of the dynamics of the situation, of the total male movement into and out of employment and the total cumulative impact on marital separation, but current sources do not provide appropriate flow data. Longitudinal studies could assess whether the marital separation is associated directly on an individual family basis with unemployment. Perhaps the association is only an aggregate one, indicating that rates of marital separation and of unemployment both respond to changes in the general economic climate. We also need to know whether marriages that are disrupted during periods of high unemployment are subsequently reconstituted or whether each partner goes on to a new relationship.

Good retrospective data can provide some of the answers. Good prospective data would help resolve the more intricate analytic questions. They would, for example, permit a test of Moynihan's assertion that the relationship may have broken down because of a new crisis stage in Negro community and family life. Empirically, this implies that the structure of relationships among variables has changed, that the equations formerly appropriate within the social accounting framework are no longer empirically adequate.

Development of a system of social accounts demands comprehensive longitudinal data. Such data are expensive to obtain and expensive to analyze. The cheapest approach would be to conduct limited surveys in a few strategic areas: a large northern metropolis, a southern city, a rural area. Restriction of the universe would omit some of the variability that complicates analysis. Restriction of geographic scope would also hold down interviewing costs. But I think there is a strong need for including existing variability, for developing national estimates, for being able to tie in with census analyses. Cost reduction (and perhaps better design and analysis) can be achieved by limiting the range of topics covered in any one survey. Sharply focused studies of specific crucial questions have many advantages in design and analysis over omnibus surveys. In the long run, social accounting techniques must be developed to handle masses of data and assess complex longitudinal multivariate relationships. We have not yet demonstrated the requisite skills, and it may be premature to broaden the range of data collected in any one survey too far beyond current analytic capabilities.

The major sociological studies of Negroes and race in American society have all emphasized family structure. The Moynihan report and the ensuing controversy brought Negro family structure to the forefront, at least temporarily, of political discussion and civil rights debate. The United States currently lacks any coherent policy on family structure or family rights, and hence many programs have been undertaken with individuals as the focus in ignorance of the effects on families. Why is this inadequate? Two reasons were specified by Lewis:

> It is through the family that the individual enters into the privileges and liabilities bestowed upon him as a citizen. And it is through the family that the effects of his citizen status first impinge on his inner circle and his inner self. The family acts, not merely as conduit, but rather as agent, reagent and catalyst. It defines the child's world for him; and it, initially, defines him to himself.
>
> The functions of the family are discussed chiefly in terms of what it does for children, and the emphasis is accurate. Yet the viability of the family depends on the satisfactions and supports it offers to adults, since it is they who determine whether a family unit survives or dissolves. Moreover, what the family can offer to its children depends on the psychological, social, physical and economic status of the adults who preside over it.[36]

The Moynihan report hinted at a third level of family influence: on the community as a viable organized structure of relationships:

> The fundamental problem . . . is that of family structure. The evidence . . . is that the Negro family in the urban ghettos is crumbling. A middle-class group has managed to save itself, but for vast numbers of the unskilled, poorly educated city working class the fabric of conventional social relationships has all but disintegrated. . . . So long as this situa-

tion persists, the cycle of poverty and disadvantage will continue to repeat itself.[37]

Lewis reviews a considerable body of research on family structure and its effects on children and adults, but no easy generalizations can yet be substantiated about most of the major questions. For example, the presumed deleterious effects on children of being raised by only one parent do not always reveal themselves empirically. Many children of all races and classes are raised by one parent or shift families during childhood. It is not at all clear that Negro family structure plays much of a direct role in undermining the aspirations and adaptiveness of Negro youth. The poverty, restrictions on opportunity, and social repression that presumably account for much of the Negro-white difference in family structure may also carry most of the direct responsibility for the difficulties of Negro youth. In my discussion of fertility I indicated how difficult it is to formulate questions of this type in researchable fashion, let alone to conduct appropriate research. The general aim of research is a series of multivariate expressions of family structure as consequence, cause, and intervening variable in the total social situation of Negroes.

Three types of research hold promise for contributing to this multivariate accounting framework. One type is the retrospective and longitudinal survey, which has the potential, largely unrealized, for bringing within its domain most of the postulated causes and consequences together with a variety of measures of family and community relationships. A second type is the smaller, more intimate survey or investigation in which the investigator personally tries to identify in the field the subtle interplay of social behaviors. Much of the work cited by Lewis is of this kind.

A third type is research into the operation and effectiveness of action programs. As with family planning campaigns, so with family viability campaigns, the best test of partially supported ideas may be their attempted implementation. My previous remarks concerning the need for appropriate experimentation and control apply also to family programs. We cannot afford to bet all our resources on any one action approach. The social sciences simply are not developed to the point where scientific consensus points clearly to any single means to a given end. Lewis' paper raised the question of which federal programs

seem to be moving effectively in needed directions—i.e., programs such as the following: Aid to Families of Dependent Children; public housing, and other Federal aid to housing; day care; vocational training and rehabilitation; employment counseling and services; training and use of non-professional aids; family counseling and education; medical and survivors' insurance; foster family and group family care; social and protective services for children; federal aids to education? [38]

The list could be expanded; my point is to emphasize the shameful waste occurring if any of these programs is operated without appropriate evaluation research. In turn, evaluation research is inefficient unless appropriate experimental design influences program planning from the outset. One of the great barriers to insightful social science research on practical topics and action programs is the tendency to call in the research team as an afterthought and assign it a narrow mission. Given the state of current knowledge, any program must be viewed as but one step in a continuing experimental effort. If that total effort is not appropriately designed, the successive steps will not be cumulatively sounder and more effective.

HEALTH

Illness often removes a person temporarily from participation in the normal activities of his group, and mortality removes him permanently from the population. Statistics on morbidity and mortality are woefully inadequate for the Negro population. I shall briefly sketch some of the difficulties with data and some of the problems which could be analyzed more adequately, were better data available.

There is a long tradition of registration of deaths by civil officials, but only within the past few decades did death registration become nearly complete throughout the United States. The National Center for Health Statistics compiles national mortality data from records of the various state and local registration systems. For calculation of death rates, registration figures must be related to population base information obtained from census counts and intercensal estimates. Types of undercounting and error in registration systems differ from those in censuses. Correcting both the numerator (deaths) and the denominator (population) for estimated undercount of Negroes yields rates significantly different from those using uncorrected data.[39] Comparison with death rates expected on the basis of technical demographic models indicates that official Negro death rates for 1910 to 1960 are subject to systematic biases.[40] A similar conclusion emerged from a careful analysis of yearly fluctuations in the official series.[41] Another recent study compared information on death certificates for persons dying shortly after the 1960 census with information reported for the same persons in the census. Serious distortions in such elementary items as sex and age were observed for the Negro population.[42]

Two recent reports summarize official data on levels and trends of white and nonwhite mortality.[43] Mortality rates for nonwhites are higher than those for whites at most ages, in most localities, and for most causes. Both reports presume that race differentials are attributable, at least in major part, to socioeconomic differentials, but death certificates provide little useful socioeconomic information. Hence no assessment of the magnitude of relationships between race, socioeconomic status, and mortality is possible from these sources. Neither report devotes attention to evaluation of the underlying data.

Many studies have collected morbidity data of one sort or another, but problems of standardization of procedures and representativeness of samples hamper generalization. For current information, the Health Interview Survey must be relied on as the most useful source.

> Data collected in the Health Interview Survey provide evidence that there is a marked difference in the health measures of the white and nonwhite populations. The rates of physician visits, dental visits, and hospital services are lower in the nonwhite population. Nonwhites report fewer chronic conditions than do whites, but the limitation of activity in the two groups occurs at about the same rate. The average number of restricted activity and bed disability days is higher in the white population, but the rate of work loss is higher among nonwhites.[44]

Even though they represent the best existing material, Health Interview results are difficult to interpret. Patterns of reporting of symptoms and of responding to a specific syndrome by bed rest or physician visit vary not only idiosyncratically but also according to social background and current circumstances. The recently inaugurated Health Examination Survey will provide medical information of a standardized character, but it will be some time before enough cases have been assembled to permit any significant analysis of Negro patterns or of white-Negro comparisons.[45]

In a recent review of a large number of studies of racial and socioeconomic differentials, Mechanic concluded that substantial differentials are not simply artifacts of poor data.

> These differences reflect a wide variety of factors: nutrition and exposure to disease, access to preventive medicine and medical care, protective health behavior, sanitary practices, and attitudes and ways of life. Above and beyond these factors, the data reflect further differences in mortality (especially between whites and nonwhites) which appear to be related to a deprived way of life, apathy and neglect, and a disorganized cultural pattern.[46]

Such a conclusion, even if it could be documented in a more convincing manner, does not provide the specification of relationships necessary for a social accounting system or for policy formulation.

Shortages of sound data and of research effort pose extreme difficulties in the way of advancing knowledge of relations of health and mortality of Negroes to other aspects of their social situation. One study currently being completed will contribute a significant new set of data centered on the 1960 census, and a similar project probably should be undertaken centered on the 1970 census.[47] This approach matches death certificates with census reports, thus permitting the mortality analysis to embrace the entire range of socioeconomic information collected in the census. If populations of persons suffering from certain illnesses could be identified for a time near the census date, similar matching could be undertaken to increase the scope of morbidity analysis. Retrospective inquiries directed to the person himself (or, in the case of death or debilitating illness, to a family member or other informant) can sometimes be used in lieu of matching to elicit a wider range of socioeconomic information than is included in hospital records, physicians' files, or death certificates.

Even with the best of data, there are analytic obstacles to inclusion of morbidity and mortality information in a general social accounting framework. Persons become ill or die from many different medical causes, each of which has its distinctive epidemiological pattern. To study death rates from all causes, death rates from major groupings of causes such as chronic illnesses or the cardiovascular group, disability days from all illnesses, or reported days of bed rest is to study an aggregate composed of many disparate elements. The design of action programs to reduce morbidity or mortality must be based on assessment of specific epidemiological processes. Reduction of excess Negro morbidity and mortality from hypertensive disease, for example, may require a program to increase Negro access to qualified physicians and to the appropriate treatment drugs,[48] whereas a reduction in Negro mortality from homicide may await radical change in the total societal pattern of racial discrimination.[49]

A greatly increased research effort is necessary in what may be termed social epidemiology or medical ecology. For each narrowly defined disease entity it is necessary to specify three patterns of influence: first, the effects on Negro morbidity rates and the course of the illness of insufficient access to medical care and lesser ability to carry out appropriate treatment; second, the effects of distinctive aspects of Negro life styles, including specification of the influence of residential crowding, inadequate nutrition, apathy, overwork, or other factors; and third, the character and effects of any genetic or physiological factors peculiar to the Negro population. These questions are so difficult and our current ignorance so great that quick answers cannot be expected even from a greatly expanded research effort.

MIGRATION AND POPULATION REDISTRIBUTION

During the decades following emancipation, Negroes continued as an impoverished, largely illiterate population in the rural South.[50] Most were employed as agricultural tenants or laborers. As late as 1910, 90 per cent of Negroes lived in the South, and 73 per cent lived in rural areas. In the succeeding fifty years, there were great changes in the distribution of Negro population. In 1960, 73 per cent of Negroes lived in cities, 40 per cent lived outside the South, and 86 per cent of employed Negro males were in nonagricultural industries. The Negro sharecropper virtually disappeared from the American scene, and Negroes became more urbanized than whites (73 vs. 70 per cent in 1960). These radical transformations occurred in a span of fifty years. What have been the highlights of the redistribution of Negro population?

The history of both white and Negro settlement in the United States is only a few centuries old. Most Negro immigrants, of course, were brought in as slaves. The total number of imported slaves from the first shipload in 1619 to the time of the Civil War has been estimated at about 670,000. By 1860, the total Negro population was 4.4 million, and it is apparent that most Negroes were already natives of native parentage, far removed from their immigrant origins.

The early pattern of Negro population distribution reflected the economics of slavery. Slavery spread from the Southeast to the Southwest in the early nineteenth century as cotton and tobacco cultivation expanded westward. Free Negroes were relatively few in number and were concentrated in the large cities of both North and South. On the eve of the Civil War, 11 per cent of Negroes were free, the rest slaves.

Emancipation and the subsequent period of Reconstruction engendered some alterations in patterns of race relations, but most were temporary, and there was little lasting effect on patterns of population distribution. There were no extensive organized programs to provide Negroes with new means of earning a livelihood. Urban economic opportunities for the newly freed Negroes were scarce. The process of southern economic recovery involved continued use of Negro labor on white-owned farms, under new forms of tenancy. The most striking feature of Negro population distribution in the period from 1860 to 1910 is its high degree of stability. Negroes remained heavily concentrated in the rural South.

By 1910, some indications of ensuing change were perceptible.

Negro migration from South to North was increasing rapidly, and several large northern cities had sizable and growing Negro populations. Within the South, new cities were springing up and old ones gaining population. Beginning about 1915, the rate of Negro urbanization from rural South to urban North increased to a high volume. Estimates of the net migration of Negroes out of the South indicate a volume of less than 100,000 in the 1870's and 1880's, nearly 200,000 in the 1890's and 1900's, 522,000 in the 1910's, and 872,000 in the 1920's.

Although patterns of social discrimination against southern Negroes may have been worsening, the timing of the abrupt acceleration in interregional migration clearly points to other factors as the proximate causes. New agricultural opportunities in the South had reached a peak (the number of Negro farm owners and tenants has declined steadily since 1920). A particularly severe drought and the spread of the boll weevil further depressed the economic circumstances of Negroes in portions of the South. But these "push" factors are insufficient in themselves; the radically changed circumstances seem to lie in the "pull" factors: the attractive force of northern cities. With the onset of World War I, European immigration, which had been bringing 1,000,000 persons a year into the United States, especially into northern cities, was halted. After the war, immigration resumed temporarily, only to be permanently reduced to low levels by restrictive legislation. With industrial prosperity, many northern firms turned to the Negro population as a source of unskilled labor.

The migrations out of the South sometimes assumed the character of a local exodus. Many villages and counties sent high percentages of their youth north. Between 1920 and 1930, nearly one-half of the young Negro males in the entire state of Georgia left for the North; many individual places lost at even greater rates. Not only was there an interregional movement to northern cities, but within the South both Negroes and whites were urbanizing rapidly. The urban percentage among southern Negroes never lagged far behind the corresponding percentage for southern whites. The rural Negro population of the South has been declining since 1910.

The Negro migrations of this early period remained economically rational in the sense that most migrants were able to find steady jobs, many of those who did not get along returned to the South, and the volume of migration slowed to low levels during periods of job scarcity. Total interregional migration averaged less than 100,000 Negroes a year on a net basis, well below the former volume of European immigration.

The worsening economic situation for industrial laborers may have begun slowing down the rate of Negro urbanization by the late 1920's. During the depression of the 1930's migration from South to North and urbanization within the South continued, but at substantially reduced levels. Drought combined with depression to lower drastically the economic status of Negroes in agriculture, while government welfare aid was perhaps more readily available to urban Negroes.

Despite a high rate of natural increase, the Negro population of the rural South diminished by more than 1.5 million between 1940 and 1960. The urban Negro population of the South increased by 3.0 million and that of the North by 4.6 million. Wartime industrial expansion was followed by a sustained period of postwar prosperity, and simultaneous changes in agricultural technology diminished opportunities in the South. From 1940 to 1959, the number of Negro sharecroppers in the South dropped from 299,000 to 73,000; other forms of farm tenancy dropped from 208,000 to 65,000; and Negro farm ownership dropped from 173,000 to 127,000. Urban opportunities were also changing. Negro men increasingly gained entry into the semiskilled ranks and to a lesser extent into skilled and white-collar occupations, while Negro women reduced their concentration in domestic employment.

Any migration stream which continues for a long period of time necessarily tends to alter circumstances at both place of origin and place of destination. The Negro migrations from the South to northern cities are an excellent example of this self-altering process. The out-migrations from the rural South were large enough not only to remove the natural increase but to deplete the population to the point where its ability to generate future migrants is severely limited. By 1960, 58 per cent of southern Negroes lived in cities, and the majority of the rural population was nonfarm. Furthermore there has been a rapid secular trend of improving education among successive cohorts of Negro youth. The rural supply of potential urban migrants includes fewer than ever poorly educated persons with an isolated, impoverished upbringing. Urban Negro populations, meanwhile, have reached such a large size that they produce a large volume of growth in themselves, simply by natural increase, and in-migration of a given volume now constitutes much less of a relative absorption burden than formerly.

Contemporary Negro migration takes place in the context of a highly urbanized population redistributing itself within a system of places which includes some rural counties, many southern towns, and large cities throughout the country. The type of migration which deposits illiterate peasants and farm tenants in a few gigantic metropolitan centers is no longer a major aspect of Negro population redistribution.

A comparison of northern Negroes born in the South with those born in the North shows recent migrants to be as well educated as the native northerners. Thus, in addition to the improvement over time in the educational levels of migrants and nonmigrants there has been a definite improvement over time in the educational levels of migrants relative to nonmigrants.

The best migration data refer to 1955–1960, and these document in sharp fashion the new character of Negro migration. Negroes are an urban people, and there is a sizable interchange among metropolitan areas. This interchange is selective of better-educated Negroes, who are also of higher economic status than nonmigrants and presumably are more aware of alternative opportunities. In many northern cities, the largest source of Negro population growth is natural increase. Even among the migrant component, migrants from other northern cities and from southern cities greatly outnumber migrants moving directly from the nonmetropolitan South.

Each of the large southern cities not only participates in an intermetropolitan system of exchange but also acts as a center of attraction for the remaining rural Negro population in its hinterland. These local migration streams, which, incidentally, flow in both directions, are the chief remaining ones which include significant proportions of persons with minimal educational backgrounds and little urban experience.

Urbanization of the Negro population in the United States has proceeded well beyond the stage reached by socially depressed groups in less urbanized and less industrialized nations. Even in its earlier stages, however, Negro migration appears to have been highly sensitive to economic considerations. Rather than contributing to "overurbanization," the Negro migrations may well have been salutary in reducing "overruralization." Although Negro migrants in the past were concentrated in a few large cities, in 1960, 18 cities (6 southern) had Negro populations in excess of 100,000. In 153 separate metropolitan areas, Negro population increased between 1950 and 1960 by more than 25 per cent.

For the total United States population, continued concentration in metropolitan areas has been accompanied by deconcentration within metropolitan areas. Additional population in a metropolitan area can be housed by increasing density in neighborhoods already built up or by developing new neighborhoods. The suburbanization of recent decades can be attributed in large part to the prevalence of the latter over the former. If political boundaries could be ignored, much of what is called suburbanization might be described simply as continued urbanization.

Political boundaries do make a difference—a decisive one for Negroes. Most metropolitan Negroes live within the central cities. Except for public housing projects, most Negro residents in large cities occupy older housing that, especially in the North, was once inhabited by whites. New housing, particularly in large developments at the periphery or in the interstices between already built-up areas, tends to be inhabited by whites only.

Residential segregation will be discussed in the section on housing. Here it suffices to note that the previously described convergence of Negro migration patterns toward those of whites refers to the dominance of intermetropolitan movement and a similarity in types of selectivities of migrants in different streams. If the focus is narrowed to intrametropolitan patterns of migration and population distribution, racial differences are striking. Negro residential areas can be viewed to some extent as subcities with the same basic patterns of population distribution and redistribution as found in the total metropolis. But constraints on Negro residential choice are so great that the analogy cannot be pushed very far.[51]

The preceding review of migration patterns and trends was based largely on regularly available census and other migration data. These data suffice for this kind of cursory review, but they are inadequate for detailed analysis, whether focused on basic research or policy issues. One of the greatest difficulties is that much of our knowledge of migration derives from information not on migration but on population redistribution. From the basic demographic growth equation, any change in population in a nation, region, state, city, or other geographic area may be allocated to natural increase plus net migration. Estimates of net migration, often by race, sex, and age, have been prepared for many places for many time periods. Useful as these estimates may be, they are of limited utility for the study of migration. The migration process is carried on by in- and out-migrants; there is no such person as a net migrant. Net migration for an area represents a balance between in- and out-migration. Net migration data do not permit identification of specific moves or specific migrants and do not permit analysis of characteristics of moves or migrants.

In the national data system, moves and migrants are identified primarily by census and Current Population Survey questions on residence at a fixed previous time (currently five years ago for the census and one year ago for the Survey).[52] If current and previous residences differ, a move from the latter to the former is assumed to have occurred. This identification of moves and migrants is imperfect. Persons who moved more than once may be misidentified. The net result of two or more moves may be treated as a single direct move from one place to another. These errors are assumed to be of small import, but four additional limitations of census and Survey data are more serious.

1. Particular categories of migrants are sometimes small in number relative to the volume of nonresponse to the migration question. This is more likely to be true for a one-year migration interval than for the five-year interval, but it is also troublesome, for example, in data for individual census tracts in poorly enumerated sectors of large cities. In addition to general improvement in enumerative procedures, special effort should be devoted to questions such as previous residence, which pose difficult problems of recall and correct response.

2. An individual's previous migration history is presumably of major relevance to his current and future migratory behavior; yet each move tends to be treated in isolation. The census or other general survey is not the place for a detailed residence history, but it could help greatly to specify the urban or rural character of birthplace (or other childhood residence).[53] Current practice identifies state of birth, a useful item permitting identification of southern-born Negroes living in 1960 in northern cities by residential location in 1955. Sociologically it would be interesting to know the type of place and not only the state in which an individual was raised. There is already evidence to suggest that the farm-born now in cities have much lower occupational status and much higher fertility than the "second-generation" urbanites. Certainly there are many questions about the adjustment of Negroes to urban life for which some specification of residential background would be highly useful.

3. The ahistorical character of much migration analysis is further exemplified by the tendency to treat migration separately from other forms of social mobility. Census information on changes in residence is not accompanied by parallel information on changes in marital status, family composition, occupation, industry, income, or type of housing. As a minimum for the census, major activity five years ago should be collected along with residential location, simply to identify roughly those migrants who were entering or leaving the labor force, school, or the armed forces.[54] Other studies must pursue the collection and utilization of more complicated life histories. As discussed in the section on family patterns, techniques of analysis of such life histories must be developed further before it will be warranted to request their regular inclusion in large-scale surveys.

4. Official statistics and many migration studies view the individual rather than the family or other social group as the unit of analysis. Thus there has developed a vast amount of material on patterns of

migration by age and sex, but there is no recognition in these data of the very obvious fact that most minor children and many women who move simply accompany a male family head. A recent national study of migration of family heads showed that "half of all the most recent moves in the last five years involved a married couple plus children. Only about two out of ten moves involved a single individual."[55] Because migration is frequently accompanied by the disruption and reformation of family units, and not all members of a migrating family may move at the same moment, it is difficult to establish simple procedures for delineating appropriate social units. Until this is done, however, only limited progress is possible in the specification of types of migrants and their characteristics.

I have emphasized national data needs because the analysis of migration patterns is peculiarly dependent on large national samples. It is usually desirable to specify migration streams according to characteristics of the places of origin and destination and to reconstitute the origin population at the beginning of a migration interval from destination data collected at the end of the interval. Local studies and small-scale studies simply cannot provide the basic data.

There are many specific issues concerning migration which are amenable to small-scale focused research, at least in the early stages of inquiry. The social psychology and economics of geographic mobility have both profited from small survey studies.[56] With respect to policy issues concerning Negro migration, current attention seems to be centered on two questions: how to reduce rates of movement to major urban concentrations and how to improve adjustment of migrants who nevertheless arrive in cities. In many large cities, the rate of in-migration of Negroes has slowed recently, and I suggest the first question should be redirected to places of origin. What is the social and economic outlook for Negroes remaining in the rural and small-town South? How has the social and economic structure of these areas been affected by previously high rates of outmovement?[57]

Helping new migrants adjust to city life is certainly a worthy endeavor, and studies of the adjustment process are a necessary accompaniment of any action program. For general social accounting purposes, however, I wonder whether migrants should be singled out for special study in lieu of more thorough examination of the various socialization processes continually occurring in cities. After all, the Negro youth brought up on Chicago's South Side may objectively be just as poorly prepared as the new migrant from Atlanta for exploiting the opportunities available to him. He may need just as much help learning to utilize employment services, realtors, city agencies, and the whole gamut of other adjustment services. The new migrant at least knows that he must seek alternatives.

HOUSING

The nation's housing stock may be viewed as a population of geographically distributed housing units that receives additions and deletions. Study of this population can rely heavily on various objective data collected in the decennial censuses (a Census of Housing accompanies each Census of Population) and in other federal surveys. At a national level, and in outline for individual large metropolitan areas, differences between units occupied by whites and those occupied by nonwhites have been delineated.[58] Housing occupied by nonwhites is older, in poorer condition, less well equipped with plumbing and other amenities, more likely to be crowded (in terms of persons per room), and more likely to be rented rather than owned.

With the accumulation of data from three decennial housing censuses it is past time for a comprehensive series of statistical analyses of race and housing. (A monograph based on the 1950 Census of Housing barely mentioned race.[59]) I shall comment briefly on four approaches that such analyses should emphasize: disaggregation, longitudinal analysis, geographic distribution and redistribution, and treatment of housing as a factor in social organization and disorganization.

Despite the proliferation of housing census data for specific localities, there has been little intensive analysis of areal data. One application for disaggregated data would be explanation of areal variation. Why are white-nonwhite differences more pronounced in one place than in another? Do cities which developed with an established Negro population differ from those in which Negroes came later and accommodated to an existing residential pattern? A second concern with disaggregated data is the opportunity for intensive analysis at the local level. In the early 1960's social scientists at the University of Chicago's Chicago Community Inventory prepared a proposal for analyses of residential patterns of race and ethnic groups, to be financed by the City of Chicago as part of its Community Renewal Program.[60] The first phase of work, relying on published data, was to entail updating *The Negro Population of Chicago*, analyzing in similar fashion the census data on the major groups of foreign stock (data last available for 1930), examining patterns of public- and private-school enrollment for small areas, and studying related topics.[61] The second phase of work was to be based on special tabulations that would link population census data for the members of a household with housing census data for their housing unit. These analyses, for one large city, were envisaged as a three-year project for two professional researchers. The proposal was not funded; the work was not carried out for Chicago; and I know of no similar analyses done for any other city.

Many more studies of race and housing must be given a longitudinal character. This is quite feasible with existing housing data. Directly designed for this purpose are the National Housing Inventories.[62] Each housing unit in a current survey is compared with that enumerated at the same place at a previous point in time. A determination is made of the reason for each addition to, or deletion from, the housing stock. Housing units may be born by new construction, conversion of a nonresidential structure, conversion of one unit into two, and so forth. Housing units may die by demolition, fire, combining two units into one, and so forth. The inventory permits specification of the frequency of each type of change and, in addition, permits cross classification of each unit by race of head at the earlier time and race of head at the later time. These data have proven useful in previous work on race and housing, but only a small share of their potentiality for intensive analysis and local studies has been realized.

A second type of longitudinal study takes the neighborhood as the unit of the analysis. The data may come from historical records or surveys on individual units (as in the Inventories), aggregated for street fronts, blocks, or other meaningful groups. Laurenti's analysis of price trends in neighborhoods to which a Negro family had moved partakes of this character.[63] The data may also come from putting together successive cross-sectional studies. An example is the Taeubers' analysis of changes in condition of units and in level of room crowding for census tracts classified by type of change in racial composition.[64]

Some neighborhoods are initially built up during a short time period and begin with a high degree of homogeneity in type of structure and price. Each such neighborhood may be viewed as a cohort of housing units entering the market at roughly the same time and sharing certain features of design, location, and other circumstances. The families or individuals initially attracted into a neighborhood may be somewhat homogeneous as to certain social and economic characteristics. Through time, it should be possible to trace changing characteristics of the housing and relate them to changing characteristics of the occupants. Some neighborhoods seem to be relatively stable, retaining not only their initial character but, in significant measure, their initial occupants for many years. The neighborhood and the residents grow old together. Other neighborhoods retain their character by continually serving as a transient location for families or individuals at a particular stage in the life cycle. Still other neighborhoods deteriorate and at successive points in time serve the residential needs of different types of clientele.

To assertions that a change from white to Negro occupancy accelerates housing deterioration, liberals commonly reply that deterioration antedates Negro occupancy and accelerates only to the extent that governmental or private maintenance and rehabilitation funds are unavailable to Negro areas. This kind of argument tends to proceed in a factual vacuum, for there simply has not been enough analysis of neighborhood dynamics. Which neighborhoods are maintained, and which deteriorate? What are the determinants of private and public allocation of resources to regular maintenance and to spot rehabilitation? How do the life cycles of neighborhoods relate to the life cycles of their inhabitants? [65]

One of the most controversial and most studied aspects of neighborhood dynamics is the change in housing price accompanying change in racial occupancy. Laurenti's analysis of *Property Values and Race* now stands as the chief evidence that the presence of Negroes in a neighborhood typically does not depress property values.[66] On the basis of this research and its extensive review of previous work, I suggest that the evidence is insufficient to support sweeping conclusions. Without asserting that Laurenti's results are erroneous, I believe the ready academic acceptance of the conclusions is a function of their conformity with what most of us hoped to be the case. If a study proposed that the presence of even an occasional Negro resident depressed neighborhood sales prices, there probably would be infrequent citation of this work and many harsh reviews of the fragile structure of evidence. I believe we all suffer from a tendency to accept at face value the results we anticipate or seek and to search diligently for biases and analytic subtleties casting doubt on findings we did not anticipate or do not approve of. With respect to the particular issue of race and sales prices, there is need for consideration of a much greater variety of neighborhoods and Negro "invasion" situations, with more attention to the sociological dynamics of the individual situations.

With respect to rental housing and race, the focus of attention has been not on whites but on Negroes and the premium they are presumed to pay because of the restricted supply of housing made available to them. In a cross-sectional analysis for Chicago in 1956, Duncan and Hauser identified an apparent $15.00 monthly higher rent for Negroes than for whites occupying substandard housing of a given number of rooms.[67] Examining changes in rents in selected Chicago neighborhoods from 1950 to 1960, Muth reached a different conclusion: "In summary, it would appear that there is no race differential in housing prices insofar as tenant-occupied housing is concerned. The tendency for average contract rents to rise slightly more rapidly in areas which switched to Negro occupancy than in those remaining in white occupancy during the fifties would appear to be due to increased crowding." [68] Muth's argument, based on his regression analysis, is that Negroes, for whatever reasons, tend to have larger households or more persons per unit than do whites, that greater crowding increases the rate of deterioration and the cost of maintenance, and that rents increase accordingly. As he goes on to note, however, "it is difficult to separate out statistically the effects of Negro occupancy and the condition variables."

Again we are confronted with methodological complications. Race is not distributed randomly with respect to all necessary control variables that should be included in our analyses. Hence appropriate statistical matching or control for intervening variables may be difficult or impossible. In the face of such obstacles, it is all the more important to have a variety of studies, utilizing differing methodologies and drawing on differing sets of data. By paying attention to the likely types of bias in data and method of each study, it may be possible to cumulate a number of weak studies into a stronger whole. Laurenti's monograph represents one such attempt, not fully successful. An impressive example of successful cumulation has occurred in work on smoking and lung cancer. No single study is without serious faults, but the presumptive biases differ from study to study. Discounting one finding therefore tends to strengthen another. This example suggests a value to varied efforts at evaluating a single thesis, particularly if no decisive empirical evidence can feasibly be obtained.

The central policy aspect of the geographic distribution of housing is racial residential segregation. The universally high degree of racial residential segregation in United States cities has been well documented.[69] Trends over time are diverse, but generally upward in degree, and there is no current indication of any significant success for any desegregation program. Although residential segregation shows some tendency to diminish in response to a loose housing supply and to improving Negro economic status, other societal forces are sustaining patterns of rigid segregation. Analysis of trend data demonstrates that no feasible indirect attack on residential segregation, such as income maintenance, rent supplements, or maintenance of a high aggregate rate of housing supply, is likely to reduce drastically the degree of segregation.

Certain desegregation programs are undoubtedly having some degree of success. Many Negro families have felt an expanded freedom of residential choice, and many white families have felt relief at successful "integration" of their neighborhoods. The aggregate effect on housing patterns, however, has not yet been measurable in any city. This pessimistic conclusion may be in error, but it entails assessment of census data through the mid-1960's.[70] Before an immediate harsh judgment is rendered on existing approaches to residential desegregation, account should be taken of the recency of most such efforts, the minuscule resources devoted to the cause, and the rather slow pace at which residential patterns can be expected to change. Nevertheless an analogy may be in order with the family planning movement, which, in response to its very sense of success, has come under increasing attack.[71] There are grounds for concern that the legal approach to residential desegregation and the emphasis on aiding individual families and neighborhoods may be insufficient. To a large extent the locus of the problem is in the racial prejudice of the white population. One path to solution might be sought in principles of social psychology, entailing analysis not merely of prejudice in general but of how it relates to views of home, house, and neighborhood.

Public attitudes toward racially mixed neighborhoods are mediated in large part by the organized real estate industry. Public concern about housing values and the propriety or decency of neighborhood diversity has been fostered and maintained by the actions of the industry. More research might fruitfully be directed to analysis of the housing market as a social institution.[72] Real estate agents, for example, may be viewed as gate-keepers, allocating people to residences according to a shared perspective on how this allocation should be accomplished.[73] Any assumption that the agent represents merely the wishes of his clients is a gross understatement of his role, but careful research is needed to delimit the powers he uses to perpetuate the industry view and, more important to policy, the powers he might use to alter traditional practice. The whole gamut of sociological approaches to study of occupations might be called into play. What are the patterns of selective recruitment into the real estate business? What are the mechanisms of socialization and social control of agents? What pronouncements or policies of organizational leaders can affect the day-to-day operation of the market so as to reduce the attention paid to race?

One assumption underlying many attitudes of the public at large as well as of the real estate industry is that residential neighborhoods not only should be but are in fact homogeneous. This homogeneity is presumed to pertain not only to race but also to housing type, economic status, and other attributes of the housing and its occupants. The empirical question of the degree and character of neighborhood homogeneity is rarely asked and has not been answered. To be sure, there exists a modest literature on the degree to which census tracts are homogeneous units, but this research begins with the homogeneity assumption and directs attention to the apparent ineffectiveness of census tract mapping as a means of delineating homogeneous neighborhoods.[74]

I referred previously to my view that Negro poverty has little to do with residential segregation. The argument supporting that view also casts doubt on the basic homogeneity assumption.[75] The argument has two facets: the first being simply that although Negro mean incomes are much lower than white mean incomes, there is nevertheless considerable overlap in income distributions and many Negro families are economically able to compete with whites for housing in the middle- and low-price ranges. The second part of the argument is that low-rent housing is not highly segregated from high-rent housing. Spatial distributions of low- and high-rent units differ, of course, but to nowhere near the degree observed for white and Negro units. If every Negro family were poorer than any white family, economic considerations still would not suffice to explain Negro residential segregation. The postwar Levittown, the Park Forest inhabited by William H. Whyte's organization men, the exurbia described by A. C. Spectorsky—these are not typical urban neighborhoods. Neither are the Manhattan tenement or the Chicago public housing project. The degree of residential homogeneity of socioeconomic groups is easily exaggerated. My analyses were not focused on the homogeneity issue, but they suggest the need for more careful consideration of the facts of urban structure. In addition, questions may be raised concerning the more subtle realms of the role of "the neighborhood" in allocating prestige, determining friendships, and so forth. If the homogeneity assumption must be abandoned, or at least seriously restricted, the character of such neighborhood effects should be reassessed. Research on these topics must embrace not only the special settings of the public housing project, the new town, or prototypical suburbia but also the typical urban conglomerate neighborhood.

There is a tendency for policies toward race and poverty to become intermingled. In particular, there is a tendency to look "beyond race" to see patterns of socioeconomic segregation as an underlying or emerging policy issue. At least with respect to residential segregation, however, it is not necessary to confront the socioeconomic patterns before it is possible to deal with racial residential patterns. It would be a major accomplishment indeed to reduce racial housing segregation to the level of socioeconomic segregation.

Racial discrimination is such an important cause of residential segregation that the existence of segregation in any city may be taken as prima facie evidence of inequities in the operation of the housing market. The antecedents of residential segregation, therefore, are clearly appropriate objects of public policy. How about the consequences of residential segregation? Do they give rise to policy issues? The answer is obvious, but precise specification within the social accounting framework is difficult. Residential segregation is the *de facto* segregation underlying segregation in schools, stores, places of employment, and many other institutions. Yet each of these other types of segregation has additional support from the general racism of the society and from various specific social patterns. Analytically, one cannot measure the degree to which residential segregation is a necessary or sufficient cause for any of the related patterns of segregation. We do not know what would happen if residential segregation were largely eliminated without simultaneous major changes in other types of segregation. The very notion seems a bit absurd.

Sociologists typically subscribe to the notion that any society must meet certain fundamental needs of man, among which is the provision of shelter. Sociology has little else to say about the relevance of housing patterns to other aspects of social organization or to the dynamics of interpersonal relations. The presumed deleterious consequences of segregated living are legion, but no general background of work in the sociology of housing exists to support empirical research and specification of these consequences.[76]

My own work on the measurement of residential segregation has focused on segregation as the phenomenon to be explained. I know of no good work treating it as an explanatory variable in the study of Negro political power, degree of racial tension, Negro occupational structure, white occupational structure, personality development, family stability, or health. For that matter, we cannot yet specify whether the types of housing occupied by Negroes have deleterious consequences independent of other disadvantages to which Negroes are subject. To be sure, the worst housing is distinctly unhealthy—there can be no controversy about rat bites. There must be study for both white and Negro populations of the consequences of high residential density, inadequate facilities, disrepair, and the like. (Analysis for the Negro population would be especially difficult because of the confounding of race with the suspected consequences of bad housing.)

Housing quality may be a symbol to oneself as well as to others of one's social situation, but aside from extreme instances of obvious danger to health and safety it has not been documented that varying degrees of housing quality have varying degrees of impact on social-psychological or organizational processes. I do not doubt that some such effects can be demonstrated, but the research effort to date has been grossly inadequate.

As an appendage to a discussion of demographic issues, this review of race and housing has assumed a very particular character, quite different from that it would have had as an appendage to the chapter on economics or politics or social psychology. Yet it belongs equally as well with any of them and might justifiably have been consigned, like education, to a separate chapter. My comments on housing have deliberately avoided review or evaluation of existing governmental housing policies. These exist in profusion, as witnessed by the cabinet-level Department of Housing and Urban Development. A correspondingly large literature has grown up around these policies, some of it empirically grounded, but much of it exhortatory. Most housing issues are linked with racial issues and might have been included in this discussion. They were excluded partly because I lack the competence for essaying a meaningful brief résumé of the many ongoing and proposed programs. Further, I believe that except for specific antidiscrimination policies, race is more of a complicating factor than a basic stimulus to policy. Programs to increase the supply of housing at lower values and rents, to increase demand for housing and improve mechanisms for matching supply and demand, to eliminate slums and facilitate rehabilitation—these are all complex, difficult, and necessary regardless of race.

CONCLUSION

I have indicated many needs for new data and many ways to spend money, but the greatest shortage is good people to conduct the research. Unfortunately, the kind of research called for is a voracious consumer of the limited time of researchers. These are not structured topics to be treated mechanically by research assistants.

From the perspective of those trying to foster policy-related research, one of the most pressing problems is the allocation of scarce research manpower to crucial research tasks. Researchers tend to define tasks as crucial in conformity with their own interests and sense of what is feasible. One approach to encouraging individuals to discover interests and define topics that contribute to a cumulative enterprise is to foster communication on the state of the general research enterprise. In addition to conferences, there may be pay-offs from selected efforts to pull things together by means of review monographs on topics such as Negro fertility, Negro family patterns, and neighborhood life cycles. Granted that each such topic needs much more research, relatively short-range efforts at systematic review of existing knowledge and cursory exploitation of unmined resources might be worthwhile. Such works tend to provide a common basis for discourse. Simply by their existence, if at all well done, they call attention to gaps in knowledge, to the state of the art, and to central research possibilities. The stimulus thus given to the total research enterprise—including the encouragement to graduate students seeking thesis and dissertation topics—may be more important than the direct utility of the monograph as a statement of current knowledge.

Competent established investigators can usually get money for their work; it is difficult for agencies, even well-funded ones, to attract qualified researchers to topics the agency thinks necessary. One approach is to facilitate mutual contact among investigators who happen to be working on related topics and keep them under pressure to interpret their findings in terms of policy issues. A second is forthright use of a carrot approach to encourage competent researchers to choose selected topics. The carrot must be both money and a convincing demonstration of professional and social urgency. This requires an appropriate mechanism to delineate research needs, select prospective personnel, and dangle carrots. Merely waiting for research proposals to come in will not suffice.

From experience in the process of recruiting faculty for a university, I know there are outstanding younger scholars to whom such carrots would have particular appeal. Once baptized on one of these topics, their own interests might develop in related areas, thus producing long-run research dividends on the initial investment. A comprehensive social accounting framework cannot be constructed in a hurry; but if it does emerge, younger scholars will participate as both architects and builders.

•NOTES

1 O. D. Duncan, "Discrimination against Negroes," *The Annals*, CCCLXXI (May, 1967), 87.

2 U.S. Department of Labor, Office of Planning and Research, *The Negro Family: The Case for National Action* (Washington: Government Printing Office, 1965), p. 43. (The so-called Moynihan report.)

3 D. M. Heer, ed., *Social Statistics and the City* (Cambridge: Joint Center for Urban Studies of the Massachusetts Institute of Technology and Harvard University, 1968), pp. 174–175. In addition to the conference proceedings, see P. Demeny and P. Gingrich, "A Reconsideration of Negro-White Mortality Differentials in the United States," *Demography*, IV (1967), 820–837, and R. Farley, "The Quality of Demographic Data for Nonwhites," *Demography*, V (1968), 1–10.

4 D. J. Bogue and E. M. Murphy, "The Effect of Classification Errors upon Statistical Inference: A Case Analysis with Census Data," *Demography*, I (1964), 35.

5 *Ibid.*

6 P. K. Whelpton, *Cohort Fertility: Native White Women in the United States* (Princeton: Princeton University Press, 1954).

7 R. Farley, "Negro Cohort Fertility," unpublished dissertation, University of Chicago, 1964. This work has been revised and considerably extended in a forthcoming monograph, *Negro Fertility*.

8 A. S. Lunde, "White-Nonwhite Fertility Differentials in the United States," *Health, Education, and Welfare Indicators* (September, 1965).

9 Farley, *op. cit.*, p. 172.

10 *Ibid.*, pp. 169–170; and C. V. Kiser, "Fertility Trends and Differentials among Nonwhites in the United States," *Milbank Memorial Fund Quarterly*, XXXVI (April, 1958), 190–195.

11 W. H. Grabill, C. V. Kiser, and P. K. Whelpton, *The Fertility of American Women* (New York: Wiley, 1958), pp. 365–371.

12 R. A. Easterlin, *The American Baby Boom in Historical Perspective* (Washington: National Bureau of Economic Research, 1962). Occasional paper No. 79.

13 P. K. Whelpton, A. A. Campbell, and J. E. Patterson, *Fertility and Family Planning in the United States* (Princeton: Princeton University Press, 1965).

14 *Ibid.*, p. 369.

15 A. Lee and E. Lee, "The Future Fertility of the American Negro," *Social Forces*, XXXVII (March, 1959), 231.

16 Farley, *op. cit.*, p. 179.

17 W. Ryan, "Savage Discovery: The Moynihan Report," *Nation* (November 22, 1965), p. 381.

18 *Ibid.*

19 L. Rainwater and W. L. Yancey, *The Moynihan Report and the Politics of Controversy* (Cambridge: M.I.T. Press, 1967), pp. 220–232.

20 N. B. Ryder, "Illegitimacy," 1960 (hectographed manuscript).

21 Whelpton, Campbell, and Patterson, *op. cit.*, pp. 428–432.

22 Farley, *op. cit.*

23 C. F. Westoff and N. B. Ryder, "United States: Methods of Fertility Control, 1955, 1960, and 1965," *Studies in Family Planning*, XVII (February, 1967), 1.

24 "United States: The Chicago Fertility Control Studies," *Studies in Family Planning*, XV (October, 1966), 1–8.

25 *Ibid.*, p. 8.

26 P. M. Hauser, "Family Planning and Population Programs," *Demography*, IV, No. 1 (1967), 397–414.

27 *Ibid.* and P. M. Hauser, "On Design for Experiment and Research in Fertility Control," in C. V. Kiser, ed., *Research in Family Planning* (Princeton: Princeton University Press, 1965). A devastating critique of programs focused only on contraception is given by K. Davis, "Population Policy: Will Current Programs Succeed?" *Science*, CLVIII (1967), 730–739.

28 Rainwater and Yancey, *op. cit.*

29 Jessie Bernard, *Marriage and Family among Negroes* (Englewood Cliffs, N.J.: Prentice-Hall, 1966), p. ix.

30 *Ibid.*

31 These suggestions draw on a manuscript by I. B. Taeuber being prepared for publication as a "Census Monograph."

32 K. E. Taeuber, W. Haenszel, and M. G. Sirken, "Residence Histories and Exposure Residences for the United States Population," *Journal of the American Statistical Association*, LVI (December, 1961), 824–834.

33 The Pruitt-Igoe housing projects in St. Louis are the locale of much of Lee Rainwater's recent research; see his "Crucible of Identity: The Negro Lower-Class Family," *Daedalus*, XCV (Winter, 1966), 172–216.

34 Westoff and Ryder, *op. cit.*

35 Quoted in Bernard, *op. cit.*, p. 22.

36 H. Lewis, "The Family: Resources for Change," reprinted in Rainwater and Yancey, *op. cit.*, p. 317.

37 U.S. Department of Labor, Office of Planning and Research, *op. cit.*, Preface.

38 Lewis, *op. cit.*, p. 316.

39 Farley, "The Quality of Demographic Data for Nonwhites." See also R. D. Grove, "Vital Statistics for the Negro, Puerto Rican and Mexican Populations: Present Quality and Plans for Improvement," in D. Heer, ed., *op. cit.*, pp. 100–117.

40 Demeny and Gingrich, *op. cit.*

41 R. F. Tomasson, "Patterns in Negro-White Differential Mortality, 1930–1957," *Milbank Memorial Fund Quarterly*, XXXVIII (October, 1960), 1–25.

42 Oral communication from E. M. Kitagawa, based on work to be sum-

marized in E. M. Kitagawa and P. M. Hauser, *Social and Economic Differentials in Mortality*, in preparation for the American Public Health Association "Vital and Health Statistics" monograph series.

43 H. C. Chase, "White-Nonwhite Mortality Differentials in the United States," *Health, Education, and Welfare Indicators* (June, 1965), pp. 27–37; E. P. Hunt and E. E. Huyck, "Mortality of White and Nonwhite Infants in Major U.S. Cities," *Health, Education, and Welfare Indicators* (January, 1966), pp. 1–19. Also see M. S. Goldstein, "Longevity and Health Status of the Negro American," *Journal of Negro Education,* XXXII (Fall, 1963), 337–348.

44 G. A. Gleeson and E. L. White, "Disability and Medical Care among Whites and Nonwhites in the United States," *Health, Education, and Welfare Indicators* (October, 1965), pp. 1–10.

45 U.S. National Health Survey, "Plan and Initial Program of the Health Examination Survey," in National Center for Health Statistics, *Vital and Health Statistics* (July, 1965), Series 1, No. 4.

46 D. Mechanic, *Medical Sociology: A Selective View* (New York: The Free Press, 1968), p. 257.

47 Kitagawa and Hauser, *op. cit.*

48 J. Howard, "Race Differences in Hypertension Mortality Trends," *Milbank Memorial Fund Quarterly*, XLIII (April, 1965), 202–218.

49 Mechanic, *op. cit.*, pp. 256–257.

50 The description of Negro migration trends is adapted from K. E Taeuber, "Perspectives on the Urbanization of the Negro Population in the United States," mimeographed reprint from United Nations, *World Population Conference*, 1965. See also K. E. Taeuber and A. F. Taeuber, "The Negro Population of the United States," in J. P. Davis, ed., *The American Negro Reference Book* (Englewood Cliffs, N.J.: Prentice-Hall, 1966), pp. 96–160, and *idem,* "The Changing Character of Negro Migration," *American Journal of Sociology*, LXX (January, 1965), 429–441.

51 K. E. Taeuber and A. F. Taeuber, *Negroes in Cities: Residential Segregation and Neighborhood Change* (Chicago: Aldine, 1965).

52 A comprehensive methodological and substantive review of official sources is included in H. S. Shryock, Jr., *Population Mobility within the United States* (Chicago: Community and Family Study Center, University of Chicago, 1964).

53 K. E. Taeuber, W. Haenszel, and L. Chiazze, Jr., *Migration in the United States: An Analysis of Residence Histories*, Public Health Monograph No. 77 (Washington: Government Printing Office, 1968).

54 A question of this type is currently scheduled for inclusion in the 1970 census.

55 J. B. Lansing and N. Barth, "The Geographic Mobility of Labor: A Summary Report," *Economic Redevelopment Research* (September, 1964), p. 8.

56 *Ibid.*, and P. Rossi, *Why Families Move: A Study in the Social Psychology of Urban Residential Mobility* (Glencoe, Illinois: The Free Press, 1955).

57 Simple demographic analyses and projections could usefully be supplemented by linkage with econometric studies such as R. H. Day, "The Economics of Technological Change and the Demise of the Sharecropper," *American Economic Review*, LVII (June, 1967), 427–449, or socioeconomic surveys such as M. J. Bowman and W. W. Haynes, *Resources and People in East Kentucky* (Baltimore: Johns Hopkins Press, 1963).

58 For one example, see the U.S. Housing and Home Finance Agency pamphlet, *Our Nonwhite Population and Its Housing: The Changes between 1950 and 1960* (Washington: Government Printing Office, 1963).

59 L. Winnick, *American Housing and Its Use* (New York: Wiley, 1957).

60 Collaborating in these plans were B. Duncan and P. M. Hauser.

61 O. D. Duncan and B. Duncan, *The Negro Population of Chicago* (Chicago: University of Chicago Press, 1957).

62 U.S. Bureau of the Census, "Components of Inventory Change," *U.S. Census of Housing: 1960* (Washington: Government Printing Office, 1962), 4, Series HC(4).

63 L. Laurenti, *Property Values and Race* (Berkeley and Los Angeles: University of California Press, 1960).

64 Taeuber and Taeuber, *Negroes in Cities*, Part 2.

65 For a pioneering study of limited aspects of neighborhood life cycles and references to related work, see B. Duncan, G. Sabagh, and M. D. Van Arsdol, Jr., "Patterns of City Growth," *American Journal of Sociology*, LXVII (January, 1962), 418–429.

66 Laurenti, *op. cit.*

67 B. Duncan and P. M. Hauser, *Housing a Metropolis—Chicago* (Glencoe, Illinois: The Free Press, 1960).

68 R. F. Muth, "Housing Prices and Race in Chicago," September 25, 1962, p. 13 (mimeographed).

69 Taeuber and Taeuber, *Negroes in Cities*, Part I.

70 R. Farley and K. E. Taeuber, "Population Trends and Residential Segregation since 1960," *Science*, CLIX (March 1, 1968), 953–956.

71 See my preceding remarks on strategies of family planning programs and the cited articles by Davis and Hauser.

72 For an early study in this vein, see E. C. Hughes, "A Study of a Secular Institution: The Chicago Real Estate Board," unpublished dissertation, University of Chicago, 1928. For recent surveys of the sparse literature, see R. Helper, "The Racial Practices of Real Estate Institutions in Selected Areas of Chicago," unpublished dissertation, University of Chicago, 1958; and D. McEntire, *Residence and Race* (Berkeley and Los Angeles: University of California Press, 1960), Part 3.

73 S. H. Palmer, "The Role of the Real Estate Agent in the Structuring of Residential Areas: A Study in Social Control," unpublished dissertation, Yale University, 1955.

74 See, for example, J. K. Myers, "Note on the Homogeneity of Census Tracts: A Methodological Problem in Urban Ecological Research," *Social Forces*, XXXII (May, 1954), 364–366.

75 Taeuber and Taeuber, *Negroes in Cities*, Chapter 4.

76 See "Social Aspects of Urban Housing and Redevelopment," in N. P. Gist and S. F. Fava, *Urban Society*, 5th edition (New York: Crowell, 1964), Part 5.

5 Charles C. Killingsworth

Jobs and Income
for Negroes

INTRODUCTION

In July, 1967, employment in the United States reached a new all-time high, and the national unemployment rate was a little below the 4 per cent level which many economists accept as a measure of "full employment." In the same month, there were riots in the predominantly Negro slums of more than a score of American cities. By any measure, the Detroit riot was the worst in the nation's history. In commenting on the riots, Martin Luther King, Jr. said the following: "Every single breakout without exception has substantially been ascribed to gross unemployment, particularly among young people." This comment underscores a paradox and a peril of American prosperity. Although Negroes generally have benefited from more than six years of record-breaking economic expansion, the large gap in economic status between Negroes and whites remains virtually unchanged.

The national average unemployment rate for all of 1967 was 3.8 per cent, which was the lowest annual average since 1953. The white unemployment rate for 1967 was 3.4 per cent. The Negro rate [1] was 7.4 per cent, and the teenage Negro rate was 26.5 per cent. Thus, the overall Negro rate in this year of "full employment" was higher than the white rate in any postwar recession year, and the teenage Negro rate was higher than the national unemployment rate in the worst years of the depression in the 1930's. The roughly two-to-one ratio between white and Negro unemployment rates has been widely publicized, and some otherwise well-informed persons have gathered the impression that this relationship has "always" existed—at least as far back as the figures go. That is not so. The two-to-one ratio first appeared in 1954, and it has persisted through good years and bad since then. But the ratio was only about 160 in the 1947–1949 period; the 1940 census reported a ratio of 118, and the 1930 census showed a ratio of 92.

Although unemployment rates have some important limitations, they have come to be generally accepted as the most significant measure of relative disadvantage. Other measures do not tell a substantially different story. The median income of Negro families is only a little more than half that of white families, and this ratio has been fairly steady throughout the postwar period. The progress of Negroes up the occupational ladder was rapid during the 1940–1950 decade; although this progress continues, it has slowed in recent years. Negroes are still greatly overrepresented in low-skilled and menial occupations and greatly underrepresented in the professions and other white-collar occupations. The educational attainment of Negroes has been rising more rapidly than that of whites for many years. In 1965, however, fewer than four out of ten Negroes in the labor force had twelve or more years of education; more than six out of ten white workers had that much education.

If we compare the present economic status of Negroes with what it was a century ago, we can conclude that their progress has been most impressive and undoubtedly greater than any reasonable person would have anticipated at the end of the Civil War. Then, 80 per cent of the Negroes were totally illiterate; they were heavily concentrated in the rural South, and most were landless and destitute. For a few of them, conditions today are almost as bad as then. But a majority of Negro families have risen above the poverty level; Negroes are now more urbanized than the white population; less than a tenth of the Negro labor force is still in agriculture; and there are now more Negroes living in the North and the West than in the Old Confederacy. The progress of the past, however, as we have newly learned, does not console those still deprived for the great inequalities that remain. As has happened in other parts of the world, recent political and economic progress has helped to create a "revolution of rising expectations."

This rise in expectations has developed at a critical juncture in national affairs. Some of the programs that have especially benefited younger Negroes—particularly Neighborhood Youth Corps and Job Corps—are being drastically reduced in order to finance an untested program to aid the "hard-core unemployed." And demographic and labor market trends now also threaten to erode further some of the hard-won gains in the fight on Negro unemployment. If present trends continue unchanged to 1975, according to an estimate of the Automation Commission in 1966, the Negro unemployment rate will rise to about two and one-half times the rate for the labor force as a whole [2] (in other words, about three times the white rate).

That prospect unquestionably establishes the necessity for some new forms of social intervention to prevent its realization. There is no present shortage of new proposals in this field, and it is frequently urged that we do not need any more studies or investigations; we already know all that we need to know to justify massive new programs. No doubt there is a reasonable basis for suspicion that some calls for further studies in this field mask a desire to postpone action. But recent experience with action programs suggest that our understanding of the causes of Negro economic inequality is not as adequate as some people now say it is. We have recently achieved much tighter labor markets; we have enacted many antidiscrimination laws; and we have substantially increased our spending for schools and training programs for the disadvantaged (especially Negroes). These efforts and others, both private and public, have undoubtedly contributed to improvement in the economic status of Negroes. Yet it seems fair to say that the results, by and large, have fallen considerably short of what had been predicted by the advocates of these "obvious" remedies. This shortfall and the magnitude of the inequalities that remain suggest that our understanding of the nature of the problem is still superficial and that, as a result, we have tackled only its more visible and accessible causes. We need not postpone all further action pending further analysis. But we are not likely soon to commit all the resources needed to pursue with maximum vigor all the lines of action currently advocated. We must develop criteria for determining priorities in this field. The criteria must be derived from a deeper understanding than we yet have of the basic sources and the incidence of economic disadvantage, particularly unemployment, among Negroes.

The conventional analysis, at least in broad outline, has become almost painfully familiar by constant reiteration. It is well known that Negroes have been leaving the South in large numbers ever since the Civil War. It is believed that they have been driven out of the South mainly by racial discrimination and have been drawn to the North by better living conditions and better jobs. But, the conventional wisdom holds, most of the migrants are poorly educated and unskilled, and therefore they are at a disadvantage in competing for jobs in the northern labor market. Moreover, as the "last hired," the Negroes are the "first fired," and for this reason, it is believed, general slack in the labor market creates disproportionately heavy rates of unemployment among Negroes. Continuing racial discrimination, even in the North, is also believed to add to the economic disadvantages of Negroes. Therefore, the conventional prescription is more antidiscrimination laws, even tighter labor markets, and even more years of schooling to enable Negroes to overcome those disadvantages.

No doubt the conventional analysis and its prescription rest on some important aspects of reality. Yet that analysis leaves some vital questions unanswered. Today we have much broader and more effective antidiscrimination laws than we had a quarter-century ago; the Negro-white differential in educational attainment is now greatly reduced; and we have had nearly seven years of record-breaking economic expansion, with the tightest labor markets since the Korean War. Why, then, is "gross unemployment" still the prime economic problem of the Negro, and why does it threaten to become worse, not better, over the next few years? The period of most rapid gains in the Negro's economic status was from about 1940 to the early 1950's; why? Younger Negroes are now predominantly city-bred, and they have much more schooling than their parents; yet Negro teenagers have shared scarcely at all in the employment gains of the current boom. Why?

We cannot answer these questions and others like them unless we examine more closely the forces in the labor market and the larger society which, in earlier eras, helped Negroes to reduce the gross economic inequalities that were the heritage of slavery. We must also consider with care some unexpected and significant consequences of the great Negro diaspora of the last half-century. Then, with a better understanding of the etiology of Negro unemployment and economic insecurity, we can proceed more confidently and more effectively to an evaluation of proposed remedies and an indication of the areas in which our knowledge is still insufficient for adequate evaluation.

NEGRO ADAPTATION TO A CHANGING
LABOR MARKET

Negro Migration

Let us begin with a fundamental if obvious truth: The present economic status of American Negroes can be understood only by understanding the nature and consequences of slavery. Under that institution, the overwhelming majority of Negroes were farm laborers in the South. They were illiterate, propertyless, and generally without the skills wanted in towns and cities; there were only a few exceptions: some house servants and some craftsmen who had been allowed to learn their trades in order to make plantations self-sufficient. After the Civil War ended, most of the former slaves had no choice but to continue to grow cotton, mainly on the white man's soil. They became farm tenants, sharecroppers, or hired laborers under a system which resembled peonage. Thus, most of the Negro population remained ignorant, destitute, and tied to the southern soil for the first half-century after the Emancipation. There was some migration from the rural South, but the numbers involved were small. Then, in the second half-century, the flow of migration increased and in some decades became a flood. Although the census figures of fifty and a hundred years ago are not of impeccable accuracy, we can get a useful impression of gross changes in the distribution of the Negro population by comparing three censuses and three broad classifications of residence in the following tabulation. (The figures are in millions.)

	1860	1910	1960
Rural South	3.9	6.9	4.7
Urban South	0.3	1.9	6.6
North and West	0.2	1.0	7.2

Thus, a Negro population which a hundred years ago was highly concentrated in southern agriculture has become predominantly urban, but without completely correcting its overrepresentation in southern agriculture.

As the figures above show, the redistribution of Negro population was far greater in the more recent half-century than in the 1860–1910 period. The greatest change from 1910 to 1960 was the more than sevenfold increase of Negroes in the North and West. This was an increase almost entirely among city dwellers, because only 2 per cent of the Negroes outside the South live in rural areas. It was also an increase that resulted mainly (though by no means exclusively) from long-distance migration. When we examine estimates of net migration by decades, we find that the movement has not been a steady flow. Pulling together estimates from various sources,[3] we get the following round numbers for net movement of Negroes from the South:

1910–1920:   450,000

1920–1930:   750,000

1930–1940:   350,000

1940–1950: 1,600,000

1950–1960: 1,500,000

Thus, the migration in the 1940's alone exceeded the total for the preceding thirty years. Although the total for the 1950's was almost as large, one study suggests that most of the movement was crowded into the first half of the decade, because there was apparently a marked decline in Negro mobility after about 1957 or 1958. Another source shows a reversal of the relationship between white and Negro interstate migration rates between the 1940's and the 1950's. Between 1940 and 1947, 14 per cent of the country's nonwhites and a little less than 10 per cent of the whites migrated between states; from 1955 to 1960, the percentages were 6.1 for nonwhites and 9.2 for whites.[4]

Furthermore, there had been an important change in the character of Negro migration by the mid-1950's. A study of nonwhite in-migrants to thirteen large metropolitan areas from 1955 to 1960 concluded that, in the northern and border metropolises, the in-migrants had a somewhat higher educational and occupational status than the resident nonwhite population, and the migrants from other metropolitan areas generally outnumbered those from the rural South.[5]

As we shall presently see, by most measures the economic status of the Negro is much higher in the North than in the South. In the past, northward migration has been a crucial factor in raising various national averages for Negroes. Why, then, has there been unevenness in the flow, and why has it slackened in recent years? Stated more precisely, what are the conditions that have been most favorable to Negro advancement by means of regional migration, and what recent changes have occurred in those conditions? The answers to these questions have great relevance to the evaluation of one of the prime remedies for the Negroes' economic disadvantages: economic growth and its concomitant, tight labor markets.

One powerful influence on Negro migration has been the continuing decline of southern agriculture, especially in cotton. Around 1915, a series of natural disasters hit southern cotton plantations: the boll weevil, floods, and droughts. White as well as black farmers were pushed off the land. Meanwhile, a labor shortage was developing in the North, the product of a war boom and the shutting off of European immigration. Therefore, many of the Negroes who were pushed off the land in the South were pulled into industrial jobs in the North. Through the 1920's, this push-pull interaction continued. The cotton culture of the South suffered further reverses: falling prices; growing competition from abroad, from the Southwest, and from rayon; and soil exhaustion and erosion. In the North, a great postwar boom was under way. The prosperity of the automobile industry was stimulating growth in other sectors, such as steel and road building, and American industry generally was learning to apply mass production techniques which required large numbers of low-skilled workers. Hence, Negro migration to the North continued and accelerated during this decade.

The experience of the 1930's seems to show that the push off the land in the South could not by itself maintain the high rates of Negro migration that had prevailed for the previous fifteen or twenty years. The Great Depression intensified some of cotton's old problems and added new ones. As world demand for cotton fell, competition intensified for the market that remained. Rayon continued to displace cotton for many purposes. There is evidence that the federal agricultural adjustment programs were administered in a way that was particularly disadvantageous to Negroes in the South. One effect was to make it profitable for the landowners to substitute machines for tenants or sharecroppers, and the traditions of the South dictated that whites rather than Negroes should run the machines.[6] Hence, the push off the land in the South was not lessened by the Depression. The pull of jobs in the North was almost eliminated, of course. The combined result was that northward migration of Negroes during this decade was reduced to about one-half the rate of the preceding decade. Perhaps the marvel is that it did not decline even more in view of the heavy unemployment in the North. One reason for continued migration was that relief standards were more generous in the North than in the South.

The great flood of northward migration by Negroes that developed after the outbreak of World War II suggests that some part of it must have been deferred from the 1930's. The wartime labor shortages drew into northern factories and shipyards many hundreds of thousands of southern Negroes who had long since lost their traditional means of subsistence in southern agriculture. After the end of World War II, pent-up civilian demand fueled a great postwar boom; and when it was faltering, the Korean War helped to prolong its life. The great northward migration continued into the 1950's. Then, as noted above, the rate slowed, although it probably remained considerably higher than in the Depression years.[7] The slowing cannot be attributed to any marked improvement in the employment prospects in southern agriculture. Mechanization and other labor-saving techniques flourished in the South, as elsewhere in the nation's agricultural sector. Despite many years of heavy migration, Negroes were still overrepresented in southern agriculture. Obviously, one major factor retarding Negro migration between regions in more recent years was the growing volume of Negro unemployment in the North and West. Analysis of the causes of this growth of unemployment, and of the present distribution of unemployment among various categories of Negroes, is of central importance to this discussion. Before undertaking that analysis, however, we must summarize the changes in Negro occupational status, income, education, and population growth, all of which have been considerably affected by the urbanization and regional migration of Negroes.

Negro Occupational Mobility

By almost any concept of measurement, the movement of a worker out of agriculture and into some nonagricultural employment is a rise in the occupational structure. In a sense, then, the long decline in the manpower needs of southern agriculture was an important factor in the occupational upgrading of the Negro labor force. Throughout the first half of this century, Negroes were leaving agriculture at a considerably greater rate than whites. The Negro "departure rate" reached a peak in the 1940–1950 period, which was also the decade of heaviest regional migration. In the ensuing decade, the rate of Negro departure from agriculture declined somewhat, and for the first time the white "departure rate" from this sector rose above the Negro rate.[8] It seems clear that the reason for this development is that changing technology started pushing up the productivity curve in most branches of farming after 1947, while total demand for farm products grew more slowly; in these circumstances, agricultural manpower needs dropped much more rapidly than in the earlier decades of the century. To anticipate somewhat, the large influx of white farmers into the urban labor market in the years after 1947 increased the competition for the least-skilled nonfarm jobs and was one factor in the rising Negro unemployment rate in the 1950's.

The Negroes who left southern agriculture in such large numbers after 1910 had, on the average, much less education and training than the labor force in the urban areas to which they migrated. Hence, most Negroes found jobs only at the bottom of the occupational hierarchy. In the South, particularly, this tendency was reinforced by racial discrimination, which had created a tradition of "Negro jobs." These were generally the heaviest, most disagreeable, and most hazardous jobs available—street cleaning, construction labor, logging, longshoring, and the like, or, in the case of Negro women, domestic service. As the southern economy has developed, the tradition of "Negro jobs" has weakened in some fields, less from Negroes moving up than from whites taking over some of the jobs; for example, the job of fireman on diesel locomotives. Negroes were largely excluded from textiles, the great growth industry of the South in earlier years.[9]

In the North, Negroes found that jobs in a greater variety of industries were open to them. During World War I and the 1920's, they got at least a foothold on the lower rungs of the ladder, to be sure, in two of the great growth industries of the times: automobiles and steel. In some plants, they were hired originally as strikebreakers and then kept on; in some others, they were hired because employers believed that their presence would hamper unionization. The great break-through, however, came during World War II. The combination of a general labor shortage, vigorous antidiscrimination measures of the federal government, and government-subsidized training programs made it possible for Negroes to enter many occupations and industries in which few members of their race had previously been employed. In particular, they improved their share of the so-called semiskilled jobs, especially in manufacturing. But their advancement was fairly general in all occupational classifications, including many of the white-collar fields, in all regions of the country. After the war ended, many of the conditions that had facilitated the absorption of millions of Negroes from the rural South into urban labor markets continued. Moreover, many of the returning Negro war veterans had learned marketable skills in the armed forces.

The conditions which had favored Negro occupational upgrading weakened or were offset by other forces around the middle of the 1950–1960 decade. The result, it must be emphasized, was not a total cessation of progress up the occupational ladder; rather, it was a slowing of the rate. Indeed, it is easy to find comparisons that suggest dramatic progress in the recent past. For example, the number of Negroes in white-collar jobs increased by about 50 per cent between 1955 and 1962, while the number of whites in such jobs increased only by 20 per cent. But this "great leap forward" for Negroes involved such small absolute numbers that, after the leap (that is, in 1962), there were still twenty-eight times as many whites as Negroes in the white-collar field.[10] Furthermore, "white-collar jobs" is an exceedingly broad classification that covers many different kinds of work, and a finer breakdown within the white-collar category strongly suggests that Negroes have found places predominantly in its lower fringes.

Any effort to measure in quantitative terms the Negro's progress up the occupational ladder faces great difficulties. Nevertheless, several ingenious efforts have been made, using various classification and weighting systems.[11] These studies, despite differences in methodology and time spans covered, appear to permit two main generalizations: that the Negro's over-all position improved quite substantially during the 1940's and that the improvement was much less during the 1950's. There is further finding of significance regarding Negro men in two studies of the 1950's.[12] Although the figures for the nation as a whole show some improvement in their occupational position in this decade, the story within states and regions is quite different. At that level of disaggregation, the figures show that little or no change occurred. All or practically all of the improvement in the national figures for Negro men during the 1950's must be attributed to their continuing migration from states and regions where they were low in the occupational structure to the areas (the North and West) where they are generally higher. Apparently Negro women, however, improved their occupational position somewhat in all major regions as well as in the nation as a whole.

Despite their great advances in the past quarter-century, Negroes are still greatly overrepresented in jobs that are low on the occupational ladder. One way to demonstrate the point is to divide all occupations into only two categories: less-skilled and more-skilled. The less-skilled group includes operatives, domestics and other service workers, laborers and all farm workers; the more-skilled group includes all white-collar jobs and the skilled and supervisory blue-collar jobs. This basis of classification is admittedly rough and ready, but it facilitates a gross kind of comparison of the whites and nonwhites. The following figures tell the story as of 1965: [13]

PER CENT IN LESS-SKILLED JOBS

	White	Nonwhite
Men	40	73
Women	38	76

This occupational distribution helps to explain why Negroes have higher rates of unemployment and lower earnings than whites. Less-skilled workers generally have more unemployment and get paid less than more-skilled workers. But it must be pointed out that the rise in Negro unemployment rates relative to white rates occurred in a decade when Negroes were still improving their representation in the more-skilled category. Occupational upgrading of Negroes relative to whites

might have been expected to reduce Negro unemployment rates relative to white rates. The opposite happened.

Negro Income

In some respects, earnings figures measure the progress and the continuing disadvantages of Negroes in the labor market even better than
unemployment or occupational status figures. There are no reliable figures for early years, but there are reasonably good estimates
from government sources going back to 1939. There is an embarrass-
ment of riches in more recent years; we must choose among many
different measures. One basic conclusion is supported by all the available measures: both in absolute terms and relative to the white majority, Negro income has improved tremendously in the past quarter-
century. In 1939, Negro families and individuals had a median annual
income from wages and salaries of $489, which was 37 per cent of the
white median. In 1963, the median for Negroes was $3,088, and this was
53 per cent of the white median. However, the period of most rapid
progress in closing the relative income gap was between 1939 and 1954.
By the latter year, the Negroes had achieved a ratio of 56 per cent.
Over the next dozen years, that ratio was not exceeded; in fact, in most
years the ratio was slightly lower, as in 1963.[14] In 1966, the white-
nonwhite ratio for families only (excluding unattached individuals)
rose to 60 per cent for the first time.[15]

Thus far, we have been considering what might be called "global"
figures—those for the entire nation—and medians. In the interests of
relative brevity and comprehensibility, the retailer of government statistics must resist the lure of more and more disaggregation. But two
points of finer detail are essential for subsequent analysis. The first is
movements in the white-nonwhite income ratio at the regional level;
the second is the relative incidence of poverty. One investigator has
studied changes in income from all sources by region between 1949
and 1959.[16] He found that the white-Negro income ratio for men in
the United States as a whole did not change significantly in that ten-
year period, but that within each of the major regions, the relative
income of Negro men declined significantly. Other data, on median
family income for 1960–1964, show a similar pattern with one significant exception: the ratio rose in the South while declining in the other
three regions.[17] Despite the rise, the ratio in the South (at 49) was still
17 to 29 points below the ratios of the other regions.

Income ratios may be taken as a measure of relative deprivation.
"Poverty" is also a relative concept; the poverty floor tends to rise over

time, and some of the American poor are undoubtedly better off than the great majority of the population of some underdeveloped countries. Nevertheless, the poverty concept obviously has some basis in objective reality. The poverty line is drawn at the level which most Americans accept as the minimum necessary to meet basic needs in contemporary society. The most widely used figure is $3,000 (in 1962 prices), postulated by the Council of Economic Advisers.[18] By this measure, the incidence of poverty among nonwhite families has decreased in the postwar years. In 1947, two-thirds of all nonwhite families lived in poverty; by 1962, less than half (44 per cent) fell below the poverty line. But demography played a wry trick in this time span. Total nonwhite families increased so rapidly that the actual *number* in poverty in 1962 was only 3 per cent less than in 1947.[19] White families were moving out of poverty at a more rapid rate, and their total was increasing at about half the rate of nonwhite families. Therefore, by 1962 nonwhite families were a larger proportion (22 per cent) of all poor families than in 1947.[20]

Recently the Bureau of the Census has developed more elaborate standards for the determination of poverty incomes. A recent census release announced that from 1959 to 1966, the total number of white Americans living in poverty decreased from 28 million to 20 million, while the number of Negroes in poverty decreased only from 11 million to 10 million.[21] Children under 16 are disproportionately represented among the nonwhite poor, and the poor nonwhite family head is more likely than his white counterpart to be working full time.[22]

Negro Educational Attainment

Historically, school attendance rates and the years of school completed by the adult population have been higher in urban than in rural areas and higher in the North and West than in the South. Hence, Negro migration patterns have strongly favored improvement in educational attainment. And there has been improvement. Some discussions of the Negro's economic and social status have placed much emphasis on this improvement as one of the most hopeful long-run aspects of the Negro's situation. On closer examination, the facts seem to justify less optimism than has been commonly expressed. It is true that, between 1940 and 1960, the median years of education completed by the adult nonwhite population rose by nearly one-half: from 5.8 to 8.2 years. But the white majority was also improving its educational attainment during those years; the white median rose from 8.7 to 10.9 years. Thus, after two decades of heavy migration, the white-nonwhite differential had been reduced only from 2.9 years to 2.7 years, and the nonwhite of 1960 was still substantially below the white median of twenty years before.[23]

Improved educational opportunities affect the young almost exclusively. Very few persons acquire any formal education after age 25. Therefore, the median educational attainment for an entire population group rises only as the oncoming generation acquires more education than its parents and grandparents and as the older, less-educated members of the group die. In some ways, we can get a better impression of recent progress by examining the educational attainment of the age group 25 to 29 years. This age group has largely completed its formal education, but has been subject to the influences of the recent past. In 1940, the difference between the white and nonwhite medians in this age group was 3.7 years; by 1962, the difference had been reduced to 1.3 years. The white median had risen by 1.8 years and the nonwhite by 4.2 years.[24] Hence, these figures might lead to the conclusion that young Negroes are rapidly approaching equality with young whites in educational attainment. The conclusion would be unjustified, however, in two important respects. The first is that the narrowing of differentials for this age group has been accomplished primarily by virtual equalization of school attendance rates in the elementary and junior high-school years.[25] Quite substantial differences persist at the higher levels of education. In 1962, only four out of ten nonwhites, but seven out of ten whites (in the 25 to 29 years age group), had completed at least four years of high school; and more than twice as large a proportion of the whites (27.1 per cent) as nonwhites (12.9 per cent) had had some college training. At these higher levels of education, the nonwhite percentages in 1962 were roughly the same as the white percentages in 1940.[26] To complete the picture, however, it must be noted that this nonwhite age group had more than tripled its high-school completion rate between 1940 and 1962, and the percentage with some college training had almost tripled. The high-school completion rate for whites had increased from 40.9 per cent in 1940 to 69.3 per cent in 1962, and the percentage with college training roughly doubled. Thus, by these measures, young nonwhites had gained ground fairly rapidly during this period; but even these crude figures, which relate only to the age group most recently completing its education, suggest that a substantial gap still remains.

In a second important respect, the comparison of median years of education completed, even for the 25 to 29 age group, is misleading. A "year" in an all-Negro school in the rural South, where Negroes are still disproportionately represented, is not the same as a year in an all-white school in a wealthy suburb in the North. The school year in the rural South may be five or six months or less. Despite significant efforts in some areas of the South to upgrade the all-Negro schools to meet the "separate but equal" standard, by most criteria those schools generally have been much more separate than equal. For example, in many southern states the percentage of Negro high schools that are accredited is less than half the percentage for white high schools in the same state; in Mississippi, less than 3 per cent of the Negro high schools were accredited in 1959.[27] But *de facto* segregation in the North has also helped to impede the achievement of real equality of educational opportunity for Negroes. The extent of inequality was documented by the recent Coleman report, which found that Negroes in the twelfth grade in the metropolitan Northeast had a median score 3.3 years behind whites in the same region on standard achievement tests. Southern Negroes in the twelfth grade had a median score 1.9 years behind northeastern Negroes.[28] There is no suggestion in the report that these differences in median test scores reflect any innate "racial" differences. The point here is simply that the discussion in earlier paragraphs, which concentrates on years of school completed, considerably understates the real inequalities of educational preparation which must still be overcome even by young Negroes.

Negro Population and Labor Force Changes

From 1960 to 1965, the nonwhite population aged 15 to 19 years in the central cities of the United States increased by 52.7 per cent. Nearly three-quarters of this increase was due to natural growth and the remainder to migration. During the same period, the total nonwhite population of the central cities increased by about 16 per cent, and their white population decreased slightly as out-migration exceeded natural growth.[29] It is hardly an overstatement to call the increase of younger Negroes in central cities a population explosion. Taken together with the decrease in white population, these figures go a long way toward explaining the crisis in the cities and the economic difficulties of the Negro population. If there is now, in the late 1960's, a "Negro revolution" in the cities, some of its roots lie in the Negro demographic revolution of the past quarter-century.

Although the main ingredients of that demographic revolution are now reasonably familiar, the outcome is quite different from what would have been predicted a quarter-century ago. During the first third of the twentieth century, the Negro population of the country was declining relative to the white population. Although this trend was reversed in the 1930's, past experience with the urbanization of peoples would have suggested that the large-scale migration of Negroes to cities would reduce their birth rates. Instead, urbanization has increased Negro birth rates, and they have risen more rapidly than white birth rates.

Important though the higher Negro birth rate has been, a decline in the Negro death rate has been an even larger factor in the growth of their total population and changes in its age structure. At the turn of the century, the death rate per thousand whites was 17; the nonwhite rate was 25. In 1960, the white rate had dropped to 9.4 and the nonwhite rate to 10.0.[30] The life expectancy of Negroes at birth has almost doubled since 1900, and the difference between whites and Negroes has dropped from 14.6 years to 6.6 years in 1960. The most rapid improvement for the Negroes occurred in the 1940's, which coincided with their greatest migration.

One study has shown that Negro migration rates tended to be highest among young adults.[31] Thus, Negro migration transferred not only population as such; it also transferred a substantial part of the reproductive capacity of the rural southern Negro population. Greater access to health facilities—even though it was still less than white access to the same kinds of facilities—substantially reduced maternal and infant mortality rates. More mothers survived to have more children, and more children survived to become teenagers. Thus, in the decade from 1950 to 1960, the total white population of the United States increased by 17.6 per cent and the Negro population increased by 25.4 per cent, a rate half again as high as the white rate.

One result of such sharply different rates of population growth, especially when the increase of Negro population is the combined result of a higher birth rate and a falling death rate, is large differences in the age distribution of the white and nonwhite population. As of mid-1963, government estimates were that almost 40 per cent of the nonwhite population, compared with about 30 per cent of the white population, was under 15 years of age. Only a third of the nonwhites were age 35 and over, compared with 43 per cent of the whites. The median age of the nonwhite population was more than seven years less than the white median, 22.2 years and 29.5 years, respectively.[32]

A faster rate of Negro population growth might be expected to produce a faster growth rate in the Negro labor force as well. Yet in recent years the difference between the rates of increase in the white and Negro components of the labor force has been surprisingly small. From 1960 to 1965, the white labor force increased by 7.1 per cent and nonwhite by 8.2 per cent.[33] Two factors have tended to hold down the growth of the nonwhite labor force: (1) the greatest increases in total nonwhite population have taken place, naturally enough, in the very young age groups; and (2) the percentage of the nonwhite population of working age that is in the labor force—the labor force participation rate—has declined. There has also been a decline, but a lesser one, in the participation rate of the white population. On the basis of relatively optimistic assumptions concerning future participation rates, Department of Labor technicians have prepared projections of the composition of the labor force by color for 1970, 1975, and 1980.[34] According to these projections, the nonwhite labor force, and especially its teenage component, will grow much more rapidly than the white labor force during each of these five-year periods. Thus, between 1965 and 1980, "the total nonwhite labor force will have risen by 41 per cent compared with only a 28 per cent increase in white workers." Nonwhite workers under 25 years of age are expected to increase by about 30 per cent between 1965 and 1970 and another 33 per cent in the decade following, compared with expected increases of 20 per cent and 16 per cent for young white workers during these time periods.

As already noted, these projections rest on relatively optimistic assumptions concerning nonwhite participation rates in the future. We must pause briefly to consider the recent behavior and the significance of participation rates. To begin with, we must recognize that the concept of the "labor force" has some elements of arbitrariness. The labor force is composed of the employed plus the unemployed. It is relatively easy to count the employed, but some rather arbitrary definitions must be applied in order to distinguish the "unemployed" from those who are "not in the labor force." Basically, the test that is applied in practice is whether the individual who is not currently employed has recently engaged in an active search for a job. Those who are able and willing to work, but have become sufficiently discouraged about their prospects to give up an active search for a job, are not counted among the unemployed. This system of classification results in an understatement of the number who would be available for employment if more jobs of the right kinds were available. This group of potential workers has come to be called "the hidden unemployed."

It is possible to estimate the size of this group by comparing participation rates for specific groups in the population—by age, sex, color, education—at one stage of the business cycle with another stage or at one point in time with a later point. A number of recent studies have demonstrated that certain groups in the population (particularly the young, the old, and women) increase their labor force participation rather sharply when jobs are readily available, and vice versa.[35] There is also evidence that chronically adverse labor market conditions have had a cumulative effect on Negro participation rates in the postwar years. For example, in 1948, Negro men in the prime working ages, 25–64, had a participation rate that was approximately the same as the rate for white men in the same age group. By 1966, the Negro rate had fallen substantially below the white rate. The same pattern of change is clear in the rates for Negro teenagers compared with white teenagers. Adult Negro women have a different pattern; their participation rates have always been generally higher than the rates for white women of the same ages. However, the white women's rates have risen substantially in the postwar years, while the Negro women's rates have risen by much less.[36] There is persuasive evidence, I believe, of the growth of hidden unemployment in the population at large since the late 1940's and early 1950's.[37] The distinctive trends in the nonwhite participation rates in the postwar years appear to show that the increase in this form of unemployment has been substantially greater among nonwhites than among whites.

Negro Unemployment

Although there has been growing discussion of Negro unemployment in recent years, there has been little attention to its development and its present structure. If unemployment rates are taken as one important measure of disadvantage in the labor market, it is imperative to try to discover the sources of this kind of disadvantage for Negroes. Such an examination may appear to be another laborious investigation of the obvious; is it not common knowledge that Negro unemployment is the result of the racial discrimination of the whites and the low educational attainment of the Negro? As often happens in the social sciences, careful examination of the facts reveals that "common knowledge," while not entirely lacking a basis, fails to provide an adequate explanation for some important characteristics of Negro unemployment.

We can seek clues to the sources of Negro labor market disadvantage first by examining the behavior of white and nonwhite unemployment rates over time. The rates for both groups are greatly affected by the business cycle; but we can partially eliminate the influence of that variable by calculating the ratio between nonwhite and white unemployment rates. We shall begin with the "reported" rates for both groups; then we shall "adjust" the nonwhite rates (to the extent possible) to reflect the greater growth of hidden unemployment among the nonwhites. We shall also consider the nonwhite-white ratios by age and by level of educational attainment. Finally, we shall briefly consider differences in these ratios in different regions of the country. This method of analysis will enable us to trace the growth of nonwhite disadvantage and to identify the groups of nonwhites that are most disadvantaged, both in relation to other nonwhite groups and in relation to white groups with the same general characteristics.

As was mentioned earlier, the 1930 census showed a lower unemployment rate for nonwhites than for whites, and the 1940 census reported a nonwhite rate only 20 per cent higher than the white rate.[38] Annual figures are available from 1948 on. They are shown in Table 5–1.[39]

TABLE 5–1 *White and Nonwhite Unemployment Rates, 1948–1967*

| | UNEMPLOYMENT RATES | | RATIO |
	White	*Nonwhite*	*Nonwhite/White*
1948	3.6	5.9	164
1949	5.6	8.9	159
1950	4.9	9.1	186
1951	3.1	5.3	171
1952	2.8	5.4	193
1953	2.7	4.5	167
1954	5.0	9.8	196
1955	3.9	8.7	223
1956	3.7	8.4	227
1957	3.9	8.0	205
1958	6.1	12.6	207
1959	4.9	10.7	218
1960	5.0	10.2	204
1961	6.0	12.5	208
1962	4.9	11.0	224
1963	5.1	10.9	214
1964	4.6	9.8	213
1965	4.1	8.3	202
1966	3.3	7.3	221
1967	3.4	7.4	218

These figures relate to men and women of working age. They show a pronounced increase in the *relative* unemployment rates of nonwhites since the late 1940's, but little apparent change since about 1955. However, this comparison leaves out of account the greater growth of hidden unemployment among nonwhites, in recent years, to which we shall return shortly. These aggregate figures also conceal the somewhat different experience of teenagers. In 1948, the unemployment rate for nonwhite teenagers was only a little higher than the white teenage rate; but in 1954, the nonwhite rate was about a third higher than the white rate; and since 1958, the nonwhite rate has been roughly twice the white teenage rate. Furthermore, the rates for both white and nonwhite teenagers have been markedly higher in the 1960's than in the preceding decade.[40]

Now let us consider hidden unemployment. The measurement of this form of labor market disadvantage necessarily rests on assumption and inference concerning "abnormal" behavior of participation rates. My own analysis begins with the observation that, in the late 1940's, participation rates of Negro men in every age group were either close to or considerably higher than the participation rates of white men in the corresponding age groups. In recent years, the Negro men's rates have been substantially lower than white rates in virtually all age groups.[41] We also know that participation rates for men tend to vary by level of education as well as by age. My adjustments for differential hidden unemployment among nonwhite men proceed on the basic assumption that where the participation rate for a particular age and educational attainment classification of nonwhites is currently lower than for the corresponding classification of whites, the difference must be attributable to the greater prevalence of hidden unemployment among nonwhites.[42] By raising the nonwhite participation rates by age and education to the white levels (where the former are lower) and applying them to reported population totals, we can get "adjusted" labor force figures and then deduct employment figures to get "adjusted" unemployment totals, from which "adjusted" unemployment rates for nonwhite men can be computed.[43] There is undeniably a margin of error in the adjustments. Although I have followed the established convention by presenting results in the following tables to the nearest tenth of a percentage point, it should be understood that the real significance of the adjusted figures is as approximate indicators of relative orders of magnitude.

My approach, as implied above, permits detailed computations only for men. The most recent time for which the necessary data are available is March, 1964, and these are for those aged 18 years and older.

The adjusted unemployment total for Negro males by this method is 217,000 higher than the reported total, an increase of approximately 50 per cent. The nonwhite-white unemployment rate ratio rises to 287. The revised unemployment rates and ratios by age are shown in Table 5–2.

T A B L E   5 – 2   *Unemployment Rates of the Male Civilian Labor Force, 18 Years and Over, by Age and Color—Reported White Rates and Adjusted Nonwhite Rates, March, 1964*

| | UNEMPLOYMENT RATES | | |
| | White (Reported) | Nonwhite (Adjusted) | RATIO Nonwhite/White |
Age			
TOTAL	4.7	13.5	287
18–24	10.4	20.7	199
25–34	3.6	14.1	392
35–44	3.5	10.5	300
45–54	4.0	10.4	260
55–64	4.5	13.9	309
65 and over	4.9	11.4	233

The census undercount of young nonwhite males probably causes a spuriously low adjusted unemployment rate and nonwhite-white ratio for the 18–24 age group; but, in any event, the ratio is low primarily because of an extremely high (reported) unemployment rate for the whites in this age classification. It should be noted that the highest adjusted unemployment rates are for the under-25 age group among the nonwhites; the second highest rate is for the 25–34 age group among the nonwhites, while this age group of whites has the second lowest rate. While the pattern of age differences for nonwhites does not lend itself to succinct generalization, we can perhaps say that unemployment is most excessive among the under-35 age group. It is also noteworthy that the *lowest* nonwhite rate happens to be exactly the same as the *highest* white rate.

It is worthwhile to examine the *reported* unemployment rates for both whites and nonwhites by level of education before considering the *adjusted* nonwhite rates, for the reason that the data do not permit as detailed a breakdown of the adjusted rates as is possible for the reported rates. Table 5–3 shows those figures.

TABLE 5-3   *Reported Unemployment Rates of the Male Civilian Labor Force, 18 Years and Over, by Years of School Completed and Color, March, 1964*

Years of School Completed	UNEMPLOYMENT RATES		RATIO Nonwhite/White
	White	Nonwhite	
TOTAL	4.7	9.4	200
Elementary School			
0–4 years	10.4	7.7	74
5–7 years	7.1	10.5	148
8 years	6.5	10.6	163
High School			
1–3 years	5.9	11.3	192
4 years	3.8	8.7	229
College			
1–3 years	3.6	7.3	203
4 years	1.3	4.3	331

The most striking feature of this comparison is the difference between the white and nonwhite pattern. Among whites, the highest unemployment rates are those for the least-educated, and there is a reasonably smooth progression of rates downward for each higher educational classification, with the lowest rate for the college-trained males. Among nonwhites, the highest rate is for high-school dropouts. The nonwhite rate for the least-educated (less than five years of schooling) is actually lower than the rate for whites with the same education; only nonwhites with college training have lower rates than this least-educated group. So far as nonwhite-white unemployment ratios are concerned, it is clear that the relative disadvantage is far greater for the better-educated nonwhites than it is for the less-educated.

One of my primary reasons for investigating differential hidden unemployment among nonwhite males was the hypothesis that adjustment of the nonwhite unemployment rates by the method previously described would bring the pattern into closer conformity with the white pattern—that is, would raise the rates for the least-educated far more than for the better-educated. That did not happen. Data limitations made it necessary to combine the least-educated classifications (those with eight years or less of schooling) and the most-educated classifications (those with *any* college training). Nevertheless, it is clear that hidden unemployment is fairly evenly spread among nonwhite men up to (but not including) those with some college training. The adjustment for hidden unemployment raises the unemployment rates for the lower educational attainment groups by 40 to 50 per cent, but by only a negligible amount for the college-trained group. Table 5–4 shows these results.

TABLE 5–4   *Unemployment Rates of the Male Civilian Labor Force, 18 Years and Over, by Years of School Completed and Color —Reported White Rates and Adjusted Nonwhite Rates, March, 1964*

Years of School Completed	UNEMPLOYMENT RATES White (Reported)	Nonwhite (Adjusted)	RATIO Nonwhite/White
TOTAL	4.7	13.5	287
0–8	7.2	14.3	199
9–11	5.9	16.0	271
12	3.8	13.0	342
13 and over	2.3	5.8	252

Thus, the distinctive nonwhite pattern is not greatly changed by the adjustment. The most disadvantaged group remains the high-school dropouts, and the rate for those with high-school diplomas is only a little lower than the rate for the least-educated. The *relative* disadvantage is least for the nonwhites with the least education: it is greatest for the better-educated.

The nonwhite female unemployment rates have not been consistently higher or lower than nonwhite male rates over the years, although there has been some tendency for the female rates to be lower than male rates in recession years and higher than male rates in prosperous years. Among whites, female rates have been consistently higher than male rates during the postwar years. The nonwhite female unemployment rates by age are broadly similar to the nonwhite male rates, except that the female teenage rates have been consistently and substantially higher than male teenage rates. Nonwhite female rates by education depart markedly from the white pattern in essentially the same way that nonwhite male rates do. The unemployment rates for less-educated nonwhite females (eight years or less of schooling) are *less* than the average, and rates for the better-educated are higher than the average except for college graduates. The nonwhite-white ratio is much higher for the better-educated nonwhite females than for the less-educated.

Hidden unemployment among nonwhite women cannot be measured by the methodology used for nonwhite men, and quite different conclusions can be reached by reasoning from various plausible assumptions. Nonwhite female participation rates for most age groups have risen somewhat in the last twenty years, although generally by considerably less than the rates of white females of the corresponding ages. The much higher unemployment rates of nonwhite females may have held their participation rates below what they would have been if jobs had been more available; but it is also possible that their participation rates are approaching some kind of upper limit. It is reasonably clear, however, that there must be substantial hidden unemployment at least among nonwhite female teenagers. Their participation rates have fallen almost precipitously in the past two decades, although those of white girls have risen; and the reported unemployment rates for nonwhite teenage girls have been the highest for any age-sex-color group: around 30 per cent in recent years. It is perhaps safe to assume, at least for this group, that greater availability of jobs would draw substantially more of them into the active labor market.

There remain for consideration differences in unemployment rates by region and place of residence. Readily available data are sparse. The Department of Labor has reported some computations from the decennial censuses which show substantially higher nonwhite unemployment rates in the non-South than in the South going as far back as 1930.[44] These computations show nonwhite-white unemployment ratios in the non-South rising as follows: 1930, *155*; 1940, *201*; 1950, *233*; 1960, *210*. These figures may not be very reliable. The conceptual basis and age range of the 1930 figures differ substantially from the later ones; the 1940 figure relates to a situation in which the national unemployment rate was close to 15 per cent; and it is generally accepted that there was a serious undercount of unemployment in the 1950 census, which conceivably could have distorted the nonwhite-white ratio. There was apparently some undercounting of unemployment in the 1960 census as well, but much less than in 1950. We can further break down the 1960 figures by major region and calculate Negro-white unemployment rate ratios which are as follows: [45]

	Men	*Women*
Northeast	200	160
North Central	280	260
West	230	180
South	170	170

The 1960 nonwhite unemployment rate in the South was also lower in absolute terms (7.4 per cent) than in the rest of the country (10.1 per cent). Part of this difference, we can speculate, must be due to the large number of Negroes still in agriculture in the South (and almost nowhere else). By this view, what appears to be a regional difference in unemployment rates and ratios may be to a considerable extent a place-of-residence difference. Some support for this view is provided by a Department of Labor survey of employment conditions in the slums of a number of major cities.[46] Three-quarters of the residents of these slums were nonwhites. The over-all unemployment rate (using the standard definitions) in these slums was close to 10 per cent, almost three times the national average at the time (November, 1966). There was little difference between the rates of whites and nonwhites in these slum areas. In the one southern city included in the study (New Orleans), the slum unemployment rate was quite close to the average of all the cities studied. The Department of Labor also calculated what it called a "subemployment" rate, which takes into account involuntary part-time work, substandard earnings, part of the hidden unemployment, and an estimate of the "undercount" group, that is, those not found by census takers. New Orleans had one of the highest "subemployment" rates.

To round out the picture of the labor market disadvantage of Negroes, brief mention should be made of the fact that they are disproportionately represented, in good times as well as bad, among those who are working part time when they would prefer full-time work; among those with three or more spells of unemployment during the year; and among the long-term unemployed.[47]

THE SOURCES OF NEGRO DISADVANTAGE IN THE LABOR MARKET

The Salient Facts

The primary purpose to this point has been description: a survey of the statistics and the studies that measure the growth and map the present structure of Negro disadvantage, especially relative to whites, in the business of making a living. It has not seemed feasible or desirable to postpone all aspects of interpretation; but neither has it been possible to undertake a coherent analysis of the sources of Negro disadvantage in the labor market until the salient facts had been described. Now it is time to shift the emphasis to analysis and interpretation. The objective is to provide a basis for evaluating the relative effectiveness of the great variety of proposals for new or enlarged forms of social intervention to reach and mitigate, if possible, the sources of Negro disadvantage.

The descriptive survey has revealed what appears to be long-term growth in the Negro unemployment rate, not only relative to the concurrent white rate but also relative to earlier Negro rates. The persistence of excessive unemployment among Negroes has led to the growth of hidden unemployment, at least among males and teenage females. It is reasonably well established that there is hidden unemployment among whites as well; but we have seen that consideration of only the "excess" hidden unemployment among Negro males—that is, its greater incidence as compared with white males of the same age and educational attainment—raises the officially reported unemployment rate for Negro males by about 50 per cent. Most of this hidden unemployment has developed since the mid-1950's. Therefore, although the reported Negro unemployment rate has remained about double the white rate since 1954, consideration of the added dimension of hidden unemployment (among Negro males, at least) reveals a *continuing* growth of relative disadvantage. Studies of occupational upgrading among Negroes show that the greatest improvement occurred during the 1940's, with considerably slower progress since that decade. In absolute terms, average Negro income has increased greatly since the end of the depressed 1930's; but the Negro-white income ratio rose most rapidly between 1939 and 1956, and in most recent years that ratio has been somewhat below the peak reached in the 1954–1956 period. Large numbers of Negroes have been moving out of poverty as a result of rising incomes, but the very large increases in Negro population have prevented substantial reductions in the total number of Negroes still living in poverty.

The present distribution of unemployment among Negroes differs significantly from white patterns. Taking into account hidden as well as counted unemployment among Negroes, younger Negro men have unemployment rates substantially above the average rate for all Negro males; and Negro men in the 25 to 34 age group have a rate that is almost four times the rate for white men in that age group. The most striking difference between Negro and white unemployment patterns is by educational level. Among whites, the highest unemployment rates have been for those with the least education, and the lowest rates have been reported for the best-educated. Among Negroes, the least-educated have relatively low unemployment rates; only the most-educated Negroes have lower rates. In relative terms, the ratio between

Negro and white rates is highest for the best-educated. Adding in the hidden unemployment of Negro males does not significantly change the Negro pattern or the relationships between white and Negro rates. Considering both unemployment rates and the Negro-white ratios that measure relative disadvantage, it is clear that the unemployment problem is worse for better-educated Negroes—especially those with nine to twelve years of schooling—than for the least-educated or the college-trained. Finally, there are large regional differentials in Negro unemployment rates. Of the four main regions of the country, the South has the lowest Negro unemployment rate, and the ratio between white and Negro rates is lowest in the South. The North Central region, which has the largest number of Negroes outside the South, has the highest Negro-white unemployment ratio.

The Role of Racial Discrimination

In the view of a great many people, specialists as well as laymen, racial discrimination is the principal source of economic disadvantage for Negroes. From the historical standpoint, this view is unquestionably valid. The fact that virtually the entire American Negro population was held in slavery for two and a half centuries obviously placed an enormous burden of disadvantage on them when they were finally freed. American slavery, unlike the institution in some other places and times, imposed a subhuman status on the enslaved; education, marriage, a normal family life, and ownership of property, among other human rights, were systematically denied American slaves. And no doubt many white people even today are influenced, consciously or unconsciously, by the doctrine of Negro inferiority which was one of the rationalizations for American slavery. More basically, it is obvious that one major reason why Negroes generally are still so far behind whites generally by most measures of economic well-being is that they were even farther behind when they were emancipated. They have made enormous progress in their century of freedom, but whites have been improving their economic status too. In a real sense, the large gaps today between Negroes and whites are a part of the heritage of slavery, and slavery was a comprehensive and virulent system of racial discrimination. Undeniably, racial discrimination is still widely prevalent in important areas of American economic life. Housing is one of the worst areas, but there are many others. Some industries and some firms employ many fewer Negroes than other industries and other firms with apparently comparable requirements.[48] There are still some "lily-white" union locals.[49] Segregated education has been and

remains a great impediment to the economic advancement of Negroes. Despite all this, and despite the continuing necessity for efforts
to eliminate racial discrimination, there appears to be a reasonable
basis for doubting that this factor is the principal *present* source of
economic disadvantage for the Negro. If it is not, continuing insistence
that it is may well divert attention and effort from other more important sources and remedial measures.

There is no way, of course, to calculate a quantitative measure of
the present importance of racial discrimination in Negro disadvantage compared with other factors. Most observers would probably
agree, however, that this country has made significant progress in recent years in reducing most forms of overt discrimination. There is
undoubtedly less discrimination today than there was a quarter-
century ago or even a dozen years ago. Yet the economic progress of
Negroes was greatest, by most measures, from 1940 to 1953. Since then,
relative unemployment of Negroes has risen, occupational upgrading
has slowed, and the narrowing of the relative Negro-white income gap
has slowed or stopped. These changes in the rate of Negro progress
cannot be correlated with changes in the relative intensity of discrimination. Furthermore, differences in the impact of discrimination do
not appear to explain why the incidence of unemployment is greatest
for younger Negroes, better-educated Negroes, and northern Negroes.
Unless we can explain that pattern of incidence and the postwar
changes in the rate of Negro progress, we risk neglecting what appear
to have been the most important sources of Negro disadvantage in
recent years.

The Role of Migration

There are factors other than discrimination that seem to have a
closer relationship to the changes in the rate of Negro progress in the
years since 1940. It is clear that interregional migration has been a
significant factor in those changes. Negro income levels are higher in
the North and West, and Negroes are higher in the occupational
structure there than in the South. As long as migrants are able to
achieve approximately the same income and the same kinds of jobs as
the Negroes already outside the South, the migration process will raise
the national averages for Negroes. There is another side of the coin,
however; it appears that for many decades the Negro unemployment
rate has tended to be higher in the North and West than in the South.
This tendency is readily understandable when we consider that Negroes in the South have been and still are overrepresented in agricul-

ture and that the sharecropper or tenant farmer will not usually be counted as unemployed even if he and his family are on the edge of starvation. Scarcely any northern Negroes work on farms. The migration of Negroes from farms and to the North has also had an important long-run effect on educational attainment. Families on farms often keep their children out of school to help with the crops, and children who expect to spend their lives on farms often see little need for extended schooling.

Thus, long-distance migration has had an important role in the complex pattern of changes in the Negroes' economic status in the past quarter-century. Unfortunately, there does not appear to be any solid basis for assigning a quantitative value to migration relative to other factors. For example, we do not have any way of determining year-by-year changes in unemployment rates by color and region.[50] The decennial census figures can show the changes from one census year to another, but they leave us uninformed about the changes within the decades between censuses. Furthermore, changes in Negro migration rates are not a completely independent variable. The enormous change in the volume of Negro migration from the decade of the 1930's to the following decade was largely a response to the great increase in jobs and the development of a labor shortage in the North, and not a response to a sudden worsening of the Negro's position in the South. The slowing of migration in the late 1950's and in the 1960's was largely a response to less favorable labor market conditions in the North.

The attribution of some part of the rise in the relative Negro unemployment rate to migration from a low-unemployment region to a high-unemployment region is not intended to minimize the problem, although this explanation seems to allay the concern of some economists. It may be true that the unemployed Negro in a northern city is better off in some ways than the underemployed sharecropper in the rural South and that the rising relative unemployment rate for Negroes might be viewed to some extent as merely the exchange of a greater kind of disadvantage for a less serious kind. Such a view ignores an important set of psychological factors. The sharecropper or tenant farmer may be on the ragged edge of existence, but he usually has less trouble keeping busy than the unemployed city worker, and he has a kind of identity which comes from his occupation. He may also be sustained by the hope that if he can somehow manage the move to the North—"the promised land"—things will be better. The man who is already in the promised land and is unemployed there may feel a bitterness and disillusionment, and a sense of rejection, that he would not have felt in the rural South. He is also bombarded by hard-sell advertising on all sides that is cleverly contrived to whet his yearning for fancy cars, fancy clothes, fancy women—all the requisites of the sweet life—and he constantly sees friends and neighbors who "have it made." [51] Our preoccupation with the national unemployment rate as the most important indicator of our economic well-being reflects in some measure our subconscious realization that, in a modern economy, the jobless man or woman is truly an outsider.

Demand for Labor, 1940–1953

The most basic causes for changes in the rate of economic progress for Negroes must be sought in changes in the labor market. And, as the beginner in economics learns, beyond the "market" lie the forces that determine the supply of labor and the demand for it. We have seen that, by almost any conceivable measure, Negroes improved their economic status rapidly in the 1940's, with some kinds of improvement continuing until the end of the Korean War. Many economists attribute this progress to a "tight labor market," [52] and they argue that the quickest and surest way to improve the economic condition of Negroes today is to stimulate aggregate demand sufficiently to achieve a tight labor market again. This prescription will be examined with care in an ensuing section. At this point, it is pertinent to inquire what brought about the tight labor market of the 1940's, what loosened it in the 1950's, and what factors other than mere over-all tightness or looseness had a significant effect on the economic fortunes of Negroes.

In 1940, recovery from the Great Depression was incomplete. Nearly 15 per cent of the labor force was counted as unemployed. By 1943, the unemployment rate had dropped below 2 per cent, and by 1944 it had reached an all-time low of 1.2 per cent. This enormous change is usually attributed to the gigantic increase in government spending for war goods, and the conclusion is often drawn that a sufficiently large increase in aggregate demand can reduce unemployment to any desired level. Whatever the merits of the theoretical argument, it must be noted and emphasized that something more than a large increase in aggregate demand was at work in those years.

The size of the armed forces was increased by about 11 million men and women, and many of them came directly out of the civilian labor force. Despite a large inflow of women, teenagers, and elderly people, the civilian labor force was smaller in 1943 than it had been in 1940, and it shrank even more in 1944 and 1945. Between the year of the

Pearl Harbor attack and the year of V-E Day, unemployment decreased by 4.6 million workers, but civilian employment increased by only 2.4 million. The point to be emphasized is that reductions in the *supply* of labor were a larger factor in the tight wartime labor market than were the increases in the *demand* for labor. Later, during the Korean War, there was a comparable development on a smaller scale: a large increase in the armed forces from 1950 to 1952, a shrinkage in the civilian labor force, and a reduction in the number of unemployed that was larger than the increase in employment.[53]

The great demand for war goods had a substantial effect on the *patterns* of demand for labor. Although there was a slight decline in total employment from 1940 to the peak of the war production effort in late 1943, employment in manufacturing industries increased by 7.3 million, and four-fifths of this increase was in production workers in durable goods industries. The transportation equipment division, which includes trucks, tanks, airplanes, ships, and boats, increased to approximately five times its prewar employment total.[54] Such massive increases in the scale of operations made it feasible, and in some cases essential, to redesign production systems. Shipbuilding and aircraft production, in particular, had been low-volume, custom-fabrication operations before the war; but mass production made it possible to subdivide many formerly skilled jobs into simple components that could readily be taught to inexperienced, low-skilled workers who had never before seen an airplane or a ship. Moreover, many of the traditional concepts of economics were set aside for the duration in most of the war plants. Some of these plants were wholly owned by the government and operated by private industry on a "cost-plus" basis—that is, with the government paying all costs of production plus a fixed fee or a percentage of cost as profit to the private firm. Some privately owned plants operated on the same cost-plus basis. Under such an arrangement, all costs of recruitment and training were usually reimbursed by the government. The normal incentive to weed out substandard or incompetent workmen was greatly diminished, if not eliminated, by the cost-plus arrangement.

The point which is almost always overlooked in contemporary discussions of the "tight labor market" during World War II is that the conditions of that time were the product of a great deal more than a massive increase in aggregate demand. There were also a massive reduction in the civilian labor force; a massive restructuring of demand, resulting in the massive creation of low-skilled, repetitive jobs; massive government subsidies, both direct and indirect, for recruitment and training of inexperienced workers; and a massive increase in tolerance of low productivity. Probably never before in history had the opportunities been as good for the low-skilled, poorly educated workers who remained in civilian life. A somewhat lower percentage of Negro men of military age than of white men were drafted into the armed forces. The rejection rate of Negroes (especially for mental or educational deficiencies) was especially high in the Southeast.[55] The opportunities were most numerous in the great centers of manufacturing activity in the Northeast and North Central regions; the Negroes were most numerous in the South; therefore, a record volume of migration ensued.

The economic distortions induced by war continued for a time after the war, although in modified form. Unemployment increased three-fold from 1944 to 1946, but remained at about the 4 per cent level for the next two years. The depression of the 1930's, followed by wartime shortages of consumer durables, had created a great backlog of unfilled needs; and the great wartime increase in the employment of low-skilled workers at high wages had added a new stratum to demand. A large number of returning veterans chose to take advantage of their educational benefits instead of entering the labor force immediately. Many of the Negroes who had been drawn to the North by war work were able to find jobs in the booming peacetime industries, like automobiles. There was a recession in 1949. Then, as previously mentioned, the Korean War revived some of the characteristics of the World War II economy, although on a smaller scale.

Demand for Labor after 1953

After 1953, as we have seen, improvement in the relative income of Negroes ceased, occupational upgrading of Negroes stopped within the regions, and Negro unemployment rose both relative to the earlier experience of Negroes and relative to contemporaneous white unemployment rates. As already noted, many economists attribute this change in the Negro's economic fortunes simply to the development of a "loose labor market," and they ascribe that in turn to the failure of government to maintain aggregate demand at a high level. Undoubtedly a part of the Negro's economic difficulties can properly be attributed to a loose labor market. But it is also true, as in the earlier period, that some special factors were at work on both the demand and supply sides of the labor market which had a special impact on Negroes.

One of the important factors on the demand side was a change in the nature of defense spending. The emphasis shifted from aircraft, ships, and wheeled vehicles to missiles, atomic weapons, electronic equipment, and similar sophisticated gear; and these trends were reinforced by the new undertakings in space flight. The employment growing out of these new emphases and interests was heavily weighted toward the engineer, the technician, and the skilled craftsman rather than the low-skilled assembly-line worker. Manufacturing industry generally exhibited some of the same trends, although to a lesser degree. The white-collar component of manufacturing employment continued to show a strong growth, but the employment of blue-collar production workers showed a downward drift over time (although, of course, there were ups and downs associated with business cycle peaks and troughs). Thus, in late 1965, the long boom, plus a new war, pushed total employment in manufacturing industries above the previous all-time high which had been reached in 1943; but in the 1965 total were 2.1 million more white-collar jobs and 2.1 million fewer blue-collar jobs than in 1943.[56] Since the Negroes in manufacturing were almost exclusively in blue-collar jobs, the long-term downward trend in this segment of demand for labor operated with special force against them. There were also declines in the less-skilled segment of the labor force in other industries; for example, railroads.

Other changes in the patterns of demand for labor also operated against Negroes. Manufacturing industries such as automobiles undertook a postwar program of decentralization as part of their capital expansion; they wanted to locate new plants in the areas where their markets were growing most rapidly, and this led them to favor the South, the Southwest, and the West rather than the old centers of manufacturing activity in the Northeast and North Central regions. There was also a growing tendency for new stores and plants to locate in the suburbs and satellite cities rather than in the central city, especially in the great capital investment boom of the 1960's. "Between 1954 and 1965, almost two-thirds of all new industrial buildings (measured by valuation) and a little over half of all new stores were constructed outside the nation's central cities."[57] Finally, the greatest growth in employment was in the service-producing industries, including government. One of the significant characteristics of services is that they must generally be performed where the consumers are instead of being fabricated in some central location, like steel or automobiles, and then transported to the customer.

The one post-1953 labor market factor which has received most attention from economists, to the point of virtual exclusion of consideration of the foregoing changes in the pattern of demand, has been inadequate over-all economic growth. The lagging growth rate has been attributed to an excessively passive fiscal and monetary policy by the federal government, especially the failure to correct the effects of what has been called "fiscal drag." In the view of many economists, the federal tax system has had a tendency to generate added revenues for government at a faster rate than government expenditures increase as the economy moves toward full utilization of its productive capacity. The draining off of purchasing power by government without any offsetting increases in government expenditures has choked off expansion of the economy in the past and has created a chronic inadequacy of aggregate demand (that is, the total of all expenditures by individuals, business, and government). One of the consequences of inadequate demand, it is argued, has been a continuously loose labor market.

It should be emphasized that there has been scarcely any disagreement among economists concerning the existence of fiscal drag and its adverse effect on economic growth. There has been disagreement, however, concerning the extent to which fiscal drag *alone* has been responsible for the disproportionately high unemployment rates of such disadvantaged groups as Negroes. This matter will be considered in more detail in a subsequent section of this chapter. At this point, it is sufficient to note that there was fairly general agreement by the end of 1966 that fiscal drag had been fully remedied; indeed, the advocacy of a tax increase by many economists as early as the beginning of 1966 implied that the growth of aggregate demand had already outrun the ability of the economy to produce goods and services. Nevertheless, Negro unemployment, especially among teenagers, remained an urgent problem.

Changes in Labor Supply

Now let us turn to the supply side of the labor market during the years since the Korean War. One development of major importance to Negroes was the sharp rise in agricultural productivity after 1947. In the 1950's white farmers left the land and entered urban labor markets at a rate which exceeded the Negro rate for the first time in the period for which data are available. The displacement of farmers was especially great in the North Central region. This region had contributed only 6 per cent of the total reduction of agricultural employment in the 1940–1950 decade; but in the 1950–1960 decade, this region contributed 28 per cent of a much larger total reduction.[58] This large influx of white farmers into the urban labor market intensified the competition for less-skilled jobs in manufacturing and service-producing industries.

Despite decidedly less favorable job prospects for Negroes in the North and West in the 1950's and early 1960's, their migration from the South continued; but there were changes in rate and direction. The average number of Negro migrants per year from the South during 1960–1963 was less than half the average annual number during the 1940–1950 period; more of the migrants were going to the Northeast and West; and, surprisingly, there was net out-migration from the North Central region.[59] The earlier rates and patterns of Negro migration were having a delayed effect, however, on local labor markets in the North and West, in that natural increases in the Negro population had become increasingly important as a source of growth in the Negro labor force. Thus, despite net out-migration of Negroes from the North Central region after 1960, its share of the total Negro population of the country increased significantly between 1960 and 1964.[60] In all central cities of the United States, about 40 per cent of the growth in Negro population (15 years and older) from 1960 to 1965 was attributed to natural increase, and in the youngest age group, 15 to 19, more than 70 per cent of the very large growth was the result of natural increase.[61]

There is a widespread belief that the essence of the Negro unemployment problem is continued heavy migration of poorly prepared, displaced farm families from the South to the large cities. The facts appear to show that increasingly it is the children of the migrants of a generation ago who have the most severe employment problems, although there appear to be some variations from region to region.

Interpretation of Negro Unemployment Patterns

We come now to a consideration of the present patterns of Negro unemployment, particularly as they differ from white patterns. The earlier discussion has emphasized the great relative disadvantage of younger Negroes, better-educated Negroes, and Negroes in the North. How can we explain these distinctive patterns of disadvantage in the light of the labor market developments of the past two decades?

Some reasons for a lower relative Negro unemployment rate in the South have already been suggested: Negroes there are still overrepresented in agriculture. Not only is there overrepresentation compared with Negroes in the North; a larger proportion of southern Negroes than of southern whites remain in agriculture. As discussed earlier, few farmers are counted as unemployed, even though they may be seriously underemployed. The extremely low earnings of Negroes in the South, relative not only to southern whites but also to northern Negroes, are suggestive of widespread underemployment, among other

things. The occupational distribution of the South also provides some
evidence of the survival of the tradition of "Negro jobs" in the nonfarm sector there. There is even greater overrepresentation of Negroes
in common labor and service jobs in the South than in the North, and
the likelihood is that segregation practices provide some protection for
Negroes against white competition for such jobs. Moreover, the proportion of Negroes in the population has been steadily declining in
the South while it was rising in all the other regions; migration has
carried off much of the natural increase of the Negro population of the
South. Finally, employment growth in the South during the postwar
period has consistently exceeded the average growth rate of the country. On balance, the southern Negro has been improving his economic
status in recent years (especially in the 1960's) more rapidly than
Negroes in the rest of the United States; but the southern Negro
started from such a low level of economic security that, despite his
recent progress, he is still far behind Negroes in the North and the
West. In 1964, for example, median family income of Negroes in the
North Central region was above $5,000; in the South, the median
was below $3,000.[62] The lower unemployment rate for Negroes in the
South is not evidence of their better economic status there. It is, in-
stead, evidence that economic inequality takes a different form in the
South.

The higher unemployment rate of Negroes in the North—especially
the North Central region—can be explained to a considerable degree
by reference to the same factors that create the opposite situation in
the South. Negroes have virtually no representation in northern agriculture. "Negro jobs" protected from white competition are rarer in
the North. The heavy displacement of white farmers in recent years,
especially in the North Central region, has intensified the competition
for low-skilled urban jobs, and Negroes are highly concentrated in
cities, especially large cities, in the North. The northern regions of
largest Negro population have been the regions with the slowest postwar growth rates in total employment—no doubt largely because of
the decentralizing tendencies of industry discussed earlier. The heavy
northward migration of a generation ago, which involved disproportionate numbers of Negroes in the childbearing ages, is now yielding
very large increases in the Negro labor force, especially in the large
cities and particularly in the younger age groups.

The greater relative disadvantage of younger Negroes is in part
attributable to their large numbers in the big cities of the North. If we
assume that young workers, especially teenagers, seek distinctive kinds
of jobs (for example, those in which the experience requirement is

minimal or nonexistent), it should follow that a large concentration of young workers in particular labor market areas will create intense competition for those kinds of jobs and will tend to raise the unemployment rate for such workers. It should be recalled that nonwhites aged 15 to 19 years increased by more than 50 per cent in the central cities of the nation from 1960 to 1965; the nonwhite age group 20 to 24 years also increased, by more than 26 per cent, in the same period. In earlier years, most Negroes of these ages would have had work experience at least on farms; today, many of them reach their twenties with little or no experience in conventional employment and without having developed acceptable work habits. Older Negroes are more likely to have had work experience, especially if they were among the 1940–1953 migrants, and their experience, plus possibly seniority rights, gives them a substantial advantage over younger Negroes. Moreover, demography favors the Negro in his middle years; his numbers have been thinned by the lower birth rates and higher death rates of earlier times.

Negro unemployment rates by level of education show the greatest departure from white patterns, especially if the greater hidden unemployment among Negro males is taken into account. Relatively, the least-educated Negroes are considerably better off than the moderately well-educated—that is, those with some high-school training or a high-school diploma. The least-educated Negro has a lower unemployment rate than his white counterpart; the best-educated Negroes—those with at least a year of college training—have an unemployment rate equal to the rate for white high-school dropouts.

What could explain the relatively low unemployment rates of the least-educated Negroes? It seems quite probable that they are considerably overrepresented in southern agriculture and thus escape the unemployment count. The least-educated Negroes who are in the North and outside agriculture probably compete with their white counterparts on more equal terms than the terms on which the better-educated Negroes must compete. A mature worker with only four or five, or perhaps even six or eight, years of education is disqualified for most jobs with any significant educational requirement. Furthermore, the Negro who is a functional illiterate probably has lower expectations than his white counterpart and may be more willing to accept the hard-to-fill, low-paid, undesirable jobs.

A substantial part of the great relative disadvantage of better-educated Negroes is undoubtedly the result of the failure of the educational system to help Negro students to overcome the handicap of a deprived background. As was noted in an earlier section, the recent

Coleman report revealed that even in the metropolitan Northeast, Negro students in the twelfth grade had median scores on standard achievement tests that were 3.3 years behind those of white students in that region, and southern Negro students were even farther behind. It is also noteworthy that, according to this study, the achievement differential is less at the lower grades. For example, Negroes in the Northeast had median scores that were 1.6 years below median white scores in the sixth grade, and in the ninth grade the difference was 2.4 years.[63] It seems reasonable to assume that these achievement differentials are not a recent development, even though the reported findings related only to a single point in time. It is also important to emphasize, as the Coleman report does, that the tests were not intended to "measure intelligence, nor attitudes, nor qualities of character. . . . What they measure are the skills which are among the most important in our society for getting a good job and moving up to a better one, and for full participation in an increasingly technical world."

If we apply a 25 to 35 per cent discount to the Negroes' reported years of schooling to make a rough adjustment for an assumed average difference in achievement, we reduce substantially the differences in Negro and white unemployment rates by level of education; but we do not eliminate them. Hence, other factors are also at work. There is a much larger percentage of high-school dropouts in the Negro labor force than in the white labor force; and in recent times, at least, the Negro high-school dropout rate has been significantly higher in the North and West than in the South. Therefore, the greater employment difficulties of Negroes in the North are reflected in some measure in the very high unemployment rates for high-school dropouts and even graduates.

There is another factor which apparently cannot be substantiated by statistical data but which competent observers believe to be significant both in the non-South and the South; that is the higher occupational aspirations of the Negroes, especially younger ones, who have invested a large number of years in schooling. These better-educated Negroes are far less willing than their less-educated parents to accept menial, low-paid, low-status, dead-end jobs. They try to compete at a higher level of the labor market, and this often means in the white-collar sector. Here, most of them face an important handicap in addition to deficient educational achievement. The great majority of young, better-educated Negroes come from blue-collar families, while the majority of better-educated young whites come from white-collar families. In most white-collar occupations, the employer, whether rationally or not, tends to require certain modes of behavior, dress, deportment, and speech that are thought to be distinctively white-collar. Whites generally tend to absorb these modes within the family; Negroes generally do not. Thus a kind of class discrimination appears to be at work in the white-collar sector.

The facts that Negroes at the middle levels of educational attainment—that is, nine to twelve years of schooling—suffer the highest unemployment rates, and that Negro college graduates suffer disproportionately high rates relative to whites, are the most disturbing aspect of Negro unemployment patterns. It has always been part of the American dream that the poor but industrious student could rise in the world by investing sufficient time and effort in education. The dream comes true much more often than not for the white student. But when Negroes invest an equal number of years of their lives in formal education, the results are highly unequal in terms of employment security. Quite possibly it is this aspect of inequality more than any other that sustains the widely held belief that the chief impediment to Negro progress is still racial discrimination. No doubt racial discrimination plays some part in this inequality of results, but its effect must be more indirect than is generally recognized. It is difficult to see why direct racial discrimination should be less at the lower levels of educational attainment than at the higher levels. It seems more probable that segregated housing for Negroes, which is responsible for *de facto* segregation in education, and possibly the race and class prejudices of teachers [64] contribute to the failure of Negroes' schools to develop their potential as effectively as do the schools of the whites. Whatever the causes of this inequality of results, the pattern of Negro unemployment rates by number of years of school completed should teach us that it is now less important to urge Negroes to put in more years in today's schools than it is to find ways to make the schools far more effective than they have been in providing true equality of educational opportunity for Negroes.

Summary

This extended analysis of the sources of Negro disadvantage in the economy has led to conclusions which, in some respects, are at variance with the conventional wisdom on the matter. Of course, there is no reasonable basis for assigning numerical values to the various sources of disadvantage; but there is fairly reliable evidence on which to base judgments concerning their relative importance. Examination of this evidence has led to the conclusion that racial discrimination, as a *present* source of economic disadvantage, is probably less important than is commonly assumed. This conclusion does not deny that discrimination persists; it does not deny that discrimination makes important indirect contributions to Negro disadvantage through segregated housing and segregated education; nor does it deny the necessity for continued educational and legislative efforts to combat discrimination. What the conclusion does imply is that an antidiscrimination campaign by itself, no matter how effective, is not likely to improve the Negro's economic status significantly, at least in the short run.

If we are to understand the basic causes of the Negro's present economic disadvantages, we must explain the great changes in his rate of progress in the past quarter-century. We must understand the causes of his unmatched progress from about 1940 to about 1953 as well as the slowing or stopping of progress on many fronts since then. The analysis here supports the view that the primary causes must be sought in a complex set of labor market interactions. It is commonly recognized that World War II created an acute labor shortage; what is not so commonly recognized is that the shortage resulted not only from a great increase in government spending but also from a massive withdrawal of men from the civilian labor force. There is almost no recognition that the needs of war production massively distorted the patterns of demand for labor. The transportation equipment industries, in particular, offered more jobs than ever before or after. Enormous growth, new plants, new products, and a pervasive system of government subsidies made it possible to redesign production techniques to utilize vast numbers of low-skilled workers.

The unprecedented increase in opportunities for workers with little or no previous industrial experience induced an unprecedented flood of northward migration by southern Negroes whose means of livelihood had been undermined by the long decline of agriculture in the South— a decline which had been reinforced by the long depression of the 1930's. The migrating Negroes were drawn to the big, established centers of heavy industry, especially in the North Central region and on the East Coast. The seeking of their own kind and the patterns of segregated housing directed the migrants into the "central cities." Even after the end of World War II, accumulated backlogs of demand for durable goods provided jobs for most of the wartime migrants and even for new migrants from the South; and the Korean War postponed the transition to more normal peacetime conditions.

Even before the end of the Korean War, Negroes were adversely affected by the influx into the urban labor market of white farmers who had been displaced by the technological revolution in agriculture. The white competition in the low-skilled segment of the urban labor market was especially intense in the North Central region, which by 1950 held the largest Negro population outside the South. After Korea, the demand for less-skilled workers in manufacturing began a long secular decline. The industrial investment boom of the 1950's hastened the decentralization of manufacturing activity, to the disadvantage of the old industrial centers and the Negroes who were massed in them. The central cities of large metropolitan areas grew less attractive as locations for new stores and offices, partly because whites were moving to the suburbs in large numbers. Deterioration of public transportation facilities increased the Negro's isolation from the growing suburbs. After the great investment boom of the 1950's ended, "fiscal drag" contributed to slack in the lower strata of the labor market.

Some of today's "gross unemployment" among Negroes can be traced fairly directly to their eager response to the distorted patterns of demand in the labor market during World War II. In the 1950's, when these patterns finally started changing in conformity with long-run, fundamental trends in the economy, Negroes were in the places and the occupations that had the greatest burdens of adjustment. Those burdens were increased by continuing migration, even though the volume and the direction of migration finally changed in the late 1950's and early 1960's as the economic climate in the North, especially the North Central region, changed. By that time, some demographic consequences of the great war-induced migration had become increasingly important. That migration had transferred a substantial part of the reproductive capacity of the entire Negro population of the country to the big cities of the North. In the ensuing years, a falling death rate and rising birth rate combined to create a population explosion among big-city Negroes. The public schools were inundated; *de facto* segregation of the schools spread rapidly; and the schools increasingly failed to pay off with greater social and economic mobility for Negroes, although they had paid off in that fashion for earlier waves of migrants. In the late 1950's and early 1960's, the first shock waves of the Negro population explosion started hitting the labor market. Despite sharply reduced participation rates among young Negroes, despite a new boom of record duration, despite special employment and training programs, despite a new war with huge draft calls, the reported unemployment rate among young Negroes rose to disastrous levels. The major trends that have been analyzed in this discussion appear to guarantee that "gross unemployment" among young Negroes will persist or even worsen as the very large numbers of Negro children now in the big cities reach working ages and that this blight will spread as today's teenage Negroes grow older.

This summary may suggest pessimism, or perhaps fatalism, concerning the prospects for reducing economic inequalities for Negroes. That is not the intention. Neither is it the intention to excuse the public and official complacency which has allowed this menacing problem to grow to its present size despite the lengthening shadow that has been visible for a long time to anyone who cared to look. Least of all is it the intention to suggest that the problem is now irremediable. On the other hand, it would be a dangerous error to underestimate the stubbornness and the size of the problem.

STRATEGIES FOR IMPROVING THE ECONOMIC STATUS OF NEGROES

General

To many people, there is no mystery at all about how to improve the economic status of Negroes. More and better jobs for those that can work and more money directly from the public purse for those who cannot work: these are the obvious answers, are they not? One is reminded of the immortal remark attributed to Calvin Coolidge: "When a great many people are unable to find work, unemployment results." The result may be entirely clear, but merely describing it leaves unanswered the difficult question: how is it brought about?

There appears to be fairly general agreement that there is no single, easy answer, although there are a number of prescriptions for "the single most important step"—most of them, unfortunately, sharply in conflict with each other. Those who have examined most closely the complex factors that have interacted to impede Negro progress toward economic equality recognize the necessity for what is sometimes called a "total program," which means a number of different approaches with careful co-ordination among them. For example, there is little point in getting employers to agree to hire more Negroes if there are no qualified Negro applicants; and on the other hand, job training which fails to lead to jobs is dangerously frustrating. If the hallmark of the scholar is the call for further research, the hallmark of the activist is insistence on immediate action. At this point in history, it seems likely that the turmoil in the cities will yield, among other things, increased opportunities both for activists and for scholars: many new programs will be proposed and some will be started, and some existing programs will be enlarged; but the need for evaluation, for measuring results, for diagnosing causes of failure, for pointing out unmet needs, and for fitting together many pieces into a meaningful whole—grist for the mills of scholars—will also grow.

The formulation of a detailed blueprint for the achievement of Negro economic equality would be beyond the scope of this chapter even if the present state of knowledge gave hope for success in such an endeavor. The analysis of the sources of Negro disadvantage, however, provides a basis for suggesting some broad lines of strategy, their respective limitations and relationships, and some emerging questions of basic importance on which research is essential. Not all important areas will be covered here. Radical improvements in Negro education and Negro housing must obviously be a major part of any "total program"; but that is discussed elsewhere in this volume. Continued pressure—economic, educational, legal, and social—is essential to reduce and, if possible, eliminate all forms of racial discrimination in American life; but this area of action is not treated at length here because, in the first place, extensive programs are already in existence and will certainly grow in effectiveness, and in the second place, it is my conviction that other relatively neglected areas should be given greater attention at this point in time. There are no homilies here on the importance of "self-help" by the Negroes. Someone has aptly observed that it is not possible for a man to lift himself by the bootstraps if he has no boots. I believe that the history of the Negroes in America—especially the history of the 1940–1953 period—demonstrates that they are as ready as any group in the population to grasp opportunity when it is within their reach.

One more preliminary observation is in order. The three main lines of strategy discussed in ensuing sections are not "Negro" programs in the sense that only Negroes would benefit from them. Whatever may be the merits of the radicals' demand for "reparations" for Negroes, there appears to be little chance that any overtly racist program (even if racist-in-reverse) will be accepted by the white majority in the foreseeable future. Nevertheless, the strategies discussed here have a special impact on Negroes. There are many more poor white families than poor Negro families; but a much larger proportion of Negro families are poor. There are many more unemployed white workers than Negroes; but unemployment hits more than twice as large a percentage of Negroes. Programs to reduce poverty and unemployment will (if they succeed) help a larger *number* of whites than Negroes, but the *proportion* of Negroes helped will be larger. Such is the arithmetic of disadvantage.

Economic Expansion

Late in 1964, some members of the Johnson administration were
pushing hard for a request to Congress for a $2-billion work program,
to be directed primarily to the big-city slums. The proposal was de-
bated at some length within the administration and was finally rejected. The argument which did the most to defeat it, according to a
report shortly after the event, was that such a proposal might jeopar-
dize the top-priority item in the economic program, which was a reduction in excise taxes. The argument was not, it should be noted, that
with such a proposal there would be no excise tax cuts; rather, it was
that pushing the job proposal might result in tax cuts of only $2 billion
rather than the hoped-for $4 billion. The sequel to the story came
three years and many riots later: In 1967, the Urban Coalition (an *ad
hoc* group of business, labor, educational, political, and civil rights
leaders) proposed immediate adoption of a program to provide at
least one million jobs in the public sector. The administration did not
respond directly, but was reported to believe that such a major new
proposal would be inconsistent with what was then the top-priority
item in the economic program, which was an increase in taxes to hold
down inflation.[65]

The 1964 decision did not reflect any lack of concern within the administration for the unemployed and the poor. Instead, it was responsive to the strong belief held in some groups within the administration
that general stimulation of the economy is a more effective and more
desirable remedy for unemployment than the direct creation of jobs in
the public sector. Such general stimulation, it is often argued, will especially benefit the groups in the labor force (such as Negroes) that
have particularly high unemployment rates. This was a major argument advanced in support of the large cut in personal and business income taxes which was enacted early in 1964,[66] and it was urged with
undiminished assurance when the excise tax cut was under consideration in 1965. There is good reason to expect that the argument will be
used yet again when the Viet Nam War ends and permits a large reduction of military spending. It is important, therefore, to examine the
basis for that belief and the extent to which it is supported by recent
experience, particularly recent changes in Negro unemployment.

The belief is derived from the teachings of J. M. Keynes. Stated
quite briefly, the argument begins with the proposition that the level of
employment—and therefore the level of unemployment—is determined by aggregate demand (which means simply total spending,

both for current consumption and for investment, by individuals, businesses, and governments). If productive resources, including labor, are not fully employed, the remedy is to increase aggregate demand up to the point where as much as the economy can produce will be bought. Government can add to aggregate demand either by increasing its own expenditures for goods and services—for example, by spending $2 billion on a work-relief program without increasing taxes—or by reducing the taxes that it levies on businesses and individuals without reducing its own expenditures. In short, government fiscal policy—what it does about spending and taxing—is a key determinant of the level of employment.

The contention that it is the most disadvantaged members of the labor force who will realize the greatest improvement in their situation from general stimulation of the economy (that is, an increase in aggregate demand) rests on certain basic assumptions about how the labor market operates. These assumptions, it must be noted, are usually stated not as assumptions but as established fact, as in the following passage:

> It is the proper function of a market to allocate resources, and in this respect the labor market does not function differently from any others. If the available resources are of high quality, the market will adjust to the use of high quality resources; if the quality is low, methods will be developed to use such resources. . . . In a slack labor market employers must have some means of selecting among numerous applicants, and it is not surprising that educational attainment is often used as a convenient yardstick, regardless of its direct relevance to the requirements of the job.
>
> We have found it useful to view the labor market as a gigantic "shape-up," with members of the labor force queued in order of their relative attractiveness to employers. . . . The total number employed and unemployed depends primarily on the general state of economic activity. The employed tend to be those near the beginning and the unemployed those near the end of the line. Only as demand rises will employers reach further down the line in their search for employees. . . . And because workers of low educational attainment are the least desirable to employers, nonwhite and older workers are concentrated at the rear of the line, not only because of their lower educational attainment, but also because of direct discrimination.[67]

These assumptions have been tacitly relied on for an explanation of the Negro's economic fortunes in the past quarter-century by Professor James Tobin, a former member of the Council of Economic Advisers. He writes as follows:

> The most important dimension of the overall economic climate is the tightness of the labor market. . . . Because of the heavy demands for

labor during the Second World War and its economic aftermath, Negroes made dramatic relative gains between 1940 and 1950. Unfortunately this momentum has not been maintained, and the blame falls largely on the weakness of labor markets since 1957. . . . I conclude that the single most important step the nation could take to improve the economic position of the Negro is to operate the economy steadily at a low rate of unemployment.[68]

Perhaps the most crucial of all the assumptions underlying this theory of the labor market is that the *patterns* of demand for labor are almost entirely determined by the state of the labor market. If it is a slack market, employers can be highly selective and impose exaggerated requirements of education, training, and experience; if it is a tight market, employers will be forced to tailor their requirements to the existing supply of labor—redesigning production processes where necessary, providing on-the-job training, and upgrading their present employees. In earlier days, it was standard procedure in economic theory to assume that labor was homogeneous. The present procedure, it may be suggested, is to assume that the labor market is an all-powerful homogenizer of labor, in the sense that market pressures are presumed to induce actions on the part of employers that make low-skilled workers readily substitutable for the unavailable high-skilled workers.

It is consistent with this view of the labor market as a great homogenizer to argue further, as most economists of this persuasion do, that it makes no real difference what the government spends money for and that there is no significant difference, so far as the effects on the employment level are concerned, between government spending and private spending. The next step in this chain of reasoning is that increases in government expenditure and tax cuts which stimulate private spending are equally effective methods of increasing aggregate demand. Since there is no economic basis for preferring one over the other, this reasoning concludes, it is proper to consider political expediency (among other things) in making the choice.

The arithmetic of politics virtually ensures that the choice, posed in these terms, will be for tax cuts rather than expenditure increases. Almost everyone is believed to benefit from a tax cut. Even the unemployed who pay no taxes will get jobs as a result of tax-cutting, it is argued. On the other hand, an expenditure program—for example, work projects in the slums—visibly and certainly benefits only the small minority that is enabled to move from unemployment into employment.[69] Furthermore, it has always been a high-priority item on the conservative agenda that taxes, no matter what their level, are too high and should be reduced. Thus, what has come to be called the

"New Economics" finds ready allies among the conservatives when the choice is to cut taxes, whereas it is assumed that conservatives would powerfully and no doubt successfully oppose expenditure increases. There is yet another, perhaps subtler, consideration which predisposes many economists in favor of tax-cutting, and that is a rather more sympathetic view of the private sector than the public: it is believed that resources are always allocated in the private sector in response to the choices of consumers, which has a kind of sanctity in economic theory that is not accorded to choices made by the political process as in the public sector.[70]

The analysis of Negro unemployment which has been set forth in the preceding sections of this chapter has undoubtedly made it clear that I do not accept the notion that the labor market always functions as a great homogenizer. Virtually the only empirical evidence that is ever cited to support that view is what happened during World War II. As previously related, there was a vast creation of low-skilled jobs during that conflict; but it was most notable in industries with a fivefold or greater expansion of employment, new product lines, new plants, and cost-plus contracts. As an arbitrator in the wartime shipbuilding, ordnance, steel, and other industries, I saw multitudinous examples of job and process redesign which were undertaken for the express purpose of making it possible to meet production schedules with unskilled and inexperienced labor. During many years as an arbitrator in the peacetime automobile, rubber, steel, household appliance, and other mass production industries, I have *never* seen a peacetime example of a job being redesigned for the specific purpose of making it possible to fill the job with unskilled rather than skilled labor. Job changes are exceedingly common, of course, in peacetime industry; but all the thousands that I have seen have been incidental to process changes, equipment changes, new products, and the like, with no evidence of any conscious effort to shape job requirements to utilize available unemployed labor.

To be sure, one man's observation can cover only an infinitesimally small fraction of total experience. For years, however, a standard feature of labor economics textbooks has been a long section summarizing the many studies of particular labor markets and their "imperfections" —lack of knowledge, immobility, noneconomic behavior, noncompeting groups, the effects of monopoly and monopsony, and so on. Reynolds states the consensus of those who have made empirical studies of labor markets when he writes as follows: "One can say, indeed, that labor markets are less adequate than any other type of factor or product market in the economy." [71]

There has been scarcely any recognition of the extent to which the latter-day advocacy of tax-cutting as the preferred method of stimulating aggregate demand and relieving unemployment rests on the mystique of the market and in particular on the view that the labor market is a great automatic homogenizer of labor. Since this dependence has not been recognized, there has been little questioning of the assumptions on which the view rests. In my opinion, it is most remarkable that economic policy choices with such a heavy impact on millions of people have so consistently been made on the basis of assumptions that are not only without relevant empirical support but even in conflict with what factual evidence is available concerning the actual operation of labor markets.

One of the urgent research needs of the day is for further studies of contemporary labor markets, updating and broadening the pioneering studies of a decade or two ago. Among the questions to which answers should be sought are the following: How do employers in diverse industries and diverse geographic locations react to shortages of labor, either skilled or unskilled? What magnitudes of increase in demand make it feasible to redesign production systems to utilize lower grades of labor? In what industries, and under what circumstances, has such redesign taken place? Are hiring standards generally without particular relevance to the job or jobs to be filled? How valid is the common employer complaint that the lower jobs in many promotion sequences are permanently occupied by men who lack the ability to advance, thus thwarting the training of others? Have employers actually relaxed hiring standards in recent periods of labor shortages, and if so with what results? These questions are intended, of course, to be suggestive and not exhaustive. And I do not mean to suggest exclusive attention to employer practices. It would also be useful to know more about what the factors are that have kept the unemployment and underemployment rates very high in (for example) the Chicago ghettos while there were acute shortages of all grades of labor, including unskilled, only twenty-five miles away in the Gary area steel plants.

Let us now turn from assumptions to performance. How much has the general stimulation of demand—first by successive tax cuts, then by large increases in defense spending—contributed to the reduction of unemployment, especially Negro unemployment? We can begin by considering unemployment rate changes between two periods: the first quarter of 1964, when the large reduction in personal and corporate income taxes was enacted, and the fourth quarter of 1966, when the long period of expansion reached its peak (most of the indices of economic activity flattened or declined in the following quarter). The changes are shown in the following tabulation.[72]

| | | | PERCENTAGE CHANGE |
Unemployment Rate	IQ, 1964	IVQ, 1966	IQ, 1964—IVQ, 1966
All groups	5.5	3.8	−31
All whites	4.9	3.3	−33
Teenage whites	13.6	10.0	−26
All nonwhites	9.8	7.5	−23
Teenage nonwhites	22.7	23.5	+3

Thus, during this period, the group that had the lowest unemployment rate to start with ("All whites") experienced the largest relative drop; the group that was most severely disadvantaged in the 1964 quarter, teenage nonwhites, had an even *higher* rate in the 1966 quarter. As will be pointed out shortly, it is unjustifiable to assume that these relative unemployment rates were responding only to economic expansion. Nevertheless, even if we make that assumption *arguendo*, it is quite clear that one of the major predictions of the demand-stimulation school was flatly wrong. Increasing the pressure of demand did not permit the labor market to function as a great homogenizer and absorb the disadvantaged at a more rapid rate than the advantaged. What happened was the opposite of that prediction; the most advantaged had the greatest proportionate improvement, and the most disadvantaged had the least proportionate improvement. Unemployment was even more heavily concentrated among the most disadvantaged at the end of 1966 than at the beginning of 1964. Most groups did have lower unemployment rates in 1966, but this was not true of the most disadvantaged group of all: nonwhite teenagers.

The aspect of performance that is most frequently emphasized in current discussions of unemployment developments is the relatively low figure of 3.8 per cent that had been achieved by the end of 1966. This figure is slightly below the administration's "interim full employment target" and is often cited as evidence of the effectiveness of the fiscal and monetary policies of the Kennedy and Johnson administrations. It is important to realize, however, that policies and programs that had no connection at all with fiscal and monetary policy (as usually defined) had a substantial effect on the over-all level of unemployment, and more particularly the unemployment rates of the disadvantaged groups. The point cannot be fully developed within the confines of this chapter, but it can at least be illustrated by reference to two kinds of programs.

The first is the expansion of the armed forces.[73] There appears to be a widespread, though unexamined, assumption among economists that this factor has no significant effect on the unemployment rate. One searches in vain through the current literature, including government reports, for any discussion of the matter. As was pointed out in an earlier section of this chapter, it is obvious that draft calls were one important factor in producing extremely low unemployment rates during World War II and again during the Korean War. The Viet Nam War has caused another large increase in the armed forces, and this increase in turn has contributed to a lowering of the over-all unemployment rate.

The net increase in the armed forces from the first quarter of 1964 to the final quarter of 1966 was, in round numbers, 600,000.[74] If we added this number of persons to the civilian labor force and to the unemployed total, the unemployment rate would be 4.5 per cent rather than the 3.8 per cent that was actually reported for the fourth quarter of 1966. No doubt, reasonable arguments can be made against adding all of the 600,000 to the unemployed total. Nevertheless, most of these young men were in the civilian labor force prior to their induction or would have been had they not anticipated induction; very few, if any, were students taken straight from school or college in this period. There is no reason to assume that there would have been any more jobs available in the civilian economy if these young men had not been inducted. If they had remained in civilian life, the majority would probably have been employed; but if so, they would have displaced some other workers. Some of the inductees might have dropped out of the labor force and joined the hidden rather than the counted unemployed, and so might some of those who had replaced the inductees.

We must also give brief attention to an indirect effect of selective service deferment policies on labor force growth. As already suggested, during the period under consideration deferment was virtually automatic for students. In consequence, there was a quite large increase in full-time male students, ages 18–25, in the fall of 1965. (I refer to those without even part-time employment and thus counted as "not in the labor force.") The increase in this category of students was about 300,000 more than a year earlier, whereas an increase of only about 115,000 would have been expected on the basis of population growth. Most of the excess of about 185,000 must be young men who would have been in the labor force had it not been for the Viet Nam War and higher draft calls.

Thus, between early 1964 and late 1966, about 785,000 young men were affected directly or indirectly by the draft calls for the Viet Nam War. How many of these would have been in the civilian labor force had it not been for the war? It seems quite conservative to estimate that between a half and two-thirds of them would have been net additions to the labor force—let us say 450,000 in round numbers. On the assumption that each of these young men would have displaced someone else from a job or would have been unemployed himself, the national unemployment rate would have been about 4.3 per cent in the last quarter of 1966, instead of 3.8 per cent. In other words, the effects of the Viet Nam War on the supply of labor contributed about 30 per cent of the reduction in unemployment rates during the period under consideration. I readily concede that more detailed analysis of these effects would be desirable; my simple calculations are not intended to provide more than an approximation of the orders of magnitude involved. Not only the past but also the future may be involved here. If a time comes when we can reduce the size of the armed forces, we shall have some basis for estimating the effects on the size of the labor force and the level of unemployment.[75]

The other kind of program that had a major impact on unemployment rates in the 1964–1966 period includes those sometimes identified as "structural": manpower training, Neighborhood Youth Corps, Job Corps, College Work-Study, New Careers, and others. To illustrate their impact, let us consider the Neighborhood Youth Corps (NYC) and Job Corps. It is well known that these programs are quite similar to two depression-era work-relief programs, the National Youth Administration (NYA) and Civilian Conservation Corps (CCC). In the historical statistics, enrollees in work-relief programs were (and still are) counted as "unemployed." Since sometime in 1965, however, the official statistics have counted NYC enrollees as "employed," and Job Corps enrollees have been classified as "not in the labor force." As a first approximation, we can simply recalculate unemployment rates on the basis of the old definition. It may be noted that the principal qualification for these two programs in particular is a lack of qualifications that are useful in the regular labor market. About 90 per cent of NYC enrollees are teenagers, and 46 per cent are nonwhite.[76] Job Corps enrollees do not differ markedly in their characteristics except that they are generally even more disadvantaged than the NYC group. Neither program was in existence in 1964; in the fourth quarter of 1966, average monthly enrollment in NYC was about 163,000, and Job Corps enrollment was slightly less than 40,000.[77] Counting the enrollees in both programs as "unemployed," as under the old definition, raises the national unemployment rate for the fourth quarter of 1966 to a little more than 4 per cent. However, because these programs concentrate on the heavily disadvantaged, the effect is much greater when we consider the nonwhite teenage unemployment rate. That rate (for fourth quarter, 1966) increases from 23.5 per cent to 33.2 per cent when the old definition is applied. The net increase in employment for nonwhite teenagers from 1964, first quarter, to 1966, fourth quarter, was 68,000; of this increase, 67,300 was attributable to NYC enrollment. Again, it might be argued that not all of these enrollees would be counted as "unemployed" according to the official definition if the NYC and Job Corps programs had never been started, but obviously all of the enrollees are able and willing to work.

There are many other manpower programs, of course, that place special emphasis on help for the disadvantaged. Nearly 400,000 workers have completed training programs under the Manpower Development and Training Act since that legislation became effective late in 1962. The great majority of these trainees were unemployed before they entered the program, and the great majority were employed after completion of training. Nonwhites, younger workers, and poorly educated workers were substantially overrepresented in the enrollments.[78] Comparably detailed enrollment figures for the College Work-Study program are apparently unavailable under present data-gathering procedures, but the total enrollment has been estimated at about 180,000 in the fourth quarter of 1966.[79] Various programs under the Office of Economic Opportunity provide direct employment for many tens of thousands of poor people, mainly as "program aides."

There is a pressing need for further collection, refinement, and analysis of data concerning these programs, in order to gauge with greater accuracy their impact on the over-all unemployment rate and the rates for particular disadvantaged groups. Even on the basis of present data, however, it is difficult to see how anyone who is familiar with the facts could reasonably dispute the conclusion that at least half of the reduction in the over-all unemployment rate between early 1964 and late 1966 was brought about by armed forces expansion and structural programs in the manpower field. In other words, in the absence of these important factors, the unemployment rate would have been somewhere between 4.5 and 5 per cent by the end of 1966. The growing concentration of unemployment on the most disadvantaged groups would have been even more pronounced than it was by the end of 1966 had it not been for the "structural" programs. Nonwhite teenagers—the most disadvantaged group in the labor force—would have had an unemployment rate about half again as high as the 23.5 per cent rate that was officially reported.

In view of the facts just reviewed, the current position of the leading advocates of general demand stimulation as the prime cure for unemployment—especially the unemployment of the most disadvantaged —is quite surprising. Generally, their analysis of developments since early 1964 (or some early date) is highly simplistic: unemployment has been reduced greatly and is now below the "interim full employment target" of 4 per cent; all of this improvement is attributable to tax-cutting plus increased defense spending; therefore, it is now beyond dispute that tax-cutting is the best remedy for unemployment. Three recent quotations—brief, but fully representative of their context—will illustrate the position:

> The economists said all along that use of fiscal and monetary policy to stimulate demand would cure unemployment, automation or no automation, and they have been proved 100 per cent right.[80]

> Employment developments in 1965–66 rendered a clear-cut verdict on the structural-unemployment thesis: the alleged hard core of unemployment lies not at 5 or 6 percent, but even deeper than 4 percent—how deep still remains to be ascertained.[81]

> It is as clear today as it can possibly be that, in the situation of 1961 [*sic*], the inadequate demand camp was right and the structuralists were wrong.[82]

The reliance of these writers on *post hoc, ergo propter hoc* reasoning necessarily implies that they support the proposition that armed forces expansion of 600,000, the draft-related increase of 185,000 in full-time student status among young men, the enrollment of more than 300,000 young people in work-relief programs, the retraining of 400,000 workers, and so on, made no significant contribution to the reduction of unemployment. I trust that the proposition is so untenable that further discussion would be superfluous.

If this fallacious view related only to some obscure point of economic doctrine or to some controversy of the dim past, there would be little cause for wide concern. But the fallacy lies at the heart of contemporary employment policy. To paraphrase one of the authors just quoted, it is as clear today as it can possibly be that, in the situation of 1965, the inadequate demand camp was badly mistaken in insisting on a $4-billion excise tax cut instead of a smaller tax cut plus a $2-billion work program. Yet even before the excise tax cut had become fully effective, the administration was publicly discussing which taxes to cut next.[83] It seems reasonable to assume that if the Viet Nam escalation had not precluded further tax-cutting, this approach to full employment policy would have continued to hold the top-priority position in the administration's economic program. But as this is written, it is an anti-inflationary tax *increase* to which all other economic proposals must be subordinated.

Superficial analysts have concluded that the alleged conflict between the demand-stimulation thesis and the structural thesis can easily be resolved by the simple formulation that employment policy must include both fiscal policy measures, to maintain aggregate demand, and manpower programs, to improve the employability of the most disadvantaged members of the labor force. This simplism ignores the basic point of disagreement, which relates to the more difficult question, how much of each? Which kind of measure should be given priority at a given level of unemployment? The demand-stimulation school has conceded the desirability of manpower programs, but would give them low priority until the last ounce of benefit has been wrung out of measures to increase aggregate demand; and some members of this group appear to be convinced now that fiscal stimulus alone can drive the unemployment rate to some point well below 4 per cent. The structural school [84] has conceded the continuing need for fiscal stimulus, not only to reduce the unemployment rate but to generate additional jobs for a growing labor force; but this school has also insisted that fiscal policy alone would not be likely to reduce the average unemployment rate much below 5 per cent, that disproportionate benefits would go to the relatively better-off groups in the labor force, and that greatly increased emphasis on manpower programs would be essential as the average unemployment rate dropped below 5 per cent.

The pragmatism of American politics and the exigencies of international relations have given the country an employment policy mix which is substantially different from what either the demand-stimulation thesis or the structural thesis prescribes. In the past five years, tax cuts have been enacted which have a current annual value of close to $25 billion, and defense expenditures have risen by $21 billion since fiscal 1965.[85] Economists are substantially in agreement, as this is written, that further expansion of demand may cause politically embarrassing inflation; hence, it seems clear that demand expansion through fiscal policy has been pursued to the maximum feasible extent, at least for the time being. Also in the past five years, manpower programs per se have been expanded—by considerably more than is implied by the demand-stimulation analysis, but by considerably less than is urged by the structural analysis. Even if the 600,000-man expansion of the armed forces and its indirect effects are included as a temporary and unwelcome supplement to other kinds of manpower programs, there is no basis for any belief that the manpower program component of employment policy is near any kind of feasibility ceiling. Instead, it can readily be demonstrated that all the manpower programs currently in operation are serving only a fraction of their respective "target populations."

Whatever may have been the merits in earlier years of the advocacy of "tighter labor markets" as the "single most important step" to remedy Negro disadvantage, further pursuit of that course is now obviously inappropriate. The burden of Negro disadvantage remains unacceptably and dangerously high. Thus, recent experience has confirmed, at least with regard to Negroes, the research findings of the past decade or so which emphasized the imperfections, rather than the homogenizing power, of the labor market. The most important lesson of recent experience is that special manpower programs, tailored to the special labor market handicaps of Negroes, must be developed on a much larger scale than in the past if we hope to avert the ominous rise in Negro unemployment which labor force projections foretell.

Transfer Payments

The renewed interest in recent years in the problems of poverty has stimulated discussion of a variety of proposals which are designed to transfer money income from the affluent majority to the impoverished minority. Like economic expansion, these proposals would affect more impoverished whites than Negroes; yet a disproportionate number of Negroes would be among the recipients of such transfer payments. In 1966, there were 29.7 million persons, including family members as well as persons without families, living below the poverty level. Approximately a third of the total were nonwhites. However, the incidence of poverty among whites was 11.8 per cent, and among nonwhites the incidence was 41.4 per cent.[86]

There is considerable variation in the proposals. No attempt will be made here to present an exhaustive compilation or to consider all the questions raised by the proposals.[87] Rather, the proposals will be divided into three main categories, and some general questions will be asked concerning each category. The three categories are the following: guaranteed annual income, negative income tax, and family allowances. Although there is some overlapping, the central ideas of all three are different.

A guaranteed annual income has been advocated most vigorously by Robert Theobald.[88] His basic premise is that revolutionary technological changes are creating the possiblilty of general abundance, but are also making it impossible to provide jobs for all who seek them. Therefore, he argues, it is essential to break the link between jobs and income. He proposes to do so by establishing "an absolute constitutional right" of every citizen to receive from government an income sufficient to permit him to live with dignity. For illustrative purposes, he suggests that at the outset allowances should be $1,000 per year per adult and $600 per year per child, or $3,200 per year for a man and wife with two children. Any family of that composition which had "private income"—that is, earnings from work or returns from savings or investments—which was less than that amount would be entitled to a make-up payment to bring the total to $3,200, plus a 10 per cent "premium" on the private income. Thus, he proposes that 90 per cent of "private earnings" be offset against the guarantee. To use his example, if the assumed four-person family had private income of $2,000, it would be entitled to $1,200 as a make-up payment, plus $200 as a "premium" on private earnings, and its total income would be $3,400. There would be a considerable "notch" effect under this scheme. The family of four with private earnings of $3,199 would collect a make-up payment of $1 plus $319.90 as a premium, for a total income of $3,519.90; but the family with private earnings of exactly $3,200 would presumably get nothing. Therefore, a diminishing premium close to the $3,200 earnings figure would probably be necessary. The net cost of this plan has been estimated at about $28.8 billion per year, but a substantial part of this estimate rests on the assumption that the working poor would be induced to leave the labor market voluntarily. Under different assumptions, it is possible to reduce the estimate to about $11 billion per year.[89] The plan would gradually replace Social Security, unemployment compensation, relief payments, and the like; but this substitution would not reduce the net cost, because Theobald envisages a gradually rising level of guaranteed income. The feature that distinguishes the guaranteed annual income plan from the negative income tax proposals is the emphasis of the former on a payment which is sufficient to permit the recipient to live with dignity—or, more explicitly, the complete elimination rather than the reduction of the poverty gap in incomes.

It is important to emphasize the extent to which Theobald justifies this approach by his basic assumption that we are entering an era of massive, permanent, and growing unemployment. On that assumption, it is unjustifiable to count as a cost of the program the production lost by the induced withdrawal of the presently working poor from the labor market. Theobald's answer would be that any who do not "voluntarily" withdraw will soon be forced out anyway. Hence, the assumption renders irrelevant any alleged "disincentive" effects of the proposal. A detailed consideration of the merits of the assumption is beyond the scope of this essay, although I will permit myself the observation that I am unable to accept the inevitability of massive unemployment in the near future as a consequence of technological change. The case for Theobald's assumption rests much more on assertion than on evidence at this point, and the kind of problem that he foresees seems more possible in the distant rather than the immediate future.

Among the leading proponents of a negative income tax are Milton Friedman,[90] Robert Lampman,[91] and James Tobin.[92] The terms of various proposals vary considerably, and some authors present several different plans. The basic approach may be briefly summarized as follows: The first step is to designate a poverty-level income (the most popular figure is $3,000 for a family of four). The next step is to determine what *fraction* of the poverty gap (the difference between the actual income of a poor family and the poverty floor, $3,000 in this illustration) is to be filled; a popular fraction is 50 per cent. The final step is to determine the rate or rates at which other income is to be offset against the allowance. In the simplest plan, this rate is 50 per cent. Thus, the family of four with no income would receive an allowance of $1,500; if the family's income were $1,500 to start with, half of that income would be offset against the allowance and it would become $750, which would result in total family income of $2,250. Some plans, however, provide for a variable rate of offset, such as 75 per cent on the first $1,500 of nonallowance income and 25 per cent on the next $1,500. Generally speaking, an integral part of the plans is self-reporting, commonly through the completion of a tax return, with eligibility for the allowance resting solely on the amount of income reported. It is usually contemplated that the plan should be administered by the Internal Revenue Service.

The principal attraction of the negative income tax proposals is that they promise to correct with a single stroke, so to speak, some of the greatest shortcomings of the present system of assistance to the needy. The negative income tax would provide payments as a matter of right, with inadequacy of income the sole criterion, thus eliminating residence requirements, ability of some family members to work, family assets, and other considerations that are relevant under many other assistance programs. It is sometimes argued, indeed, that the negative income tax would eliminate the humiliating "means" test that is almost universal today in other programs; this argument, however, seems to go too far, at least with respect to most of the current proposals. We shall return to this point shortly. Another unquestionable advantage of the negative income tax is that it would provide a nationwide minimum of income, in contrast to the great present variations under locally administered assistance programs. The minimum would be universally available to those eligible, while at present about half of all poor persons receive no relief or other government payments at all. Finally, the point that is usually most strongly argued is that the negative income tax would eliminate or at least mitigate what is regarded as a strong disincentive to work under present programs, which generally deduct 100 per cent of any earnings from the amount that might otherwise be allowed.

The list of possible disadvantages of a negative income tax plan is also impressive. As some proponents and critics have recognized, any scheme of income supplementation must strike a balance between three partially conflicting objectives: adequacy, incentive, and economy. Any scheme which is *adequate,* in the sense of filling all or practically all of the poverty gap, is thought to weaken if not destroy the *incentive* to seek and continue employment. To maintain this incentive, it is thought necessary to provide something considerably less than an adequate income and to permit the recipient to retain a substantial part of whatever earnings he may be able to obtain from employment. The conflict between adequacy and incentive could theoretically be resolved by providing allowances that would fill *all* of the poverty gap and in addition allowing the recipient to retain a percentage of his earnings above the poverty minimum; but this choice would involve the payment of substantial amounts to people who are not poor, and thus it would conflict with the objective of *economy,* which in this context means transferring dollars only to those who are actually poor. To the extent that any two of these three objectives are realized, the third is sacrificed. In the usual formulation, a negative income tax plan strives to achieve economy and to preserve incentive; and the result is an allowance that would be less than adequate to relieve the poverty of many recipients.

Under these circumstances, it is especially pertinent to ask what evidence supports the basic proposition that existing welfare arrangements weaken or destroy the incentive to work. The answer is that there is virtually no empirical evidence. The proposition rests almost entirely on assumption. It does seem reasonable to assume that a "tax" of 100 per cent on earnings would deter people from working. It once seemed equally reasonable, however, to assume that high tax rates on high incomes would reduce the work effort of those who had to pay the high rates; but it has proved to be quite difficult to find clear evidence of such an effect in actual practice, and it seems justifiable to conclude from the studies that have been made that the effect is probably much less than is generally assumed.[93] Obviously, the response of low-income persons may be different from that of high-income persons, but the few available studies which touch on this matter even tangentially provide a less than satisfactory basis for firm conclusions. There appears to be a pressing need for further study of work incentives among low-income workers and the possible effects of various types of income supplementation on such incentives. Unverified assumption is an indefensible basis for policy decisions that affect the standards of living of millions of human beings.

There is another respect in which the emphasis of the negative income tax proposals on work incentives is a serious weakness. It has been estimated that nearly half of all poor families are headed by persons who are not in the labor force. Many poor families have no members who are capable of paid employment; all are too old, too young, disabled, or responsible for the care of very young children. For most of these families, an incentive to work is either meaningless or undesirable.

The effort to provide a putative work incentive under the negative income tax plans has yet another important consequence. As already noted, the allowances that are contemplated under most versions are *fractional* in the sense that they fill only a part of the poverty gap for the individual or family. Therefore, as one analyst has demonstrated, the allowances would be substantially less than is currently paid to the needy under many present assistance programs in many states.[94] This fact reveals an unpleasant dilemma: if the negative income tax is to replace all present assistance programs, such replacement will drastically reduce the present living standards of many poor persons, some of whom are completely unable to respond to the alleged incentive to go to work; or, if the assistance programs are retained in order to avoid placing large numbers of people in a much worse position than at present, the means test has not been abolished—although this is one of the advantages frequently claimed for the negative income tax.

It seems clear that some of the more enthusiastic proponents of the negative income tax have considerably overstated its advantages and, for the most part, have ignored its substantial disadvantages (not all of which are discussed here). The negative income tax is not the "ultimate weapon" that will ensure victory in the war on poverty. Possibly this device could play a useful if limited role in a pluralistic system of assistance to the poor; but little consideration appears to have been given thus far to the possibilities and problems of meshing the negative income tax with other programs. It is also desirable to consider the extent to which the most important objectives of the negative income tax could be achieved by modification of existing assistance programs.

There have been limited experiments with simplification and deper-
sonalizing of the means test, reducing it to a simple affidavit not very
different from the tax return that is contemplated under the negative
income tax. Deduction of only part of any earnings from assistance allowances is also being tried. No doubt the isolated and small-scale experiments that have been undertaken thus far do not justify any broad
generalizations, except possibly the observation that the continuation
and careful analysis of such experiments is highly desirable. Consideration should also be given to ways of achieving another significant objective of the negative income tax: a national minimum standard of
assistance, readily and equally available to all the needy. Obviously,
there are substantial political difficulties in the way of achieving this
objective while retaining the present system of assistance payments;
but it is not clear that the political difficulty of enacting a negative income tax plan would be significantly less. Perhaps in the long run it
will appear that the greatest contribution of the negative income tax
proposals has been to focus attention more sharply than before on the
inadequacies, inequities, and irrationalities of the existing system of
transfer payments to the poor.

Another kind of proposal merits brief attention. The United States is
one of the few countries in the Western world without some system of
family or children's allowances. This fact has prompted the suggestion
that we should adopt such a system, and it is sometimes offered as an
alternative to a negative income tax. Moynihan has proposed a plan
under which parents would receive an allowance of eight dollars per
month for each child under the age of 6, and twelve dollars for each
child aged 6 to 17. He estimates that payments under this plan would
come to about $9 billion per year. He would make the payments to all
families, regardless of other income, presumably to avoid the attachment of any stigma to the payment and also to gain political support
for the plan.[95] This and similar proposals for children's or family allowances appear to have considerable sentimental appeal; but the
Moynihan proposal in particular would be a remarkably inefficient way
to do something about poverty. Despite the large expenditure that is
proposed, it would contribute little to the relief of poverty. Only about
16 million of the country's 69 million children live in poor families;
therefore, more than three-quarters of the payments under this scheme
would go to families that are not poor, and only a fraction of the expenditure on the nonpoor would be recovered through income taxes.[96]
Furthermore, the Moynihan proposal would fill a much smaller fraction of the poverty gap for most poor families than would even the
negative income tax. It would be difficult to argue that this kind of

children's allowance would have a significant effect on incentive; but it certainly fails the adequacy and economy tests.

Not only the Moynihan proposal but all the other transfer payment programs involve very large amounts of money. One study analyzed probable expenditures for a number of plans under various assumptions and derived estimates which ranged from $4.4 to $51.3 billion per year, with most of the plans falling between $6 billion and $20 billion per year.[97] Economists can and do argue that the size of the expenditure is not a proper measure of the *cost* of a transfer payment program; the real income of the nation may not be significantly affected at all by a $20 billion transfer of income from the affluent to the poor. In this view, there would be a real cost only if the program induced some people who would otherwise be employed to withdraw partially or completely from productive labor. Nevertheless, for those from whom income is being transferred, the tax cost is very real. It is not actually an answer to point out that federal tax revenues show a strong tendency to rise over time without any change in tax rates and to argue that this kind of plan could be financed out of that kind of rise in revenues. Expenditure for this purpose must compete not only with other programs in the federal budget but also with proposals for tax reduction. Hence, the amount of expenditure that is contemplated for a transfer payment program is one aspect that is appropriately considered in making a choice between this strategy and other possibilities.

Work, Training, and Services

Galbraith once described a pilot program as a technique for creating the appearance of action without really spending money. It would be unfair to say seriously that the training and employment programs of the last half-dozen years have failed to progress beyond the pilot stage thus defined; but it is beyond dispute that these programs have remained very small relative to their respective "target populations." Even though these programs have generally devoted disproportionately large shares of their resources to Negroes (because of the relative disadvantage of the Negro population), only a small fraction of the eligible population has been served. Thus, during 1966, the average level of officially reported Negro unemployment was 621,000, but only 47,000 received training under the Manpower Development and Training Act. It is estimated that about 300,000 Negro youths met the eligibility requirements of the out-of-school Neighborhood Youth Corps, and 33,000 were actually enrolled. More than half a million Negroes were eligible for the Work Experience and Training program, and

17,000 were enrolled. Around 30,000 Negroes were employed as "aides" of various kinds under the Community Action Program, although the eligible population was about 3.5 million. Despite talk of a "War on Poverty," the appropriation for the Office of Economic Opportunity during fiscal 1968 amounted to $57 per poor person.[98] The cost of the war in Viet Nam during that fiscal year approached $2,000 per South Vietnamese.

There are undoubtedly good reasons for starting an entirely new program at a relatively low level of funding. Staff must be recruited, procedures developed, facilities obtained, clients located, and so on. Then, after these initial steps have been completed, it can be argued that expansion of the program should await demonstration of results. There has been a reasonable demonstration of results so far as most of the programs are concerned, but a complex of factors has prevented a substantial expansion of their appropriations.

One major factor undoubtedly has been the excessive faith of the Johnson administration in fiscal policy as a cure for unemployment. Thus, in early 1966, the Department of Labor presented to the Joint Economic Committee of Congress an estimate that the over-all unemployment rate would drop to 3.5 per cent by the end of that year and that, as a result, the nonwhite unemployment rate would decrease to "significantly less than double the white unemployment rate for the first time since the Korean period." [99] By late 1966, it was clear that both aspects of this estimate had been overoptimistic. The chairman of the Council of Economic Advisers then stated that the time had finally come to shift to a major emphasis on so-called "structural" remedies for unemployment; [100] but, as already noted, the proposal for a tax increase to combat inflation then became the top-priority item in the administration's economic program. This priority, and congressional insistence on accompanying expenditure cuts, made it seem unlikely that any substantial increase in expenditures would be realized for the manpower programs under discussion here; indeed, the avoidance of crippling reductions became the realistic goal. There is now some tendency, although mainly among the uninformed, to conclude that the epidemic of urban riots has demonstrated the failure of the war on poverty and the manpower programs which predate it. It is more reasonable to conclude that these efforts had been so consistently underfinanced that their impact on the employment and income problems of the slums was minimal.

Is there any basis for thinking that larger programs would have a proportionately larger impact? For some programs, perhaps a negative answer would be indicated by presently available evidence; but for most of them the response can be more favorable. Parenthetically, it must be noted that one of the common weaknesses of these programs is that something less than ideal provisions have been made for evaluation of them. Some do not even collect the operating data necessary for adequate evaluation. This criticism is less applicable to the programs under the Manpower Development and Training Act (MDTA) than to most others.

Training under the MDTA began in late 1962, at a time of fairly high unemployment. There was apparently some tendency toward "creaming" the client population in the beginning—that is, concentrating on the training of those who were already the best-qualified and the most employable. But as appropriations have been modestly increased, as general unemployment has declined, and as the goals of the program have been more precisely defined, the emphasis has shifted toward the training of the disadvantaged. Thus, the percentage of non-white enrollees in institutional training courses increased from 27.2 in 1963 to 40.1 in 1966. The smaller on-the-job training component increased its percentage of nonwhites from 14.9 to 18.0 in the same years.[101] The available studies appear to show that MDTA trainees who complete their training courses have, on the average, higher earnings and greater employment stability than they experienced prior to training, and their experience appears to be significantly more favorable than that of control groups with comparable characteristics who have not had such training. Unhappily, the programs appear to benefit nonwhites less in these respects than whites, but even the nonwhites experience a betterment of their pretraining status.[102]

The Neighborhood Youth Corps (NYC) was established by the Economic Opportunity Act of 1964, but its administration has been delegated to the Department of Labor.[103] The NYC provides work opportunity and (to a limited degree) training for in-school and out-of-school youth from families with poverty-level incomes. Another aspect of the program has been summer employment for eligible youths. Unlike some other manpower programs, NYC has enjoyed congressional favor to the extent that its appropriation for fiscal 1967 considerably exceeded the administration's request; the funds available for its third year of operation were almost three times as much as in its first year. Even so, it still enrolls a small fraction of those who are potentially eligible.

One of the main goals of the in-school program is to reduce the dropout rate among enrollees. There is no comprehensive measurement of its success in achieving this goal, but two fragments of evidence suggest the desirability of further investigation of this point. The Washington, D.C. schools found that its NYC students, although selected from among those "judged to be potential dropouts," actually had a dropout rate which was about one-tenth that of non-NYC students in the three high schools covered by the study. A city-wide study in Pittsburgh, involving a much larger number of NYC enrollees, found that they had a dropout rate which was exactly half the city-wide average.

The out-of-school program had hoped to provide "supportive services" (remedial education, medical care, job training and counseling) in addition to useful work experience. However, the inadequacy of funds forced a choice between maximum enrollments with minimum supportive services and much smaller enrollments with adequate services; and the program administrators chose to emphasize maximum enrollment. Hence, for most of the out-of-school enrollees, NYC provided only a job to tide them over pending the time they could find a better opportunity. It has been suggested that, for these enrollees, the NYC served as an "aging vat," but the validity of the concept has been challenged.[104] Young Negroes are overrepresented in the program; they were about 40 per cent of the in-school enrollees and slightly more than half of the out-of-school and summer enrollees in a recent period. But apparently no separate study has been made of the effects of the program on Negroes. In any event, it is reported that nearly five out of six former out-of-school enrollees believed that they needed more education or training to get the kind of job that they wanted. It seems reasonable to conclude that all three facets of NYC—in-school, out-of-school, and summer—have made a modest contribution to the alleviation of the problems to which the program is directed, but that the potential contribution with more adequate funding is considerably greater.

The Job Corps has been one of the smallest, most expensive, and most controversial of the new manpower programs.[105] Its purpose is to provide remedial education, medical attention, and vocational training in a residential setting for the most severely disadvantaged youths. By mid-1967, its total enrollment was close to 40,000, and approximately two-thirds of the enrollees were nonwhite. Males are divided about equally between urban and conservation (rural) centers, but women are placed only in urban centers. The urban centers are operated by contractors—universities, nonprofit organizations, and business firms—and the conservation centers are run by the Department of Agriculture, the Department of the Interior, and in a few instances by states. Costs, especially in the urban centers, turned out to be unexpectedly high and attracted much critical comment. Some of the criticism was unfair in that it ignored the fact that per enrollee start-up costs would inevitably be much higher in the early phases of the program than when it reached full strength. Nevertheless, the total annual cost per enrollee in fiscal 1967 was more than $8,000. As some critics were fond of saying, a student could be sent to Harvard for much less; the Job Corps offered to send any enrollee there who could get accepted, but apparently none could make it.

There has been no evidence of scandalous extravagance in the operation of the program. The unhappy fact is that this kind of training, in a residential setting with medical and dental repairs thrown in, is necessarily quite expensive. From one standpoint, the costs involved are an indication of the relative deprivation of the enrollees, for there has been no accusation of "creaming" the applicants for the Job Corps. A great many of the enrollees are severely retarded in reading and arithmetic ability—much more than expected—and some are actual or potential delinquents. Disciplinary problems were serious in the early days in some of the centers, and the result was a bad press and often bad community relations. With more experience, and with the replacement of some of the contractors, the disciplinary problems have generally been brought under control; but the unfavorable image remains to threaten the future of the program. There have been careful follow-up studies of former enrollees, and it is clear from these that the Corpsmen do benefit substantially from the program, especially if they complete the normal course (the dropout rate is disturbingly high). Nevertheless, a not unfriendly analyst concludes that the case is not yet conclusive that this costly program is fully justified in view of the alternatives that are available.[106] Congress expressed its reservations concerning the program by cutting back its third-year appropriation by about one-third from the second-year level.

There are many other specialized, often local and private programs to provide training or jobs or both for the hard-core unemployed.[107] Indeed, one of the most widespread criticisms of the whole manpower development effort has been that the proliferation of specialized programs and agencies, with a great deal of overlap in their aims and target populations, has created confusion and wasteful duplication of effort. In my judgment, this kind of difficulty is probably inevitable and incurable as long as Congress insists on a multiplicity of separate authorizations for programs for separately described populations and as long as a conscientious effort is made to involve state and local agencies in program planning and administration. No doubt the federal organization chart could be tidied up, and some of the concern in Congress might be allayed by such a reorganization; but the fundamental sources of difficulty are not likely to be reached by reshuffling federal bureaus.

No effort will be made here to describe all the functioning or proposed programs in this field. There is one experimental program, however, which seems to have great potential if certain difficulties can be overcome. The basic idea, simply stated, is to hire and train the poor to help the poor. One of the great needs of the slums is for more "helping" services of many kinds, it is argued—in health, education, recreation, sanitation, counseling, and so on. But in all these fields there is a shortage of professional personnel that will be intensified by efforts to expand such programs. Therefore, the rationale runs, let us split up the job of the professional, or at least split off some simpler aspects of it, and train the "indigenous poor" to perform these tasks under the supervision of a professional. Furthermore, let us design into the program a substantial training element, and let us make clear provision for a ladder of advancement for such subprofessional workers so that ultimately, with experience and training, they will have the opportunity to advance into the ranks of the professionals. This approach has been named the "New Careers Movement." [108] The approach has been endorsed by the Senate Subcommittee on Employment and Manpower,[109] by the Automation Commission,[110] and by Congress, which established a "pilot program" embodying this approach in 1966 amendments to the Economic Opportunity Act.[111]

The difficulties that confront the New Careers Movement should not be underestimated. Much more than merely appropriating money, making grants, and establishing slots will be necessary. A new and sophisticated kind of engineering will be required to split up existing professional jobs into components that can be performed acceptably by subprofessionals with professional supervision. Possibly many of the professionals will resist the movement; they could quietly sabotage it. Carefully designed, long-term, on-the-job training will be essential. Hastily organized projects which fail to make adequate provisions for the solution of these difficulties may lead to disillusionment with the approach before it has had a fair trial. Yet some experiments have already been undertaken which demonstrate that the problems are not insoluble.

The potential of the New Careers approach is suggested by a comparison with the wartime experience in industry. One of the major lessons of that experience is that a vast expansion of the scale of operations makes feasible a redesign of jobs which might not otherwise be possible. The opposition of highly trained workers to "job dilution" is minimized when it is obvious that the available work greatly exceeds the capacity of the available fully qualified workers. It is possible that most of the fully qualified professionals may welcome the opportunity to concentrate most of their time and energy on supervisory and instructional tasks, particularly if this recasting of their function is accompanied by appropriate increases in salary levels. Finally, and most important, this approach to job creation is more consistent with the present patterns of unemployment among Negroes than most other "public works" kinds of proposals. As we have seen, unemployment rates are highest for the relatively better-educated younger Negroes in the urban North. It seems entirely possible that Negroes with these characteristics would have little enthusiasm for make-work, dead-end, manual-labor jobs. They would be more likely to respond favorably to jobs offering a substantial training component, possibilities of advancement, a modicum of respectability, and a chance to wear dress clothes rather than overalls or aprons. If the great bulk of unemployed Negroes were illiterate rural migrants, as the popular misconception has it, the New Careers approach might be impossibly idealistic; but the peculiar concentration of unemployment among the relatively better-educated Negroes can be converted into an advantage for this program. And to the extent that the program succeeds, the product will be not only paying jobs for some slum dwellers but also a more adequate level of helping services for all slum dwellers.

It would be a serious mistake, of course, to place exclusive or even primary reliance on the New Careers approach at this stage of its development. Although it deserves a major trial, other kinds of programs are needed to meet the needs of other groups of unemployed, some of whom are indeed illiterate and unqualified for any but the simplest manual tasks. An adequate job-creation program must provide a number of different kinds of jobs, plus some arrangements for referring the job candidate to the kind of program for which he is best suited.

Experience will probably show that there is a not inconsiderable role for private enterprise in the solution of the unemployment problems of the slums. No doubt some form of government assistance for private efforts in this area will be essential, in the form of either tax incentives, direct subsidies, or both. This approach also should be given a fair trial in order to determine how large or how small this component of the total program should be. There is reason for much concern about the recent decision of the administration to place a very heavy emphasis on this approach, even before the returns are in on some experimental programs of this kind, and to get part of the money for this new and untested approach by sharply reducing the expenditures on Neighborhood Youth Corps and Job Corps. Not only is this robbing Peter to pay Paul; it is paying Paul before you know how much—if anything!— he is going to be able to accomplish.

Conclusion

The underlying theme of this section has been that there is no single policy measure that will remedy all or most of the complex problem of the economic inequality of Negroes. The problem is much less one of selection from among competing programs than it is one of co-ordination of complementary approaches. This theme may appear to be so noncontroversial that it is actually trite. But the support for this theme by those who discuss employment and income policy is usually more verbal than practical. The common formula is: my proposal will not do the whole job; other programs will be needed too; but what I advocate is the most important thing that we can do, and we should give this priority.

This pattern has been clear in the advocacy of stimulation of aggregate demand as a solution for unemployment. Although the advocates of demand stimulation by tax-cutting were careful to state that other programs would be needed for a full solution to the problem of Negro economic inequality, they laid heavy emphasis on the prediction that Negroes would reap disproportionate benefits from this approach, or, in particular, that the Negro unemployment rate would fall more rapidly than the over-all rate. The political appeal of tax-cutting, and more recently the escalation of the Viet Nam War, have made it possible to test the full potential of demand stimulation as a remedy for Negro economic inequality. Widespread reliance on the *post hoc, ergo propter hoc* fallacy has considerably exaggerated the effect of demand stimulation on Negro unemployment and income. Even so, the exaggerated results fall considerably short of the predicted results. Negro unemployment rates have fallen, but relatively less than white unemployment rates, and the two-to-one ratio persists despite repeated predictions of its imminent reduction. Unemployment remains at disastrous levels among slum dwellers, especially young Negroes. Negro income levels have not markedly improved relative to white income levels; and since 1959, the number of whites living in poverty has decreased by almost 30 per cent, while the number of Negroes in that condition is down by less than 10 per cent.

Scarcely any informed person today would question the proposition that maintaining an adequate level of aggregate demand is an essential component of employment policy. The achievement of that objective primarily through tax-cutting is much more questionable, especially when, as in recent years, the political price for tax cuts is excessive restraint on expenditures. It is reasonably clear that the growth of more direct, "structural" remedies for unemployment and low incomes among Negroes has been stunted by the excessive expectations raised by the demand-stimulation protagonists and the excessive restraints on expenditures which they accepted in order to get tax cuts. In the shaping of employment policy in the future, it is as important to emphasize the costs and limitations of tax cuts as it is to recognize the essentiality of an adequate level of aggregate demand. There is some danger that the recent emphasis on the virtues of tax-cutting will obscure the elementary fact that a new $5-billion income maintenance program, plus a new $5-billion job-creation program, would provide at least as much stimulation to aggregate demand as a $10-billion tax cut.

There appears to be a similar danger of overemphasis in the growing discussion of the negative income tax as "the single most important" step toward the elimination of poverty. Unquestionably, there is an urgent need for remedies for the inequities, inadequacies, and irrationalities of present income maintenance programs; and a program which seems to promise a full set of remedies with a single stroke of the pen, so to speak, has great appeal. But there is an inherent problem of balancing considerations of adequacy, incentive, and economy in any system of income maintenance. The solution offered by the negative income tax relies heavily on assumptions about incentives among the poor that are unverified with regard to some of the poor and irrelevant to the circumstances of others. And the size of the federal expenditure that is contemplated by most of the negative income tax proposals might preclude adequate funding of other approaches to the relief of poverty and unemployment.

No doubt a large program of transfer payments could make the statistics on poverty look a great deal better in a short time. Furthermore, it has been contended that there is no other really practical way to relieve poverty. Moynihan, for example, has argued that "our problem has been too much concentration on doing things for the poor and not enough concentration on giving them money." We lack the trained professionals to provide all the services that are needed; therefore, Moynihan argues, we should give the poor more money instead of more services.[112] It is a short step from this position to the argument that "the market" is generally the most responsive and accurate apparatus for providing the things that people really want and that the poor will be better off getting what they want through the market instead of having it prescribed for them by social workers; this rationale has led the conservative Milton Friedman to advocate the supposedly radical negative income tax.

What this approach ignores is that some needs are not met at all, or are met most inadequately, by the market. The most spectacular failure of the market, for example, has been in the provision of low-cost housing for the poor; and for another example, it is hard to believe that the market could effectively organize a system of remedial education for slum dwellers. A transfer payment system is likely to leave untouched the root causes of poverty. At best, such a system will maintain its clients at a level a dollar a year above the poverty line. The transfer payment improves the buying power of the poor; remedial services seek to improve the earning power of the poor. The transfer payment improvement is tangible and immediate; but the improvement is permanent only if the payment itself is permanent. Remedial services provide a benefit that is long-run and perhaps speculative; but if they achieve their objective, they need not be provided permanently to the same individual. There are some poor people who can be helped only by money, and most of them need much more than they are now getting; but there are others who can and should be made self-supporting.

Some of the unemployed Negroes can be helped to find jobs in the private sector. But the serious shortages of trained professionals in most of the social service professions make it logical to launch a major effort to apply the concepts of the New Careers movement: to hire and train the poor to help the poor. Other, less demanding kinds of jobs should also be created for the lower strata of the labor force. Recently, currency has been given to the concept of "the government as the employer of last resort." Insofar as the concept advances the idea that government should guarantee a meaningful job for every person who is able and willing to work, perhaps it is a useful addition to public discussion. But it seems to reflect the kind of "private sector bias" previously discussed. Perhaps as our thinking matures we shall succeed in outgrowing the notion that there is something inherently less noble, less worthy, and less desirable about public employment than private employment.

All that has been said up to now leaves essentially unanswered the basic question: how much of each? The tentative answer is, of course, more of all. Only in the area of aggregate demand stimulation is there evidence that our efforts have reached the outer limit of practical feasibility. Almost all of our direct, structural kinds of programs could be doubled or even quadrupled in size without running into any kind of feasibility limit; for some, a tenfold increase could be justified. We should have learned by now that we must have more doors than one out of poverty and many more than one out of unemployment. There may be merit in efforts to determine the optimum emphasis of various forms of income maintenance, training, and job-creation programs. If such efforts serve no other purpose, they should serve to reveal the vast disproportion between the needs and the resources that we have thus far directed toward meeting those needs. But another important purpose might well be to reveal the central importance of the integration and interaction of programs for the relief of Negro poverty and Negro unemployment.

Several years ago, Gunnar Myrdal remarked that the American "under-class" had been the most inarticulate and apathetic in the world. Nevertheless, he warned, "There is an ugly smell rising from the basement of the stately American mansion." [113] The ugly smell has given way to thick smoke, and sirens and fire bells now rend the air. The superficially inert "under-class" shows signs of spontaneous combustion. The Negroes are clearly the most combustible element. We have made progress toward finding and remedying some of the sources of Negro inequality in recent years. But "some" is obviously no longer enough.

·NOTES

1 The quoted figures are for "nonwhites," a statistical classification which is about 92 per cent Negroes. Throughout this chapter the terms "Negro" and "nonwhite" are used interchangeably unless otherwise specified. The source of the unemployment figures for 1967 is *Manpower Report of the President and a Report on Manpower Requirements, Resources, Utilization and Training* by the U.S. Department of Labor, April, 1968 (hereafter cited as *Manpower Report,* 1968 or 1964 or 1967 as appropriate), Tables A–1, A–5, and A–11.

2 National Commission on Technology, Automation, and Economic Progress, *Technology and the American Economy* (Washington: Government Printing Office, 1966) (hereafter cited as *Automation Commission Report*), I, 31.

3 Only for recent years are reasonably accurate statistics on net migration of Negroes available. Not until the 1940 census were statistics gathered comparing the current residence of persons with earlier places of residence. Estimates of net migration for earlier periods vary considerably. Some estimates covering the earlier years are found in G. Myrdal *et al.,* *An American Dilemma: The Negro Problem and Modern Democracy* (New York: Harper and Row, 1944 and 1962), pp. 1229–1231. No estimate is specifically presented for the 1910–1930 period. However, the 1910–1940 migration is estimated to be 1,750,000, and the estimate

of 1930–1940 migration is 317,000. The authors recognize considerable margins of error in the estimates. More recent estimates by E. S. Lee *et al.* yield the following figures for net migration of Negroes from the South (including migration to western areas): 1910–1920, 455,264; 1920–1930, 750,826; 1930–1940, 347,741. See E. S. Lee *et al.*, in S. Kuznets and D. S. Thomas, eds., *Population Redistribution and Economic Growth, United States, 1870–1950* (Philadelphia: American Philosophical Society, 1953), Vol I, Reference Table P–1. More recent decades are covered in U.S. Bureau of the Census, *Statistical Abstract of the United States,* 1964 (hereafter cited as *Statistical Abstract*), Table 33. Negro migration to the western states reached major proportions for the first time in the 1940–1950 period, and it continued to be a substantial part of Negro migration in the 1950's.

4 The decline after 1957 or 1958 was reported by E. Mueller and W. Ladd, *Negro-White Differences in Geographic Mobility* (U.S. Department of Commerce, Area Redevelopment Administration, 1964), p. 8. The statement in the text is subject to some reservations: the cited study deals with intercounty migration rates, which are not necessarily the same as interregional rates; the study does not show precisely when the slowdown occurred; and some of the findings, especially those referred to later, are based on interviews with an extremely small, though carefully selected, sample of white and Negro families. The 1940–1947 and 1955–1960 comparison is from U.S. Department of Labor, *The Economic Situation of Negroes in the U.S.*, Bulletin S–3, revised 1962, p. 2.

5 K. E. Taeuber and A. F. Taeuber, "The Changing Character of Negro Migration," *American Journal of Sociology*, LXX (January, 1965), 429–441.

6 Myrdal *et al., op. cit.*, Chapter 12.

7 One recent estimate of nonwhite migration from the South in 1960–1963 gives an annual average of 78,000—about half of the annual average in the 1940's and 1950's and about the same as in the 1920's. U.S. Department of Labor, *The Negroes in the United States: Their Economic and Social Situation,* Bulletin No. 1511 (1966), Table IB–2.

8 D. L. Hiestand, *Economic Growth and Employment Opportunities for Minorities* (New York: Columbia University Press, 1964), pp. 15–17.

9 Myrdal *et al., op. cit.*, Appendix 6, "Pre-War Conditions of the Negro Wage Earner in Selected Industries and Occupations," pp. 1079–1124, provides a comprehensive treatment up to about 1940.

10 M. A. Kessler, "Economic Status of Nonwhite Workers, 1955–62," *Monthly Labor Review* (July, 1963), pp. 780–788, at p. 780.

11 G. S. Becker, *The Economics of Discrimination* (Chicago: University of Chicago Press, 1957); E. Rayack, "Discrimination and the Occupational Progress of Negroes," *Review of Economics and Statistics* (May, 1961), pp. 209–214; H. P. Miller, Statement, *Hearings on Equal Opportunity,*

Subcommittee on Employment and Manpower, U.S. Senate, 88th Congress, 1st session, July 31, 1963, pp. 321–374; and N. D. Glenn, "Some Changes in the Relative Status of American Non-Whites, 1940–1960," *Phylon* (Summer, 1963), pp. 109–122.

12 Miller, *op. cit.;* Glenn, *op. cit.*

13 Calculated from U.S. Department of Labor, *The Negroes in the United States, op. cit.*, Table IIB–1.

14 *Poverty in the United States*, Committee on Education and Labor, House of Representatives, 88th Congress, 2d session, April, 1964, Table 18, p. 268.

15 Time will tell whether the 1966 figure is a one-year aberration of the kind frequently observed in the past or a movement to a permanently higher ratio. The year-to-year fluctuations in this ratio from 1950 through 1966 are shown in a table in *Social and Economic Conditions of Negroes in the United States*, BLS Report No. 332; Current Population Reports, Series P–23, No. 24; October, 1967, p. 15.

16 A. B. Batchelder, "Decline in the Relative Income of Negro Men," *Quarterly Journal of Economics* (November, 1964), pp. 525–548.

17 *The Negroes in the United States*, Table IIIA–4.

18 U.S. President, *Economic Report of the President*, 1964, pp. 57–58. This is the figure for a four-person family.

19 *Poverty in the United States*, Table 7, p. 16.

20 *Ibid.*, Table 8, p. 17.

21 Bureau of National Affairs, Inc., *Daily Labor Report* No. 163, August 22, 1967, B–6.

22 *The Negroes in the United States*, Tables IIIC–2 and IIIC–3.

23 *Statistical Abstract*, 1964, Table 146.

24 Kessler, *op. cit.*, p. 788.

25 *Statistical Abstract*, 1964, Table 142.

26 D. J. Johnston, "Educational Attainment of Workers, March 1962," *Monthly Labor Review* (May, 1963), pp. 504–515, Table 2. For further development of the "time-lag" comparison, not only in education but in a number of other realms, see R. Fein, "An Economic and Social Profile of the Negro American," *Daedalus* (Fall, 1965), pp. 815–846.

27 *Manpower Report*, 1964, p. 99.

28 J. S. Coleman *et al.*, *Equality of Educational Opportunity* (Washington: Government Printing Office, 1966), pp. 20–21. Two qualifications are noted: many Negro students scored above many white students; and some part of the regional difference for Negroes may result from a substantially higher Negro dropout rate in the North, which probably removed many of the low achievers from the testing in the North.

29 *Manpower Report*, 1967, p. 92. The white population aged 15 to 19 in the central cities increased by 14.6 per cent during this five-year period.

30 U.S. Department of Labor, *The Economic Situation of Negroes in the U.S.*, Table 2.

31 The study, by Kuznets and others, is summarized by I. B. Taeuber, in "Migration, Mobility and the Assimilation of the Negro," *Population Bulletin* (November, 1958), pp. 127–151.

32 *Manpower Report*, 1964, Table H–2, p. 271.

33 Calculated from *The Negroes in the United States*, Table IIA–1.

34 S. Cooper and D. J. Johnston, "Labor Force Projections, By Color, 1970–80," *Monthly Labor Review* (September, 1966), pp. 965–972. The relatively optimistic assumptions are that unemployment will remain at about the 4 per cent level; that participation rates for most nonwhite male age groups will rise from the 1965 level; and that the rates for nonwhite female age groups will decline only slightly, or, in a few instances, rise moderately.

35 C. Killingsworth, "Unemployment and the Tax Cut," appears in Hearings before the Subcommittee on Employment and Manpower, 88th Congress, 1st session, Part 5, pp. 1787–1794. Others include: T. Dernberg and K. Strand, "Cyclical Variation in Civilian Labor Force Participation," *Review of Economics and Statistics* (November, 1964), pp. 378–391; T. Dernberg and K. Strand, "Hidden Unemployment, 1953–62: A Quantitative Analysis by Age and Sex," *American Economic Review* (March, 1966), pp. 71–95; A. J. Tella, "The Relation of Labor Force to Employment," *Industrial and Labor Relations Review* (April, 1964), pp. 454–469; A. J. Tella, "Labor Force Sensitivity to Employment by Age, Sex," *Industrial Relations* (February, 1965), pp. 69–83; W. G. Bowen and T. A. Finegan, "Labor Force Participation and Unemployment," in A. M. Ross, ed., *Employment Policy and the Labor Market* (Berkeley: University of California Press, 1965), pp. 115–161; J. Mincer, "Labor Force Participation and Unemployment: A Review of Recent Evidence," in R. A. Gordon and M. S. Gordon, eds., *Prosperity and Unemployment* (New York: Wiley, 1966), pp. 73–112.

36 *Manpower Report*, 1967, Table A–4, p. 205.

37 Killingsworth, *Hearings, op. cit.*

38 These figures were computed by the Bureau of Labor Statistics and reported in the so-called Moynihan report: U.S. Department of Labor, Office of Planning and Research, *The Negro Family: The Case for National Action* (Washington: Government Printing Office, 1965), Table 10, p. 66. The 1930 figures are based on a "gainful worker" concept and include persons 10 years of age and over.

39 Figures for 1948–1965 from *Manpower Report*, 1966, Table A–11, p. 166; figures for 1966 and 1967 from *ibid.*, 1968, Table A–11, p. 234. The 1966 and 1967 figures are not completely comparable with those for earlier years, because they exclude the unemployed who are 14 and 15 years old, and the figures for earlier years include this age group.

40 Rates for 1948 are from Kessler, *op. cit.*, Table 4. Rates for 1954–1967 are from *Manpower Report*, 1968, Table A–5, p. 226. The 1948 rates for both whites and nonwhites have not been adjusted for the 1957 change in definition; the 1954–1967 rates for both groups have been so adjusted.

41 Detailed data are found in *Manpower Report*, 1968, Table A–4, p. 225. The exceptions are ages 18–24 and possibly 65 and over. The relationship shifts from year to year for the latter age group, probably because of high sampling error. The figures are probably unreliable for nonwhites, ages 18–24, because the census undercount of nonwhites is generally believed to be especially serious for this age-sex group.

42 Other explanations might suggest themselves. For example, school attendance rates of young nonwhites have risen more rapidly than the rates of whites; but this would affect only those in the 18–24 age group, in which (as pointed out in the preceding footnote) the reported nonwhite participation rate is still higher than the white rate. (My adjustments, because of data limitations, are applied only to men 18 years of age and older.) Again, it may be pointed out that disability is probably more prevalent among nonwhite men than among white men; but there is no reason to think that there has been a differential *increase* in disability rates among nonwhite men compared with white men since the late 1940's, when the nonwhite participation rates were predominantly higher.

43 These calculations are based on unpublished data for March, 1964, supplied by the Bureau of Labor Statistics. I have made the same calculations with data from the 1960 census, which is derived from a larger sample and presents more detailed age and educational attainment breakdowns by color and sex than the BLS data. The over-all results from the 1960 data are quite similar to those reported in the text. For example, the reported unemployment rate for white males (age 14 and over) was 4.6 per cent, and for nonwhite males (same ages) it was 8.7 per cent; the adjusted rate for nonwhite males was 13.6 per cent. Despite the lack of comparability of the data and the difference in dates, the general similarity of the magnitudes is somewhat reassuring.

44 *The Negro Family*, Table 10, p. 66.

45 Batchelder, *op. cit.*, p. 542. These ratios are for Negroes, not nonwhites.

46 The survey findings (and the findings of some comparable independent surveys) are summarized in *Manpower Report*, 1967, pp. 73–92. Cf. J. R. Wetzel and S. S. Holland, "Poverty Areas of Our Major Cities," *Monthly Labor Review* (October, 1966), pp. 1105–1110.

47 *The Negroes in the United States*, Tables IIA–1, IIA–16, and IIA–26.

48 The point is documented in a report prepared by the Equal Employment Opportunity Commission, "Nine City Minority Group Employment Profiles," Research Report 1967–19–A, August 6, 1967 (mimeographed). There are also extensive documentation and a useful bibliography in D. D. Wachtel, *The Negro and Discrimination in Employment* (Ann Arbor

and Detroit: Institute of Labor and Industrial Relations, University of Michigan–Wayne State University, 1965).

49 The most recent comprehensive study is by R. Marshall, *The Negro and Organized Labor* (New York: Wiley, 1965). Historical sections of this book draw upon the earlier literature, which is cited in numerous footnote references.

50 The monthly and annual reports on unemployment do not provide a regional breakdown. The decennial censuses do make it possible to calculate regional differences in unemployment by color; but the reliability of some of the census counting of certain categories of the unemployed is open to serious question, and the month in which the census is taken may not be representative of the year, not to mention the decade.

51 See, for example, the poignant work by C. Brown, *Manchild in the Promised Land* (New York: Macmillan, 1965).

52 An example is Rayack, *op. cit.*, especially pp. 211–212.

53 The relevant statistics are summarized in *Economic Report of the President*, 1967, Table B–20, p. 236.

54 The data are found in U.S. Department of Labor, *Employment and Earnings Statistics for the United States, 1909–66*, Bureau of Labor Statistics, Bulletin No. 1312–4, October, 1966, pp. 705 ff.

55 E. Ginzberg, *The Negro Potential* (New York: Columbia University Press, 1956), pp. 66, 81.

56 See source cited in note 54. I have undertaken an analysis of the developments responsible for the decrease in blue-collar jobs in C. Killingsworth, "Structural Unemployment in the United States," in J. Stieber, ed., *Employment Problems of Automation and Advanced Technology* (London: Macmillan; and New York: St Martin's Press, 1966).

57 *Manpower Report*, 1967, p. 87. For regional variations in employment increases, see pp. 26–28.

58 Calculated from *Statistical Abstract*, 1964, Table 321, p. 243.

59 *The Negroes in the United States*, Table IB–2, p. 74.

60 *Ibid.*, Table IA–3, p. 65.

61 *Manpower Report*, 1967, Table 3, p. 92.

62 *The Negroes in the United States*, Table IIIA–4, p. 139.

63 Coleman, *op. cit.*, pp. 20–21.

64 This point is strongly emphasized by K. B. Clark, *Dark Ghetto* (New York: Harper and Row, 1965), Chapter 6; and by J. Kozol, *Death at an Early Age* (Boston: Houghton Mifflin, 1967).

65 A large-scale job creation program was also recommended in *Report of the National Advisory Commission on Civil Disorders* (New York: Dutton, 1968), which was issued after the text of this chapter was written. The administration was equally cool to this new recommendation.

66 Thus, in testimony before the U.S. Senate Subcommittee on Employment

and Manpower on October 28, 1963, the chairman of the Council of Economic Advisers predicted that one of the effects of the proposed tax cut on unemployment rates would be "that the sharpest declines will occur where the incidence of unemployment is the highest: among teen-agers, the Negroes, the less-skilled." This testimony is reproduced in *Economic Report*, 1964, Appendix A; the quoted passage appears at p. 173.

67 *Automation Commission Report*, I, 23.

68 J. Tobin, "On Improving the Economic Status of the Negro," *Daedalus* (Fall, 1965), pp. 880, 884, 887.

69 Economists would recognize, one hopes, that a $5-billion work program would provide at least as much stimulus to the economy as a $5-billion tax cut; but the line of reasoning required to support this proposition is apparently regarded as too tenuous to be very effective in politics.

70 Consider the following statement by W. W. Heller, former chairman of the Council of Economic Advisers and a chief architect of the "New Economics": "It is often said that the study of economics makes people conservative. In the microeconomic sense, it undoubtedly does. It is hard to study the modern economics of relative prices, resource allocation, and distribution without developing a healthy respect for the market mechanism on three major scores: first, for what Robert Dorfman calls its 'cybernetics,' for the incredible capacity of the price system to receive and generate information and respond to it; second, for its technical efficiency and hard-headedness as a guide to resources and a goad to effort and risk-taking; and third, for its contribution to political democracy by keeping economic decisions free and decentralized." W. W. Heller, *New Dimensions of Political Economy* (Cambridge: Harvard University Press, 1966), p. 8.

71 L. G. Reynolds, *Labor Economics and Labor Relations*, 4th ed. (Englewood Cliffs, N.J.: Prentice-Hall, 1964), p. 375. See also L. G. Reynolds, *The Structure of Labor Markets* (New York: Harper and Row, 1951); G. F. Bloom and H. R. Northrup, *Economics of Labor Relations*, 5th ed. (Homewood, Illinois: Richard D. Irwin, 1965), Chapter 8; R. A. Lester, *Economics of Labor* (New York: Macmillan, 1941), Chapter 5; E. W. Bakke *et al., Labor Mobility and Economic Opportunity* (New York: Wiley, 1954). Most of these works have bibliographical references and discussions of the studies in this field.

72 Data from *Employment and Earnings and Monthly Report on the Labor Force* (January, 1967), Tables 18 and 24, pp. 114, 116. The unemployment rates are seasonally adjusted. Neither set of figures is affected by the new definitions that were adopted in January, 1967.

73 The ensuing discussion of armed forces expansion is based on data provided by the Department of Defense, specifically, estimates of the size of the armed forces in January, February, and March, 1964, and

October, November, and December, 1966, classified by age, sex and color.

74 Because of a strong upward trend in the figures the difference between January, 1964, and December, 1966, is considerably larger: 670,000.

75 Nonwhites accounted for 11.8 per cent of the increase in the armed forces during this period, although nonwhite males were only 10 per cent of the civilian male labor force in 1965. Hence, it is reasonable to infer that there must have been a somewhat larger effect on the unemployment rate of nonwhite males than on white males.

76 *Manpower Report,* 1967, Table F–4, p. 279.

77 Neighborhood Youth Corps data supplied by Manpower Administration, U.S. Department of Labor; Job Corps data, by Office of Economic Opportunity.

78 These data are cumulative, from August, 1962, to April, 1967, and were provided by the Manpower Administration. Annual data show a sharp increase in emphasis on the training of the more disadvantaged groups in more recent years.

79 Data from an unpublished paper by M. S. Cohen (U.S. Bureau of Labor Statistics) entitled "The Direct Effects of Federal Manpower Programs in Reducing Unemployment." Cohen estimates that the four programs which he analyzed (Neighborhood Youth Corps, On-the-Job Training under MDTA, Community Action, and College Work-Study) led to a reduction of 0.4 per cent in the national unemployment rate in the first quarter of 1967—that is, in the absence of these programs, the national unemployment rate would have been 4.2 per cent rather than the reported 3.8 per cent. He does not attempt to measure the direct and indirect effects of armed forces expansion; but if my estimate of an effect of about 0.5 per cent is added to his estimate, the conclusion is that in the absence of these programs, the national unemployment rate would have been at least 4.7 per cent ("at least" because the armed forces were larger in the first quarter of 1967 than in the fourth quarter of 1966).

80 E. L. Dale, Jr., "Can We Manage Prosperity?", New York *Times Magazine,* March 6, 1966.

81 Heller, *op. cit.,* p. 64.

82 G. Ackley, Address at Southern Illinois University, October 26, 1966 (mimeographed).

83 On June 17, 1965, the New York *Times* carried a front-page news story headed, "Fowler [Secretary of the Treasury] Predicts Income Tax Cuts." As late as October 5, 1965, the *Wall Street Journal* was reporting that "Administration Studies Further Cuts in Levies for Individuals, Firms."

84 It is important to distinguish between the "structuralists," among whom I would include Myrdal, Martin, and Killingsworth, among others, and the "permanent unemployment" school, as represented by Theobald and others.

85 The estimate of the increase in defense expenditures is from R. P. Oliver, "The Employment Effect of Defense Expenditures," *Monthly Labor Review* (September, 1967), pp. 9–20.

86 These figures are from a Bureau of the Census release, printed in *Daily Labor Report* No. 163, August 22, 1967, B–6 to B–8.

87 The most comprehensive treatment of recent proposals in this field is by C. Green, *Negative Taxes and the Poverty Problem* (Washington: Brookings Institution, 1967). This valuable study includes a summary of the discussion at a Brookings conference on the subject in June, 1966. For a critique of a number of proposals in this field, see G. H. Hildebrand, *Poverty, Income Maintenance, and the Negative Income Tax* (Ithaca: School of Industrial and Labor Relations, Cornell University, 1967).

88 R. Theobald, *Free Men and Free Markets* (Garden City, N.Y.: Doubleday, 1965); see also R. Theobald, *The Guaranteed Income* (Garden City, N.Y.: Doubleday, 1966).

89 Hildebrand, *op. cit.*, pp. 49–50. Hildebrand supports the higher estimate.

90 M. Friedman, *Capitalism and Freedom* (Chicago: University of Chicago Press, Phoenix Books, 1963), pp. 190–192.

91 R. J. Lampman, "The American System of Transfers: How Does It Benefit the Poor?", in L. Goodman, ed., *Social Welfare and Economic Progress* (New York: Columbia University Press, 1966); see also C. Green and R. J. Lampman, "Schemes for Transferring Income to the Poor," *Industrial Relations* (February, 1967), pp. 121–137.

92 Tobin, *op. cit.*; also J. Tobin, "The Case for an Income Guarantee," *Public Interest* (Summer, 1966), pp. 31–41; A. L. Schorr, "Against a Negative Income Tax," and J. Tobin, "A Rejoinder," *Public Interest* (Fall, 1966), pp. 110–119.

93 Green, *op. cit.*, pp. 115–117, summarizes three studies and quotes the conclusion of Good that the effect of taxation on work incentives is unclear and "may be weaker than popular discussions imply."

94 Hildebrand, *op. cit.*, pp. 56–59.

95 "The Case for a Family Allowance," New York *Times Magazine*, February 5, 1967, pp. 13, 68–73.

96 It would be possible, of course, to revise the individual income tax in such a way as to recapture a larger proportion of the payments to non-poor families. Schorr, *op. cit.*, proposes to eliminate all tax exemptions for children and to make children's allowances ($50 per month for each child under 6, $10 for each older child) taxable. The effect on the family's tax liability would depend on the age of the children as well as the number and on the family's other income; some high-income families would have a higher tax liability than before, even after crediting the children's allowances; and some middle-income families would find that their children's allowances would be larger than their new tax liability. Thus this plan would involve substantial payments to those who are not

poor and a significant increase in net tax liability for some taxpayers, which would be a substantial revision of the tax structure.

97 Green, *op. cit.*, Chapter 9.

98 S. A. Levitan and G. L. Mangum, "Programs and Priorities," *Reporter* (September 7, 1967), pp. 20–21.

99 "January 1966 Economic Report of the President." *Hearings* before the Joint Economic Committee, 89th Congress, 2d session, Part 2, pp. 366–367.

100 G. Ackley, speech cited in footnote 82.

101 *Examination of the War on Poverty: Staff and Consultants' Reports,* Subcommittee on Employment, Manpower, and Poverty, U.S. Senate, 90th Congress, 1st session, II, Appendix I. Summarizes a great deal of information on MDTA operation, much of it previously unpublished.

102 G. L. Mangum, "Manpower Programs in the Antipoverty Effort," *Examination of the War on Poverty*, II, 245–246; Appendix I, pp. 352–357, 377–379.

103 Much of my discussion of the Neighborhood Youth Corps draws upon S. A. Levitan, "Neighborhood Youth Corps," *Examination of the War on Poverty*, I, 43–56.

104 H. L. Sheppard, "Neighborhood Youth Corps," *Examination of the War on Poverty*, I, 31–39.

105 The most useful evaluation of the Job Corps is by S. A. Levitan, "Job Corps," *Examination of the War on Poverty*, I, 1–27. See also C. Weeks, *Job Corps: Dollars and Dropouts* (Boston: Little, Brown, 1967), a detailed account by a person closely involved in the administration of the program.

106 Levitan, "Job Corps," pp. 22–23.

107 Four such programs are evaluated by A. Nemore, "Transferability of Manpower Programs," *Examination of the War on Poverty*, II, 199–232.

108 The best description of the program and of some experimental applications of the ideas is in a book by A. Pearl and F. Riessman, *New Careers for the Poor* (New York: The Free Press, 1965). Professor Riessman, now of New York University, has also written a number of subsequent papers on the subject which are available from him in mimeographed form.

109 Subcommittee on Employment and Manpower, U.S. Senate, *Toward Full Employment: Proposals for a Comprehensive Employment and Manpower Policy in the United States*, 88th Congress, 2d session, 1964, pp. 58–60. The emphasis here was on the creation of unskilled jobs for such tasks as physically cleaning up the slums; the New Careers concept was not mentioned, but the principles recommended clearly imply support of this approach.

110 *Automation Commission Report*, pp. 35–37.

111 Under the Nelson-Scheuer amendment, $36.5 million are available for

New Careers–type programs, and an equal amount is allotted for beautification and community betterment projects. Under the Kennedy-Javits amendment, $25 million are available for combined private and public programs to alleviate the problems of urban areas with high concentrations of the unemployed.

112 D. Moynihan, "The Case for a Family Allowance," New York *Times Magazine,* February 5, 1967.

113 G. Myrdal, *Challenge to Affluence* (New York: Random House, 1963), pp. 49 *et passim.*

6 *James S. Coleman*

Race Relations and

Social Change

INTRODUCTION

The problem to which this chapter is addressed is a very general one in all societies, though more acute in some than others. It is the problem of how a distinct subgroup in society, without power and without the direct resources for gaining power, can nevertheless come to gain power, either individually or as a group. My use of the term "power" here is not in the sense of power over another group. I mean a position in society having as much power over one's own life and over community and national actions as do other citizens; in short, a position in society that makes real, rather than potential, the power of each individual implied in a document like the United States Constitution.

This problem may be described in such general terms because of its applicability to many societies. In many Latin American societies, a large mass of people lives in poverty, with little effective political power, with little economic strength, with little education, while a small elite controls the society. In South Africa, the division is a racial one, with the large mass of colored and blacks remaining without political power or economic resources. In England, the line of demarcation is defined by social class and family, but still with the consequences of effective lack of resources by those on the wrong side of the line. In the United States, the most important line of demarcation is a color line. Despite the fact that there exist wide variations within the group of whites and within the group of Negroes, it is nevertheless true that the cluster of high political power, economic well-being, education, and effective opportunity (for all these things go together) is found principally among whites, while a large proportion of Negroes is characterized by the cluster consisting of little political power, poverty, poor education, and lack of effective opportunity. Since the United States has long been a land of absorption of impoverished immigrants, this clustering of disadvantages in an ethnic group has been a frequent occurrence in our history. Negroes, however, were an immigrant group with three particular disadvantages: they came from tribal societies without a culture of written language; they were black in a land of whites; and they were confined for generations as slaves. These three differences have combined to make the problem faced by Negroes in gaining constitutional power and economic opportunity a particularly difficult one.

Though I shall address myself wholly to this single problem—that of Negroes gaining power in American society—many of the points will be of general relevance for the problem of bringing power to groups in society without it, whether it be Brazil or Britain.

First I shall present a general framework within which the problem of social change in relation to Negroes can be viewed; then review research and theory relevant to this framework; and finally discuss the research necessary to make this framework useful for policy.

Any discussion of purposive social change implies some ideas, at the very start, of just what the desired or optimum state of the future is toward which change might be directed. However, to specify such an optimum in any detail would obviously lead to endless debate, for each of us has his own vision of the future, and each will differ from the others. It is possible, however, to list the political, economic, and social resources which together constitute the individual's position in society —resources of which the average Negro has fewer than Americans generally. These lower levels of resources constitute deficits, relative to other Americans, experienced by Negroes in America. These deficits, then, are the focal points of change. For it is these deficits which define the condition of Negroes relative to the remainder of American society, and it is only elimination of them that will provide that equality of opportunity that is central to any of the optimum future states we might define. This is not, of course, to imply that every aspect of Negroes' lives is marked by a deficit compared to other Americans, but rather that it is the deficits that constitute the focus of change. Certain resources held by Negroes may be tools to aid in effecting the elimination of the deficits.

The general framework involves two sets of resources in society. One set consists of all the resources held by a group that are desirable in themselves—resources which, if deficient relative to others in society, constitute deficits in that group's power or opportunity in society. The second set consists of all the resources that have the potential for generating resources of other types, that is, as a cause of change. This second kind of resource can constitute an asset whose value lies in its conversion to assets of other kinds. Some resources are in both these sets, for first, their relative size compared to that for other persons in society constitutes a measure of deficit; and second, they constitute assets that are convertible into assets of other types. In the discussion below, no distinction will be made between resources that serve both as measures of relative position and potentially as convertible assets and resources that serve only the latter role, because it is not important to the framework itself, but only to its subsequent use. In principle, then, the framework would be used with any one or any subset of resources as the desired end products of change, the resources whose deficit position for a population group relative to others in society is the measure of desired change.

After outlining in Part I the state of the system of resources, I shall examine in Part II the question of convertibility of assets of each type into assets of another type. It is here that most of the theories of social change come to be directly relevant. These theories hypothesize certain conversion processes by which assets of one type generate assets of another type.

Such "conversion of assets" occurs in distinctly different types of action situations. As a consequence, I shall consider next, in Part III, the different contexts of action through which the conversion occurs. These action situations, or arenas of action, constitute a kind of system of production, within which resources of one type are converted into resources of another. As such, their results depend on particular combinations of resources, and not on single resources taken alone. The creation of certain assets, such as economic power, occurs through individual action in an occupational context, depending on both individual productivity and job opportunity. Other assets, such as organized political power, are created principally in a context of collective action and depend on a combination of individual resources and laws regarding assembly. Still other assets, such as intellectual achievement, are created principally in the institutional context of the school and the context of the home and depend on both individual resources, such as strength of motivation, and the school's or home's intellectual resources.

Finally, after presenting this over-all framework, within which are located various theories and hypotheses about social change, I shall turn in Part IV to research, asking how research may add certain assets that can aid in the elimination of the deficits in question. The research results themselves can constitute part of the system of assets of change, and it is within this framework that I propose to examine research. Therefore I shall discuss research programs, not as they will contribute to general knowledge, but as the results will constitute valuable assets for the reduction of deficits currently held by Negroes.

At the outset, then, I propose to list a set of resources relevant to the general areas in which Negroes currently experience a deficit compared to other Americans. Some of these resources are of intrinsic value, while some may be merely of value in bringing about the desired change. Some of these resources are largely absent or exist at a lower level and thus create a deficit for Negroes relative to other Americans. Some are at a high level. Any of them can constitute assets through which other resources can be generated.

PART I—LEVELS OF RESOURCES

The Resource Deficits

Freedom of Social Action as a Consequence of Skin Color

I use the phrase "freedom of social action" rather than "civil rights" or "social integration" or "discrimination" partly because these other terms have come to have special connotations in recent usage, but partly because this phrase expresses the essential attribute of which the Negro, as a Negro, has been deprived in American society. The general condition includes segregation, but it is not limited to it. It consists of all constraints and strictures placed on an individual's action because his skin color categorizes him as Negro: the lack of freedom to associate with whom he wants, the unavailability of certain jobs, the impossibility of joining certain clubs or organizations or of being served at certain places of business, discrimination in housing, and the enforced payment of deference by Negroes to whites in the South. Some of these deficits in freedom of action, or in "civil rights," have been reduced in recent years, but many remain.

I do not mean to include here the strictures on freedom of social action that arise from other aspects of most Negroes' condition: poverty, poor education, and the like. These attributes bring their own consequences, some of which are identical to those described above, but it is important to separate analytically those that arise from skin color itself, because the elimination of Negro poverty would not directly eliminate these; and conversely, the elimination of lack of freedom due to skin color will not eliminate the strictures on social action imposed by poverty.

Although this point is an elementary one, it is important to make it clear, because not long ago many persons held the simple assumption that elimination of the strictures on action directly due to skin color would somehow erase all the social deficits held by Negroes. Though the elimination of skin-color constraints is far from realization, enough such change has occurred, principally through legal action and legislation, to make quite clear that the other deficits will not be automatically erased, even if skin color comes to play no part in human interaction.

Economic Power

The deficit in economic power held by Negroes in American society can be measured in a variety of ways: by average income, relative rates of unemployment, occupational distribution, ownership of wealth by Negroes, control by Negroes of economic institutions such as manufacturing firms or retail stores. Economic power constitutes both a resource desirable in itself and a source of other resources, for it is a very versatile power, able to bring social position or political strength as well as direct satisfaction from consumption.

Political Power

As with economic power, the political power held by Negroes is less than that of most other Americans. The average Negro is much less likely to be registered to vote, and less likely to vote if registered, than other Americans. He is less likely than a white to write letters to his congressman and knows few effective ways of influencing those in government (with exceptions, described below). At the state and local levels of government, his political power is likely to be reduced through gerrymandered districts and underrepresentation. In addition, Negroes are most often in a minority in any political unit and thus stand the likelihood of losing on political issues in which there is a direct confrontation of racial interests. Negroes have less experience in holding office and in the organizational skills necessary to gain and hold office. Except in districts where Negroes constitute a majority, a Negro is unlikely to be nominated to candidacy for political office.

Two factors provide a partial balance for this lack of individual and collective political power. First, most Negroes are more sensitive than most whites to racial issues and even as a minority may provide the balance of power that will elect a desired candidate when the whites are split. Second, and more important, the organized direct action of

Negro civil rights groups has come to constitute enormous power at the national and local levels. Although Negroes' political power and efficacy through usual channels of democratic politics, such as voting, is low, collective Negro political power through the effective use of direct action has come to be very great.

The importance of political power is as obvious as the importance of economic power: it can affect greatly the other social and economic conditions that characterize the Negro. One evidence of this is the change in appeals and actions of political candidates in the districts of the South where increased Negro registration has made the Negro vote for the first time important enough to be sought after. Another evidence is the recent change in behavior of some congressmen from the urban North, pushing Negro demands in Congress because of the new-found political strength of Negroes in their constituencies. Presently the least politically powerful Negroes are those in the traditional situation, the rural South, where many Negroes are not now and never have been registered to vote and where there is frequently no organized civil rights activity.

Community Cohesion

A fourth resource largely missing among Negroes in America is social cohesion that characterizes neighborhoods and communities. American communities, particularly in urban areas, have a generally low level of community cohesion; but this absence of cohesion is far more pronounced in most Negro communities. This particularly characterizes the slums of the urban North, where transiency and other conditions make community solidarity difficult to achieve. Such cohesion or solidarity would constitute a great asset, for it would give Negroes collective strength both in making external demands (as on city governments or landlords) and in enforcing internal constraints (for example, against delinquency and crime). Community solidarity would create an enormous asset, as well, through the creation of community institutions that would provide a variety of services and aids that could partially compensate for the absence of individual economic resources. Its relative absence leaves the individual urban Negro particularly vulnerable to organized economic and governmental forces and to individuals from outside the Negro community, as well as to the unrestrained predations of persons within it. In many underdeveloped areas that share with American Negroes a lack of political and economic power, community solidarity constitutes an important asset in the struggle toward development. The examples of the solidarity of ethnic groups such as Jews and Chinese indicate the tangible assets this solidarity provides: mutual aid groups, lending arrangements, economic assistance for establishing businesses, and community disciplinary forces that reduce the costs of crime to near zero.

Family Cohesion

Closely related to community cohesion, but distinct from it, is family cohesion. The Negro family pattern, in both urban and rural America, is marked by the breakdown of the nuclear family unit and the substitution of a matriarchal three-generation family. The weakness of the conjugal bond among Negroes has consequences for the economic stability of the family, its ability to socialize the young, and the whole set of functions that the family provides for its members in modern society. In addition to the weakness of the conjugal bond and the relatively unimportant position of the male in the household in Negro families of low economic status (attributes that to a lesser extent characterize many lower economic groups other than Negroes), there is as well a cultural or normative poverty in the Negro family. The relative absence of a cultural tradition with a strong family unit means that the Negro mother is more nearly cast on her own unaided resources in maintaining the family and socializing the children. This is a powerful liability particularly because of the importance of these functions for the next generation.

The three-generation pattern of family life, with matrilineal kinship bonds, does provide some assets that partially substitute for others. For example, this kinship structure often makes it possible for the female head of the household to hold a full-time job, while the children are attended to by the mother's mother or others in the matrilineal kinship group.

Personal Resources

The average Negro in America suffers serious deficits of personal resources relative to other Americans—resources that could generate some of the other resources described above. The average Negro has a relatively low level of academic achievement in school, preventing further education and narrowing the range of available jobs; a lack of organizational skills; lack of information that could make possible rational action; and absence of the feeling that he can affect his own situation. The absence of these resources is symptomized by mental illness, crime, and such self-destructive actions as delinquency and addiction to drugs and alcohol. The deficits of personal resources are partly due to the absence of resources of the types above; but in turn, they help perpetuate those deficits. For example, the low level of personal resources in one generation of females makes it impossible for that generation of females to compensate for the absence of family cohesion in socializing the next generation. The lack of personal resources in males makes it impossible for them to take full advantage of greater freedom of access to jobs as patterns of discrimination are reduced.

This description of the personal resources of Negroes that are in short supply does not imply the absence of personal assets, though it does imply that the liabilities far outweigh the assets in providing the Negro with a competitive position in society. It implies that the balance of liabilities and assets is such that even if all other resources, including political and economic power, were equal at a given point in life, the average Negro in America could not maintain these resources at the same level as could the average non-Negro.

Attributes of the Larger Society That Constitute Liabilities for Negroes

White Prejudice

An important liability for Negroes is the prejudice of many whites that leads them to act differently toward Negroes than toward other whites. This prejudice, both as it is directly acted on and as it constitutes an expectation which even unprejudiced whites will use as a basis of action (for example, in panic selling of houses when Negroes move into a neighborhood), is the principal source of the first-listed deficit, lack of freedom of social action. The elimination of anti-Negro prejudice would have an important effect in increasing other resources held by Negroes. This is not to say that the most efficient way to generate certain of those resources is to eliminate prejudice, for prejudice is itself partly caused by the Negro's present position in society. And whatever its cause, prejudice may be one of the slowest elements to change. Nevertheless, certain actions such as school integration may be important assets for reducing the liability of prejudice.

Occupational Structure

A second important attribute of the larger society that constitutes a liability for Negroes is the present state of the occupational structure. This structure now, more than at any time in the past and more than that of any other nation, has a paucity of unskilled and semiskilled jobs requiring little education. Such jobs have been the first occupations after immigration for many immigrant groups. They offer an entry into the employed labor force and often a training ground for other occupations. For many persons, they have been the first rung on the ladder of economic independence. Now that rung is less often available than in the past.

Division of Labor

A third characteristic of American society that constitutes a liability for many Negroes is that the economy itself is far from a subsistence economy and has a very high level of division of labor. This means that many necessities of life which in a subsistence economy can be provided by the individual's own labor must be purchased with money. For a simple example, in many cities in other societies, working-class families are able to keep chickens in the back yard and to raise a few vegetables. In the rural areas from which urban Negroes have migrated, this pattern is even more frequent. But in the parts of the urban North to which Negroes have migrated, such partial direct subsistence by one's own labor is not possible. The necessities must be obtained indirectly through work at a job which is paid by money.

The nonsubsistence character of the American economy increases sharply the impact of conditions that lead to unemployment, such as slowdowns in the economy or lack of personal resources necessary to hold a job. The importance of money for subsistence living acts as a multiplier of the impact of certain economic conditions and personal resources on resources in other areas.

There are many more attributes of the society that constitute liabilities for Negroes, but without a more adequate theoretical framework for relating them to other elements, it is probably not useful to list them. The three attributes listed above provide some idea of the range they cover. Although no list of such attributes will be given, certain of them will be mentioned at later points when appropriate.

The list of current resources held by Negroes in America and liabilities of the larger society point to areas in which social change is necessary to make it possible for Negroes to have the same balance sheet in life as do non-Negroes. The missing assets and the liabilities range all the way from conditions existing in the white community or in institutions controlled by whites to the personal characteristics of Negroes. Some of the resources are important as desirable in themselves; all are important through their effects in increasing or reducing other resources. The question then becomes one of how the existing deficits of Negroes relative to other Americans are to be overcome. What resources or assets can be used to generate resources of another given type; and in turn, how will that change provide assets that eliminate certain of the other deficits described above? The problem appears an enormous one, but it should be placed in some perspective. There are at present certain great assets that did not exist some years ago. Some of these assets will be described below.

Assets Held by Negroes

Political Assets

In at least three ways, there have been recent sharp increases in the political power of Negroes. First, the migration of Negroes into the urban North gave political strength to Negroes in Congress through congressmen whose political interests came to be dependent on Negroes' interests. Second, there has been an increase in personal resources on the part of some Negroes in both the South and the North due to urbanization and education. Third, the northern migration has led to an increasing focus of attention on the condition of Negroes in America by whites, particularly younger whites with high organizational and political skills and the absence of an opportunity to use these. This sympathetic attention itself constitutes a resource that was absent only a few years earlier. These last two changes—an increase in personal resources of some urban Negroes and an increase in attention from resourceful whites—led to the civil rights movement and the enormous political power that movement has created. This in turn has itself decreased the deficit in freedom of action of Negroes (through protest movements at the local level and legislation at all levels) and the deficit in political power (for example, through voter registration drives in the South), and it has created personal resources by giving Negro activists organizational skills and a belief in their ability to affect their situation. Thus at present there are political assets that did not exist some years ago, which offer a potential resource for conversion into assets directly held by the average Negro.

Expanding Wealth of the Nation

An important asset currently held by Negroes in America is the rapid expansion of wealth in the society. At first glance it appears that this asset is valuable principally in making possible subsidies to education, housing, family support, health, and other welfare measures which can create certain resources and facilitate the growth of others.

However, to look at the question in this way is to take a too narrow view, for the rate of expansion of wealth of the country has indirect consequences as well. An example is the passage of the Civil Rights Act of 1964. This bill required no allocation of the country's wealth. It was not a public welfare measure, but merely a redistribution of political resources. Yet one action that made this bill possible was the passage of a Cotton Act to aid cotton-growing states. The Cotton Act, itself made possible by expanding economic resources, reduced opposition of southern legislators to the Civil Rights Act to a level that made possible its passage.

The general principle of which this is an example is that at a time of expanding resources, conflict in which one side must lose can be readily transformed into action in which both sides gain. If resources are expanding, an action is possible that makes both sides better off than they were before; if resources are stable or contracting, no such action is possible. It is important to note that the crucial variable which allows action is not the absolute size of the economic resources, but their rate of expansion.

This principle has special relevance to the problem of reducing Negro deficits, for if the set of resources in the nation were fixed, no matter at how high a level of economic wealth, increase of the resources held by Negroes could come only through reduction of the assets held by whites. Since it is not fixed, actions can be taken to increase resources of Negroes without reducing the assets of whites. In short, it means that actions can be taken that would otherwise confront immovable opposition.

An excellent example of this principle is found in the problem of school integration in northern cities. Negro demands for such integration have been quite powerful. Yet in their period of greatest power they were not powerful enough to bring about integration in the face of opposition by whites. It is likely that whatever measures were instituted, at a local, state, or national level, to bring about integration, white parents would find a way around them (for instance, middle-class parents can now afford private schools), so long as they felt their children were being hurt by integration. Since there is evidence that a child's achievement is affected by the socioeconomic level of his fellow students, and since, in addition, many white parents are racially prejudiced, they are likely to feel that their children are being hurt by integration.

A viable solution would appear to be to *accompany* school integration with an improvement in the quality of the school that at least compensated for the reduction in school quality that occurred with the introduction of large numbers of lower-class children. That is, the fact of integration acts to increase resources available to Negro children; but in order for this to be possible, it must be done without greatly reducing assets of the white children necessary to it. In a system of expanding economic resources, this is possible, simply by allocating some portion of this increment in wealth to the creation of schools that are both integrated and greatly improved.

I have listed two types of current assets held by Negroes that can aid in overcoming deficits. This list is, of course, only a beginning; and any systematic analysis would require the list to both longer and more systematic. In this chapter, it is possible only to give an outline of the kind of approach that appears possible and useful. The two assets listed above will serve the purposes of that outline.

PART II—THE CONVERSION OF RESOURCES

In gaining some idea of the efficacy of various types of social action and social policy toward erasing the deficits described above, the most important question is the convertibility of assets of one type into assets of another. For example, if the deficits in freedom of action held by Negroes because of skin color were to be erased, what would be the extent and timing of reduction of deficits in economic power? The answers to these questions of convertibility of assets are most important for public policy.

I suggest that the general framework within which these interdependencies can be usefully considered is the system of resources implied above. A variety of hypotheses and theories of social change will be discussed below. Each of these, in effect, hypothesizes certain convertibilities. Many of these hypotheses are in implicit or explicit conflict, and therefore a primary order of business is to gain a better idea of the convertibility of assets in each of these areas to assets in others.

Resources of Negro Communities

It was indicated earlier that Negroes have a low level of community cohesion in Negro residential communities. It is useful to spell out in some detail the kind of assets that can be provided by a community and the use that may be made of such assets.

The Level of Interpersonal Trust in a Community

The quantity of trust existing in a community is a resource more directly related to a community's financial capital than is ordinarily realized. Nearly all economic transactions involve a time difference between the delivery of goods by one party and that by the other. The institution of metallic or commodity money facilitates such transactions by providing a medium that is accepted by one party to the transaction in lieu of goods. But transactions are even further facilitated if promises to pay, or debts, can be accepted to cover this time discrepancy. In small, close communities, such as the modern financial community in Wall Street, or in some primitive tribes, debts or promises do circulate in much the same way that money does. But in the larger society where partners to an exchange have no basis of trust for accepting such promises, the government or a central bank itself acts as the debtor and makes the promises, embodied in paper money, and commercial banks make further promises, embodied in bank credit. These monetary systems are at bottom based on trust—trust of institutions such as the government or a bank. This trust makes possible a far greater flow of economic activity than could otherwise occur and constitutes a definite capital asset of the society. In modern society, it is usual to conceive of such economically productive systems of trust in terms of the existing monetary system. But in subcommunities of the larger society, systems of trust may exist which constitute just as definite an economic capital asset. Two examples will illustrate this. In Lancashire around 1800, manufacturers had little trust in local merchant banks and even less in the central Bank of England. Yet they had great need for money to facilitate economic activity. They developed the use of bills of exchange, with these bills or promises to pay circulating from one manufacturer to another as payment for goods received and guaranteed by each party through whose hands they passed. Had it not been for the existence of widespread mutual trust among these men, economic development could not have taken place with such rapidity.[1]

The second example is the revolving credit associations existing in villages and towns of southeast Asia and Africa, as described by Geertz.[2] The associations consist of a circle of friends and neighbors who, in social gatherings at a member's house, make weekly or monthly contributions to a common fund that is then given to each member in turn, through some predetermined order or by lot. Though these systems vary widely, they all take the form of steady contributions and lump-sum payments. Geertz describes the institutions as a means of saving, that is, of accumulation of sufficient capital to make a major purchase, such as a bicycle, that could not be purchased otherwise. But the associations depend wholly on a system of mutual trust, which in effect constitutes a capital asset of the community. In a community without such trust, individuals would not be willing to take the necessary chance of loss, and no association could develop.

If, instead of the revolving credit association of primitive Asia and Africa, Negro slums in America are saddled by the numbers racket and other gambling schemes, the result is a great economic loss to the community instead of a capital gain. In both cases, the individual pays steadily a small amount, in the prospect of receiving a large lump sum. But in the Negro community, in which the numbers racket is prevalent, the concentration of resources provided by the lump-sum payment is so uncertain that it leads to squandering rather than productive uses, and the payments returned are so small compared to the sum invested that the racket constitutes a serious economic drain on the community.

A further contrast can be drawn by considering the revolving credit associations as mutual loan associations and comparing them to the loan facilities in lower-class Negro neighborhoods in America. The revolving credit associations are ordinarily initiated by one person who needs a loan for establishing a small enterprise or meeting an emergency. He receives the first payment of the revolving fund. The resulting interest he pays is to his neighbors; thus it remains within the community and is at a lower rate than that offered by the commercial moneylenders. In the absence of the system of trust on which such associations are based, lower-class Negroes in America must pay exorbitant rates of interest to a criminal-sponsored loan industry. This interest leaves the community and is very high, imposing a tax that constitutes a direct economic deficit for the community.

Examples similar to the revolving credit associations may be found in many communities. Certain craft workers have developed mutual benevolent societies to insure them against extremities of ill fortune. Among immigrant groups to the United States, as one family of immigrants became established and economically self-sufficient, they would bring friends and relatives, helping them until they were established. In Amish communities, a man's barn or house is built by a collective enterprise consisting of the whole community. In such religious communities, in fact, the principal economic asset is the cohesion of the community, allowing it to confront all problems, internal and external, as a collective body.

In every group with little economic capital, such mutual help arrangements develop, and they provide as definite a source of capital assets as does the more formal money that we ordinarily think of as capital. The point is that although they develop wherever monetary capital is scarce, their extent varies widely in different groups, depending on the system of trust that exists in the community. Although they do exist in Negro communities as a substitute for monetary capital, they often have a meager foundation of trust and are consequently poorly developed. The transiency that characterizes much of the Negro urban North, and in some cases the personal disorganization manifested in delinquency, crime, gambling, drug addiction, and alcoholism, inhibit the development of community institutions based on trust.

The community institutions discussed above have all been rather direct substitutes for economic capital. But many community institutions based on mutual aid, and thus ultimately on mutual trust, provide assets of other kinds. The collective confrontation of government officials, landlords, or merchants may provide improved living conditions that no individual could bring about. The presence of a community newspaper can conserve each individual's resources by sharing information that he could obtain only with difficulty. The existence of a strong parents' group can both exert pressure on the school for results and aid it in gaining those results.

Yet all these activities depend on an extensive system of mutual trust —a belief in my mind, so to speak, that if I aid you today, you will aid me when I am in need, and thus a willingness to make such an investment of resources in one's neighbors.

It is important to recognize that the benefits of community trust and cohesion depend on both the existence of the resource in the community and the cohesion that allows its sharing. In upper middle-class American communities, it is often remarked that resources existing in the community, in the form of occupational skills of adult males, are wholly unavailable to the children. Sometimes, attempts are made to bring these resources to the children through a "careers night," or a similar exercise, at the school. But on the whole, one can say that these resources are of very little use to the community as a collectivity. A friend of an architect's son hardly knows what his friend's father does and is almost never able to benefit from it—to be stimulated by it or even informed about the kind of work it entails.

In such communities, a set of individual resources that might be a community asset cannot be so, because of the lack of community cohesion and the particular structure of activities that separates the youth from adults other than their own parents. In contrast, in many village communities the social cohesion exists, so that the youth are in contact with adults outside their family; but the variety of resources is missing, so that this child too fails to learn about what an architect does.

This example of sharing of occupational information (or the failure to do so) in upper middle-class communities shows a case in which the potential community asset is not so directly economic as in the previous examples. The principle of shared resources holds quite independently of the kind of asset; the important point is that the resource *exist* in some members of the community and that the community social organization be *cohesive* enough to allow its sharing. An important case is that of socialization and discipline of children. Where the family has extensive resources for controlling the actions of its children, these may or may not be shared throughout the community, depending on its cohesion. In a cohesive community, a parent need have little concern about his child's activities, because he soon learns from neighbors if the child has misbehaved. This may be absent because of the lack of community cohesion, as it tends to be in upper middle-class communities; or it may be absent because of the absence of the basic resource of discipline within the family itself. In lower-class urban Negro neighborhoods, both the essential requirements appear to be missing.

Another important example is the care of children and households in emergencies. In the absence of hired resources, complicated welfare schemes, which seldom function adequately, must be devised to meet the emergencies that occur, or else the deficit is transferred to the children left to roam in the streets. In every case, the community deficit in cohesion becomes converted into deficits that are directly experienced by individuals, unless some other asset is substituted in its absence.

In short, it appears that the provision of any community asset requires two kinds of element: it requires first of all some set of individual resources that *can* be shared (such as the small money incomes of Asian villagers or the architect's skills in the hypothetical example above) and the community cohesion, institutions, and system of trust that allow these resources to serve the whole community. In the United States, middle-class communities have a wide variety of resources, but lack the cohesion to allow their utilization by the community. Negro lower-class communities lack the cohesion and trust; and except for purely economic resources (which are far more abundant than in a southeast Asian village), they lack many of the resources as well. Thus both of these elements are deficient, and both must be supplied if a given community asset is to come into existence. The community cohesion and trust act as a "multiplier," multiplying the assets of individuals by the number of individuals, to make the assets of all available to each; but for this multiplication to provide a significant asset as a product, both terms must be of some size.

My use of the imagery of multiplication here is no vague analogy. This situation is a case of what economists describe as the problem of "supply of public goods." Public goods, such as a fire department which serves the whole community alike, will not be provided without either formal tax enforcement or informal community norms that constrain each person to pay his share. A rotating credit association or a mutual benefit association is like a public good in that each person contributes to it, and each receives a return worth more to him than his contribution (a lump-sum payment or insurance against a catastrophe).

The multiplication of individual resources by the size of the community in the case of perfect sharing of resources indicates the interaction that exists between different types of resources. In this case, the creation of a capital asset depends on the existence of both the resource of community cohesion and individual resources. More generally, community cohesion and trust act both as a multiplier of assets and a facilitator of social action. As indicated in the examples, this is an asset that is directly translatable into economic capital or political power.

There appears to be little question about, and little need for, research concerning the multiplier effects of the assets of community trust and cohesion. The principal research questions here seem to be how the cohesion and trust are themselves created and what the resources are that lead to their development in a community.

Family Resources

The importance of the family as the principal socializing agent of the child is, of course, well known. What has only recently become evident is the great strength of the family's influence in relation to other socializing agents. For example, several studies comparing the relative importance of variations in family background and variations in school quality on the achievement of children in school show the much greater effects of variations in the family.[3] Jackson and Marsden show the continuity of the family's socializing effects over two or more generations, as reflected by the ability of families displaced from the middle class in one generation to guide their children back to it in the next.[4] More general evidence on the socialization patterns of ethnic groups shows the relation of strong families to high achievement and low delinquency for different ethnic groups.

As a determinant not only of achievement but of a child's personal resources generally, the family appears to have a degree of importance not approached by any other factor.

This is a sword that cuts both ways, for it means not only that the assets of the family will be transmitted to the child but also that the liabilities of the family will become the liabilities of the child. Family resources cannot be supplied or withheld by government policy, as can some other resources. And it is family resources in which Negroes have probably the greatest liability. They are both cultural (the absence of cultural traditions that guide and assist parents in socializing their children) and structural. The structural liabilities consist in the absence of a strong male role in the family and the number of families in which the father is absent entirely or only intermittently present. Moynihan and others argue, with some evidence, that it is particularly the structural defects which prevent the growth of economic and socialization resources.[5]

This set of conditions creates a difficult situation for social change. The effect of family resources on personal resources is quite clear and evidently quite strong, but lack of family resources appears to be a major liability for lower-class Negroes and one which is at least as difficult to modify as a lack of personal resources themselves.

Such a situation would appear to lead to three possible avenues of change: attempts to increase family resources and, at one remove, the personal resources; attempts to reduce the strength of the family's effect on the child's personal resources, either by greatly increasing the strength of other socializing agents or reducing the child's contact with the family; or finally, provision of external aids, which allow families with a low level of resources to nevertheless socialize their children more effectively. An example of the latter is effective community or police action to control delinquent behavior, which aids parents otherwise unable to insulate their children from delinquent influences.

Modern totalitarian regimes have faced the problem of breaking the strength of family socialization in the period immediately after taking power. This was done both in Hitler's Germany and in Stalin's Russia through the use of boarding schools and strong youth associations acting as age-specific autosocializing groups. Though it is not a question of breaking a family's socialization power here, it is a question of breaking into a pattern in which one generation's liabilities are carried over into those of the next. American society has shown little imagination and little application in facing this problem of missing family resources. It appears quite possible that an assessment of alternative socializing mechanisms for children (such as organized peer groups), and ways of increasing the socializing resources of families, would provide ideas that could greatly aid the socialization process.

Apart from the effects of families in socializing their children and thus transmitting assets or deficits to the next generation, family resources serve in other ways: in particular, as an alternative or substitute for personal resources or community resources. A strong family constitutes a kind of social insurance that cushions against reversals of fortune, illness, or any other events that tax or overwhelm the individual's resources. Because resources of a strong family may be concentrated to aid any single member, the family acts like the community described in a preceding section: as a multiplier of individual resources, allowing each individual to use his own resources to the limits, secure in the knowledge that the family reserve can aid him if necessary. A simple example will give the idea concreteness: a merchant with relatives who can provide him quick loans if necessary can make immediate commitments on bargain or large-lot purchases, which he could not do if forced to depend on the formal banking system.

Yet family resources can supplement not only personal resources but community resources as well. Many activities may be alternatively carried out by the community or the family, with either substituting for the other: disciplining children, controlling crime and enforcing social norms, sheltering or aiding handicapped or otherwise dependent members, and the variety of other functions that communities and families perform. The family and community differ in size and in strength and permanence of attachment; but their potential functions are similar, except for the child-socializing function in which the community seldom substitutes for the family.

Personal Resources

A number of theories of social change give primacy to personal qualities of one type or another. The advocates of this basis of social change include the sociologist Max Weber,[6] the revolutionary Mao Tse-tung,[7] philosophers Sorel [8] and Sartre,[9] and the psychologist McClelland.[10] All these men have in common the view that social change is produced by personal qualities on the part of some number of the population. I shall give a brief account of the various types of such theories before discussing research strategy.

The Achievement Orientation Theories

One general thesis argues that the personal qualities of hard work, thrift, and orientation to achievement, whether derived from religious values, family cultural traditions, explicit training, or some other source, are essential elements in much of social change. This thesis has gained its greatest psychological sophistication and most intensive study in the work of McClelland.[11] His thesis is that the "need for achievement" (which is similar to Weber's concept of the "Protestant Ethic") differs widely in different cultures and within a culture and that individuals and societies (seen as aggregates of individuals) with high need for achievement will in fact achieve highly. McClelland has carried out a number of experiments and action programs that appear to confirm that need for achievement can be considered a general personality trait, that it can be induced by training, and that such induced need for achievement does lead to an increase in actual achievements in the real world. The sociological counterpart of such research is that begun by Weber in his linking of the Protestant emphasis on individualism and individual responsibility for one's fate to the rise of capitalism in Western society. The Protestant Ethic thesis has been subjected to both reexamination (as by Tawney [12]) and further research effort since Weber's time. The point of greatest question appears not to be the psychological linkage between the individualism of Protestant sect religion and a strong orientation to achievement, but the social and institutional linkage between such achievement orientation and economic growth.

Besides the general face validity of the argument that those who are achievement-oriented will achieve, much evidence indicates that personality differences, resulting from different family backgrounds, have a powerful impact on achievement, as indicated in the preceding section. A number of research results show that among different ethnic groups, those with families that impose the strongest demands on their children, and are themselves strongest (in particular, Jews, Chinese, Japanese), show the highest achievement, while those with the weakest and least demanding families (Negroes, American Indians) show lowest achievement. Within ethnic groups, as well, the relation holds: the social and economic level of the family, which is associated with the strength of the family and the strength of demands it makes on its children, accounts for more variation in school achievement and occupation than do any other environmental factors. Altogether, the impact of childhood experience within the family on a generalized personality trait of achievement orientation appears to be quite strong.

The psychological constellation leading to high achievement among Negroes appears to be somewhat more complex than suggested by the notion of an achievement orientation or need. The aspirations toward achievement held by both Negro adults and children, particularly aspirations to educational achievement, appear to be rather great even among those whose achievement is low and stationary. This is obviously a psychological oversimplification, for such Negroes might well score low in McClelland's n-Ach measures. Yet there is a peculiar and ill-understood phenomenon that appears to characterize many Negro adults and youths: an unrealistically high, idealized aspiration, relatively unconnected to the actions that ordinarily lead to achievement of a goal.

A personality characteristic related to, but slightly different from, n-Ach has appeared in several studies to be a strong determinant of Negro achievement.[13] This is a sense of "fate control" or of "personal efficacy"—a sense that the environment will respond in an orderly fashion to one's actions. Its high relation to achievement, and the lesser relation than is ordinarily supposed between self-esteem and achievement, or aspirations and achievement, may offer some hints about the motivational constellation that operates for these children.

The propositions under discussion here are of three orders: the first is a very straightforward proposition about the effect of personality characteristics ("values" or "motives") on individual achievement. This proposition can be directly studied by psychological research in the laboratory or in schools. It appears, as indicated above, that the psychological determinants of achievement may be somewhat different for Negro children than for white children in the United States.

A second proposition, or set of propositions, concerns the determinants of the psychological states leading to achievement. The strongest evidence in this area indicates the importance of the family; but the effect of other experiences has been studied by McClelland and others; and work by Weber and others has shown the importance of religious ideology in shaping these attitudes.

The third proposition concerns the aggregation of individual achievement into societal achievement. The proposition is that significant change in the rate of economic development in a society comes about as a result of increases in, or a higher level of, the relevant personality characteristics. These characteristics are seen as assets that can be converted not only into individual achievement but also into economic development of the society or subsociety. As McClelland states the hypothesis, "The shortest way to achieve economic objectives might turn out to be through changing people first." [14]

The Revolutionary Transformation Theorists

A second major variety of the thesis that social change derives from personal qualities is of a somewhat different sort and, as will be evident, more sociologically complex. It is the set of hypotheses characterizing "revolutionary" theorists such as Sorel, Sartre, and Mao Tse-tung. The hypothesis that all these theorists hold in common (and is most emphasized by Sartre and Sorel) is this: Participation in revolutionary action transforms the previously apathetic masses by giving them a goal and the hope of achieving the goal. The revolutionary action itself and the rewards of success it brings to hard work create men who are no longer bound by traditional customs, inhibited by ascribed authority patterns, and made apathetic by the lack of hope. This psychological transformation, according to these authors, is a necessary prerequisite to the social and economic transformation. Applied to the case of

Negroes in the United States, it would state that the real benefit of the civil rights movement is the psychological change it has produced and is producing in those Negroes active in it. A more radical application would be that only by engaging in a real revolution will Negroes be psychologically transformed in such a way that they can achieve their goals. For these theorists, the revolution plays the same role that individualist religion did for Weber, or family socialization for McClelland. The psychological mechanism is somewhat different, however, because it predicates psychological change as a result of the individual's own action, not as a result of his social or institutional context. It is an "action-affects-beliefs" hypothesis: the revolutionary action will change the personalities and belief systems of the revolutionaries. This hypothesis, which is stated with different emphasis by Sartre and Sorel, is related to certain social-psychological theories that emphasize the effect of action in changing attitudes (see Festinger [15]). A second element in the hypothesis is identical to that of the achievement orientation theorists discussed earlier. It states that the changed personalities will then constitute a human capital that can be transformed into economic productivity and social change.

Some of the "revolutionary" theorists include an additional element in their theories, to the effect that the revolutionary ideology must include a total commitment of the individual to the collectivity. It is logically unrelated to the hypothesis of a psychological transformation. A total submission of the individual will in the collectivity is essential to this theory of social change, so that the collectivity becomes a single-minded instrument of change. This principle implies a need for abdication of the right of individuals to hold diverse views, either about goals or about means, and the consequent transformation of the revolutionary group into a single force that can be directed at the enemy. The extent of this ideological directive is well illustrated by a recent attack in China on President Liu Shao-chi by the Maoists. Liu had written, "As Communist party members shoulder the unprecedentedly 'great office' of changing the world, it is all the more necessary for them to go through such steeling and self-cultivation in revolutionary struggle." This statement reflects fully the psychological transformation in the revolutionary theorists' work, but it is now seen as too individualistic. It has been interpreted by Maoists to mean that one should "suffer a little to gain a lot" and is seen as a perversion of Mao's teaching that one must be totally selfless and "be the first to suffer and the last to enjoy." [16]

The revolutionary theory of social change constitutes a sharp contrast with the theory of social change which depends on the Protestant

Ethic or individualistic achievement. It is a peculiar combination of individual responsibility and collective authority. The two theories begin together, in that they imply a transformation in the values or personalities of individuals (the one through religious beliefs or childhood socialization, and the other through participation in a revolutionary struggle), and in both theories the transformation includes the belief that one's individual effort can have great effects on one's fate and on the world. The psychological transformation can be an enormous one, because the social structures in which economically depressed populations have often subsisted are feudal and traditional structures with ascribed status, which inculcate a belief in a static order rather than in change, and a belief that one could not and should not by his own efforts alter his position in life. These conditions in the United States have been most closely approximated in the rural South, which has been the most economically static region and the one closest to a feudal order in its social structure. It is under these conditions that, until recently, the large majority of Negroes in the United States lived.

Viewed in a slightly different way, these theories of social change all are predicated on the imposition on the individual of a powerful and unchallengeable norm. In the theories based on family socialization, the norm is internalized through family training. In the theories based on religious ideology, the norm is imposed by the religious belief. In the theories based on revolution, the norm is imposed by the demands of the revolutionary struggle and enforced by the revolutionary group.

Beyond their common psychological core, the achievement theory and the revolutionary theory diverge sharply. The first is wholly individualistic, the second wholly collective in orientation. The first focuses on the free individual, able to respond to opportunity without regard for obligations or ties to others, able to migrate to cities or to new jobs. The absence of such individualism is often used to account for lack of economic development in primitive societies, societies which are burdened by social values that inhibit the individualistic response to opportunity. The achievement-motive theory emphasizes as well a freedom from constraints by fellow workers to limit work. (Max Weber cites in *The Protestant Ethic* the experience of Methodist workers, embracing the new ideology, having their tools broken by fellow workers for working too hard and producing too much.)

The revolutionary theory is wholly collective, denying the individual member of the revolutionary effort any freedom of direction. It emphasizes selflessness, the strength in unity, the necessity to "stand together or fall separately," the enormous power that a single-minded collective body exhibits. Thus these two theories share a common element of individual psychology and are diametrically opposed in their social psychological premises.

Another way of looking at the similarities and differences between the achievement and revolutionary theories of social change or approaches to change is to say that they both postulate the disciplined effort of individuals as the essential resource that produces change. For the first, the market system, with its possibilities of individual mobility through individual effort, acts as the mechanism to induce this self-discipline and effort. The second depends on collective identity, and the existence of a collective enemy to overcome, as the source of self-discipline and effort. This second approach to change tends to arise when the market system has broken down for an identifiable group, thus providing the basis for such collective identity. It appears as well to have an inherent instability, because of the special conditions necessary to maintain the collective identity.[17]

It is true that these two theories have often been applied to different situations of social change. The Protestant Ethic or individual achievement theories have been more often applied to social change within social structures that have been most open, most characterized by a division of labor, least characterized by a fixed hierarchical order in society. The collective force theories have more often been applied to social structures closer to a fixed hierarchical order. Nevertheless, there are large areas of overlap: the collective force thesis has been applied to systems with an advanced division of labor, though its notable successes have been in the hierarchically organized peasant societies. Similarly, the individual achievement thesis has been applied to the whole range of social systems, though its greatest successes have been in the least hierarchically organized, most open societies.

This partial consistency of theories and social structures is reasonable, but it should not lead to a false sense of closure, for this dialectic, or one directly analogous to it, arises in all phases of Negro action. The problem at a personal level confronts every middle-class Negro: should he strengthen his individualism, discard all past associations, make white friends when he has the opportunity, and let the social change for Negroes be the aggregate change due to achievements of himself and others? Or should he bind himself to the Negro community, a part of a single-minded collectivity, advancing only as it advances? The only ambitious Negroes for whom this question does not arise are the leaders of the Negro movement, for their personal achievements, including sometimes great status and power, arise only through the collective achievements of Negroes as a group.

This is the question as it confronts individual Negroes. A modified version of the question confronts the collective Negro movement as well: whether to take collective action leading as quickly as possible to a dismemberment of the collectivity through integration, or to take collective action leading to a strengthened collective identity and a continued collectivity with increased power. The first strategy characterizes most groups in the Negro movement and is perhaps best represented by the NAACP. The second strategy characterizes, at the extreme, the Black Muslims and Black Nationalists and some youth groups such as SNCC. It should be noted that among all the non-English white national groups in North America, the only one whose leaders have often pursued the second strategy is French Canadians, particularly in Quebec. Except for French Canadians, change has occurred through individual achievement and individual assimilation into the larger society.

A similar question confronts the larger society as a collectivity: which goal on the part of Negroes is most beneficial to the society? Which aim should be facilitated? The answer in this case is quite clear: the first goal, of individual achievement, destruction of collective identity whenever it impedes integration into the society, is always the society's desired goal. (The insistence on maintaining a strong collective identity is one reason that Jews have always constituted such a thorn in the flesh to governments.)

From the point of view of the most efficient reduction of current Negro deficits, this question in modified form also arises. The question here is not ultimate goals, but means. Taking the goals as both the erasing of the deficits described earlier and the ultimate goal of the society as a collectivity—social integration—the answer about means is not so clear. For example, the increase in collective identity of Negroes that has been partly responsible for the Negro movement has been a major asset both in generating other resources and in establishing the conditions for integration. Yet further increase in this collective identity has led to an ideology of separation, of anti-integration and black racism.

The answer must therefore be complex, differing according to the type of deficit attacked and the stage in erasing these deficits that has been reached. For example, collective action appears to have been an extremely powerful asset in reducing the deficit in freedom of social action, but a less important asset in increasing the economic power of Negroes.

Legal and Legislative Resources

Certain theories of social change in the direction of economic development stand at the opposite pole from those that give personal qualities the primary place in social change. They can be well exemplified by an analysis that Berle and Means [18] and Commons [19] have used to account for the growth of the modern corporation in the United States. The argument is somewhat as follows. The owners of a company are concerned with the rate of profit on the investment, that is, the rate of return in dividends on the market value of stock. Managers of a company are concerned first with total profit, the difference between expenditures and income, and beyond that, with expansion of the resources under their control. Thus a corporation in which the policies are closely controlled by the owners will tend to make larger profit yields on capital investment, but smaller total profits, and will less likely reinvest profits or borrow for capital expansion than will a corporation in which managers are free from control by the owners.

The joint-stock corporation, with ownership dispersed among many investors, provided an organization where managers were relatively free from control by owners. In addition, incorporation of such firms is done in the United States by states, not by the federal government. During the growth of capitalism in the late nineteenth and early twentieth centuries, states competed with one another to obtain the incorporation of firms, and since the managers had most control over the place of incorporation, they were able to select a state which allowed a corporate structure giving them most freedom from owners. This freedom included the use of proxy voting, increased discretion by directors in management, the change from unanimous to majority stockholders' votes, the issuance of stock warrants and nonvoting stock, the freedom to enter into new kinds of business, and the freedom to amend the charter itself by majority vote. The consequence of this was the existence of a corporation governed by those whose principal aim was growth and whose policies were designed to maximize growth, regardless of its effect in depressing the profit yield on investment.

This example is not of direct applicability to the present situation; it is useful for the contrast it implies to the "personal quality" theories. It proposes that change, growth, or development is due to a particular organizational structure (the competitive structure among states and the subsequent autonomy of corporation managers in use of corporate resources). Implicitly, it is assumed that men appropriate to the role will come to occupy it, given the distribution of personalities in society, and that the crucial element is the organizational, or ultimately the legal, structure in creating roles that generate a given motivation. It attributes the rise in capitalism in the United States to the appropriate institutional structure, while Weber attributed it to an appropriate psychological structure of individuals.

How are theories of this sort different from the theory behind much civil rights activity: that if the white community's barriers to opportunity for Negroes are removed, Negroes will seize the opportunity and thus overcome the economic, political, or social deficit? The similarity, of course, lies in the implicit assumption that the principal barrier to social change is the absence of the appropriate roles, or to use recent sociological terms, the absence of an appropriate opportunity structure. In part, the difference between the theories is one of numbers: the corporate growth theories imply that *there exist* at least a few men in society who will pursue the goals relevant to the role; the civil rights theory implies that a *large number* of Negroes will be able to fill adequately a new set of roles that are opened up to them. In part, the latter theories imply an additional strong condition: that since Negroes must compete for these newly open roles with whites, they can effectively do so, despite other liabilities. Obviously, this is a very strong assumption that few persons would make; and it is an assumption not made by the corporate growth theory.

Thus it is evident that theories which disregard individual personal qualities differ in their assumptions about the supply of implicitly required qualities. Some make only very weak assumptions about this supply, while others make very strong assumptions.

The most prevalent theory in the area of race relations that does not depend on personal resources is a generalization of the Berle-Means and Commons theory of corporate growth. In that theory, the legal statutes, which themselves derived from a particular political competition among states, were responsible for the structure of control of the corporation and thereby its growth. Generalized, the theory is that social change can be effectively brought about through legal statutes aimed at prohibiting certain actions, enforcing others, or allowing still others. The Supreme Court decision on school desegregation of 1954, and statutes in the Civil Rights Act of 1964 prohibiting discrimination of various sorts, are examples of actions guided by such theory. This theoretical position is widely held by lawyers, who see it as the principal mechanism for change. In this theory, the arena of social action is the court, and any advocate of social change implements his advocacy by obtaining court rulings. A theory of slightly differing content is held by some legislators, who see the same process, though the principal arena of social action is the legislature, and social change is implemented by change in the law.

The evidence of this theory is quite mixed. In certain cases, legal action has created great social change. For example, the National Labor Relations Act in 1935 changed the terms on which management and labor could legally negotiate, giving legality to certain actions of labor that it had previously not had. The formal power provided by this act did result in more favorable negotiations for unions and was followed by large increases in the numerical size of unions.

On the other hand, the Supreme Court school desegregation decision had practically no direct effect on school desegregation in states of the deep South: ten years after the decision, less than 1 per cent of all Negroes in these states were attending school with whites, and in some states the percentage was zero. Its only direct effect on desegregation of schools was in border states. It is possible, of course, that this decision comes to have an ultimate effect through indirect means, such as by changing the expectations and thus the demands of Negroes and sympathetic whites, which then create the political power necessary for enforcement of the decision. But if this is so, the importance of the legal action as the source of change is far less than its protagonists allege, because first of all it is itself in part determined by social conditions, and second, it depends for its effects on the presence of a variety of additional factors.

Knowledge about the conditions under which a change in the law will have greater or lesser effects is very weak. Certain obvious points can be stated, however. First of all, if the agent to carry out the action is under direct control of the policy-makers, the action will occur. For example, Britain is undergoing a currency change to a decimal standard. There is great controversy over the details of the change. But once the law is passed, it will be implemented, merely because its implementation lies wholly in the hands of a bureaucracy under the control of the government. Similarly, if the United States school system were a national one instead of a set of local ones, with each superintendent removable by the national government, the Supreme Court decision would have been implemented immediately. This is easily seen by comparing the school systems on military bases, which are responsible directly to the national government. These schools did immediately desegregate.

Thus a general principle can be stated: *the more nearly a legal action requires implementation by a set of actors who owe no responsibility, direct or indirect, to the lawmakers, the less likely that the action will have an effect.*

But even if we assume a lack of direct responsibility to the lawmakers, a situation may be distinguished in which legal action may be expected to have rather strong and immediate effects. This is the situation in which *implementation of the legal action involves at least one party in whose interest it lies and who is prepared to implement it.* In this case, the legislation places a weapon in the hands of one party to a conflict, who is prepared to use it. The National Labor Relations Act of 1935 was like this. The law redefined the rules under which collective bargaining could take place, giving more weapons to labor than it currently had. The law was effective because the interested party, labor, was already well enough organized and prepared to take advantage of these new conditions. Similarly, civil rights legislation which allows persons with a discrimination complaint against a place of business to bring the complaint to court can he highly effective when Negroes are prepared to press complaints, but not unless they are so prepared. In a differentiated urban environment, social pressure to prevent such complaints can be used only with difficulty, and thus a Negro is free to press a charge; in closely knit rural communities, this is seldom so. Also, in some contexts there exist the organizational skill and resources to press the charge effectively; in other contexts, these are absent. As a consequence, the effectiveness of such a law will vary greatly from one locale to another, merely because in one locale it places a weapon in the hands of the parties prepared to use it, while in another no one is prepared to use the new weapon.

Apart from these two principles about the agents of implementation of a legal action, there are certain types of legal action that create an immediate social change. One of the most important of these involves *situations in which one person loses if he changes alone, but no one loses if all change.* This may be termed the "innovator loss" situation. The best example of this in recent legislation is laws against discrimination in places of business that serve the public, such as restaurants or commercial apartments. Without a law, restaurant owners may not individually desegregate, because if any one does, he feels that he stands to lose some of his white customers to other restaurants. But if all do, this will not occur, except where attitudes of white customers are very intransigent. The customer knows that Negroes are admitted in all restaurants and thus cannot escape by shifting his patronage. Under such conditions, the peculiar paradox may arise, as it has in some localities, in which no single businessman will admit Negroes; yet the association made up of the same businessmen favors legislation prohibiting discrimination in their places of business. This kind of paradox can be expected to hold when there is a situation of innovator loss; and when such a paradox arises, legislation ordinarily has a quick and permanent effect.

On the other hand, if customers are very prejudiced, there will probably come to exist certain ways around the law: the formation of private restaurant clubs that exclude Negroes from membership, the use of normative constraints by customers determined to keep a place of business all white, and the flight of whites from restaurants in which Negroes have gained a stable foothold, thus encouraging a further increase in Negro patronage.

This example indicates that even given a particular structure of implementation—the innovator loss situation, for instance—a legal action may or may not have an effect. In this case, implementation depends not only on the owners, who face no loss if all integrate, but also on the customers, whose attitudes may be strong enough to lead to countering action.

There is a surprising number of situations in race relations that involve innovator loss. This arises because much discriminatory behavior occurs not directly through prejudice, but through fear of a prejudiced reaction on the part of another with whom one wants to maintain good relations. For example, real estate salesmen, who show a high amount of discriminatory behavior, do so not because of an intrinsically high amount of prejudice, but because of a belief that they would lose business from other customers if they did not discriminate. Similarly, a girl may refuse to date a Negro boy, not because of prejudice, but because she fears that she may lose dates from other boys and be excluded from social occasions by other boys. The principal difference between these two cases is that the latter is not a situation for legal action, though real estate selling might be; yet in the case of dating, just as in the case of real estate selling, the fear of *others'* reactions prevents the individual from acting freely in accord with his own desires. In certain cases of this sort, the intent of a law may be not to compel, but to release individuals from an informally imposed compulsion. Yet the unfortunate character of such situations is that freedom from social compulsion imposed by others' prejudice often can arise only by an opposing compulsion. Just as the social compulsion does not allow the individual the freedom to act in a nondiscriminatory way, the legal compulsion does not allow the freedom to act in a discriminatory way. If this were not so, such remedies could be applied in many instances where individual freedom from social constraint is desirable, but not if it is to be immediately subject to legal compulsion in the opposite direction.

These examples suggest the general way in which legal power should be seen. Its effectiveness is not independent of other conditions, but depends greatly on them. Yet this has seldom been recognized: the advocates of legal action assume that it is automatically effective; the opponents assume that "every action produces an equal and opposite reaction" and that the system will adjust so as to maintain its equilibrium and prevent any change. The matter is in fact much more complex and is amenable to careful investigation, which can show the conditions in which the assets of legal or legislative power have a high convertibility toward erasing deficits in other areas.

Economic Resources

Theories of social change as applied to underdeveloped countries sometimes take economic resources as a principal independent variable in social change. In this approach, only economic factors are important, and rapid economic growth is contingent solely upon the existence of economic capital.[20] Similar assumptions are behind the idea of creating economic development through the investment of foreign capital. The general thesis is that underdeveloped countries suffer a deficiency of economic resources with which they can create the means for production. The ideas are, of course, considerably more complex than this simple view, but at this superficial level, the evidence is quite mixed. In some countries, like Puerto Rico, Mexico, Israel, and the nations of postwar Europe, there is strong positive evidence of the effect of external capital in reducing social deficits. In others, such as India, Egypt, Ghana, and numerous other countries of Africa, Asia, and South America, the evidence is just as strongly negative. The external capital provided to western Europe through the Marshall Plan after World War II was highly effective in fostering massive social and economic change in western Europe. Economic aid with similar purpose in Asia, Africa, and South America has usually been ineffective in producing change, even when accompanied by technical assistance far more extensive than that provided under the Marshall Plan.

It seems clear even at this superficial level that the efficacy of economic resources from the outside depends very greatly on other factors in the society. There are enough cases of three types to allow a definite conclusion: type 1 cases, in which social and economic change occurred even without external economic resources; type 2 cases, in which change occurred in the presence of external economic resources, but not without it; and type 3 cases, in which change did not occur even in the presence of external economic resources. From these cases, it is clear that for societies as wholes, external economic resources are neither necessary nor sufficient for change that reduces social deficits, but can aid in bringing about change if "other conditions" are present. This, of course, does not carry matters very far, but it does suggest a simple two-factor conception of change at the most superficial level: a given system of personal, social, and economic organization has the capacity to convert a unit of economic resources into x units of output per unit time.[21] If there are c units of economic capital, the output per unit time, which determines economic growth, is xc. In some systems, the addition of external capital, c', will lead to rapid increase in growth because the conversion capacity of the system is great and the capital is low. The countries of western Europe were in this situation and thus made remarkable gains in only four years of Marshall Plan aid. In other systems, it is this conversion capacity itself that is deficient, and the addition of external capital will have little effect on growth. This way of looking at change in a system as a product of economic resources and the system's conversion potential is little more than a formalization of common sense; but it is common sense that has often been missing from foreign aid programs; and it does sensitize one to the importance of both elements and the fact that the absence of growth may be due to the absence of one or the other or both.[22]

The reduction of deficits of groups *within* a society through economic resources involves several different kinds of social policy, with different theoretical assumptions underlying them. Three somewhat different sets of assumptions can be identified by rough description of three policies as those that provide *jobs,* those that provide *money,* and those that provide *goods and services.* In the normal economy of the household, an outside job brings money income which is used to buy goods and services, which in turn sustain and improve that labor. That is, productive labor is an asset converted into money which is converted into goods and services, which provide the sustenance for further productive labor. In a household that is not economically self-sufficient, additional inputs must be made at one of the three points in this cycle: jobs, money, or goods and services. It is the lack of goods and services that constitutes the directly experienced economic deficit for certain households, but different policies have aimed not only at supplying these directly but at providing either jobs or money.

In this chain of resources, it is useful to identify several different hypotheses implied by policies that provide inputs at each point. First, however, there must be a division between policies designed to reconstitute a self-sufficient cycle, the household becoming independent of external inputs, and policies designed to provide permanent continued inputs of resources to the cycle. The latter policies envision a permanently dependent set of households supported by public funds; the former envision a final state in which all households are independent of external support.

Permanent Dependency

In the case of a permanently dependent population, the appropriate policy obviously depends on what resources in this cycle are seen as the ultimate resource satisfying primary needs. Ordinarily, this is seen as goods and services themselves, so that direct provision of the goods and services that constitute the necessities of life automatically overcomes this deficit. Sometimes, however, the primary needs are seen to include the autonomy to consume what one wishes, the autonomy to make one's own consumer choice. For example, Macdonald argues this in expressing the belief that in an affluent society, the standards of support for the poor ought also to be affluent enough to allow expenditures on desired nonessentials.[23] Macdonald's general view appears to be one of accepting permanent dependence of a segment of the population. There are also many policies of governments that provide direct money inputs to the household with no aim of re-creating a self-sufficient economic unit, but with the idea of permanent dependency: aid to dependent children in the United States, family allowances in France, disability payments under Social Security. Proposals like that of a negative income tax constitute similar devices.

Finally, productive work and the self-respect it entails are sometimes seen to be an ultimately desirable resource. In this case, neither provision of preselected goods and services nor provision of a direct money income, but only jobs themselves, would satisfy the primary needs.

Thus, even if one has a conception of a permanently dependent segment of the population as a final state, different beliefs about what constitute primary needs will imply different policies in supplementing the resources of the household economic cycle. Little research has been done on the question of where the input should best occur, for it is difficult to define operationally just what is meant by a primary need, and also research has often confused the goal of maintaining a dependent population with that of re-creating a self-sufficient household. One comparative measure would be the over-all level of satisfaction of persons supported in each of these three ways at equal levels of public cost. Another would be the use of child rearing as a kind of litmus paper test: at the same level of expenditure of public resources, which of the sets of families supported in these three ways provide their children with the greatest personal resources with which to enter the larger world? The crucial difference between the criteria here and those under the "self-liquidating support" assumption to be discussed below is that here the criteria do not include the movement toward self-sufficiency, but only the stable level of satisfaction for a given degree of public support. If, for example, goods and services are directly supplied through subsidies to housing, food, and other commodities, does this give as high a level of satisfaction as if the consumer made his own choices? Or if money is directly provided, will this be spent in a way to best increase over-all satisfaction, or to satisfy an artificially created demand and whims of the moment? Or if jobs are provided, either through a greater demand for labor or through sheltered jobs in public works outside the labor market, will there be anyone from the most economically deficient households able to hold even a sheltered job? It is these kinds of questions, even given the goal of permanent dependence, that must arise in assessing the relative virtues of various types of economic inputs to the production-consumption cycle of the household.

One might dismiss this general perspective as envisioning a set of second-class dependent citizens inappropriate to a conception of the good society, except for several points. One is that in some economies, subsidies to workers are designed to support certain industries by allowing direct wages to be low. Housing and food subsidies to those with low incomes, for example, are rather standard partial substitutes in European countries for wages. Such subsidies, used as wage supplements, are not really support for households but a subsidy to low-wage labor-intensive industries. The cost of the subsidy must then be compared to other forms of income maintenance, for such income supplements may be an alternative to higher levels of unemployment if the noncompetitive industries are forced out of business by higher wages. The question becomes a complicated one for joint study by economists and sociologists: to estimate the total cost to the economy of maintaining noncompetitive enterprises and to balance this against an estimate of the costs of permanent maintenance of noncompetitive workers and their households (and any loss in satisfaction due to a permanent dependent status), in an economy where industry is highly competitive and only highly productive workers are employable. For the basic problem is that although noncompetitive or subsidized industries may constitute a drain on the economy that is removed when they are forced out of business, noncompetitive workers and their households constitute a drain that is not removed unless they can be brought to a level of competitive productivity.

To state the matter differently, a society must accept the idea of a set of partially or totally dependent households either through direct payments or disguised by subsidized noncompetitive industries or public works, unless it is able to train noncompetitive workers to a level of productivity that allows them to be competitive.

Re-creation of Self-Sufficiency: Self-Liquidating Support

Policies designed to reconstitute a self-sufficient household by supplying inputs that will be self-liquidating involve research questions of considerably more interest and complexity. To provide jobs that supply money, or money that will buy goods and services, or goods and services that will sustain and improve labor—each implies assumptions about a point of deficiency in the economic cycle of the household. I shall suggest assumptions implicit in each policy and then turn to research results bearing upon each set of assumptions.

The economic cycle of the household can be conveniently described in terms of four variables: two on the productive side and two on the consumption side. On the productive side, one variable can be described as a general level of productive potential, and the second as opportunity for its employment. These will be labeled x and c for convenience. On the consumption side is, first, the amount of money, and second, consumer skill in purchasing the goods and services that will augment productive potential. The money and consumer wisdom will be labeled m and w for convenience. Then the normal cycle is one in which the product of x and c generate m; and the product of m and w augments x. If the processes are operating at a level too low for household maintenance, the family is not self-sufficient. In an urban money economy, there is a discontinuity in the relation that does not exist in a rural subsistence economy: if the product of potential and opportunity, xc, is above a given point, the worker holds a job; if below this threshold, he does not. The hypotheses discussed below involve assumptions about deficits in particular ones of these variables.

Increasing Job Opportunity through Increasing the Demand for Labor

This policy assumes in the set of relations above that job opportunity c is the one variable whose low level prevents functioning of the cycle. If this opportunity is increased, all the other variables are sufficiently high to create a self-sustaining household (and, by increasing the level of economic demand, to maintain high levels of c). In this view, the only deficit is a deficit of the economic system, which determines the level of c.

Evidence on this assumption in the recent United States context is discussed in detail by Killingsworth.[24] In brief, the results of economic expansion since 1963 (first through a tax cut designed to stimulate demand and increase opportunity, c, and then through high demand created by the Viet Nam War) show that although Negro unemployment decreased, it remained in the same ratio to white unemployment— twice as high—and Negro teenage unemployment remained in its same relative position—more than six times over-all white unemployment. Unemployment in Negro ghettos appears not to have decreased at all, but perhaps to have increased. Thus while increasing c appears to have some effect in reconstituting the cycle of economic self-sufficiency (using continued employment as a rough indicator of economic self-sufficiency), its effect appears to be least for groups that are least self-sufficient; in this case, ghetto Negroes. Given the continued problems of economic deficits of Negroes at high levels of over-all economic activity in the United States, it is clear that for many Negroes, the economic cycle of the household is defective at other points that are not affected by increasing job opportunity.

There is one body of theory and research that regards the level of job opportunity as a determinant of resources quite outside this economic cycle, in particular, of stable personal characteristics. This is the thesis that regards delinquency and crime as principally a product of blocked opportunity (Cloward and Ohlin [25]). Evidence for and against this thesis occurs in the delinquency literature; it cannot be regarded as a well-confirmed thesis.

A corollary to this thesis, that the experience of holding a job will increase personal resources, is a relation of similar plausibility but unknown importance. The thesis at its strongest would state that experience in full-time occupations is the most important element in increasing productive potential.

Examination of work histories, even if these histories contain only minimal information (such as Social Security records), could be valuable in testing this thesis. Such examination would show how the probability of becoming unemployed is affected by the length of continuous employment, controlling for income, or by age of entry into full-time employment, controlling for income. Obviously, if this effect is a great one, policies designed to increase opportunity, c, would have special benefit, for they act to increase x as well, and thus allow self-sustenance even if the level of opportunity reduces.

Increasing Job Opportunity through Protected Enterprises

To increase job opportunity, c, through economically protected enterprises (public works or subsidized industry) will obviously maintain the household cycle, so long as the subsidy is maintained, for those who can hold the sheltered job. But if it is to be used to reconstitute economic self-sufficiency, this implies the stronger hypotheses discussed above: that occupational experience increases personal resources enough so that the subsidy is self-liquidating; or conversely, that unemployment destroys personal resources. As indicated above, research on these questions would have quite important policy implications.

Direct Inputs of Money to the Family

As indicated earlier, many policies for money supplements to the
family are designed as permanent supplements. Even so, if there are
effects of these supplements on other resources which make the household more self-sufficient, these supplements could be temporary and
self-liquidating. The literature indicates that such ideas are certainly
held by some persons. Fleisher, examining statistical correlations,
shows a relation between income and family resources and interprets
these as effects of income: "A $500 increase in family income will cause
a decline in the number of separated or divorced women over 14 by
about 2.7 per 1000." [26] Such statements certainly overinterpret the
data; but the statistical relationships exist, and research is necessary to
determine the directions of cause and effect.

Some persons go even further than Fleisher. For example, Macdonald and others argue that a very high level of income support, far
above the poverty line, would establish the levels of work motivation
and consumer wisdom (that is, affecting both x and w) necessary for
economic self-sufficiency. [27] This is probably nonsense; but it is very
likely possible to test it through careful observation of selected populations who have experienced large windfalls (such as American Indians
made wealthy by natural resources on their reservations). There does
appear to be some evidence against the converse of the thesis: that
income loss will destroy motivation and the personal resources necessary for self-sufficiency. For example, the study of Jackson and Marsden, cited earlier, of eighty-eight working-class children who went into
the sixth form of grammar school in England, the last secondary step
toward higher education, found that few of them were truly working-
class. Many were from middle-class families who for a generation
had suffered reverses and fallen into working-class occupations and income. The economic reverse suffered by these families had left them
still far better equipped to guide their children into academic streams
of education than were the truly working-class families. [28] From a similar perspective Haggstrom shows that families with self-sufficient
household economies exist at nearly all levels of income and that those
with economic dependency are also found over a wide range of income. [29] He suggests that the lack of money income can thus hardly be
used as an explanation for economic dependency. Certainly it is the
case that variations in the degree of wisdom in consumption by different households can affect the product mw and thus the productive potential just as much as can variations in money income.

The possible effects of money inputs to the family are suggested by controversies over the specific way the input is to be made. For example, Moynihan argues that the payment to mothers of aid for dependent children destroys family cohesion because it is conditional on the absence of a male potential wage earner in the household. He suggests that it further weakens the already weak position of the male in the matriarchal family of the Negro.[30] Schorr examines more generally the possible differential effects of different types of money inputs into the household.[31] Obviously, it becomes important to learn these effects if the money input is to have effects beyond that of a permanent income supplement.[32] The question of whether money input will reduce the economic dependency deficit better than job opportunity or goods and services can be answered only if these details of its effects are known.

Inputs of Goods and Services to the Family

Goods and services as inputs to overcome deficits of the household economy may cover a wide range. Most apparent are subsidies to housing and food, both of which are more widespread in Europe than in the United States. But also included in this are other services which attempt directly to affect the productivity of the household: education, health services, job training programs, child care centers, and a variety of activities of community service agencies.

As indicated above, some inputs of goods and services to the household are designed only to serve as permanent external supply of resources, and their value depends on their efficiency in satisfying primary needs. But their merit as resources that help overcome other deficits to produce a self-sufficient household is the point in question here. For this, the evidence differs according to the kind of good or service provided. There appears to be a considerable amount of evidence now that housing is a resource that has little effect in overcoming other deficits, although plausible arguments for its effects have been given by many authors.[33] Optimistic expectations that "slum clearance" and public housing would reduce crime, delinquency, and other deficits have been completely unfulfilled. Even the effect on health cannot be detected. Wilner, in a carefully controlled study in Baltimore, finds little if any effect of improved housing on health.[34] Glazer summarizes the evidence of the lack of effect of this resource on other social deficits.[35]

Health services would appear to constitute, prima facie, a resource that overcomes other deficits, since persons in ill-health frequently cannot be self-sufficient. For example, Brown examines occupational histories of persons with mental illness and finds a decline in occupational status following first admission to a mental hospital.[36] Fuchs, citing this and other evidence, suggests that the effects of health on productivity and self-sufficiency, over an individual's occupational career, is an important one.[37]

Given this evidence that health resources are important in overcoming or preventing economic deficits, one can go further and ask whether ill-health and disease constitute an important deficit for Negroes, and for nonself-sufficient households in particular. There seems to be little evidence that this is so, except in extreme situations (for example, isolated areas in the rural South). Kadushin reviews a number of studies which show little or no greater likelihood of becoming or staying ill among those at low economic levels than among those at high levels.[38] Rein, in a study of British medical services, shows that these services are utilized as fully by those at very low economic levels as by those at higher levels.[39]

Thus, despite the fact that health services, in contrast to housing, are a resource that does overcome or prevent economic deficits, there does not appear to be a widespread deficiency in these services which, if rectified, would have a strong indirect effect on economic resources.

There is one broad class of services designed specifically to increase the productive potential of the individual or household. These are disparate types of services including public education as a way of making the young self-sufficient and productive, child day care centers that allow mothers to hold a job, and job training programs for youth or for unemployed. Little can be said about the efficiency of such services in general for creation of resources; I shall mention only evidence concerning education. A massive United States Office of Education survey shows that in the urban North, Negroes at the end of high school are in about the same relative position with regard to whites as at the start of the first grade in verbal and mathematical skills: about 85 per cent of the Negroes are below the average achievement of whites; about 15 per cent of Negroes (and 50 per cent of whites) are above this average. Thus Negroes end school with the same relative deficits that their family and neighborhood conditions have imposed upon them by age 6. In the rural South, the relative deficit increases from 1 to 1½ standard deviations; only about 7 per cent of Negroes are above the white average.[40]

These statistics make it clear that the system of public education, regarded as a resource that can overcome deficits which arise in the family and community, does not do so for Negro children on the whole, but leaves them with either the same or a greater relative deficit in scholastic achievement than the one with which they began. The situation is the opposite to that of health services. Health services are effective in overcoming illness and appear to reduce economic deficits deriving from ill-health; but illness is found little or no more often among low economic groups than high. Educational services appear to be relatively ineffective in overcoming scholastic deficits, and these deficits, relative to middle-class whites, are quite great for lower-class Negroes.

Altogether, the question of convertibility of economic resources to other resources for deprived groups within a society is a varied and complex one, with no single answer. In the cycle of economic production and consumption of the home, there appear to be three points at which economic resources can be added and several ways they can be added at each of these points. Their convertibility depends on where and how they are added, as well as on existing resources of the nonself-sufficient households (for example, their productive potential, their wisdom in consumption, the resources of the family in child socialization). The answers to these questions are precisely those necessary for designing welfare policies that will most efficiently create resources that make the individual and family self-sustaining. Yet the evidence, as well as analogous data from developing countries, suggests that creation of self-sufficiency through economic inputs may have quite limited possibilities in the absence of other changes.

Political Resources

The convertibility of political assets to assets of other kinds depends greatly on the kind of political asset held. The individual vote in an election is different from the organization of votes to support or defeat a candidate, which is still different from organized collective action such as used in the civil rights movement. Perhaps it is most useful to divide the political assets held by Negroes into two classes: (1) assets that are used in the formal political processes: the vote in elections and Negro representatives in legislatures and in other political office; and (2) assets that are used outside the electoral process, usually in direct action which presses demands for change. It is the latter which have been most effectively used by Negroes since 1960. Both, however, are important resources, and both have increased greatly in recent years. I shall examine them separately, labeling the first "electoral politics" and the second "action politics." In the latter I shall include not only direct action outside legal channels but also actions which use the courts as a mechanism for effecting change. Both the extralegal direct action and the legal procedures in the courts require the organization and initiation of action, and in this both stand in contrast to the act of voting in an election, which is an individual response of an institutionalized nature.

In neither the case of electoral political resources nor that of action political resources will I examine the convertibility of legislative or legal action into resources of other kinds; that question has been discussed in the preceding section. I shall instead examine the prior step: the convertibility of political resources (political power of either of these two types) into government action.

Electoral Resources

The convertibility of the vote into government actions is, of course, not a simple matter, because the government action depends on the net result of many votes, and Negroes are in a small minority in the United States. Yet a number of important points can be stated, because that vote has more or less power in different situations.

Given a simple majority decision rule in collective choices, or, for that matter, any decision rule that requires between about 25 and 75 per cent of the vote cast in order to take action, the effective electoral power of a minority group in a democracy depends on its geographic distribution. This is less so in a system of proportional representation in the election of legislatures, for in a system of pure proportional representation, the total country is in effect one large constituency. But proportional representation does not exist in most elections in the United States, so that geographical distribution is very important in a minority's power. The principal point is that power increases with concentration, for only with concentration will the minority group be in a majority in certain constituencies and able to control the nomination and election of legislators.

In the move from the South to the urban North, Negroes have moved toward greater geographical concentration. Even though Negroes have constituted majorities in some counties and even in some congressional districts in the South, they have never been so highly concentrated that whites, aided by disenfranchising techniques, could not outvote them. In the central cities of the North, however, Negro concentration has reached in some areas the point of absolute control of congressional districts. In many cities it has reached the point of absolute control of city councilmanic districts, and in some of the largest cities, it will soon reach a majority of the total city electorate.

The functioning of the United States Congress allows minority group representation, once it reaches the point of electing a representative, a rather high degree of power. A case in point is the power of Adam Clayton Powell, Jr., both before and after his unseating in Congress, and his subsequent re-election by his constituency. A parliamentary system with strict party discipline, as in Britain, greatly reduces such minority and constituency power.

The general point then is that the convertibility of a minority group's votes into political power that can affect legislation depends, in the American political system, greatly on geographical concentration. This can be counted an important defect of a democratic system, for even apart from the techniques used to disenfranchise Negroes in the South, it has prevented Negro demands from being effectively represented in governmental decision-making bodies. However, once reaching legislative bodies, a minority group's interest does have important power in the United States governmental system. These two points together make especially important, in the estimation of future Negro political power through the vote, the projection of demographic and ecological trends.

Resources for Action Politics

One of the major changes from the 1950's to the 1960's in the set of assets and deficits held by Negroes is the development of extensive devices for exerting demands on government outside the electoral channels of politics. These have taken numerous forms, ranging from court cases challenging the legality of school districting patterns to actions which violate the law. They include nonviolent action and violent action, demonstrations aimed at changing laws regarded as inequitable, and demonstrations aimed at exerting a legally protected right.

All these actions have in common the element of collective organization, and many include as well mobilization of the populace. One of their effects may be to create personal resources in the way described earlier, but the explicit aim of most of them is to exert political pressure. The community resources of collective solidarity and trust that were discussed earlier, and described as largely missing in Negro communities, have come to exist in the "Negro movement" beyond the community level. Thus the enormous multiplication of resources that such collective cohesion provides has come to exist through this movement.

I shall not attempt to be comprehensive in discussion of these forms of political action, but shall discuss only two attributes: first, the use of nonviolence as a technique, and second, the development of the activities described as "black power."

The principle of nonviolence has been widely used in the Negro movement. When can it be a powerful tool, and under which conditions is it most powerful in gaining one's ends?

Consider a social conflict in which the lines of cleavage are drawn, with each person on one of the two sides. An aggressive action in the conflict will have two kinds of effect on the defender. The first kind of effect is to destroy, disrupt, and otherwise make ineffective the defender. The second kind of effect is to unify and intensify the defender's opposition to the aggressor, ordinarily leading to an aggressive response.

Now let us consider an asymmetric conflict situation, with one side the administrative establishment, and the other a conflict group. If the conflict group carries out an aggressive act of civil disobedience, the administration and behind them the united community will ordinarily retaliate; the conflict group will in turn be unified by the aggressive response and respond aggressively in turn; and the battle will be on. However, if the initial act of civil disobedience is not an aggressive one, and if the administration's response is not responded to in turn by aggression, but merely by refusal to obey, the second effect of an aggressive action on the administration and general community does not occur. That is, by failing to act aggressively, the conflict group does not unify and intensify the actions of its opponent, the administration. *The principal virtue of nonviolence as a strategy is that it does not serve the opponent by unifying his force and intensifying his anger, as does an aggressive or violent act.*

Given this, what does it imply about the conditions under which nonviolence will be a good strategy and the conditions that make it a bad one? The principal implication is that for a monolithic, undivided, fully unified opposition, nonviolence would be a totally ineffective strategy. For an opposition (ordinarily an administrative establishment) which was divided, for a conflict situation in which many persons were uncommitted, and in a situation where the opposition held humanitarian goals, nonviolence should be maximally effective. Nonviolence depends wholly on separation of the partially committed from the totally committed and on the further pressure of the partially committed on the totally committed to stop the conflict.

Thus, several propositions can be derived from this implication. First, the less internally mobilized the opposition, the more effective will nonviolence be and the quicker it will have an effect. Second, the more divergence in strength of commitment between the opposition actors and their potential supporters, the more effective will nonviolence be. Third, the larger the uncommitted public, and the more influence it can have on the opposition, the more effective will nonviolence be.

A quite different strategy of action from the strategy of nonviolent resistance is one which has recently developed under the label of black power. The term has widely varying definitions, ranging from those that emphasize violence to those that emphasize retail store ownership by Negroes. Its essential difference from other aspects of Negro political action, however, is its concentration on Negro action in strengthening resources of Negroes. It thus combines the two apparently incongruous aims that have always characterized the Black Muslims: great attention to personal virtues of honesty, effort, achievement; and overcoming the power of whites. It is at one and the same time a self-improvement association and a revolutionary one.

In many respects, this direction of the movement can hardly be called political, since it is largely directed to producing personal and social changes within the Negro community, to self-improvement and self-help. It is political only in the use of these resources for collectively gaining political ends, the extreme in revolutionary directions. Some of its advocates are explicitly revolutionary, taking their ideology and strategy from the revolutionary theorists discussed earlier and from very recent writings emerging from the colonial revolutions (like Fanon[41]). The general strategy can best be described as the use of the power of collective identity both to create internal changes in personal resources of Negroes and to overcome the external enemy. As such, it constitutes the concrete realization in the United States of the revolutionary theory of social change discussed earlier.

PART III—ARENAS OF ACTION

Although each of the hypotheses or theories of social change discussed in Part II claims a kind of exclusivity as the only or the principal mechanism of change, it appears quite clear that there are a number of different and important mechanisms. Consequently, the task of the theorist at this point is not to select which of the theories is correct, but rather to set up some kind of framework within which any of the processes discussed above can operate. At the extreme, this means nothing more nor less than setting up a theory of the social system as a whole. However, it is obviously not possible to accomplish this in one great leap, and the integration to be attempted here will be somewhat more modest.

The integration will take two forms: first, an attempt to discern a few principles or themes that differentiate certain theories from others, as a way of summarizing what some of the major differences are; and second, ignoring the temptation to select among these principles a set which shows "the" way to change, an attempt to set up a framework for describing more systematically the conversion of resources of all the types discussed above.

One major distinction among theories is the degree to which they interpret social change as resulting from actions of the group in question, either as individuals or as a collectivity, or from the conditions within which members of that group must act. These environmental conditions include all kinds, ranging from economic resources to freedom of action. In the first case, change is seen as originating from within the group in question; in the second, from outside. This distinction is most fully evident in contrasting the theories described under "personal resources" in Part II with those described under "legal and legislative resources" and "economic resources." Second, within the first of these two classes of theories are those which see the primary actors in the situation as individuals, acting to pursue individual interests, and those which see the primary actors as collectivities, either the community or the political action group.

This suggests, then, that these theories see three primary sources of change: the individual member of the group in question, collective actors made up of members of the group in question, and the environmental conditions within which the action takes place. In Table 6–1, these will be labeled I, C, and E, respectively.

A second major distinction between different theories of change is the different arenas of action within which the processes of change are seen to occur. These arenas of action, such as occupation, or family, or school, or political collectivities, are evident in the discussion of Part II.

In Table 6–1 are listed the various arenas of action discussed in Part II, and under these the theories and hypotheses proposed concerning each, indicating the resources that constitute the primary sources of change and the resources that are, by hypothesis, generated in the change. These resources generated by the process are indicated by the same three symbols, I, C, and E, as for the sources of change. Under each of these are a wide range of resources: under I are the whole set of personal resources discussed in Parts I and II; under C are cohesion, organization, trust, at a variety of different levels of collectivity; under E are legal actions, legislative actions, economic resources, and freedom of action.

This table provides a convenient summary of the theories and hypotheses discussed in Part II. The usual practice in sociological theory is to argue or present evidence in favor of one of these, failing to recognize that the social system functions through most or all of these processes, and under different circumstances (that is, different distributions of initial resources) different ones of these processes can assume greater importance. It is likely that the tendency among sociologists to focus on one or the other of these is either because one appears important in the particular situation at hand or else because of a confusion between theory and action in social change. Action involves choosing among these processes in a particular situation, depending on the resources at hand and the desired goals, thus involving a narrowing of focus.[42] But the theory of change should describe the processes independently of any resources that characterize a concrete situation.

TABLE 6-1 *Summary of Theories of Change*

Arenas of Action	Sources of Change	Resultant Changes	Description of Theory or Policy
Occupation	I,	E	Achievement–orientation
Occupation	E	E	Job opportunity
Family	I, C	I	Socialization
Family	E	I, C	Family welfare activities
School	E	I	School improvement
Local community	I, C	I, E	Community action
Elections	I, E	E	Liberal political theory
Legislature	C	E	Liberal political theory (legislative political action)
Courts	C	E	Court rulings
Collective political action	I, C	E	Populist political theory (civil rights movement)
Collective political action	I, C	I, C, E	Revolutionary theory (black power movement)

Thus the task becomes one of integrating these various conversion processes into a systematic descriptive framework. Two questions naturally arise: the strategic question of how far one should go in the process of integrating these ideas, and the intellectual question of what direction one should take.

In examining the first of these questions, the two extremes are provided by the discussion as presented in Part II, left in the form of Table 6-1, and at the other extreme, a mathematical model together with explicit operations for the measurement of variables entering into it. Toward this latter extreme are certain models of resource-transformation in economics, usually described as activity analysis or input-output analysis. Because of the numerous obstacles which would require much more than a short chapter to remove, I shall not go nearly so far as these models go.

In examining the list of resources and the processes of conversion in Parts I and II, several points become evident which can give some insights about the direction that an integration of ideas can best follow. First of all, it seems clear that one can usefully conceive of a system of resources which act, through certain processes, to increase or decrease other resources. Second, it appears useful to think of resources acting in a reasonably limited set of arenas of action, or contexts of action, with particular actors involved. In economic analysis, the analogue to these arenas of action is the particular production process, or activity, as it is sometimes called—an activity that is conceptually distinct both from the set of resources that serve as inputs and from the set of resources that are outputs.[43]

These arenas of action may vary from highly institutionalized ones, such as the school, to highly fluid and unstructured ones, such as political protest. But in each arena, it appears reasonable to conceive of several *kinds* of resources that affect the process. There are resources held by the *actors* in this arena and resources that characterize the *context* within which the action takes place. For example, in discussing the effectiveness of legal actions designed to bring about greater freedom of action for Negroes, such as public accommodation laws, it was pointed out that the increase in actual freedom of action depended on the conjunction of two input resources: the characteristics of the laws themselves and the presence of active individuals or organizations prepared to make use of it. Neither of these need be considered the primary resource in this situation; it seems rather that the result is a joint product of these two resources.

Interaction between these two kinds of resources can be seen by example. One of these is school desegregation. The school system plans for desegregation approved by the United States Office of Education in 1965 were of two types. One was a plan that substituted single districts for dual ones, often in stages to be completed over several years. The second was a "free-choice" plan, in which any student could attend any of two or more schools. The second plan worked differentially well in different areas. In the few areas where it produced substantial integration, the reason appeared to be the organized efforts of Negro parents, aided by civil rights groups, to send their children to previously all-white schools, in spite of physical and sometimes administrative obstacles. Thus, overcoming the deficit of racial isolation in these cases required two assets: first, the political asset at the national level, which led to the requirement for integration imposed by the guidelines, and second, the organized initiative of Negroes in the local community. In communities where the latter asset was not present, the former asset was not effective.

A second and similar example occurred several years ago in the opening of the building craft unions in New York to widespread admission of Negroes for apprenticeship. Traditionally, apprenticeships had been held rather closely and distributed first to relatives of current union members, thus making it difficult for new ethnic groups to enter one of these craft unions. The political assets of Negroes both locally and nationally, together with the ideological asset found in more liberal union leaders, created enough pressure on the local unions to provide an allocation of a large proportion of apprenticeships for Negro applicants. But there were almost no Negro applicants, with the result that the existing economic deficit was not reduced. The specific deficits were the absence of community and family resources that would have generated the organized efforts to produce applicants and the absence of personal resources of knowledge and motivation that would have led to individual response.

However, this conception of two sets of interacting resources, those characterizing the actors and those characterizing the situation, meets with difficulty, as evidenced by the statement above that individuals *or* organizations must be prepared to act in the situation. More generally, the effect of social organization in augmenting individual resources has been evident throughout Part II. How then, can it be best introduced into description of the social processes of interest? There appear to be two alternative ways of conceptualizing the role of organizations or collectivities which act as augmenters of individual resources: as actors themselves, that is, as one of the primary components of a social process operating in a given arena of action, with resources consisting of the personal resources of individuals within them and the cohesion, trust, or other attribute of the collective body itself. Or alternatively, the individuals themselves may be seen as the primary actors, with the resources of the collectivity acting as multipliers of the personal resources of these individual actors.

A second complication in this schema is that a given arena of action may well involve two or even more sets of actors, with differing resources and with conflicting or reinforcing goals. The outcome of a protest demonstration depends not only on the organization and personal resources of the demonstrators but also on the characteristics of the police and the white community or organization who are actual or potential actors in this arena. In some situations, the characteristics of actors other than Negroes in the situation can be taken as constant; but this assumption should be clearly recognized.

It is evident that if we would attempt to go very far toward formalization of the system at the present, a whole variety of obstacles arise, even apart from problems of measurement, which we have not discussed. What is useful in this context is not to open up such a Pandora's box, but rather to attempt to create some kind of order from the chaos of theoretical ideas described in Part II. It will not help in creating this order to attempt to go too far in devising a single integrated system of ideas.

As a start toward the appropriate integration, I shall lay out three kinds of relationships in tables. The first of these, Table 6–2, is an indication of what resources appear to interact in affecting the level of operation of activities. Such interaction between two variables means that an increase in either of the variables *intensifies* the effect of the other: for example, the strength of family cohesion intensifies the effect of parental educational background on children's learning. In effect, the result depends on a new variable, which is the product of the two initial resources. As indicated above, these will consist principally of two kinds of interactions: interactions between resources of the actors in a given arena of action and the opportunity or constraints offered by the action context; and interactions which consist of the intensifying or multiplicative effect of social cohesion or organization in its various forms, and personal resources.

TABLE 6–2   *Interactions between Resources*

RESOURCES	1	2	3	4	5	6	7	8	9	10	11	12
1 Personal resources		X	X	X	X	X		X	X		X	
2 Family cohesion			X		X	X		X				
3 Community cohesion				X		X		X	X		X	
4 Political movement organization										X	X	
5 Jobs								X				
6 Money												
7 Goods												
8 Services												
9 Freedom of action												
10 Demographic concentration												
11 Legal rules, laws												X
12 Political representation												

The next table (Table 6–3) shows the resources that are the inputs for, or affect the level of operation of, each arena of action. Thus this table relates the level of operation of each arena of action to the resources which sustain that level. The final table (Table 6–4) shows the resources that are the outputs of or are produced by each arena of action. Thus the general conceptual scheme is that the resources held by actors, intensified by resources of social organization and by the opportunities which characterize the action context, determine the level of functioning in each arena of action. Each of the arenas of action then produces as outputs resources of different kinds. In all the tables, some of the resources discussed in Parts I and II are missing, such as the rate of expansion of the economy and the involvement of resourceful whites. A second omission in the tables is any indication of negative "side effects" or reduction of resources of one type through the operation of a given process. For example, the actions of black power organizations have as one consequence the reduction of personal and financial support from whites, and perhaps a reduction in freedom of action as well. Such reduction of resources or creation of liabilities is an omission from the tables that should be recognized in their use.

In Table 6–2, the interactions are generally of two different kinds: interaction between actors' resources and the opportunities provided by the situation of action; and intensification by the level of social cohesion. The resources are specified in rather gross categories, so that within each category, the specific interactions depend on the action context. For example, an interaction is indicated between "personal resources" and "jobs," which is in fact an interaction between occupational productivity and job opportunity. But since the table is intended principally as a check list for reference purposes, fine detail is omitted.

In Table 6–2, an X in a cell indicates that resources of the two types specified by the row and column appear to interact with the result of a joint effect on the level of operation of the relevant arena of action.

Table 6–3 shows the resource inputs to each arena of action. These resources ordinarily have their effect jointly with other resources, as Table 6–2 indicates; that should be taken as given in reading Table 6–3. It is also important to remember that these are in some cases heterogeneous classes of resources. For example, "services" include health services, school and child care programs, and on-the-job training programs, each of which occurs in a different arena of action. Equally, some arenas of action are heterogeneous in the variety of processes or activities that occur within them. In one case, the "family," two processes are separated out; but in the family, as in other arenas of action, there are processes that are not listed separately. As in Table 6–2,

TABLE 6–3 *Input Resources to Arenas of Action*

ARENAS OF ACTION

Input Resource	Occu-pation	Family Social-ization	Consump-tion	School	Local Commu-nity	Elec-tions	Legis-lature	Courts	Civil Rights Organ-ization	Black Power Organ-ization
Personal resources	X	X	X	X	X	X			X	X
Family cohesion		X	X	X						
Community cohesion		X			X				X	
Political movement organization								X	X	X
Jobs	X									
Money			X							
Goods			X							
Services	X	X	X	X						
Freedom of action	X			X	X	X			X	X
Demographic concentration					X	X				
Legal rules, laws					X	X		X	X	X
Political representation							X			

TABLE 6-4   Output Resources from Arenas of Action

OUTPUT RESOURCES

Arenas of Action	Personal Resources	Family Cohesion	Community Cohesion	Political Movement Organization	Jobs	Money	Goods	Services	Freedom of Action	Demographic Concentration	Legal Rules, Laws	Political Representation
Occupation	X	X				X						
Family socialization	X	X										
Family consumption							X	X				
School	X											
Local community		X	X	X		X	X	X				
Elections												X
Legislature					X	X	X	X		X	X	
Courts									X	X	X	
Political action (civil rights)	X		X	X	X			X	X			
Political action (power)	X		X	X	X			X				

an X in a cell of Table 6–3 indicates that a given resource serves as an input to the process or activity which occurs in a given arena of action.

In Table 6–4, the outputs of activities in each arena of action are listed. The table relates arenas of action to the same resources as in Table 6–3, but these resources are those either demonstrated or hypothesized to result from the given process. In some cases where an X is listed in the cell, the output is well demonstrated to exist; in other cases, it is merely claimed or hypothesized, but not proved. No attempt is made to distinguish claims from demonstrated fact or strong effects from weak ones.

These tables constitute the limits of the integration of ideas from Part II. If the framework is to be useful in any quantitative way for the study of social change, it will be necessary to specify much more precisely the form of the conversion processes and in conjunction with this to define operationally the measures of resources and the conversion coefficients in each process. It would be fortunate if the precise form of the model could be taken over from input-output analysis in economics, but this does not appear possible because of various rigidities in input-output analysis.

PART IV—RESEARCH IMPLICATIONS

If a theory of social change is to justify its existence, it must contain within it some point or points at which knowledge can affect action, which in turn affects the course of social change. One suspects this is implicit even in theories that posit deterministic forces of change. But if the theory is to be complete, or even if it is to be useful, these points in which knowledge can affect the course of change should be incorporated within the theory and not left outside. Another way of putting this is to say that a theory of directed social change, to be complete, must show how knowledge itself is incorporated into the processes of change. The agents who use the knowledge provided by the theory are themselves part of the system described by the theory. Thus the theory should show how such knowledge affects these actors' actions and thus the course of change. In the present framework of theory, this implies that knowledge, in the hands of particular actors, is itself an input resource for certain processes.

Economists concerned with directed economic change ordinarily leave this element outside their theories, for they implicitly assume that there is someone with power to manipulate the independent variables of their theories. Since theories of social change are concerned with the whole social system, including the structure of power in the society, sociologists cannot as justifiably leave outside their theory a specification of how the knowledge it provides enters the system and initiates a chain of action, unless they are merely programs for action written implicitly for the use of someone in a given position of power or aspiration to power in society.

Consider, for example, one type of theory which at first appears least deterministic because it focuses on individual personal resources as the locus of change: the theory that social change is brought about by a high achievement orientation, which in turn is created by certain socialization processes. If the theory is to do more than describe an inexorable fate or be designed for consumption by a person in a particular position of power as a how-to book for his use, it must include as well propositions about how such information can enter and affect the system, ultimately leading to an increase in achievement motivation.

The first point is to recognize that the research product must itself be located as an element in the system of resources, for in this perspective, the research results themselves can constitute assets that, in combination with other assets, help bring about change. This is often implicit in applied research programs; but I suggest it is better made explicit, so that the research programs can then be evaluated in terms of the kind and amount of assets they can be expected to produce.

I shall not go beyond the first step in locating the research product, or knowledge generally, in the system of action, for to do so would require taking the theory of the system considerably beyond its present point. I shall simply indicate the points at which the research product, considered as a resource, can enter into the system and affect the course of change.

The first step in embedding the potential research products in the system of resources is to note that the principal effect of this asset is in modifying the distribution of other resources. That is, the whole aim of this framework of research is to show the connection between inputs to the system and resulting changes. Thus the implicit use for which it is created (besides showing the expected future state of the system under existing resource allocation) is to show how different resource allocations might be expected to lead to different profiles of assets. Thus it is the actions of those actors who have control over various resources that the research product should affect. These actors include many different persons, Negro and white, in all branches of government and in organizations of the Negro movement, as well as private organizations of other types, who control any resources that can be allocated in the various arenas of action described in Part III.

Given this general view of where the research product is itself located in the system of resources, it is necessary to examine more closely just what research activities will give useful resources that can affect the course of change. One point emerges immediately, and that is the over-all perspective that has been presented: the rather simple idea of viewing the state of Negroes in American society through a set of accounts that lists levels of resources (together with relative positions of Negroes on those resources that are desired in themselves). This perspective has served to provide a framework within which processes of social change can be viewed. If the perspective is developed with care and imagination, it could have long-range value as a theoretical framework for social change of the types here examined. But its principal present virtue is as the basis for a descriptive set of accounts that can be used for recording changes in the state of Negroes in America and as guides for action.

The first necessary research activity, then, is a wholly descriptive one: to set up a system of accounts, based on careful and frequent observations, showing the deficits of Negroes in America, as measures of the current conditions characterizing Negroes, relative to other Americans, and the resources that can effect change.

In setting up such a system of accounts, the headings used in this chapter are gross ones; the actual accounts would consist of much more detailed categories. For example, under "personal resources" would come occupational productivity, organizational skills, achievement motivation, educational achievement, and other areas. In addition, regional variations, rural-urban variations, and measures of the spread of the distribution as well as the average are necessary. The degree and type of subgroup disaggregation required remains an open question.

The second necessary research activity is measurement of the conversion factors or transformation coefficients through which certain resources are created from others. This is research of the type that sociologists most often engage in to learn the effects of certain variables on others. Yet there is required much more sophistication in conceptualization, in research design, and in measurement if the results of the research are to be quantitatively useful in providing measures of the conversion of resources.

A third kind of research activity, which goes beyond the measurement of existing conversion factors, is the measurement of effects of new processes; that is, the existing institutional structure constitutes a kind of current technology within which the system operates in each arena of action. Yet if certain conversion processes are very inefficient (for example, if current schools appear to be relatively ineffective in producing achievement in lower-class children), experiments with new techniques may be tried in a given arena. The estimate of conversion factors for these new institutional arrangements or techniques is necessary to show their potential effect on the entire set of assets and deficits.

A final research activity is one implied by all that has been already stated: the use of the research results above in a model that will allow forward projection of the system of resources under a variety of assumptions about changes in input resources or setting up new institutional arrangements. Such projections allow the use of these research results in social policy by showing the expected consequences of various alternative policies.

Altogether, the research activities implied by the framework laid down in Parts I, II, and III can probably be seen best by thinking of two kinds of entities: the level of resources of various types existing in the system at any point in time, and the mechanisms through which resources are converted into new resources and the arenas of action within which these mechanisms function. The first research activity is simply a periodic measurement of the state of the resources in the system. The second type of research is measurement of the mechanisms of resource conversion. The third type of research is measurement of the effects of changes in a given arena of action—changes in the institutional arrangements or techniques which modify the mechanism of conversion. The fourth activity is the use of all this information in giving alternative projections of the system under different resources allocations and in some arenas of action with new institutional arrangements. I shall not describe in detail each of these research activities, for each constitutes in itself a research program of some complexity. However, I shall indicate in the following sections a few salient points concerning each of these areas.

A System of Accounts over Time

The set of resources described in Parts I, II, and III play two roles in the system. Certain of them are the measures of deficits held by Negroes in American society. They are the final criteria in terms of which goals or desired changes are stated. At the same time, most or all of the resources are inputs to the social processes through which changes take place.

In their role as current deficits, the resources require a *relative* measurement. The measure of deficit is the relative position of Negroes compared to non-Negroes or of certain subgroups of Negroes compared to other Negroes and non-Negroes. It is this relative position which is a measure of their effective power over their own lives and over actions of the community and nation.

However, considered as resources that can generate other resources, a measure of the absolute level of the resources is necessary. In this measurement, a fully satisfactory operational definition of the resource is not possible until the form of the conversion process is known. A simple analogy from industrial conversion will indicate how this is so: in the conversion of iron ore into iron, the weight of the iron ore is not a sufficient measure of the resource; necessary also is the proportion by weight of iron in the ore. An example in social conversion processes in schools is similar: as a measure of school resources, it is not sufficient only to know the resources provided by the board of education; the social background and motivations of other students in the school constitute a resource that enters into the conversion process for any given student.

It is necessary, then, to carry out measurement of resources in intimate communication with analysis of the processes themselves, for the processes give appropriate definitions to, or descriptions of, the resources that affect their results. This is not to say that measurement of the resources should wait upon analysis of the relevant processes or be carried out in conjunction with them. The development of this research tool is a bootstrap operation, and each research activity will be continually refined by the results of complementary activities. It is likely that the measurement of resources should in fact be carried out independently of the analysis of conversion processes, because of the different types of research design implied by the goals: one an extensive estimation of population characteristics, and the other an intensive investigation of the conversion process.

Conversion of Assets

The second general type of research complements the system of accounts described above. It is research on the convertibility of resources of one type into resources of another type. It is this question, in different terms, to which most of the hypotheses or theories of social change are directed. These hypotheses have been discussed in the earlier sections, and I shall make no attempt to review them here.

My general perspective here, and the perspective I suggest in the design of research in this area, is to start by laying out the classes of variables that constitute assets and to specify the known relations among them. Then the questions that need to be answered by research are specific details about the form of these processes and quantitative estimates of conversion rates, for those that are known, and exploratory information for those that are quite unknown.

The starting point in this research should be the hypotheses described in Part II and the evidence on which they are based, together with the further discussion of Part III. As is evident, such research constitutes a very large program, and selectivity is necessary. It is possible, however, to begin by obtaining rough estimates of a large number of the conversion processes, rather than by attempting to obtain precise information on a few. For example, census data can be used to obtain a rough estimate of the convertibility of years of schooling into income and the convertibility of freedom of social action by virtue of skin color into income, and some work of this kind has been done.[44] There are numerous possibilities for further estimates from administration statistics and census data, and these estimates are crucial for filling out the matrices described in Part III.

There are several additional points that should be noted in research on conversion of assets, and these are listed below.

Some of the relationships under investigation have their effect quickly, while others operate only after some delay. Thus it is necessary to design both short- and long-range research. For example, the effect of increased achievements in education on a Negro's economic earning power is an effect that occurs only over a period of time. Similarly, the effect of various school conditions on achievement in school operates over a period of several years. In both of these cases, fortunate circumstances may have made it possible to carry out comparative analysis without examining the same persons over time; but often circumstances are not so fortunate. Thus some research design should include rigorous controls and provision for passage of the necessary time, recognizing that research results based on cross-sectional comparative analysis may often fail to provide conclusive evidence.

A second general point is that any research program must recognize that there are several distinctly different environments in which Negroes are concentrated. The urban North and the rural South are the two most important; but many Negroes are in the urban South as well. A second distinction is between the lower class and the middle class, for the resources of the middle class are different from those of the lower class. Still a third distinction is a generational one. The attitudes of each generation of Negroes are shaped by the events that occurred while they were growing up. Thus we may expect the young, when they are adults, to have political views different in many respects from those of their parents today. Still another important difference is the one between an environment that is predominantly Negro and one that is predominantly white. The actions of any minority group are greatly shaped by its size, and Negroes are no exception.

A third general point is that studies of the convertibility of resources are often best carried out as tests of the use of alternative resources for the same purpose, rather than as single separate tests. This arises from the fact that research methods often do not allow precise quantitative estimates of conversion parameters. Thus results of two studies, each of which examines the conversion of one type of resource, and both with the same output, will often yield results that cannot be directly compared. Consequently, given the crude state of present measurement, it is often best to test such processes against one another.

For example, the hypothesis implied by some economists who attribute unemployment to lack of aggregate demand is that a strong demand creates employment opportunities which give jobs to persons "unemployable" in times of weak demand, and these marginal jobs in turn provide training for more highly skilled jobs. Further, in times of high demand, employers will train workers on the job, while they will not do so in times of weak demand. The hypothesis held by economists who attribute unemployment to "structural" reasons is that the formal educational system is the principal path of entry into the labor force and that persons untrained in the formal educational system will not be able to recover in the labor force itself. These alternative and competing hypotheses imply different convertibility of educational and economic resources into occupational skills and can probably best be tested *against* each other by appropriate statistical studies.

A final and more extended point in the discussion of research on conversion of resources concerns the social organization of Negroes. It is apparent in much of the preceding discussion that some of the most important existing and potential assets among Negroes lie in organization and cohesion. As indicated earlier, the effect of this organization can be to reduce deficits in freedom of action and political power and also in personal resources. Or roughly, it can exert power both to the outside, to change the larger white community, and to the inside, to change Negroes themselves. The organization of the Negro movement, the community cohesion of Negroes, and the family cohesion are all quite important in this: the first, the Negro movement, exerting its direct effects on the outside, the family cohesion exerting its direct effects on Negroes themselves, and community cohesion exerting its direct effects in both directions.

Because of their present and potential importance in reducing deficits of Negroes, research on the organization of the Negro movement, the Negro community, and the Negro family demands special attention.

Most organizations in the Negro movement were born as conflict groups. This gives them certain special characteristics: their goals are to win in a social conflict; they tend to be sustained by conflict; leadership of the organization lies with those who are most successful in conflict; and each organization tends to develop particular styles, strategies, and arenas of conflict.

Conflict organizations tend to be shaped and structured by their opposition and by the terms of the dispute. This is most obvious in the effect of a polarization on the nature of leadership: as a dispute becomes polarized, leaders who urge collaboration and compromise can no longer gain the support of the followers, and radical leaders take over. It is remarkable that in the civil rights movement the polarization process has waxed and waned; it has not moved inexorably forward, as is often the case in conflicts. In Little Rock, Arkansas, at the height of the dispute there was no place for moderates, either white or Negro; the intensity of the conflict destroyed the audience and thus the power of the moderates. Yet since then there have been many subsequent rises and falls in the intensity of the conflict and in the ability of moderate leaders to gain a following.

It is important to understand far better than we presently do the processes that often carry a conflict into greater and greater intensity, often pushing a conflict group into greater and greater radicalism. I say "push" advisedly, because the competition for leadership can push leaders into more violent and radical activity than they themselves desire, merely in order to hold the attention of the followers. It is useful to note that there have been some remarkable Negro leaders in this movement who have managed to maintain their positions of leadership while holding firmly to moderate strategies of conflict; perhaps the best example was Martin Luther King, Jr.

The basic point is that a situation of protracted conflict such as occurs in the Negro movement is a very delicately balanced one, which can easily erupt into violence, as has occurred sporadically in this conflict. Yet too little is known about the conditions that upset this balance and the conditions that maintain it. In general, Negro conflict groups have shown great restraint. But what are the factors, besides the personalities of particular men, that have allowed this restraint? And what changes in the structure of the Negro movement would upset it? An example of the kind of problem to be studied here is the conditions of increasing or decreasing radicalism of Negro conflict groups. Increasing radicalism might be explained by the competition for leadership among different groups in the movement. Certainly such competition exists, and its effect is in the direction of increasing radicalism. But why in the direction of increasing radicalism? What determines the direction in which such competition leads? And since the radicalism has waxed and waned and moderation had often prevailed, there are countering factors, some of which may lie in the larger society (for example, the fact that moderate means have succeeded in gaining legislative action), but some of which may lie within the movement itself.

For these reasons, it is important to have better knowledge of the internal functioning of these conflict groups and the processes that lead toward and away from violence. The Negro movement constitutes perhaps the most important current asset by which the deficits of Negroes can be overcome. It could perhaps become an even more effective asset for this purpose (for example, in conjunction with information of the sort discussed in other parts of this research section). But it could also run wholly out of control of its present leaders and bring in response a wave of repression that would wipe out the current assets.

Study of the Negro neighborhood and community is of a very different sort. The first research task here is merely a descriptive one: to chart the ecology of mutual trust in Negro communities, as well as the kinds of institutions it has spawned—all the way from help between neighbors to investment in a community co-operative. Little is known, in simple descriptive terms, about the pervasiveness of trust and the kinds of community institutions it has bred. It is evident that this will vary widely from South to North, from rural to urban, from low-density to high-density Negro neighborhoods.

The direct value of trust-based institutions as capital assets in an economic sense is so important that simply a description of these assets is a valuable research result. But a second research aim should be to discover to what extent a trust basis exists, without as full a development of mutual aid institutions as the base would allow. Such results would show the opportunities for appropriate social policies to build on the basis of trust; or conversely, they would show what social policies might be expected to fail because of the absence of a sufficient base.

A still deeper research aim in this area would be to learn the deterrents to a system of trust, the principal community deficits that undermine the extensive development of a system of trust.

Many Negroes are effectively undermined in their attempts at achievement by the disorganization in their communities. There would be much support from such Negroes for efforts to create neighborhood cohesion; but there are many impediments in the way. Since such cohesion could be a valuable asset to Negroes, it is important to examine in detail the impediments.

There have been many action programs in Negro communities designed precisely to foster such neighborhood self-help. The combined experiences of these programs should itself be a worthwhile research result—giving some evidence of what the major impediments are, whether it is in fact feasible to overcome them in all settings, or whether community organization is an asset that can be achieved only as a result of reducing all the other deficits first.

Similar questions can be asked about the Negro family. The effectiveness of strong families is evident in much research; what is not known is how the family can become a strong unit. The Moynihan hypothesis is that reconstitution of the role and importance of the male in the family through greater economic opportunity is an important element. Certainly further data beyond those presented by Moynihan can be brought to bear on this question. More generally, what are the principal impediments to the development of a strong family among Negroes?

Many of the questions posed here about organization among Negroes at these levels ranging from family to political action group are mere repetitions of what has been said many times before; and certainly there is research in progress on many of them. The most important point of this section, however, is that the results of such research should be seen not as isolated results, but rather as aids for developing organizational assets that are themselves known to be important aids in overcoming other deficits. Many of the questions that arise in government action and in actions of the Negro movement are questions about allocation of resources: given a limited set of resources, what is their most effective use to overcome Negro deficits? It is questions like this for which the results of research on Negro national, community, and family organization are necessary.

Changes in Conversion Processes

Each arena of action can be conceived as a context within which various conversion processes occur. The family is one such arena in which a wide range of conversion processes take place, the most important being the creation of personal resources in childhood.

In using the system of resources discussed in the pages for creating or modifying change, two kinds of modifications of the existing system are possible. One is a modification of the distribution of input resources. The simplest example of this is in shifting government appropriations between services such as education or job training and money income supplements such as family allowances or a negative income tax. Another example is the shifting of the use of the personal resources of Negro leadership from the arena of the local community in community development programs to the Negro civil rights or black power movement.

But a second kind of modification of the existing system is one that changes the very processes or mechanism in a given arena. One example is the development of quite new kinds of educational institutions. Another is the institution of the poverty program, which created new mechanisms of change within local communities.

This second kind of modification, viewed in the framework of the matrices and sector of Part III, is a modification not of the vector of resources, but of the matrices of conversion coefficients. This may state the matter too simply and may overstate the difference between the two cases, but the difference is important.[45] The research required for these changes in process is actual experimentation with the new institutional arrangements: empirical examination of the effects of Head Start, or the Job Corps, or a new Negro action group, or a new community center program. Given the present state of knowledge, it is seldom possible to predict the effects of such processes from the combination of resources that goes into them.

Altogether, then, there is one principal point concerning changes in the conversion process: these changes require more than observation of the ongoing system; they require experimentation with the changed processes themselves, whether in the form of new organizations or institutions, or as new techniques within existing organizations.

Contingent Projections and Optimization

The fourth major type of research depends on the first and second (and makes use of the third), but goes beyond them. It is the projection of what can be termed "contingent trends" by use of the current accounts of assets and deficits and knowledge about conversion of assets. Such projections are simulations of future states, contingent on different actions being taken in the present.

In principle, it is easy to see how such projections or simulations can proceed. If one knows the detailed current state of relevant variables and the relations between them, it is in principle possible to project that system of variables to show the effect of changes in one on changes in others. In practice, it is more difficult. Although it is frequently done in natural sciences, economics provides the only example in the social sciences. Input-output analysis has been designed for just that purpose and has been used in several economies for modeling the effects of different economic policies. But the difficulties that input-output analysis has encountered, although the conversion factors for resources of one type into resources of another are much better known, show the problems that can be expected to arise in making such contingent projections.

The principal rule that must guide work in this area is that action will be taken with or without such explicit projections, and action taken without them will be based on implicit assumptions and implicit mental projections. Thus, to be valuable, the explicit contingent projections need not be perfect, but need only be better than the implicit ones otherwise used. Thus they should err on the side of simplicity rather than complexity, to provide modest improvements on the implicit mental projections.

There are examples of such projections that can be made on the basis of existing data and some that have been done. Ecological-demographic projections, for example, show the consequences of current birth rates and residential patterns for the ecology of metropolitan areas some years hence. Another is educational-occupational. Using information about the current structure of the labor force, the rate of change in this structure, current occupational distributions of Negroes and whites, the relation between education and occupation, trends in educational achievement for Negroes and whites, and projected numbers of Negro and white entrants and leavers of the labor force, it would be possible to project the occupational distribution of Negroes and whites into the future.

Such projections can become contingent projections by the use of alternative assumptions about certain trends. The results would be of the form, "If it were possible to change the educational achievement of Negroes over the next five years in a different way than expected on the basis of extrapolation of past trends, the effect on the occupational distribution fifteen years hence would be . . ." They can become optimization models by starting at the other end: by taking as given a desired profile of assets and asking what distribution of resources will give that profile in the shortest period of time, or a related optimization question.

Such simulations or projections would obviously require mounting a serious and intensive research effort, using skills and experience from econometric analysis as well as sociological skills. The value of the results would be, as in the earlier types of research, to provide the informational base for legal, governmental, and Negro-organizational action, as well as to inform the political pressure that can affect such action; in short, to inform those who control particular resources.

•NOTES

1 T. S. Ashton, "The Bill of Exchange and Private Banks in Lancashire, 1790–1830," *Economic History Review*, Vol. XV, Nos. 1, 2 (1945), reprinted in T. S. Ashton and R. S. Sayers, eds., *Papers in English Monetary History* (London: Oxford University Press, 1953).

2 C. Geertz, "The Rotating Credit Association: A 'Middle Rung' in Development," *Economic Development and Cultural Change*, X (1962), 241–263.

3 J. S. Coleman, E. Q. Campbell, C. J. Hobson, J. McPartland, A. M. Mood, F. O. Weinfeld, and R. L. York, *Equality of Educational Opportunity* (Washington: Government Printing Office, 1966), Chapter 3; Department of Education and Science (England), *Children and Their Primary Schools* (called the "Plowden Report") (London: Her Majesty's Stationery Office, 1967), Vol. II, Appendix 4; U.S. Commission on Civil Rights, *Racial Isolation in the Public Schools* (Washington: Government Printing Office, 1967), Vol. II, Appendix C3.

4 B. Jackson and D. Marsden, *Education and the Working Class* (London: Routledge and Kegan Paul, 1962).

5 U.S. Department of Labor, Office of Planning and Research, *The Negro Family: The Case for National Action* (Washington: Government Printing Office, 1965). (The so-called Moynihan report.)

6 M. Weber, *The Protestant Ethic and the Spirit of Capitalism* (London: Allen and Unwin, 1948).

7 Mao Tse-tung, *The Political Thought of Mao Tse-Tung*, edited by S. R. Schram (New York: Praeger, 1963).

8 G. Sorel, *Reflections on Violence* (London: Allen and Unwin, 1925).

9 J. P. Sartre, *The Problem of Method* (London: Methuen, 1963).

10 D C. McClelland, *The Achieving Society* (Princeton: Van Nostrand, 1961).

11 *Ibid.*

12 R. H. Tawney, *Religion and the Rise of Capitalism* (London: Murray, 1927).

13 Coleman, *op. cit.*, Section 3.26; R. M. Bear, R. D. Hess, and V. C. Shipman, *Social Class Differences in Maternal Attitudes toward School and the Consequences for Cognitive Development in the Young Child* (Chicago: Urban Child Center, University of Chicago, 1966, mimeographed).

14 McClelland, *op. cit.*, p. 337.

15 L. Festinger, *A Theory of Cognitive Dissonance* (Evanston: Row, Peterson, 1957) (reprinted by Stanford University Press, Stanford, 1962).

16 Reported in the New York *Times,* March 3, 1967, p. 8.

17 A very reasonable interpretation of the activities of the Red Guards in China is the attempt by Mao Tse-tung to recreate the collective identity which was earlier created by the revolution itself.

18 A. A. Berle and G. C. Means, *Modern Corporation and Private Property* (New York: Macmillan, 1932).

19 J. R. Commons, *Legal Foundations of Capitalism* (New York: Macmillan, 1924); and J. R. Commons, *The Economics of Collective Action* (New York: Macmillan, 1950), pp. 297–335.

20 One economist who does not make such a simple assumption, but nevertheless sees economic capital as a primary factor, is W. W. Rostow, *The Stages of Economic Growth* (Cambridge: University Press, 1961).

21 If we think of economic production as consisting of a sequence of stages from raw materials to final product, and each of these stages requiring a certain mode of industrial organization or productive potential, then x_i is the productive potential of a given stage, and the output per unit time is the product of $n + 1$ factors: $x_1 x_2 \ldots x_n c$. This provides a more appropriate sense of the complexity of the problem than does a simple product xc of productive potential and capital. It indicates also that even the introduction of technical assistance to increase x_n and x_{n-1} along with capital resources will not affect productivity if productive potential at other stages, x_1 or x_2, is absent. Even more, if an element of productive potential is introduced from outside in the form of technical and organizational skills, without providing a means to subsequently generate it internally, its subsequent withdrawal will leave the country as unproductive as at the beginning.

22 For a further discussion of this problem, see B. Ward, "The Decade of Development—A Study in Frustration?", and P. T. Bauer, "Foreign Aid: An Instrument for Progress?", in Institute of Economic Affairs, *Two Views on Aid to Developing Countries* (London: Institute of Economic Affairs, 1966), Occasional Paper No. 9. Bauer goes so far as to argue that foreign governmental aid to underdeveloped countries is almost never of value to the recipient, and often harmful.

23 D. Macdonald, "Our Invisible Poor," *New Yorker* (January 19, 1963).

24 C. Killingsworth, Chapter 5 of this book.

25 R. A. Cloward and L. Ohlin, *Delinquency and Opportunity* (New York: The Free Press, 1960).

26 B. M. Fleisher, *The Effect of Income on Delinquency* (Chicago: Center for the Study of Social Organization, University of Chicago, 1965).

27 Macdonald, *op. cit.*

28 Jackson and Marsden, *op. cit.*

29 W. C. Haggstrom, "The Power of the Poor," in F. Reissman *et al.*, eds., *Mental Health of the Poor* (New York: The Free Press, 1964).

30 U.S. Department of Labor, *op. cit.*

31 A. Schorr, *Poor Kids* (New York: Basic Books, 1966).

32 Even, of course, if it is conceived as a permanent supplement, it is important to know the efficiency with which it satisfies wants under different methods of input. Much of the effort of economists working in this area is directed to this question.

33 See, for example, A. Schorr, in Social Security Administration, *Slums and Social Insecurity* (Washington: Government Printing Office, 1963).

34 D. Wilner *et al.*, *The Housing Environment and Family Life* (Baltimore: Johns Hopkins Press, 1962).

35 N. Glazer and D. McEntire, eds., *Studies in Housing and Minority Groups* (Berkeley: University of California Press, 1960).

36 G. W. Brown *et al.*, *Schizophrenia and Social Care* (London: Oxford University Press, 1966).

37 V. Fuchs, *The Contribution of Health Services to the American Economy* (Washington: National Bureau of Economic Research, 1966, mimeographed).

38 C. Kadushin, "Health and Social Class," *New Society* (December 24, 1964), p. 14.

39 M. Rein, personal communication, 1967; also M. Rein, "Social Science and the Elimination of Poverty," *Journal of the American Institute of Planners*, XXXIII (1967), 146–163.

40 J. S. Coleman *et al.*, *op. cit.*

41 F. Fanon, *The Wretched of the Earth* (London: Penguin Books, 1967—first published as *Les Damnés de la terre*, 1961).

42 However, more sophisticated action, based on a comprehensive theory, would very likely involve strategies that employed a number of the processes. A comparison with input-output analysis in economics is useful: for a given desired profile of final demand, the appropriate allocation of resources will ordinarily make use of all the industries in the system, except those processes which provide a less efficient output of a given resource than others in the system.

43 In most economic input-output type models, the activity is not distinguished from its single product. Only in Von Neumann's general growth model is this distinction made, in order to allow joint products from a single industry.

44 P. M. Siegel, "On the Cost of Being a Negro," *Sociological Inquiry*, XXXV (1965), 41–57; O. D. Duncan, "Discrimination against Negroes," *Annals*, CCCLXXI (1967), 85–103.

45 Some equivalences may exist between resources and conversion coefficients. If a mechanism of conversion is complex in form, with multi-

plicative relationships between resources, shifts of certain resources may, in one conceptual framework, be equivalent to changes in conversion mechanisms in another. In one conceptual system, the change of a conventional school system to an educational park might be merely a change in the distribution of input resources, while in the other, it would be a change in the mechanism or process itself. Obviously, in either case, it would be necessary to study empirically the effect of this change.

7 *Irwin Katz and Patricia Gurin*

Race Relations and the Social Sciences: Overview and Further Discussion

How can research in the social sciences help solve the problem of Negro-white inequality in the United States? More specifically, what is presently known about relations between the two groups, the causes of Negro disadvantage, the effectiveness of various types of change efforts—and what more needs to be known—to provide an adequate scientific basis for building sound public policy? Further, since scholarly and technical resources are necessarily limited, what sort of research priorities are indicated for both the immediate and long-term future? These are some of the difficult yet fundamental questions to which six social scientists have addressed themselves in the preceding chapters. In the main, each contributor has looked at different aspects of the total problem, using the intellectual tools of his own discipline. Thus Hyman examines recent trends in the study of white prejudice that begin to relate it to the changing status of Negroes in American life; Pettigrew and Killingsworth deal with policy issues in the respective fields of education and employment; Matthews provides a paradigm for studying the politics of race relations; Taeuber clarifies the essential role to be played by systematic measurement of characteristics of the Negro population and its environment; and finally, Coleman proposes an overarching conceptual framework for analyzing the major determinants of racially relevant social change.

In this chapter we shall first review the salient points in each contribution. Then we shall consider common underlying themes relating to research strategies and highlight the relevance of these strategies for public policy. Finally, we shall discuss psychological assumptions made in some of the papers that require further elaboration.

RÉSUMÉS

Hyman

Herbert H. Hyman deals mainly with the aspect of Negro-white relations in America that has traditionally received the most attention from social psychologists: white prejudice. He does not attempt to survey the entire vast literature on this topic, but limits himself to the pursuit of promising leads into the relationship between white attitudes and the changing position of Negroes in American society. Hyman begins by considering factors that may currently be causing a favorable modification of white attitudes, such as changes in the racial socialization of white children. He advances the intriguing notion, supported by some evidence from studies of nonracial socialization, that with shifting societal demands, parents begin to transmit to their children values and beliefs different from those they had internalized from their own parents. Other new types of early experience, such as increased contact with Negro age-peers and less exposure to negative stereotyping in the mass media, may also contribute to a generally more favorable socialization of racial attitudes today than at any time in the past.

Most research on white attitudes, Hyman points out, has failed to differentiate Negroes as attitudinal objects. He believes that researchers have been wont to assume that whites do not differentiate Negroes into different social-class subgroups, because until recently there was hardly any basis in reality for such distinctions. Now, as increasing numbers of Negroes enter the urban middle class, it becomes relevant to inquire to what extent the majority group's attitudes about Negroes reflect class stereotypes and to what extent they signify racial prejudice per se. Some relatively small-sample studies are cited which indicate that the perception of Negroes as middle-class has a strongly favorable influence on white reactions. But conceivably the same perception may have the negative consequence of arousing feelings of status anxiety and competitive threat. Hyman recommends that these alternative hypotheses be tested empirically.

Also discussed is Rokeach's hypothesis that intergroup prejudice is largely an effect of perceived differences in belief. This hypothesis, Hyman observes, raises two questions: one about the correctness of the hypothesis itself, and another as to whether whites, when lacking information, tend to assume that Negroes' beliefs are different from their own.

With regard to the problem of predicting white behavior in interracial contact situations, a number of useful suggestions are made for resolving observed inconsistencies between measured attitudes and overt conduct. Hyman conjectures that prejudice often does not translate into discriminatory behavior because a variety of other motives interact with the desire to manifest prejudice, with the outcome being determined by the relative strength of the forces.

Finally, there is a discussion of reference group and relative deprivation concepts as they apply to white attitudes, on one hand, and Negro passivity or militancy, on the other, with suggested directions for research.

Pettigrew

The relevance of social science to the problem of inequality of educational opportunity is taken up by Thomas F. Pettigrew. His major thesis is that racial imbalance of school enrollments, whether deliberately contrived or simply a by-product of residential patterns, constitutes a major barrier to the full inclusion of Negroes in American society. The findings of the famous Coleman survey of American public schools reveal that in all regions of the country most Negro children attend predominantly Negro institutions. Despite the gravity of the problem, relatively little research on the causes and effects of racial imbalance is currently under way. The reasons, as Pettigrew describes them, are both political-bureaucratic and technical.

What is presently known about the effect of school conditions (including racial balance of student enrollments) on Negro academic achievement? In addressing this question, Pettigrew refers mainly to the Coleman survey and a more recent report by the United States Commission on Civil Rights. Both federal reports—particularly the commission's—suggest that the Negro child benefits from attending majority-white schools, regardless of his own social-class background or the average social class of his schoolmates. White students, on the other hand, seem not to be adversely affected by the presence of Negro peers, so long as the latter remain a numerical minority. Negro children in majority-white schools also have a markedly stronger sense of personal control over their fate than do their counterparts in *de facto* segregated schools—an attitude that is closely related to actual achievement.

After reviewing various nonracial interpretations of the apparent racial composition effect, Pettigrew concludes that they do not really explain away the phenomenon. He sees the benefits of the desegregated experience as being mediated largely by the Negro pupil's social interactions with whites, which on balance appear to be positive, but which when negative can be highly detrimental to learning. Pettigrew proposes a broad "social evaluation" hypothesis, citing empirical evidence that the Negro pupils who benefit most from desegregation are also the ones most likely to have white friends.

Another set of data mentioned has to do with adult attitudes and behavior. Surveys indicate that Negro adults who attended desegregated schools have better jobs and higher incomes than those who attended racially isolated schools. Moreover, they are more likely to be living in racially mixed neighborhoods, to be sending their children to desegregated schools, and to have white friends. Similarly, white adults who experienced desegregated schooling are more favorably disposed toward Negroes than those who attended all-white schools.

Referring to recent evaluations of compensatory educational programs in segregated inner-city schools, Pettigrew points out that as currently carried on the programs "resoundingly fail" to produce lasting and significant academic gains. He strongly advocates combining compensatory services with racially balanced enrollments.

What factors determine the decisions of local communities to desegregate their schools? After considering this and related questions regarding the politics of desegregation, Pettigrew takes up the racial relevance of educational alternatives to the public schools and, finally, ideas for definitive solutions of the segregation problem, particularly educational parks in conjunction with metropolitan redistricting.

Among the items mentioned in a final summing up of research needs are demographic simulations of the racial imbalance problem's future dimensions; improved evaluations of change efforts; and theoretically oriented "process research" to identify the mediators of change.

Matthews

In his treatment of race politics, Donald R. Matthews employs a "systems theory" framework which he describes as "far from a theory in any meaningful sense" but "the closest thing political science now has to a generally accepted paradigm." As applied to race politics, the major components of the model are inputs from the environment, which take the form of either Negro demands or Negro supports; a set of authoritative decision-makers who convert these inputs into outputs, or policies; and feedback of a portion of these outputs through the environment, to become new inputs.

Among the various aspects of Negro political demands that require study are the two divergent trends in Negro leadership: separatism and black nationalism on the one hand and integrationism on the other. Another aspect has to do with the relation of Negro goals and objectives to white opinions and political demands. In the South, for example, both races apparently agree on the *direction* of change in race relations, while having sharply discrepant expectations about the *pace* of change.

Matthews discusses how such Negro resources as votes, money, prestige, skill, and information traditionally get translated into political power. Potential political power depends on how much of *all* these resources a group controls, plus its willingness to *use* the resources for political goals. He takes up in detail what may be expected from Negro voting and also points to several critical research questions on Negro leadership and effects of protest politics.

In a section on "Authoritative Decision-Makers" Matthews points out that the systems paradigm tends to focus attention on the environment in which decision-makers operate, but does not seem to throw much light on the decision-making processes whereby demands and supports are converted into policies. Little is known about the behavior of decision-makers and the structural and institutional arrangements that condition the way in which the conflicting claims of groups are handled. What is needed, he feels, is a series of detailed case studies of the processing of Negro political demands by government officials and agencies.

Matthews believes that the most important consequence for political science of a systems perspective may be the attention it directs toward outputs. Everything else now becomes significant only as it helps explain governmental actions. Though recent quantitative studies of governmental policy outputs are beset by many unresolved problems of measurement and causal inference, Matthews sees them as "a first step in the analysis of 'who gets what and why.' " But the *direction* of policy —"who gets what?"—is not the only important dimension of the problem. Also important are the *efficiency* of the policy, its *rationality* for goal attainment, its *coherence* (compatibility with other policies), and its *impact* (effectiveness in changing individual behavior and attitudes). He regards the question of impact as the one deserving the most attention and classifies its determinants into three types, according to whether they involve governmental resources, target groups, or the kind of changes required. For Matthews the most critical type of determinant has to do with the kind and amount of change the policy requires.

Taeuber

Karl E. Taeuber writes from the point of view of a sociologist who prefers a demographic mode of analysis and is concerned with selected aspects of social change. He is essentially interested in two questions: First, what kinds of quantitative information about the Negro population are needed to understand the "vicious cycle of disabilities" and how it can be broken? Second, how can these data be obtained most efficiently? He sharply distinguishes between the use of data on Negroes for primarily descriptive purposes—that is, to provide a summary "index of race relations"—and their use in analysis of causal relationships. He rejects the former on grounds that not enough is yet known about the complexities of race relations to warrant an attempt at representation through the use of a few key indicators.

Taeuber would use the individual life cycle as a broad framework for analysis. There are formidable problems having to do with the availability of good data, which he discusses at length.

Another basic frame of reference for ordering research problems is provided by the "basic demographic equation—fertility, mortality, and migration." Taeuber points out that Negro fertility presents a number of puzzles. It is not known, for example, why Negro birth rates declined sharply from the Civil War until the 1930's, rose very rapidly after World War II, and then showed a downward trend in the 1960's. Longitudinal studies are needed to clarify effects; for example, how the fertility of low-income families changes as income maintenance programs move their income upward. Longitudinal research, in conjunction with retrospective and case studies, should also be used to investigate Negro family composition. Taeuber also shows that the other components of the "basic demographic equation"—migration and mortality—are as inadequately researched or understood as fertility.

When he takes up racial aspects of housing, Taeuber states that it is "past time for a comprehensive series of statistical analyses" of the problem. He recommends local-level studies in which neighborhoods and larger areas are compared with one another and also studied historically. Such research could examine questions about the relationship between neighborhood deterioration and housing costs and changeover from white to Negro occupancy. Taeuber is pessimistic about prospects for reducing housing segregation. His own research indicates that racial segregation in housing is caused primarily by discrimination, with Negro poverty having very little to do with it. Housing segregation should also be studied as an explanatory variable with respect to a host of Negro attributes, including political power, employment, personality development, family stability, health, and so on.

Killingsworth

Why have Negro income and employment, relative to whites', shown little improvement since the mid-1950's? Charles C. Killingsworth maintains that the prime reasons are not to be found in weakness of the total economy and racial discrimination, for there are broader and more effective antidiscrimination laws today than there were twenty-five years ago, Negro-white differences in educational attainment are now greatly reduced, and there have been several record-breaking years of economic expansion. Moreover, neither general economic slackness nor discrimination can account for the peculiar patterns of disadvantage among Negroes; for example, relative unemployment rates are highest for younger, better-educated, northern Negroes.

Killingsworth's thesis is that the most basic causes of slowdown in the economic progress of Negroes are to be found in the structural changes that have occurred in the labor market. In support of this interpretation he reviews the history of the Negro labor force during the past thirty years. The great break-through into northern industry came during World War II, as a result of a general labor shortage, vigorous antidiscrimination measures of the federal government, and government-subsidized job training. The tight labor market of this period was not created by aggregate demand alone; an important factor was the enormous siphoning off of manpower into the armed forces. During the Korean War there were comparable developments on a smaller scale. But these conditions weakened or were offset by other forces somewhere around the middle of the 1951–1960 decade.

A real trend toward rising Negro unemployment in the 1960's, Killingsworth asserts, has been obscured by a serious distortion factor in reports by federal agencies. This is the practice of defining the "labor force" as composed of people who are actively seeking a job. It results in an understatement of the number who would be available for employment if more jobs of the right kind were available. Killingsworth's data analyses indicate that over the past twenty years Negro hidden unemployment has increased at a much faster rate than that of whites. Negro income and education are additional areas in which apparent gains since World War II become less impressive when examined closely.

In proposing strategies for change, Killingsworth makes the explicit assumption that Negroes "are as ready as any group in the population to grasp opportunity when it is within their reach." The aggregate demand strategy for full employment cannot provide the kind of opportunities that are needed by willing but unskilled Negro workers, he argues, because it assumes a "rational labor market," while his own experience has been that jobs are never broken down except in time of major war mobilization. Killingsworth recommends that such assumptions be tested empirically.

Killingsworth discusses the relative merits of various proposals for making transfer payments to the poor. He does not regard such plans as providing a key to solution of the poverty problem. Although some form of government subsidy is required for people who do not belong in the labor market, the main thrust of any over-all government effort must be in the direction of expanding job opportunities.

Coleman

Of all the contributors, James S. Coleman provides the most general theoretical framework for analyzing social change. It is essentially a systems analysis model in which the *inputs* are individual, collective, and environmental resources available to Negroes, the *conversion processes* occur within various arenas of action, and the *output* consists of new Negro resources of other types. Coleman draws up a "balance sheet" in which he lists the main liabilities and assets of Negro Americans. On the liabilities side he mentions *freedom of action* (every type of action and association that entails some degree of restriction due to skin color); *economic power*; *political power*; *community cohesion*; *family cohesion*; *personal resources* (low levels of education, organizational skills, information, motivation, and so on); and *attributes of the larger society* (including white prejudice and an unfavorable occupational structure). On the favorable side of the ledger he mentions *increasing political strength* and the *expanding wealth of the nation*.

Coleman hypothesizes specific types of process whereby the resources described in his balance sheet get translated into other kinds of resources, directly related to status and well-being. He gives examples of "multiplier effects," when resources interact with one another. Thus with regard to "resources of the Negro community" he points out the potential multiplier effect when individuals are able to draw upon the pooled political and economic strength and socialization skills of neighbors through collective community action and co-operative arrangements. Negroes, according to Coleman, are handicapped in doing this by the low level of trust that prevails among them. Similarly, he believes that Negroes suffer from a relatively low level of family cohesion and structural stability, which deprives them of important multiplier effects on individual resources for school and job achievement.

Theories of social change that emphasize the role of individual achievement orientation—as represented by Max Weber's Protestant Ethic and David McClelland's achievement motive—are compared with the "revolutionary collectivist" theories of Sorel, Sartre, and Mao Tse-tung. Implications are shown with regard to the goal choices that Negroes must make. Another type of theory of social change which emphasizes the influence of organizational structure on behavior is discussed in connection with legal and legislative resources.

Coleman's basic premise about the role of economic resources is that inputs of external economic resources into a group will not bring about social change unless certain internal resources provide a necessary "conversion potential." He identifies three different kinds of social policy on giving economic resources to the poor: policies that provide jobs, money or goods, and services. Each has its own implicit assumptions about social and psychological effects. In evaluating these proposals, Coleman's frame of reference is the economic cycle of the household, described in terms of four variables. The model suggests a great number of empirically testable propositions about the relative effects of putting jobs, money, or goods and services into the household system.

Ultimately Coleman organizes the various theories and hypotheses about social change in terms of types of interacting resources, the arenas of action in which the interaction occurs, and the outputs to be expected. His research suggestions are all in the direction of affecting policy decisions and of identifying points in the social system where research results could have the greatest impact. A major recommendation is that there be established a system of social accounts, kept over time.

RESEARCH STRATEGIES

All the chapters in this volume document the disadvantages faced by Negroes in numerous arenas of life, as have many other papers, books,

and government reports. These chapters stress two points: first, despite
the movement of large numbers of Negroes into more secure and desirable positions in the social structure, sizable differentials still exist in
the extent to which Negroes and whites possess the rights and rewards
valued in this society: employment, income, job status and mobility,
housing, health, education, freedom of movement, and the respect of
others; second, the comparative trends for Negroes and whites are such
that Negroes in the 1960's are relatively as disadvantaged in several of
these areas as they have ever been. The question arises, then, whether
more research is really needed. This was certainly the reaction of many
Americans after the report of the National Advisory Commission on
Civil Disorders [1] was published in 1968. Do we not really know what
the problem is? Do we not also know what the solutions are? Is not the
only issue whether the nation will do what obviously must be done?

To a large extent the parameters of the problem are known; to some
extent it is also known what kinds of solutions can be more or less
effective. Nevertheless, the preceding chapters point to numerous research needs which press for attention if the long-standing tensions
between racial groups in this country are to be resolved. The most general point of agreement among the authors is that research on Negro-
white relations must be greatly expanded and upgraded in quality.
This is not to state that nothing practical should be done while social
scientists engage in further analysis. Indeed, all the writers emphasize
a need to move ahead as quickly as possible with action programs and
new legislation while the research effort is being expanded.

It is not merely the call for more research, however, that stands out
in these chapters. More importantly, there is a good deal of comple-
mentarity and agreement about *general research strategies.* First of all,
there is consensus that research must begin to focus more sharply than
it has in the past on factors that influence the direction and pace of
change. Hitherto, much of the work on race in this country was neither
theoretically interesting nor directly relevant to policy issues. By and
large, it was restricted to descriptions of the *status quo;* that is, to comparisons of Negro and white intelligence and personality, verbal
measurements of white prejudice, impressionistic accounts of Negro
life and culture, and so on. Of course, for several decades the rigid
subordination of nonwhite minorities severely restricted the social
scientist's opportunities for meaningful research on race relations. Indeed, it was not until the first major break-throughs against discrimination occurred during and following World War II that it became possible to mount large-scale investigations of social change processes (such
as integration in the armed forces, in certain industries, and in the pub-

lic schools). But even today, as the fabric of American society is being torn by racial conflict, social science is still too closely bound by its traditional research interests. For this reason it is especially noteworthy that all the papers display a primary concern with developing fresh approaches to the study of racial inequality—approaches that employ new concepts and investigative techniques for the causal analysis of social change.

A second unifying theme is closely tied to the first. To stimulate the development of useful hypotheses about change processes, some of the writers (Matthews, Taeuber, Coleman) propose using conceptual frameworks that are similar to the systems theory model of the economists. In their theories the social, political, and economic gains of Negroes and other disadvantaged groups would be treated as outcomes of conversion processes, consisting essentially of interactions of measurable inputs. The inputs could be any group or individual attributes of the minority or any features of their environment. Furthermore, even the writers who do not explicitly formulate general models of social change tend to favor multiple-factor rather than single-factor causal hypotheses.

Third, causal analyses require data—valid and reliable measures of the variables that are thought to be interrelated. Hence, another point of agreement among the authors (with varying degrees of emphasis) is on the need for regular and systematic gathering of information about a host of social-psychological, political, economic, and demographic variables that both define and shape the life situation of Negro Americans. The main purpose of such ambitious efforts at social accounting would be to provide accurate indices of the inputs and outcomes of hypothesized conversion processes. Another possible use of the obtained information—as descriptive indicators of the status and well-being of minority groups at a given point in time—is viewed cautiously by the contributors, no doubt because of the inherent dangers of popular misinterpretation and political misapplication.

Finally, we see in all the chapters a concern that research be tied integrally to social interventions and public policy. At the most pragmatic level, there is the pressing need to evaluate effects of different programs which supposedly are aimed at the same target. Thus, Killingsworth points out how difficult it is to draw conclusions about the relative success of different job retraining programs because so little adequate evaluation has been done. Of course, we are all aware of the political conditions which hamper evaluative research. So long as funding is on an annual basis, evaluation inevitably will be limited to the study of short-range effects and will be geared to the buttressing of new requests for appropriations. Further, at least some social scientists continue to hold negative views about what they call "applied research."

To criticize previous evaluation efforts only highlights the continuing need for good evaluation research if action is to be maximally effective. Indeed, there is a more general reason why research must not be divorced from action. The contributors repeatedly call for experimental studies in which causal relationships are directly observed. All too often in the past research has been limited to statistical analyses of data gathered for some other purpose, from which only tenuous conclusions about cause and effect could be drawn. Intervention programs can be used to approximate experimental situations in which inputs are manipulated to test what actually *does* happen. Of course, there will always be difficulties in fitting action programs to the requirements of good experimental design, as Pettigrew's discussion of educational research shows so well.

The foregoing points of agreement among the contributors indicate a common perspective across the social science disciplines on the potential contribution of race relations research, if certain general strategies were to be followed. The value of these chapters lies not only in their highlighting of specific research topics but also in their suggestions for an over-all research direction. We shall examine some of the issues that they raise, turning first to descriptive research strategies and then to models for causal analyses of Negro disadvantage.

Descriptive Research: Its Future and Limitations

The very nature of the problem of Negro disadvantage dictates that there will be a continuing need for descriptive comparisons of the status of Negroes and whites. Without such descriptive comparisons, one would be unable to assess the effects of change efforts, since reductions in race differentials define the targets for change. For instance, the relative unemployment rates for Negroes and whites from 1963 to 1967 provide the criterion in Killingsworth's analysis of the 1964 tax cut's effectiveness as a remedial strategy. The fact that the tax cut did bring about an increase in number of jobs available is less relevant to the problem of Negro disadvantage than whether it resulted in reduction of race differentials in unemployment. Descriptive research must also provide periodic information about the status of Negroes in all important areas where they remain disadvantaged. Thus, regardless of how much is known about racial inequality at present, future data gathering on a continuing basis will be necessary. The chapters are helpful in highlighting some defects of current descriptive research—particularly in its sampling, data gathering, and data analysis procedures—that should be eliminated from future studies.

Sampling Issues

The contributors lay considerable stress on the importance of using samples of adequate size in research on Negroes. All too often in the past Negroes have been included in surveys almost as an afterthought, resulting in samples too small to allow meaningful generalizations to any defined segment of the Negro population. In future studies Negroes must be oversampled if estimates are to be more reliable and if detailed subgroup comparisons are to be possible. But even when numerically adequate sampling of Negroes is undertaken, there remains the problem of representative selection. Taeuber makes it clear that the problem of biased underenumeration, particularly of males 20 to 39 years of age, is a severe one. Given the demographic distribution of the Negro population, this means that rates of underenumeration are likely to be excessively high in metropolitan areas. Yet it is in this very group—young urban males—that both unemployment and riot participation are concentrated. For too long it has been assumed that underenumeration is a problem primarily for the Census Bureau; it is really a problem for every study that employs survey research methods and, as Taeuber points out, for all multivariate analyses.

Another sampling problem has to do with the kind of design that is most appropriate for attaining a particular research objective. Very often a random sampling procedure is the most suitable. But there are research objectives for which estimates of race differences need to be based on stratified sampling procedures which oversample certain subgroups of Negroes and whites. This is clearly so whenever it is the difference between a tiny minority of Negroes and a tiny minority of whites that has implications for race relations and social change. Even if only small proportions of whites and Negroes are racial extremists, they may be the groups who account for mounting conflict. Another example of the need for stratified sampling can be drawn from the papers by Matthews and Coleman. If one is trying to understand Negro and white voting, random sampling may be an adequate technique (though not necessarily). But if participation in protest politics is also a focus of research (which it must be if one is to grasp the full extent of political pressures for social change), it is crucial to oversample the subgroups from which the protest leadership has come. The summers of unrest in the decade of the sixties are a testament to the impact that a small minority can have.

Data and Analysis Issues

Related to many of the sampling issues are certain data and analysis problems. One problem has to do with the classification of nonwhite populations. The usual estimates of Negro disadvantage are based on comparisons of whites and nonwhites. Most of the chapters recommend using more finely graded classifications within the nonwhite category. When national comparisons of total populations are sought, this issue may be relatively unimportant, but it becomes highly important in analyzing data on a regional basis. For instance, it probably does not matter where Mexicans are placed in national population statistics, since their total number is small. But combining Mexicans and Negroes in the nonwhite category in metropolitan areas of California would result in very questionable estimates of both groups and make quite meaningless any comparison of whites and nonwhites in those areas. Non-Negro minority groups have special needs and problems that are just as pressing as those of Negroes.

This example points to another analysis problem that is often mentioned in this book. Far too many estimates of race differentials are based on highly aggregated data. The kinds of difficulties that can result are shown in Killingsworth's discussion of race differentials in employment. He demonstrates that the problem of Negro unemployment cannot be adequately defined until rates of joblessness in different subgroups and in different regions are compared. Figures on gross unemployment at the national level can be quite misleading. He also points out how deceptive trend analyses are unless the trends are examined region by region.

Still another source of weakness in previous research has been the grossness of the measures on which Negroes and whites have been compared. Taeuber mentions this with respect to studies of race differentials in death rates. To study death rates from all causes is to study an aggregate composed of many disparate elements. Little is learned about the nature of Negro disadvantages in the health area. Killingsworth expresses the same concern when he calls for a finer breakdown of occupational classifications in comparing the job status of Negroes and whites. On the face of it, the 50 per cent increase of Negroes in white-collar jobs from 1955 to 1962 is impressive. Yet Killingsworth questions the meaning of the gain because of the grossness of the white-collar category; detailed data indicate that Negroes are located predominantly in the lower fringes of this category. Similarly, Hyman calls for more finely differentiated concepts and measures in research on race attitudes and stereotypes. Specifically, the gross, undifferentiated attitudinal object "Negro" of most prejudice questionnaires must give way to a variety of Negro subgroups based on social-class and other differences. The same recommendation is applicable to studies of Negro attitudes and stereotypes about whites.

Finally, this summary of data and analysis problems of previous descriptive research would not be complete without a reference to the problem of bias in many of the measures on which Negroes and whites are compared. It is the kind of problem that appears in culture-bound ability tests and also in efforts to apply the same criteria of social class to Negroes and whites when there is evidence that the bases for class distinctions are somewhat different in the two groups. But even when measurement instruments are appropriate, bias can enter in other ways. At least in experimental settings, there is ample evidence from the work of Katz and others [2] that responses of Negroes differ greatly, depending on such situational variables as the race of the experimenter, the race of fellow subjects, and the race of the group with which the subjects feel they are to be compared. Although there has been little research on bias in survey interview responses due to the race or class of the interviewer, studies in other settings suggest that it may be considerable.

Limitations of Descriptive Research

Though more and better descriptive research is needed, there are dangers inherent in the use of racial comparisons. A narrow emphasis on race differentials can lend a false sense of security about the research endeavor. Race differences are easy to find and may too easily create an impression that something has been explained when a problem has merely been identified. All too often neglected is the fact that obtained race differences may have nothing to do with race. What looks like an effect of race may stand for something else, such as social class or economic status. The evidence to date is quite unclear whether race differentials define a race problem or an underclass problem in the United States. Therefore, it is unwise to assume that race differences are explainable by race itself without examining whether there is a unique race effect over and above the effects of social class and economic variables. The very fact that public attention is focused on the problem of Negro disadvantage tempts the researcher to accept race as an explanatory variable in accounting for apparent race differences even when appropriate analyses have not been done from which to draw such conclusions. Moreover, if one takes seriously the task of delineating the separate and unique effects of race, he confronts difficult methodological issues. These are ably discussed by Taeuber. One of his points is that the apparent effect of race, after controlling for other factors, may be greatly influenced by the number and variety of the control variables included in the analysis. Further, it is not clear in what sense other social status conditions can be controlled, if being Negro affects the meaning of each status.

One of the dangers in an emphasis on racial comparisons is that it can exaggerate the divisiveness in American society. When comparison is the objective of research, the tendency is to report findings of differences rather than similarities. Yet there are many values, attitudes, and behaviors which are cultural characteristics in America shared equally by Negroes and whites. We would agree with Hyman that it is incumbent on social science to study these shared perspectives across racial lines, to balance the emphasis on race differences.

Finally, focusing on race differences, particularly when the comparisons are between a dominant majority and a subordinated minority group, can lead to certain biases in interpretation of nonwhite characteristics. The mean of the majority group tends to be viewed as the standard, and minority group deviations from that standard as evidence of deficiencies. Admittedly an emphasis on deficits is not a necessary consequence of comparative studies. In fact, the pejorative sense of the word "deficit" probably does not color conclusions from comparative studies when two groups of fairly equal prestige are compared. But only rarely are race differences interpreted as indicative of strengths or resources in the Negro group and deficits in the white group. An exception is the recent focus by some writers in the poverty literature on what are called "strengths of the poor." [3] This approach has its own dangers, particularly in the tendency to romanticize conditions that may be experienced by the poor as negative. Clearly there is need of greater awareness of possible biases that comparative studies may encourage.

Perhaps the kind of comparative research that has been done with fewest invidious distinctions is the social-class analysis of emotional and mental illnesses. The approach of Hollingshead and Redlich stresses that persons from lower-class positions are not necessarily "sicker"; rather, they are more likely to exhibit certain kinds of disturbances and less likely to have others which predominate in other social groups. [4]

To conclude this discussion of the limitations of descriptive research, comparative studies of Negro and white characteristics are both necessary and desirable. However, there are dangers to guard against: allowing descriptive studies to substitute for the kinds of analysis that would get at the underlying causes of racial differences; and allowing these studies to overstate differences—particularly differences with invidious implications—while glossing over important similarities, thus perhaps fostering (in Taeuber's words) "the very racism that produces those differences."

Causal Analysis and Models for Research in Race Relations

To go beyond the mere demonstration of race differences to an understanding of causes, it is necessary to set up testable hypotheses. The contributors to this book amply demonstrate the gains to be derived from explicit formulations of good hypotheses. For generating hypotheses they tend to prefer theoretical models which permit one to assess the relative importance of several different causal factors at the same time. Matthews, Taeuber, and Coleman favor systems models in which multiple inputs are viewed as affecting a set of outcomes which, in turn, feed back as inputs. One of the issues that come up in their discussions of multivariate analysis has to do with the ways in which input factors combine to produce effects on Negro-white differentials. Certain discrepancies between Negroes and whites—for instance, different unemployment rates—may be adequately explained by simply adding together the separate effects of several factors (discrimination, disparity in educational attainment, availability of jobs, distance of one's place of residence from industrial centers, and so on). Yet Killingsworth suggests that the importance of these factors may depend on still other conditions: for instance, whether the setting in question is northern or southern, rural or urban; whether the Negro and white comparison groups are young, middle-aged, or old; whether they are male or female. If the explanation for higher unemployment rates is quite different for young Negro males in northern urban centers and for middle-aged Negro men in the rural South, the causal model must be one that takes account of this. For example, if education or availability of jobs relates to unemployment differently for these two groups of Negro men, the model must be one that specifies these interactions. And the techniques of analysis must be able to detect them.

Here is a place where social science disciplines differ greatly. In the disciplines dominated by experimental methods, particularly experimental psychology, the factorial design and analysis of variance statistics have come to dominate research. Widespread use of an analytic technique which requires the researcher to test whether the explanatory variables simply add together or interact in some manner seems to have molded an "accepted" way of thinking in experimental psychology. Interactions are taken for granted as a basic feature of reality. In contrast, the disciplines which are less experimental in nature and more concerned with real phenomena in the social world have depended largely on multivariate analysis techniques, such as correlation and regression, which assume additive relationships among variables. Therefore, nonexperimental psychologists, as well as sociologists, economists, and political scientists, often implicitly accept an additive model even if it may not fit the processes being studied. This is not to imply that technology is the only determinant of styles of thinking in social science; still, it is an important one. Only recently have multivariate statistical models which do not demand additive assumptions, but still handle large numbers of variables, become available to investigators who employ nonexperimental research techniques, such as surveys.[5] This should lead to the development of causal models which more adequately reflect reality.

Nowhere is this need to take account of interactions clearer than in Coleman's proposed model of social change. Returning to the unemployment example, we see that making interactive, rather than additive, assumptions matters greatly in this model. Consider two factors which most experts regard as important in reducing Negro unemployment: increased job opportunities and increased educational achievement. Coleman, who also looks upon these factors as important, suggests that their effect is not a simple additive one. Instead, the effect of each depends on the other. Whether an increase in job opportunities will really reduce Negro unemployment depends on whether Negroes have sufficient personal resources in the form of educational achievement to convert the new opportunities into actual job success. Conversely, whether an increase in educational achievement truly pays off into job success depends on the existence of effective nondiscriminatory policies and availability of jobs at the appropriate skill level. Neither job opportunities nor educational achievement is considered the primary resource. The effective resource for social change is their joint product. Stated this way, the hypothesized interaction appears obvious. Yet it is not obvious. Many change efforts are directed at one or the other of these factors in a way that implicitly accepts the additive assumption. Thus it is commonly assumed that either improving job skills through training programs or increasing the availability of jobs ought to reduce unemployment, although not as effectively as adopting both approaches. In contrast, Coleman's model suggests there may be no change at all in the amount of unemployment unless both factors exceed critical, or minimum, levels. A further implication of the Coleman approach is that the *rate* at which either factor translates into higher employment may, under certain conditions, be determined by the level at which the other factor is set. For example, when jobs are abundant, a *small increment* in the general skill level of the potential Negro labor force may produce a *large increment* in employment, whereas when job opportunities are scarce, the reverse relationship may obtain. Similarly, the level at which job skills are fixed in the Negro population at a given time may determine the ratio of increments in the number of available jobs to increments in Negro employment.

The interaction model may explain why action strategies aimed at a single target are often unsuccessful. For example, interaction processes probably account for some of the ineffectiveness of antidiscrimination measures, as Coleman contends. He proposes three factors that determine the impact of a legal action: (1) the extent to which it requires implementation by a set of actors who are responsible, directly or indirectly, to the lawmakers; (2) whether implementation of the legal action involves at least one party in whose interest it lies and who is prepared to implement it; and (3) whether the situation is one in which one person loses if he changes alone, but no one loses if all change. Social change is not likely to follow legislative action unless these factors are favorable. We would add a fourth: whether the legal action provides effective sanctions for noncompliance. And there may be still other important conditioners. The significance of Coleman's approach is not only in the particular causal variables he suggests but in the general notion of their multiplicative relationships.

We view the explicit concern of the contributors with the nature of the relationship among causal factors as one of their major contributions to this text. Whether the determinants of a particular phenomenon in American race relations have a summative or multiplicative effect is a matter for empirical investigation. The suggested theoretical models should prove most helpful in the task of constructing alternative hypotheses about these causal processes.

ASSUMPTIONS REGARDING THE DETERMINANTS OF PERFORMANCE

Can Negroes make the most of available opportunities for improving their lot, or are they critically handicapped by personal characteristics that are inimical to achievement in modern industrial society? The opinions of social planners who are concerned with the plight of the poor differ sharply on this question. Some are convinced that the only really important blocks to Negro advancement are in the external environment. Others believe that even if all external barriers were removed, the Negro's own values, attitudes, and habits would still hold him back. The two diagnoses of the problem generate different prescriptions for change, one emphasizing maximum expansion of the opportunity structure and the other calling for a mixture of structural reform and psychological rehabilitation. Both strategies can be seen operating in government-sponsored job training programs for ghetto youths. Gurin [6] observes that these programs have tended to reflect various administrators' assumptions about the main causes of unemployment. Some projects have focused strongly on inculcating in trainees a psychological orientation deemed essential for successful adjustment to the world of work, even to the point of neglecting to teach concrete job skills or to help graduates find suitable positions; other projects have used the opposite approach; and still others have tried to steer a middle course between these two extremes.

Generally stated, the question being considered is whether behavioral competence is mainly determined by relatively unchangeable personality traits that are acquired early in life or by certain features of the individual's contemporary environment, particularly those having to do with the availability and attractiveness of goals. While underscoring the need for further research, the contributors to the present volume who deal with Negro performance tend to favor one or the other of these alternative hypotheses.

Family Influence on Personality

The personality interpretation is most fully presented by Coleman. He states that the average Negro's personal liabilities are such "that even if all other resources, including political and economic power, were equal at a given point in life . . . [he] could not maintain these resources at the same level as could the average non-Negro." For Coleman, the root of the problem is the lower-class Negro family. He sees the family as by far the most important determinant not only of children's academic achievement but of their personal resources generally, "but family resources appear to be a major liability for lower-class Negroes, and one which is at least as difficult to modify as a lack of personal resources themselves."

Other contributors seem less impressed than Coleman by the evidence in support of the family-influence interpretation of Negro performance. Regarding the presumed deleterious effects on children of father-absence (effects which Coleman regards as well documented), Taeuber remarks that "no easy generalization can yet be substantiated." To him, it is "not at all clear that Negro family structure plays much of a direct role in undermining the aspirations and adaptiveness of Negro youth." Taeuber's point is well taken, for research findings on the relationship between family intactness and academic success are consistently negative. Neither the nationwide survey of public schools by Coleman and others [7] nor Wilson's California study [8] found the presence or absence of a father in the home, per se, to be a factor in Negro school achievement. In arguing that the high frequency of father-absence among Negroes was a prime cause of their educational and vocational difficulties, Moynihan [9] cited only one study of family structure that controlled for socioeconomic variables. This investigation, by Deutsch and Brown, [10] reported lower IQ scores for Negro children from broken homes than for Negro children from intact homes. However, in a more comprehensive follow-up study by Whiteman and Deutsch, [11] no such relationship was found. Finally, Feld and Lewis [12] reported a large racial difference in pupils' levels of school anxiety, a characteristic that was closely related to the mother's educational level, but not to family structure.

Given these negative findings in regard to the father-absence hypothesis, Taeuber proposes that the same social and economic pressures that presumably weaken Negro family structure "may also carry most of the responsibility for the difficulties of Negro youth." In a similar vein, Killingsworth concludes from his studies of Negro unemployment "that the history of Negroes in America, especially the history of the 1940–1953 period, demonstrates that they are as ready as any group in the population to grasp opportunity when it is within their reach." And Pettigrew's approach to problems of Negro achievement is also less concerned with early-acquired characteristics than with conditions that prevail in the situations where performance occurs. In-school conditions, he maintains, can have a profound effect on Negro academic attainment. Much of his discussion is devoted to an analysis of social processes in the classroom that possibly mediate the apparent beneficial effects of desegregation.

In evaluating the "personality deficit" hypothesis about low Negro achievement, one would want to ask not only (1) whether specific personality differences have been found between Negroes and whites but also (2) whether demonstrated personality differences have been related to differences in behavior. If research findings indicate, for example, that the average Negro youth does possess traits that are academically detrimental, it should then be asked (3) whether the traits have been shown to be products of early experience in the home and (4) whether the traits appear to be relatively unmodifiable, once formed. Measured by these criteria, available data provide little support for the "personality deficit" viewpoint, despite its wide currency in the literature on poverty.

Self-Esteem

Though there are personal dispositions on which Negroes and whites are known to differ, generally they have not been shown to be related to academic or vocational competence. For example, a well-established characteristic of Negro children in both the North and the South is an inclination toward hostile rejection of their own race and identification with the white majority.[13] Derogation of their own race appears in minority children as early as age 3, remaining strong until later childhood, when it tends to become less apparent. Hence the development of the characteristic cannot be attributed to school influences. Nor, on the other hand, has it as yet been related to social class or family factors. At the present time virtually nothing is definitely known about its effect on school performance. To the extent that the child believes he belongs to an intellectually inferior group, he might be expected to lack the confidence to strive for success in the classroom. However, the studies of racial identity generally have not dealt with evaluation of intellectual attributes. As Smith [14] points out in a recent paper on the socialization of personal competence, there is no compelling reason why attitudes about nonintellectual traits should be closely tied to scholastic motivation. Where *academic* self-esteem has been investigated, the findings on race differences have been equivocal, perhaps because of the inadequacy of the measurement techniques that were used. Further research, with better instruments, is clearly needed on the question of the relevance of racial self-concepts to achievement.

Motives and Values

Turning to motives and values, Negroes are often assumed to be lacking the *need for achievement,* as measured projectively.[15] There are a good many difficulties with the concept of a global achievement motive, as embodied in the fantasy-based measure, which have recently been summarized by Katz.[16] Not the least of these is the ambiguity of findings in regard to its relationship to achieving behaviors.

With respect to achievement *values,* an extensive literature on educational and job aspirations has been reviewed by Proshansky and

Newton.[17] Studies of Negro and white children and their parents generally show only small differences when social class is controlled. Comparing classes, aspirations of high- and low-income adults and children are consistently reported as high: most individuals at both economic levels desire college attendance and professional or white-collar occupations. However, when realistic expectations of achieving the goals are measured, stable class differences appear: these more *functionally relevant* goal levels are lower among low-income students and parents (though even statements of "realistic" expectation from the poor are often unrealistically high when measured against the objective availability of the stated goals or against actual striving behavior). Thus it seems that the main difference between the achievement orientations of the poor and those of the affluent lies not in the *choice* of goals, but in *expectations* of attaining them.

Sense of Efficacy

The one personality characteristic that most clearly differentiates both children and adults of the two races, and that also appears to be closely related to achievement, is Rotter's [18] sense of fate control. Individuals vary in the extent to which they feel they can extract material and social benefits from the environment through their own efforts. In its broadest meaning, the construct refers to one's sense of efficacy, or power, and readiness to accept personal responsibility for what happens to him. At several southern Negro colleges, scores on a scale of personal efficacy that was administered to entering students predicted their grade point averages as freshmen; these grades, in turn, affected the sense of efficacy, as shown by their correlation with scores on a later administration of the scale, with the effect of initial attitudinal differences partialed out.[19] In the Coleman survey of public schools the sense of fate control was found to be related to academic achievement in children of both races. Moreover, in Negro students achievement was much more closely related to this attitude than it was to any family-background factor. Also, there are strong suggestions in these correlational data regarding the relative importance of home and school determinants of the sense of control. Among Negroes it apparently was little influenced by home factors or objective school characteristics, but one condition seemed to affect it greatly: as the proportion of white schoolmates increased, Negroes' sense of internality grew stronger. In discussing this finding, the Coleman report suggests that it could be a reflection of the Negro child's *awareness of greater opportunity* in the racially integrated environment.

Thus a generalized expectation of being rewarded for one's efforts is the personality factor that research has shown most consistently to differentiate Negroes and whites and to correlate with measures of intellectual achievement. And in Negroes this attitude appears to be more strongly influenced by the immediate social environment than by early family socialization. However, the nature of the causal linkage between the sense of efficacy and achievement striving still remains to be explored. It is interesting to note that in the Negro college study mentioned above, academic grades apparently had more influence on the feeling of personal control than the latter had on grades. Similar results were obtained by G. Gurin [20] when he compared the job success of high-school dropouts with personal efficacy scores obtained before starting the job and again after having been on the job for a while.

As questions about how expectancies are acquired and how they influence behavior come under further investigation, it may quickly be discovered that Rotter's concept of a highly generalized sense of efficacy is not the most appropriate tool to use with Negroes and other minorities that experience discrimination. Greater differentiation of attitudes may be called for, as suggested by Patricia Gurin.[21] She factor-analyzed Negro college students' responses to Rotter-type items into two component orientations that were quite differently related to occupational preferences: feelings of *personal* competence, of control over one's *own* life; and beliefs about the relative importance of internal and external forces in the lives of *other people*. Another distinction that perhaps should be made is that between a person's general sense of confidence about meeting standards of excellence in performance and his expectation of being rewarded by the social environment for these attainments.

Expectancies in Specific Situations

In addition to studying general expectations, it would be worthwhile to examine expectations about specific outcomes as they relate to experience and behavior in concrete, achievement-oriented situations. This approach is exemplified by the experiments of Atkinson and his associates,[22] in which subjective probabilities of success at specific tasks are manipulated by imparting to subjects fictitious information about the difficulty of the tasks. Quality of performance, persistence, and choice of task goals have been shown to be strongly influenced by subjects' perceptions of the likelihood of success.

Another technique for studying the effect of highly specific expectancies on behavior has been developed by Mischel and others.[23] Initially, Mischel set out to show that socially disadvantaged children (lower-class and father-deprived), as compared with other children, would prefer small but immediate rewards over large rewards that entailed waiting. His original assumption was that the capacity to delay gratification was a stable personality disposition laid down in early family socialization. More recently, however, he has demonstrated that children's readiness to postpone rewards is strongly influenced by the circumstances in which the choice is offered, including the perceived probability that the delayed reward will actually be forthcoming.

As one more example of the experimental approach to expectancy processes, mention can be made of research by Rotter and his associates,[24] dealing with the effects of induced success and failure at specific tasks on subjects' expectations about future performance. These investigators are interested not only in how *levels* of expectation get changed but also in the *stability* and *generality* of the newly acquired expectations. Their findings with regard to people who initially have low general expectancies of success are particularly relevant to problems of motivation in Negroes. The experiments suggest that there will be many complexities associated with improving the self-confidence of people who have had a previous history of academic and vocational failure.

Relevant to this discussion of expectancies are Pettigrew's remarks on social comparison processes in the racially mixed classroom. He proposes that the apparently beneficial effect of integration on Negro students' achievement is due mainly to the opportunities provided for cross-racial self-evaluations of ability. Under conditions of social acceptance, and if racial differences in ability are not too large, the relatively high performance level of white classmates has an elevating effect on the Negro pupil's standards, or expectancies, regarding his own performance. His higher expectancies stimulate greater effort and accomplishment, confirming the new expectancies. Thus a benign spiral is set in motion. It follows from this analysis that an important problem for research is the empirical specification of conditions under which white peers become positive or negative referents.

Incentives

Pettigrew also makes the point that in the predominantly white school the *incentive value* of academic success may be high. The reasons are at least twofold: first, because the academic standards of these schools are also the standards of white society, success in the classroom bespeaks later success in the outside world; second, given the high prestige of white teachers and peers, gaining their approval through high achievement is a particularly attractive goal.

The topic of incentives is as complex as any topic in psychology; yet some of its least-understood problems often are not recognized by social theorists and policy-makers as problems at all. Highly tenuous assumptions become accepted as self-evident truths. An example is provided by current discussions of proposals for a federally guaranteed minimum income. Even the proponents of these plans usually take it for granted that if government payments are large enough to cover all the subsistence needs of the poor, the incentive to work will be seriously weakened. One economist, Morgan,[25] has boldly challenged this assumption. It is his belief that with a secure subsistence-level income, people "capable of working will be more, not less, willing to work, and more willing to move to new jobs and try new things, except for a few at the fringe and with a preference for the simple rural life." His unusual prediction is based in part on psychological experiments which have shown that rewards are more powerful incentive than punishments and that attainment of minimal goals has the effect of raising levels of aspiration, initiative, and effort. He also draws upon an accumulating body of fact about economic behavior, revealing, for example, that the provision of economic security through Social Security and private pensions has led to *increased* savings and *increased* purchase of private insurance.

Morgan calls attention to the importance of a person's perceptual framework in determining the strength of incentives. He points out: "Close and realizable rewards and goals are more powerful motivating forces than distant and improbable ones." Thus expectancies influence incentives. Social comparisons often furnish the perceptual framework, as Hyman notes in his remarks on relative deprivation phenomena. Combining the thoughts of Morgan and Hyman, it appears likely that as people's incomes rise, they will adopt new reference groups for defining their economic and other goals. This broad hypothesis generates an interesting array of predictions that can be tested empirically.

Implications for Public Policy

We conclude this section on Negro motivation and performance as we began: by pointing out the general implications for public policy of two alternative basic conceptions. According to one conception, the behavior of the poor is primarily determined by relatively stable, deep-rooted, and early-acquired personality factors. The other view stresses the role of ongoing experiences in situations that afford different amounts of opportunity for goal attainment. The former assumption inevitably creates pessimism among administrators and planners about the feasibility and value of instituting major structural reforms in the employment market, in conjunction with ambitious job training programs. It forces the conclusion that Negro unemployment is not primarily caused by a shortage of suitable jobs or a lack of specific vocational skills. The result is acceptance of a remedial strategy based on permanent government support of a presumably incompetent population, perhaps with some provisions for sheltered, low-level occupations.

For those who ascribe Negro poverty primarily to personality "deficits" acquired early in life in the home (as does, for example, Moynihan), any change efforts that are made should be directed primarily at the family, through child allowances, preschool day-care programs, and the like. But Killingsworth sees the problem differently. Through painstaking empirical analysis he has been able to demonstrate that even in periods of high peacetime prosperity, job opportunities for Negroes have been more apparent than real. Guided by the principle of parsimony, he concludes that the simple explanation of unemployment—lack of employment opportunities—should be tested first. Hence, he sets his programmatic recommendations accordingly, giving high priority to job-creation, manpower training programs, and improvement of ghetto schools.

ASSUMPTIONS REGARDING PREJUDICE AND DISCRIMINATION

Historically, interest in prejudice among social psychologists developed as part of a broader concern about the nature of attitudes in general.[26] An attitude was viewed as an orientation toward an object which involved belief, feeling, and action-tendency components with respect to the object. Since it had an action (or conative) element, an attitude, if adequately measured, was supposed to predict how people would behave. In fact, it was often argued that behavioral indicators were the best measures of attitudes. However, studies conducted over fifteen years ago brought into question the importance of prejudice in predicting how people will act. These studies, summarized by Hyman, indicated that whites with strong racial prejudice exhibited discrimination in some situations of racial contact, but not in others. Apparently, certain features of the situations determined whether prejudice would be inhibited or openly expressed. Although, as Hyman observes, the investigations were few in number and sampled a narrow range of contact situations (all economic in nature), their findings led some social scientists to stress the general primacy of situational determinants over attitudinal factors in predicting behavior. As applied to civil rights problems, this meant that external control of discriminatory behavior might be more effective than efforts to change the prejudice in the hearts of men. In the early 1960's the interest in direct behavioral control was further encouraged by some development in attitude-change research. Starting with experiments on modification of private attitudes by means of role playing and culminating with the cognitive dissonance studies of Festinger and his colleagues,[27] there emerged considerable evidence that attitudes which conflict with the acts one performs will sometimes change to conform with the behavior. Although very few of these experiments dealt directly with prejudice and discrimination, the implication was clear: if a prejudiced person could be induced by norms or other situational pressures to act in a nondiscriminatory fashion, he should in consequence become less prejudiced. Of course, many social scientists, particularly those influenced by psychoanalytic theory, continue to stress the primacy of attitudes over behavior. But among experimental social psychologists the tide is still running strong in the other direction.

Research interest in direct behavioral control is very much in accord with what until recently was the main target of civil rights activity. Since its inception, the NAACP has emphasized legal control of discrimination. Even the direct-action and protest groups, beginning with CORE in the 1940's and continuing with SCLC and SNCC in the 1960's, have directed their main attacks against discrimination. Yet, today the value of antidiscrimination measures is being questioned by Negro leaders. The formal legislative and judicial victories of previous years have not yielded the social and economic pay-offs that were expected of them. As both Taeuber and Killingsworth document, Negro disadvantage in most areas of life continues to be great. It is no longer possible for either activists or social scientists to adhere to the conception that the attainment of racial equality is essentially a matter of suppressing white discrimination. At the present time at least two opposing views about the role of prejudice and discrimination in American society are being voiced.

One point of view, forcefully expressed by black nationalists, is that racial prejudice is so deeply entrenched in white American society that to believe that discrimination can be eliminated is really a delusion. Social control of "racist" behavior is not possible because both the objects of control and the necessary controlling agents are incurably biased against Negroes. Another current position, perhaps also a symptom of disillusionment with the pay-offs from antidiscrimination strategies, is developed most explicitly in this book by Killingsworth. It holds that neither prejudice nor discrimination is the primary *present* source of Negro disadvantage; they are only important historically as factors in the emergence of skill and performance deficits which are a major present cause of inequities. According to this view, even if discrimination is still a significant barrier to Negro advancement, it is often so difficult to identify that research and action strategies focused on discrimination are doomed to fail. Either way, Killingsworth argues, we would be further ahead if we focused our efforts on massive educational, retraining, and recruitment programs that would put more Negroes into better jobs and thus into more advantaged economic positions. Implicit in this approach is the assumption that enough employers are sufficiently unprejudiced, or can be encouraged with appropriate incentives to act in a nondiscriminatory fashion, so that jobs will be available for the increased supply of trained Negroes.

For all their differences, both analyses of the problem appear to treat discrimination and prejudice as constants. In the "racism" argument, discrimination and prejudice are constant at a high level of intensity; they are ubiquitous, the most important source of current inequities. In the "performance deficit" argument, they are constant at a low level of intensity. Yet, from an analytical point of view, there is little to be gained from either approach, since constant factors can hardly show up as potent explanatory variables. And surely their significance does vary as a function of other conditions: region of the country, concentration of Negroes in the population, educational attainment of both races in a given situation, and whether the inequity concerns jobs, housing, education, or some other area. Killingsworth acknowledges that white prejudice is a prime cause of residential segregation. Clearly it is necessary to differentiate situations if we are to understand and curtail the negative consequences of prejudice and discrimination for Negro Americans.

Will this be done at a time when disillusionment is so great? Perhaps not, unless the effectiveness of past civil rights legislation is examined more carefully than has yet been done. As both Coleman and Matthews point out, the probable impact of antidiscrimination legislation cannot be gauged without specifying the conditions that are necessary for it to be effective. In instances where such conditions were met, legislation may well have been reasonably successful.

Further research is needed on the attitudinal and situational determinants of discrimination. It would be of practical value to be able to identify situational factors that make certain kinds of discriminatory acts unlikely, regardless of how prejudiced people in the situation are. At the same time, it is necessary to know to what extent attitudes themselves may have to be changed in order to reduce racial tensions.

Conditions under Which Prejudice Leads to Discrimination

According to Hyman, most of the reported inconsistencies between prejudice and overt behavior can probably be explained in terms of conflicting motives. Prejudiced people also hold other attitudes and motives which in a given situation may conflict with their desire to express the prejudice. Therefore, whether they act in a discriminatory fashion will depend on the relative strength of the prejudice and the countervailing tendencies. Implicit in this approach is the conception that there are three factors which together determine whether discrimination will occur. Each of these factors will be discussed.

The Intrapsychic Factor

The racial prejudice of individuals can differ along a variety of dimensions, for prejudice shows all the characteristics of attitudes in general. For instance, it is part of a larger organization of attitudes, and, for some people, it is *central in the attitudinal structure.* That is, it is so closely interlocked with other attitudes that arousal of what might seem an unrelated belief can trigger a prejudiced reaction as well. For other people, attitudes about race are more peripheral or compartmentalized and thus less subject to indirect stimulation. Fewer situations are capable of stimulating prejudice when it is not central in the person's attitudinal structure.

People also differ in the *intensity* of their prejudice. Even when prejudice is more compartmentalized, it may be felt so keenly that action inevitably follows when the prejudice is aroused. For other people the intensity is weak enough so that the same situation does not result in discriminatory behavior.

Moreover, in addition to centrality and intensity, racial attitudes may also differ in their *specificity or generality.* For some people race prejudice may be highly generalized, including all persons of a different color. For others, it may relate only to certain subgroups. Hyman's discussion of the importance of differentiating what "Negro" means to white subjects in assessing their attitudes is germane to this. Until researchers began to present as attitudinal objects Negroes who differed in social class and beliefs, it was impossible to determine how general or specific prejudicial attitudes were. Yet, highly generalized prejudice is more likely to eventuate in discriminatory behavior.

Finally, there is the question of the *function* of prejudice for the individual. Attitudes can serve quite different functions, which make them differ in how easily they are aroused and translated into action, as well as how difficult they are to change.[28] For instance, when they have an instrumental function of helping the individual attain other goals or a knowledge function of helping him organize and understand the world, they tend to be less potent stimulants of behavior and easier to modify than when they serve to protect the individual against internal conflict or external dangers. When prejudice fulfills this defensive function, as it often does in highly insecure persons, it seems to be a powerful motivator of behavior and very difficult either to control or change. Therefore, knowing something about individual differences in prejudice is important for understanding behavior, even in situations where external constraints are strong.

To summarize, when prejudice is central to the person's attitudinal structure, highly intense, broadly generalized, and defensive in nature, it will carry such force that discriminatory behavior is a likely consequence.

The Arousal Potential of Situations

It is important to know whether a given situation is likely to arouse prejudice. While this will depend on the function the prejudicial attitude performs for the individual, it does not mean that the arousal potential of situations is unique for each individual. Many functions of prejudice are not idiosyncratic. For instance, enough people apparently still use prejudice to defend against sexual and aggressive impulses or against threats to self-esteem so that we can expect situations demanding social intimacy to arouse prejudice more easily than situations allowing social distance. The difficulty in achieving housing integration, which many social scientists agree results more from white prejudice than any other factor, is witness to the arousal quality of intimate situations. So too is the slowness in integrating fire departments long after police departments have moved ahead. Any situation demanding personal relationships beyond strictly role-defined behaviors will have strong arousal potential so long as prejudice performs a defensive function for large numbers of white Americans.

Even situations where social relationships are relatively restricted by occupational or other role demands will vary in their arousal potential. For instance, if the major gratifications are based on status or power, prejudice will be aroused more easily than if there exist other sources of rewards. With regard to power, it may be noted that the intransigency of unions to broadening their membership (as in the construction industry) stems not only from economic threats but also from the threat to old members of losing their power to control union policies.

The Regulation Potential of Situations

Finally, we must also know the extent to which the situation lends itself to regulation of behavior. Two equally prejudiced people in situations with high potential for arousing prejudice may nevertheless act quite differently if one, but not the other, anticipates that the expression of prejudice will have negative consequences. The regulation potential of the situation depends, first of all, on the extent to which there exist norms which specify what is and what is not appropriate behavior. In highly cohesive groups the existence of norms per se may be sufficient to regulate behavior. But in many situations, the norms will need to be supported through the use of sanctions, either negative (fines, imprisonment, loss of status or power, and the like) or positive (such as economic, status, or power gains). As regards positive sanctions, the profit motive in a situation can be made so central that a person will curtail his prejudice for the sake of an attractive economic reward that is contingent on nondiscriminatory behavior. Most of the studies reviewed by Hyman showing inconsistencies between racial attitudes and behavior probably involved this type of sanction. Comparing the relative effectiveness of punishment and reward in controlling discriminatory behavior, psychological research on other types of behavior suggests that reward will prove more effective. Research on the use of different kinds of sanctions for discrimination in a variety of social settings is much needed. Lack of attention to sanctions has been one of the weakest aspects of prior antidiscrimination legislation. The courts and legislatures have done a better job in the past of defining norms than of providing effective sanctions.

In addition to norms and sanctions, another feature of situations that will vary is the ease with which trangressions of the norms can be identified. Prejudice is more likely to be inhibited when discriminatory acts are visible to persons responsible for enforcing the norms. Thus, in the employment situation, discrimination in promotion and upgrading may be especially difficult to regulate because decisions are frequently left to the personal discretion of supervisors throughout a company and therefore not so easily scrutinized by persons particularly responsible for nondiscriminatory policies. When there are many gate keepers with autonomy to exercise their professional and personal judgments, transgressions become very difficult to monitor.

Situations will vary in the availability of each of the regulatory devices that have just been discussed. Some situations, such as housing, are almost lacking in all of them. In contrast, integration in the armed forces, which like integrated housing demands social intimacy, has high regulatory potential. Desegregation was readily accomplished by executive order because of the traditional chain of command in the military, the powerful disciplinary structure, and the ease of behavioral surveillance. Still, one must not forget the dire predictions of chaos and violence that were made at the time President Truman issued his historic order to the armed forces. Even today many people, not realizing how effective situational controls can be, remain convinced that effective integration, involving equalitarian relationships, is not possible in nonmilitary settings.

The Significance of Attitude Change

Although more and more situations are likely to become subject to public control, there will remain a great many in which external regulation of behavior is unfeasible. In American society, with its strong emphasis on the values of personal freedom, there is widespread resistance to certain types of behavioral constraint. Moreover, there are many social situations—for example, the classroom—in which nondiscriminatory conduct cannot be readily codified. The bare essentials of school desegregation could be easily codified and regulated, were the will to do so present. The behavior demanded of school officials is simple enough: children of different races are to sit in the same classroom and be taught by members of a racially mixed faculty. It is visually apparent when this does or does not happen. But Pettigrew's discussion of school desegregation attests to the importance of nonobvious social behaviors between children and between children and their teachers, which mark the difference between a truly integrated school and one which is merely desegregated. He cites an experiment conducted by Rosenthal and his associates in which teachers' feelings about their students strongly affected student performance.[29] The children from whom teachers were told to expect unusual intellectual development did, in fact, improve their performance much beyond that of another group of children who had similar ability but were not identified to the teachers as having exceptional potential for growth. It is also known from other studies that teachers tend to underestimate the ability and motivation of children from lower-class, minority group backgrounds.[30] Thus, the average Negro student may be disadvantaged by teacher attitudes and expectations even when the formal requirements of desegregation are met. Meaningful school integration demands the kinds of behavior from white teachers and pupils that official school policies and regulations cannot guarantee unless unfavorable feelings and attitudes are changed.

Another reason why the control of discrimination requires attitude change is that public regulation of behavior itself depends on the prior existence of positive attitudes. The areas of least regulation are generally those, like housing, where white Americans are particularly unwilling to support passage of legislation that will restrict the expression of their prejudice. To assume that regulation is possible without prior support for it in a significant portion of the population is wishful fantasy. This is not to say that widespread attitude change must always precede legislative or judicial control. The history of race relations in America shows that this is not true. But certainly domestic programs of the magnitude needed to bring racial minorities out of poverty and unemployment will not be mounted by Congress in the absence of strong popular pressure. The critical question today is not whether it is necessary to change the racial attitudes of white America, but rather how to do it. Even the most extreme Negro militants acknowledge the desirability of reducing prejudice, though they despair of its ever being accomplished.

We have argued the desirability of taking a fresh look at the relationship between prejudice and behavior. Research should explore the conditions under which induced change in one will cause change in the other. In need of critical examination is the notion that once a person acts in a nondiscriminatory manner, he is likely to undergo a change in his private attitudes as well. No doubt, sometimes he will change his attitudes to make them congruent with his behavior. But there are many restrictions on this application of Festinger's cognitive dissonance hypothesis that must be recognized. It may well be true that acting in a fashion that is dissonant with one's beliefs produces pressures to achieve a new congruity between action and attitude and that this new congruity sometimes comes about through changing private attitudes to conform with behavior. But when the situation allows other alternatives—denying the dissonance between action and attitude, restricting the new behavior to one very specific situation, compartmentalizing the meaning of new ways of behaving, attributing the responsibility for the new behavior to someone else—attitude change may not be the most likely consequence.

Probably what most frequently results from behavioral regulation that is based either on material rewards or threat of physical punishment is what Kelman calls *compliance*.[31] The person who is required to act in a new, prescribed manner complies in his action and may even profess to believe what he is doing. But both the compliance in action and conformity in belief are likely to last only so long as they can be scrutinized by a controlling agent. When the person in authority leaves, there is likely to be a reversion to the old attitudes. Thus, the change is likely to be temporary, except in unusual situations where the control itself lasts a long time and covers most aspects of the person's life—what have come to be termed total institutions. In most real-life situations this type of attitude change is neither persistent nor generalizable to new and different situations. For profound attitude change to occur, other ingredients are needed, apart from regulation of behavior. For instance, when a person acts voluntarily with a sense of choice, he is likely to do more than merely comply with some external requirements. By accepting responsibility for his own behavior, he is forced to re-examine attitudes that are inconsistent with it. This may lead to lasting change in feelings and beliefs. The process is what Kelman calls *internalization*, and it can occur when a person in authority not only has the power to regulate behavior but is perceived as a trustworthy expert on issues related to the required behavior.

Kelman's distinction between compliance and internalization offers a promising approach to the study of prejudice and its reduction. Under what conditions does each process occur, and what are its consequences? In addition to questions about the permanence of racial attitude changes, there are questions regarding generalization effects— generalization from one situation to another, from one specific attitude to another, from one object to a larger class of objects. Findings from this type of research could be useful in designing education and mass communication programs and even in the shaping of civil rights legislation.

•NOTES

1 The National Advisory Commission on Civil Disorders, *U.S. Riot Commission Report* (New York: Bantam, 1968).

2 I. Katz, "Review of Evidence Relating to Effects of Desegregation on the Intellectual Performance of Negroes," *American Psychologist,* XIX (1964), 381–399.

3 W. C. Haggstrom, "The Power of the Poor," in L. A. Ferman, J. L. Kornbluh, and A. Haber, eds., *Poverty in America* (Ann Arbor: University of Michigan Press, 1965), pp. 315–334; F. Riessman, *The Culturally Deprived Child* (New York: Harper and Row, 1962), Chapter 4.

4 A. B. Hollingshead and F. C. Redlich, *Social Class and Mental Illness* (New York: Wiley, 1958).

5 J. A. Sonquist and J. N. Morgan, *The Detection of Interaction Effects*, Survey Research Center Monograph No. 35 (Ann Arbor: Institute for Social Research, University of Michigan, 1964); J. N. Morgan and J. A. Sonquist, "Problems in the Analysis of Survey Data and a Proposal," *Journal of the American Statistical Association*, LVIII (1963), 415–434.

6 G. Gurin, "An Expectancy Approach to Intervention Programs," in V. Allen, ed., *Psychological Factors in Poverty* (Chicago: Markham, 1969).

7 J. S. Coleman *et al.*, *Equality of Educational Opportunity* (Washington: Government Printing Office, 1966).

8 A. B. Wilson, "Educational Consequences of Segregation in a California Community," in U. S. Commission on Civil Rights, *Racial Isolation in the Public Schools* (Washington: Government Printing Office, 1967), Appendixes, 165–206.

9 U.S. Department of Labor, Office of Planning and Research, *The Negro Family* (Washington: Government Printing Office, 1965).

10 M. Deutsch and B. Brown, "Social Influences in Negro-White Intelligence Differences," *Journal of Social Issues*, XX (1964), 24–35.

11 M. Whiteman and M. Deutsch, "Some Effects of Social Class and Race on Children's Language and Intellectual Abilities," in M. Deutsch, I. Katz, and A. Jensen, eds., *Social Class, Race and Psychological Development* (New York: Holt, 1968).

12 S. Feld and J. Lewis, "The Assessment of Achievement Anxieties in Children," (Bethesda, Maryland: National Institute of Mental Health, 1967), manuscript.

13 See the following for a review of the research literature: H. Proshansky and P. Newton, "The Nature and Meaning of Negro Self-Identity," in Deutsch, Katz, and Jensen, *op. cit.*

14 M. B. Smith, "Competence and Socialization," in J. A. Clausen, ed., *Socialization and Society* (Boston: Little, Brown, 1968).

15 D. C. McClelland *et al.*, *The Achievement Motive* (New York: Appleton-Century, 1953).

16 I. Katz, "The Socialization of Academic Motivation in Minority Group Children," in D. Levine, ed., *Nebraska Symposium on Motivation* (Lincoln: University of Nebraska Press, 1967).

17 Proshansky and Newton, *op. cit.*

18 J. Rotter, M. Seeman, and S. Liverant, "Internal vs. External Control of Reinforcement: A Major Variable in Behavior Theory," in N. F. Washburne, ed., *Decisions, Values and Groups*, Vol. 2 (London: Pergamon, 1962).

19 Patricia Gurin and G. Gurin, "The Significance of Competence and Internal Control in the Motivational Dynamics of Negro Youth," *Journal of Social Issues* (1969).

20 G. Gurin, *op. cit.*

21 Patricia Gurin and D. Katz, *Motivation and Aspiration in the Negro College* (Ann Arbor: Institute for Social Research, University of Michigan, 1966).

22 J. W. Atkinson and N. T. Feather, *A Theory of Achievement Motivation* (New York: Wiley, 1966); J. W. Atkinson, *An Introduction to Motivation* (New York: Van Nostrand, 1964).

23 W. Mischel, "Theory and Research on the Antecedents of Self-Imposed Delay of Reward," in B. Maher, ed., *Progress in Experimental Personality Research*, Vol. 3 (New York: Academic Press, 1966).

24 J. B. Rotter, "Generalized Expectancies for Internal versus External Control of Reinforcement," *Psychological Monographs*, LXXX, No. 69 (1966).

25 J. N. Morgan, "Impact of a Federally Guaranteed Minimum Income on Economic Behavior" (Ann Arbor: Institute for Social Research, University of Michigan, 1966).

26 J. Harding *et al.*, "Prejudice and Ethnic Relations," in G. Lindzey, ed., *Handbook of Social Psychology* (Cambridge: Addison-Wesley, 1954), Vol. III, Chapter 27.

27 L. Festinger, *A Theory of Cognitive Dissonance* (Evanston: Row, Peterson, 1957); J. W. Brehm and A. R. Cohen, *Explorations in Cognitive Dissonance* (New York: Wiley, 1962).

28 D. Katz, "The Functional Approach to the Study of Attitudes," *Public Opinion Quarterly*, XXIV (1960), 163–204.

29 R. Rosenthal and L. F. Jacobson, "Teacher Expectations for the Disadvantaged," *Scientific American*, CCXVIII (1968), 19–23.

30 R. Herriott and N. St. John, *Social Class and the Urban School* (New York: Wiley, 1966).

31 H. C. Kelman, "Compliance, Identification, and Internalization: Three Processes of Attitude Change," *Journal of Conflict Resolution*, II (1958), 51–60.

Index

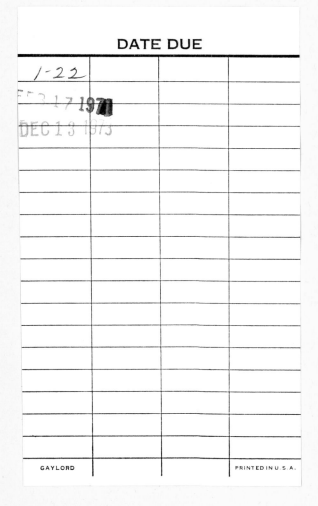

DATE DUE

1-22			
FEB 17 1971			
DEC 13 1973			
GAYLORD			PRINTED IN U.S.A.